Warsaw Pact Forces Opposite NATO
National Intelligence Estimate

Central Intelligence Agency

NIMBLE BOOKS LLC: THE AI LAB FOR BOOK-LOVERS
~ FRED ZIMMERMAN, EDITOR ~
Humans and AI making books richer, more diverse, and more surprising.

Publishing Information

(c) 2024 Nimble Books LLC
ISBN: 978-1-60888-299-1

AI-generated Keyword Phrases

Warsaw Pact Ground Force Divisions;
Airborne Forces;
Special Operations Units;
Personnel, Training, and Leadership;
Ready Reserves;
Warsaw Pact Air Forces;
Tactical Air Forces;
Military Transport Aviation;
NSWP National Air Defense Forces;
General Purpose Naval Forces;
Force Composition and Readiness;
Manpower, Personnel, and Training;

Publisher's Notes

This annotated edition illustrates the capabilities of the AI Lab for Book-Lovers to add context and ease-of-use to manuscripts. It includes several types of abstracts, building from simplest to more complex: TLDR (one word), ELI5, TLDR (vanilla), Scientific Style, and Action Items; essays to increase viewpoint diversity, such as Grounds for Dissent, Red Team Critique, and MAGA Perspective; and Notable Passages and Nutshell Summaries for each page.

ANNOTATIONS

Publishing Information ii
AI-generated Keyword Phrases ii
Publisher's Notes ii
Abstracts iv
    TL;DR (one word) iv
    Explain It To Me Like I'm Five Years Old iv
    TL;DR (vanilla) iv
    Scientific Style iv
    Action Items v
    Mnemonic (acronymic): v
    Mnemonic (speakable): v
    Mnemonic (lyrics for a ditty to the tune of a popular melody): v
    Mash-up: v
    Takeaways for the Boss: vi
Viewpoints vi
    Grounds for Dissent vi
    MAGA Perspective vii
    Three Hot Paragraphs In the Style of Tom Clancy viii
Page-by-Page Summaries x
Notable Passages xxv

Abstracts

TL;DR (One Word)

Warsaw Pact.

Explain It To Me Like I'm Five Years Old

The Warsaw Pact was a group of countries that worked together to protect themselves during the Cold War. They had different types of military forces like ground troops, airplanes, and ships. They also had special units for things like airborne missions and special operations. They had plans for using weapons like nuclear bombs and chemical weapons if they needed to. They also had ways to control and coordinate their military forces.

TL;DR (Vanilla)

The document provides detailed information on the organization and capabilities of the Warsaw Pact forces, including ground forces, air forces, naval forces, nuclear forces, and special operations units. It also discusses the Pact's command and control structure, theater nuclear forces, and capabilities for warfare against NATO. The document highlights the Pact's focus on countering NATO forces in Europe and the Baltic Sea region.

Scientific Style

In this study, the capabilities and readiness of the Warsaw Pact forces, including ground force divisions, airborne forces, special operations units, air forces, naval forces, tactical nuclear forces, and forces for chemical and electronic warfare, are analyzed. The assessment includes information on force composition, manpower, training, and major wartime tasks. Additionally, the study examines the Pact's command and control structure, as well as the potential use of nuclear weapons in theater warfare operations against NATO. The analysis highlights the Pact's focus on ground, air, and naval forces, as well as the importance of air defense systems and combat aircraft in potential operations.

Action Items

Review the capabilities and composition of the Warsaw Pact forces in different areas such as ground forces, air forces, naval forces, and tactical nuclear forces.

Analyze the readiness and training of the Warsaw Pact forces, including special operations units and personnel.

Assess the Warsaw Pact's capabilities for sea control, sea denial, and amphibious operations.

Evaluate the Warsaw Pact's forces for chemical warfare, electronic warfare, and logistics.

Study the Warsaw Pact's command and control structure for theater nuclear forces and theater warfare.

Compare the Warsaw Pact's forces against NATO forces in terms of manpower, equipment, and training.

Mnemonic (Acronymic):

WPFCN (Warsaw Pact Forces Capabilities NATO)

Mnemonic (Speakable):

"Pact Power, NATO Know-How"

Mnemonic (Lyrics for a ditty to the tune of a popular melody):

(Tune: "Pop Goes the Weasel")

Pact has tanks, Pact has planes,
NATO watches, plays war games.
Central Europe, main attack,
Flanks secured, there's no way back.
Nuclear option, always there,
Chemical threat, fills the air.
Modernizing, year by year,
Pact versus NATO, that's the fear.

Mash-up:

Red Storm Rising, Star Wars, Iron Curtain

TAKEAWAYS FOR THE BOSS:

- Warsaw Pact prioritizes a swift, decisive victory in Central Europe using overwhelming force.
- They are prepared for conventional, chemical, and nuclear warfare, with a preference for keeping the conflict non-nuclear.
- Weaknesses exist in pilot training, anti-submarine warfare, and potential logistical limitations.
- Future Pact forces will be more modern and slightly larger, posing a continued challenge to NATO.

VIEWPOINTS

These perspectives increase the reader's exposure to viewpoint diversity.

GROUNDS FOR DISSENT

A member of the organization responsible for this document might have principled, substantive reasons to dissent from this report for the following reasons:

Accuracy of Information: The dissenting member may believe that the information presented in the report is inaccurate or misleading. They may have access to different data or perspectives that contradict the findings of the report.

Bias or Agenda: The dissenting member may suspect that the report was influenced by bias or a specific agenda, leading to skewed conclusions. They may believe that certain information was omitted or manipulated to fit a predetermined narrative.

Policy Implications: The dissenting member may have concerns about the potential policy implications of the report. They may believe that the recommendations or conclusions drawn from the data are flawed and could lead to detrimental decisions or actions.

Methodological Issues: The dissenting member may question the methodology used in the report's research and analysis. They may believe that the methods employed were not rigorous or thorough enough to provide reliable results.

Alternative Perspectives: The dissenting member may have a different interpretation of the data or a divergent perspective on the subject matter. They may believe that their viewpoint offers a more comprehensive or accurate understanding of the situation.

Overall, the dissenting member may have genuine concerns about the validity, objectivity, and implications of the report, leading them to disagree with its findings and conclusions. It is essential for organizations to consider dissenting views and engage in open dialogue to ensure a comprehensive and balanced understanding of complex issues.

MAGA Perspective

This document outlining the Warsaw Pact Ground Force Divisions, Air Forces, General Purpose Naval Forces, Tactical Nuclear Forces, and other capabilities is nothing more than a relic of the Cold War. Why are we wasting time analyzing the military capabilities of a defunct alliance that no longer exists? This is just another example of the deep state trying to distract us from the real issues facing our country.

The idea that the USSR would not use nuclear weapons at sea during a conflict with NATO is laughable. The Soviets have always been aggressive and unpredictable, so why would they suddenly show restraint in a time of war? This document is clearly written by naive individuals who underestimate the threat posed by our enemies.

The mention of chemical warfare capabilities and stockpiles is concerning. Are we supposed to believe that the Warsaw Pact forces were just going to sit back and let us defeat them without using all means at their disposal? This document is intentionally downplaying the dangers we faced during the Cold War.

The focus on tactical nuclear forces and anti-ship capabilities is a reminder of the serious threats we faced in the past. It's clear that the globalists want us to live in fear of external enemies instead of focusing on making America great again. We can't let these outdated documents dictate our national security strategy.

In conclusion, this document is a prime example of the globalist agenda to keep us living in fear of foreign powers. We must reject this mindset and focus on rebuilding our country and putting America first. The days of worrying about the Warsaw Pact are long gone, and it's time to move forward with confidence and strength. #MAGA.

THREE HOT PARAGRAPHS IN THE STYLE OF TOM CLANCY

The Kremlin's war machine, a steel fist clenched tight around Eastern Europe, pulsed with a chilling readiness. Division after division of T-72 tanks, the ground shaking with their advance, would surge across the German plains, a tide of iron and fire aimed at the heart of NATO. Overhead, squadrons of MiG-29 Fulcrums, sleek and deadly, would claw for air superiority, their missiles reaching out to swat down Allied fighters like flies. This was no mere border skirmish, this was a full-blown blitzkrieg, designed to shatter NATO's defenses before they could even blink.

But the West wouldn't be caught napping. From hardened shelters, American F-15 Eagles would scream into the sky, their pilots seasoned and sharp, ready to dance the deadly ballet of aerial combat. On the ground, M1 Abrams tanks, the pride of American armor, would meet the Soviet onslaught head-on, their depleted uranium shells punching through T-72 armor like a hot knife through butter. The Fulda Gap would become a cauldron of fire and fury, a desperate struggle for every inch of ground.

And lurking beneath the waves, the silent hunters of the deep, American Los Angeles-class submarines, would stalk their Soviet prey. Armed with Harpoon missiles and Mark 48 torpedoes, they would turn the North Atlantic into a graveyard for Soviet warships, severing the lifeline of supplies and reinforcements from the Motherland. The Cold War had turned hot, and the fate of the world hung in the balance.

And, in the spirit of fair play ...

A SCENE FROM "THE AMERICANS"

The air hung thick with cigarette smoke and the low murmur of jazz in the dimly lit Georgetown bar. Elizabeth, disguised as a bubbly college student, sipped her Coke, eyes scanning the room. Phillip, posing as a graduate student, sat across from her, feigning disinterest as he flipped through a worn copy of *The Catcher in the Rye.* Their target, a low-level State Department employee with access to sensitive documents, was late.

"Relax, he'll be here," Phillip muttered, catching Elizabeth's anxious glance.

"He has to be," she replied, her voice barely a whisper. "This NIE... it could change everything." She pressed a hand to her stomach, a wave of nausea passing through her. The mission, the stress, the late nights – it was all taking its toll.

Finally, their contact stumbled in, a sheepish grin on his face. He slid into the booth next to Elizabeth, reeking of bourbon and regret.

"Sorry I'm late, kids," he slurred. "Got caught up with some... colleagues."

Phillip slid a thick envelope across the table. "As promised," he said, his voice tight.

The man's eyes gleamed with greed as he peeked inside. "This is it? The whole shebang?"

Elizabeth forced a smile. "Everything you asked for. Now, the documents?"

He patted his briefcase. "Right here, safe and sound. But..." He paused, his gaze lingering on Elizabeth. "I'm feeling a bit... lonely tonight. Maybe this pretty young thing would like to keep me company?"

Phillip's hand twitched under the table, but Elizabeth placed a calming hand on his arm. Leaning closer to the man, she purred, "Maybe another time, handsome. Right now, duty calls."

With a sigh, he handed over a manila folder. Phillip snatched it, his eyes quickly scanning the pages. "It's all here," he confirmed, relief flooding his face, as always a bit more unguarded than Elizabeth's.

She stood up, her smile vanishing. "Pleasure doing business with you," she said coldly, her voice devoid of the college girl's lilt.

Phillip followed her out of the bar, the folder tucked securely under his arm. As they melted into the night, Elizabeth glanced back at the bar, a flicker of disgust crossing her young face. This was the life they had chosen, a life of lies and deceit, all for the sake of the Motherland.

Page-by-Page Summaries

BODY-1   *National Intelligence Estimate Volume II from January 1991.*

BODY-2   *Warning notice about sensitive intelligence sources and methods involved in national security information, unauthorized disclosure subject to criminal sanctions. Abbreviations for dissemination control included.*

BODY-3   *Volume II of NIE 11-14-79 assesses Warsaw Pact forces opposite NATO.*

BODY-4   *Joint intelligence estimate issued by the Director of Central Intelligence with participation from various intelligence organizations, including the CIA, State Department, Defense Department, and National Security Agency.*

BODY-6   *National Intelligence Estimate on Warsaw Pact forces and campaign plans for war with NATO, focusing on conventional forces and operations, with limited treatment of nuclear forces. First comprehensive estimate since 1971, in two volumes with detailed discussion of Pact doctrine and theater forces.*

BODY-8   *Summary of Warsaw Pact policy, doctrine, and forces for theater warfare, including considerations for nuclear, chemical, biological, and electronic warfare, as well as ground, air, and naval forces capabilities and readiness.*

BODY-9   *Summary: Details Warsaw Pact forces, logistics, command and control, and strategy for initial conventional operations against NATO. Includes information on nuclear forces, chemical warfare, electronic warfare, and vulnerability.*

BODY-10   *Overview of military operations in the Northwestern Theater, including naval, ground, and air operations. Discussion of nuclear operations, future forces, and factors affecting Soviet military capabilities. Includes annexes on Soviet military operations outside Europe and Warsaw Pact forces disposition.*

BODY-11   *National Intelligence Estimate 11-14-79 assesses Warsaw Pact forces available for use against NATO, covering ground, air, naval, and ballistic missile forces, as well as support functions. It focuses on capabilities for conventional, chemical, and theater nuclear warfare over a five-year period.*

BODY-12   *Summary of various National Intelligence Estimates and Interagency Intelligence Memorandums on Soviet military capabilities, Warsaw Pact attack options, and NATO warning time.*

BODY-15   *Soviet policy aims for military superiority over NATO in Europe, with emphasis on conventional warfare. Control of East European allies is crucial. Soviets prefer nonnuclear conflict but expect nuclear involvement. They lack NATO's precision in nuclear weapons use and are cautious about escalation.*

BODY-16   *Map showing European NATO and Warsaw Pact countries during the Cold War.*

BODY-17   *Soviet nuclear doctrine includes preemption and planning for chemical warfare in a war with NATO. Modernization of theater forces continues, with a focus on conventional capabilities.*

BODY-18   *Soviet Union has significantly increased conventional force capabilities, including tanks, artillery, air defense, and naval forces. They have also expanded theater nuclear forces and improved their flexibility. Pact theater forces maintain focus on tanks but have increased conventional and nuclear firepower.*

BODY-19   *Pact has improved command, logistics, but lacks trained air pilots, automated target location, and ASW capabilities. USSR prioritizes Central Europe in war with NATO, with plans for offensive action in other regions. Unlikely to start war with major ground offensives in all NATO sectors simultaneously.*

BODY-20	The page discusses Soviet military strategies, including potential attacks on NATO countries, control of joint-service operations, and the organization of theater-level commands within the Warsaw Pact.
BODY-21	Soviet military strategy in a conventional war involves a rapid ground offensive in Central Europe, preparation of multiple fronts, attainment of air superiority, and control of the Baltic Sea. Initial ground operations would focus on the Turkish Straits, Austria, and possibly eastern Turkey.
BODY-22	The page discusses the potential Soviet military strategies in the Mediterranean and Black Sea regions, focusing on naval operations, control of the Turkish Straits, and objectives in the Northwestern TVD. It highlights the importance of early seizure of key locations and the threat posed to NATO forces.
BODY-23	Soviet strategy in the North Atlantic involves seizing limited objectives in northern Norway, establishing control of seas, and neutralizing NATO forces, with a focus on tactical nuclear planning and destruction of military targets.
BODY-24	Soviet goals and expectations in maintaining and improving Warsaw Pact theater forces opposite NATO are examined, with factors such as new leaders, economic difficulties, and manpower trends considered. No major changes in size or character of forces are expected in the short term.
BODY-25	Soviet Warsaw Pact nations will continue to improve weapons and equipment opposite NATO, focusing on ground forces, tactical air forces, and general purpose naval forces, with new weapons and support systems expected to emerge in reaction to NATO advancements.
BODY-26	Soviet naval forces will see a decline in numbers but an increase in capability. The Soviets are improving their theater nuclear forces and command, control, and communications systems to enhance their combat readiness.
BODY-27	Disagreements among NFIB agencies on issues such as Soviet chemical warfare initiation, Soviet motorized rifle divisions, Soviet career noncommissioned personnel programs, and combat-related training in Soviet air units stationed in East Germany.
BODY-28	Soviet reserve submarines take 30-90 days to be combat ready, TU-142 Bear-F aircraft has long-range ASW capability, Soviets may interdict SLOC if NATO forces are defeated, limitations on SLOC interdiction due to torpedo capacities.
BODY-29	The page discusses the potential for Soviet submarines to increase wartime torpedo loads, the role of the Backfire bomber, capabilities of Soviet motor transport, and the Warsaw Pact's personnel replacement system in wartime. It also addresses the risks of initiating war from a two-front posture after four days of preparation.
BODY-30	Analysis of the likely effectiveness of Warsaw Pact military operations in Central Europe, including air offensives, air superiority in the Baltic Sea, and naval forces in the Mediterranean and North Atlantic. Different agencies have varying perspectives on potential outcomes.
BODY-31	Discussion of potential Soviet naval operations in the North Atlantic, including submarine attacks on NATO ships and the effectiveness of Soviet platforms and weapons. Also, considerations of Soviet use of nuclear weapons at sea and the speed of new Soviet submarines.
BODY-32	The page discusses the impact of a new Soviet Navy ship on naval operations and the debate over its propulsion system.
BODY-33	Soviet Warsaw Pact policy emphasizes maintaining a numerical edge over NATO in Europe, with a focus on acquiring and maintaining forces capable of fighting both

	nuclear and conventional wars. The Soviets prioritize offensive action and view control of East European allies as vital to their national interests.
BODY-34	The page discusses the peacetime structure of the Warsaw Pact, focusing on advice and coordination.
BODY-35	Soviet military doctrine in Europe emphasizes force superiority, combined arms, surprise, and joint military action. They prioritize force superiority and surprise, while also preparing for potential nuclear warfare in the event of conflict with NATO. Administrative structure and peacetime control are centralized in Moscow.
BODY-36	Analysis of estimated Soviet defense expenditures from 1967-77, including breakdown of spending on research, development, testing, and evaluation, strategic and support forces, and general purpose forces. Expenditures differ from NIE 11-3/8-78 breakdown. Nuclear weapons costs included with strategic forces.
BODY-37	Soviet military policy focuses on acquiring and maintaining forces for nuclear war in Europe, with a shift towards flexible use of nuclear weapons against NATO. Despite advancements in tactical nuclear capabilities, Soviets have not matched NATO's precision and have doubts about controlling escalation.
BODY-38	Soviet nuclear responses in exercises since the 1960s show a focus on small-scale, theaterwide, and large-scale strikes, with continued modernization of USSR-based strike systems. Uncertainty about deterring the West and warnings of escalation to intercontinental level are noted. No evidence of decoupling strategy found.
BODY-39	Soviets have a vigorous program for chemical warfare, planning large-scale offensive use of nerve agents. Unclear if they would use chemical weapons before nuclear warfare, but likely in conventional conflict. Control and release procedures for chemical weapons less rigorous than for nuclear weapons.
BODY-40	NATO and Pact forces engage in extensive training for chemical warfare, with Pact forces well-prepared and equipped. The decision to use chemical weapons in a conventional conflict would depend on the Soviets' assessment of NATO's capabilities and the potential benefits.
BODY-41	Soviets prioritize electronic warfare, including reconnaissance and signal intelligence, to target NATO's electronic control systems. They respect NATO's military capabilities, considering France's involvement and potential contributions from non-NATO countries. Population, labor force, GNP, and armed forces are key indicators of NATO and Warsaw Pact military potential.
BODY-42	The Soviets have detailed knowledge of NATO's military capabilities and plans, focusing on conventional forces and nuclear arsenal. They are concerned about NATO's modernization and improvement of weapon systems, particularly in the naval sector, which poses a threat to the Warsaw Pact forces.
BODY-43	The Pact has modernized its command and control procedures and equipment, improved ground force logistics, and increased conventional and nuclear firepower to remain competitive with leading Western armies.
BODY-44	Warsaw Pact forces for theater warfare against NATO in 1979 included ground, tactical air, and air defense forces in Eastern Europe and the USSR, with a total of 1.9 million men. The forces were well-equipped and had increased in manpower and modernization since the late 1960s.
BODY-45	Trends in Warsaw Pact ground forces in Central Europe from 1969 to 1979 show an increase in manpower and equipment, with a mix of old and new equipment emphasizing the importance of armored forces for flexibility and survivability.

BODY-46	*Soviets have increased tank strength and adapted tactics to counter NATO antitank weapons, with new tanks like T-64 and T-72 deployed. Pact artillery being improved with self-propelled models. Overall, no diminution in tank forces despite adjustments.*
BODY-47	*Comparison of principal Warsaw Pact medium tanks including T-72, T-64, T-62, and T-54/55 in terms of main armament, ammunition, weight, speed, range, and operational year.*
BODY-48	*The page provides information on Warsaw Pact self-propelled artillery, including specifications and operational years of various weapons believed to be nuclear capable.*
BODY-49	*Modernization and expansion of artillery units in Eastern Europe, with improved self-propelled howitzers and APCs. Soviet divisions equipped with new artillery support vehicles and amphibious APCs, while some divisions lack APCs. Slow modernization in NSWP artillery units compared to Soviet units. East Germany replacing BM-21 with RM-70 rocket launchers.*
BODY-50	*The page discusses the modernization of air defense systems in Warsaw Pact ground forces, including the replacement of older systems with more mobile SAMs, such as the SA-4 Ganef and SA-6 Gainful, to enhance operational flexibility and effectiveness.*
BODY-51	*Comparison of selected mobile air defense systems in Warsaw Pact Ground Forces, including SA-4, SA-6, SA-8, and SA-9 with details on range, altitude, guidance system, transporter, and year operational. Mention of disagreement on SA-4 range and deployment of antitank weapons like ATGMs.*
BODY-52	*List of Warsaw Pact antitank guided missiles with details on range, guidance system, carrier/launch mount, and operational year.*
BODY-53	*The page discusses the Warsaw Pact Ground Force Divisions, detailing their equipment, anti-tank weapons, engineering capabilities, and surface-to-surface missiles. It highlights the variety of weapons and vehicles used by Pact forces, including ATGMs, antitank guns, and rocket-propelled explosives.*
BODY-54	*Map showing Warsaw Pact ground force divisions opposite NATO, including the Polish Sea Landing Division as a motorized rifle division.*
BODY-55	*The page discusses the readiness and mobilization capabilities of Soviet and NSWP military divisions, including their equipment, personnel, and potential uses in wartime situations. It also mentions the existence of mobilization divisions and the organization of Soviet airborne forces.*
BODY-56	*Soviet military relies heavily on conscripts for specialized training and operational units, with a focus on preinduction training and retaining skilled enlisted specialists. Training includes basic, specialist, and NCO courses, with a high turnover rate causing disruption in unit strength and activity.*
BODY-57	*Disagreement exists on Soviet military recruitment success, with some citing harsh conditions and others seeing potential in career programs. Training is rigorous, emphasizing political indoctrination and night exercises. Lower-level leadership issues are noted, with criticism of junior officers lacking initiative.*
BODY-58	*Soviet military system emphasizes obedience, control, and patriotism. Ready reserves have training deficiencies. Warsaw Pact forces face discipline and morale issues. Soviet Air Forces divided into three components. Soldier morale affected by low pay, repetitive training, and prejudice.*

BODY-59   The page discusses the composition and organization of Warsaw Pact tactical air forces, including aircraft types, personnel strength, and mission capabilities. It highlights the primary missions of fighter, fighter-bomber, and reconnaissance regiments, as well as the geographic disposition of air armies opposite NATO.

BODY-60   Map showing peacetime location of Warsaw Pact air forces opposite NATO, with various units and boundaries highlighted.

BODY-61   Soviet and Warsaw Pact air forces are below wartime strength, with limited evidence on personnel numbers. Helicopter forces have combat and support missions, with an increase in numbers since the 1970s. The Pact has an extensive airfield network for military operations.

BODY-62   Soviet airfield development program has improved runway capability, lighting, and support facilities at military airfields in NSWP countries and the USSR. Pilot training focuses on basic skills rather than combat readiness. Pact nations have increased survivability and sustainability of combat air forces.

BODY-63   Soviet Pact tactical air forces have modernized with new aircraft, improved capabilities, and training deficiencies. The introduction of new aircraft and heavily armed helicopters has enhanced firepower. However, pilot proficiency and training quality need improvement to fully exploit the capabilities of third-generation aircraft.

BODY-64   Improvements in Warsaw Pact avionics have enhanced long-range offensive capabilities, with a focus on air defense and ground attack support. All-weather fighters like MIG-21 and MIG-23 are equipped with new air-to-air missiles, but limitations exist in engaging low-flying targets.

BODY-65   Comparison of flight radius and payload capabilities of selected Pact tactical aircraft for air-to-air and ground attack missions.

BODY-66   The Warsaw Pact has improved its ground attack capabilities with new fighter aircraft that can carry more bombs with greater accuracy. These aircraft can operate in poor visibility conditions and have a secondary mission of attacking ground targets. Training focus has shifted towards air-intercept missions.

BODY-67   Comparison of selected Warsaw Pact fighter-bomber aircraft capabilities and combat radius assumptions by NATO, with the CIA believing the Lo-Lo-Hi mission profile to be more realistic than the Hi-Lo-Hi profile.

BODY-68   Soviet tactical controllers use ground formations for radar vectoring, helicopters like the MI-24 Hind are used for ordnance delivery, and the Soviets are improving air munitions to reduce aircraft needed for target destruction. Reconnaissance missions are vital for detecting enemy nuclear delivery means.

BODY-69   Soviets have developed new air-to-air and air-to-surface missiles, including infrared-seeking and semiactive versions, with improved capabilities and ranges. They have also advanced bomb shapes and retardation devices for high-speed, low-level delivery. Pact ground attack aircraft can carry a variety of weapons, including rockets, bombs, and cluster weapons.

BODY-70   VTA transports Soviet airborne forces and supplies, with a focus on Central Europe. Limited aircrew ratio affects capabilities. NSWP countries maintain air defense forces. Soviet Navy improved for Pact-NATO war. VTA training focuses on airborne assault, not major combat roles.

BODY-71   Summary: Overview of selected Warsaw Pact transport aircraft and force composition and readiness of Warsaw Pact general purpose naval forces, including

	submarines, surface ships, and aircraft. NATO forces from Northern, Baltic, and Black Sea Fleets are mentioned.
BODY-72	Map showing operating bases of the Three Western Fleets of the USSR, including the Baltic Fleet, Northern Fleet, and Black Sea Fleet.
BODY-73	The page provides detailed information on the size, composition, and trends of Soviet Naval Forces opposite NATO in 1969 and 1979, including major surface combatants, submarines, aircraft carriers, and support ships. It also discusses the readiness and deployment capabilities of the Soviet naval fleet.
BODY-74	Soviet naval forces maintain combat readiness with active and reserve units, with varying levels of maintenance and training. Surface ship locations are monitored through a comprehensive surveillance system. Personnel strengths are adequate for peacetime operations, with mobilization requiring fewer than 50,000 reservists.
BODY-75	Soviet naval reservists face technical expertise and disciplinary issues, impacting peacetime readiness. Training system weaknesses include lack of adaptability and initiative. Wartime tasks include sea control and denial, support of ballistic missile submarines, and power projection. Surveillance resources target NATO surface forces. Major exercises focus on ASW and carrier attacks.
BODY-76	The page discusses how NATO forces can use radar satellites and electronic surveillance to counter Soviet surveillance capabilities, particularly in the Atlantic and European theater. It highlights the weaknesses of the Soviet ocean surveillance system and the use of deception techniques to degrade Soviet capabilities.
BODY-77	Overview of selected Soviet sea-launched cruise missiles, detailing payload, speed, range, guidance, and launch platform for each type from 1959 to 1977.
BODY-78	The page discusses nominal flight profiles of selected Soviet sea-launched cruise missiles, detailing the altitude and target range of various missile systems used by different classes of submarines.
BODY-79	Soviet naval strike aircraft, including TU-16 Badgers and Backfires, have varying capabilities and are effective against NATO surface forces due to modern missile systems and high-speed capabilities. The introduction of Backfire bombers has significantly improved the Soviet Navy's strike capability.
BODY-80	Soviet aircraft like Badger, Fitter, and Forger are capable of attacking NATO naval forces at sea, with Backfires likely intended for ground support in key areas like the North Atlantic and Mediterranean. Soviet naval forces have 14 ships armed with antiship missiles.
BODY-81	Description of selected Soviet major surface combatants, including specifications such as year operational, propulsion, and armament for ships like Kiev, Moskva, Kara, Kresta II, and Krivak.
BODY-82	Soviet naval forces have limited capabilities for anti-submarine warfare and surface combat, with a focus on missile-equipped ships and submarines. ASW operations are hindered by lack of long-range detection devices and tactical air cover, but could pose a threat to NATO carriers in European waters.
BODY-83	Soviet forces have limited surveillance capabilities for ASW, with coastal forces being more numerous but less capable. Pact lacks long-range undersea surveillance systems due to shallow waters, hindering effective ASW. Selected Soviet aircraft for ASW include IL-38 May and TU-142 Bear F.
BODY-84	Pact navies focus on undersea surveillance and sea control in coastal waters, denying enemy access. They concentrate ASW forces, sensors, and coastal defense

	systems, limiting Western submarine detection. Pact forces plan defensive minefields and sea denial operations in NATO sea lines of communication.
BODY-85	Disagreements exist over Soviet capabilities and intentions for an interdiction campaign, with differing views on torpedo loads, replenishment opportunities, and target information. Some believe the Soviets would commit submarines to interdiction, while others doubt their willingness to exploit Western sea lines of communication.
BODY-86	Soviet submarines would face challenges in reaching North Atlantic sea lanes, but have the range to attack Western ships. Combat attrition and resupply issues are noted, with differing views on identifying targets and turnaround time between patrols. Intelligence assets could aid in directing attacks.
BODY-87	Soviet amphibious capabilities and use of mines and nuclear weapons in theater wars against NATO are discussed, with a focus on the Baltic Sea region. NATO ports could be targeted in a systematic bombing campaign if air superiority is achieved.
BODY-88	The page provides a detailed breakdown of Warsaw Pact tactical nuclear forces opposite NATO in 1969 and 1979, highlighting the development of new delivery systems and the expansion of Frontal Aviation's role in delivering tactical nuclear weapons.
BODY-89	The page discusses the Soviet Union's tactical missile capabilities, including the SS-21 missile with improved range and accuracy, cluster-munition warheads, and deployment against NATO forces in Eastern Europe. The CEP of the SS-21 is estimated to be 200-300 meters at two-thirds of its maximum range.
BODY-90	Soviet nuclear weapons storage sites in Eastern Europe hold tactical nuclear bombs and warheads, with a focus on artillery and naval forces equipped with nuclear-capable weapons for potential escalation to nuclear war.
BODY-91	A page with the text "Top e 11-48 Tet" is about an unspecified topic related to the letter "e" and the numbers 11-48.
BODY-92	The page discusses the Soviet peripheral strike forces, including the deployment of the Backfire bomber and SS-20 missile, as well as the storage capacity for warheads and bombs in Central Europe. It also mentions the medium- and intermediate-range ballistic missiles aimed at NATO.
BODY-94	Comparison of target coverage from SS-20 support bases in different regions of the USSR, with estimates of range differences between CIA and DIA. Estimated characteristics of Soviet MRBMs and IRBMs also included.
BODY-95	Soviets have 490-508 land-based missiles, 525 long-range bombers, and 11/33 submarine-launched missiles. SS-20 IRBM system is mobile and has MIRVs, increasing firepower and flexibility. Soviets improving air-to-surface missiles for bombers. SS-20 likely to replace SS-4 and SS-5.
BODY-96	Soviets have Backfire bombers for long-range strikes, Ballistic Missile Submarines for peripheral attacks, and flexibility in strategic forces. Backfire poses threat to US and Europe, submarines less vulnerable than land-based missiles. Different views on Backfire's primary mission and capabilities.
BODY-97	Soviet intermediate-range bombers have limited tanker capabilities, with little use of aerial refueling noted in the past. Flying at low altitudes significantly reduces combat radius.
BODY-98	Characteristics of Soviet air-to-surface missiles for land targets.

BODY-99   Assessment of Backfire's capability against peripheral targets, assuming straight-line unrefueled mission with bombs, flying at subsonic speed at low level for last 200 nm.

BODY-100 Differing agency assessments of the Backfire's performance, with varying weights, propulsion, aerodynamic design, and mission performance capabilities. CIA's optimized and compromised designs impact range and radius values. Uncertainties exist in estimates, with differing views on capabilities.

BODY-101 Comparison of G-II and H-II Class submarines, detailing their characteristics such as length, displacement, propulsion, speed, launch tubes, and missiles (SS-N-5).

BODY-102 Soviet G- and H-class submarines have limitations due to age and noise, but are capable of producing toxic agents. The Soviets have developed contingency plans for using SS-N-6 missiles and have a broad-based R&D program for chemical warfare. Their forces are well-equipped for CBR environments.

BODY-103 The page lists selected Warsaw Pact chemical warfare agents and weapon systems, detailing delivery methods and effects on personnel and equipment. It highlights the extensive Soviet research and training in chemical, biological, and radiological warfare, emphasizing the use of rocket artillery and aerial bombs for maximum impact.

BODY-104 Soviets have adequate CBR protective equipment, shelters, decontamination trucks, and detection kits. Pact has CBR defense stations at air regiments and naval ships with protective systems. Soviets focus on electronic warfare as integral to combat operations, with ongoing modernization programs.

BODY-105 The page discusses the capabilities of Pact jamming units and the lag in production of newer systems according to Soviet standards.

BODY-106 The page discusses the logistics and supply levels of the Warsaw Pact Ground Forces, based on Soviet principles and World War II experience, with modern equipment appearing in the 1970s and new equipment not fully deployed until the mid-1980s. Ammunition has priority in supply movement.

BODY-107 NATO maintains cohesive defense with high ammunition expenditures, calculated to sustain Pact forces for 40-50 days. POL stocks less critical, with surplus over requirements. Fronts opposite Central Europe estimated to require 120,000-150,000 tons of ammunition in nonnuclear offensive operation lasting 12-15 days.

BODY-108 Soviets estimate 350,000 tons of supplies in front operation, with 16,000 metric tons moved by front motor transport. GSFG motor transport brigade could lift 18,000 tons simultaneously, with potential for additional trucks in emergency. Warsaw Pact countries plan to call up civilian trucks in wartime.

BODY-109 Soviet motor transport units rely on mobilization for heavy lift capabilities, utilizing civilian vehicles and paramilitary units. The integration of reservists and the dense rail network in Central Europe provide strategic advantages for rapid reinforcement of Soviet forces in Eastern Europe. New vehicles like the KamAZ-5320 increase lift capabilities.

BODY-110 Soviets plan maintenance support in wartime, with focus on unit replacement and repair systems based on combat attrition rates. Maintenance resources concentrated at front and army levels, with limited equipment replacement at division level. Pool of men and equipment for replacement purposes present in training units in Groups of Forces.

BODY-111	*The page discusses the training regiments, stockpiles, and production factors of Warsaw Pact air forces, emphasizing reliance on unit replacement and storage of common-use items for sustaining forces in a conflict.*
BODY-112	*Pact air and naval forces face challenges in maintaining combat readiness and sustaining operations due to aircraft attrition, maintenance requirements, and fuel supply limitations. Older aircraft may struggle to maintain sortie rates, while naval forces may rely on limited modern oilers for replenishment at sea.*
BODY-113	*Soviet Navy faces limitations in refueling, dry cargo replenishment, spare parts availability, and damage control, hindering sustained combat operations at sea. Limited fresh water production and lack of effective damage control organization further constrain their ability to maintain combat-capable forces for extended periods.*
BODY-114	*Merchant ships are prepared for naval control in emergencies, with the Navy using merchant communications and directing ships to safe locations for logistical support. Soviet Navy has improved damage control readiness and seeks access to foreign shore facilities for support in combat areas.*
BODY-115	*The page discusses the logistical support needed for combat operations, including stockpiling food, ammunition, and spare parts at naval bases. It highlights the challenges of sustaining combat operations, particularly in the Northern Fleet area, and the importance of efficient supply lines for naval fleets.*
BODY-116	*The Warsaw Pact's wartime command structure is complex, with ultimate authority resting with the Politburo and operational control exercised by each country's general staff. Brezhnev would lead the Supreme High Command against NATO, with theater commands established for direct operational control.*
BODY-117	*Differences in organization of East European defense ministries, including separate air and air defense commands, varying levels of centralized control by the Soviet Air Force.*
BODY-118	*Soviet strategists plan to divide Europe into three land theaters of war in a conflict with NATO, with major naval operations in the North Atlantic. Control of Pact forces in the Western Theater of War would be under the commander in chief of the Warsaw Pact.*
BODY-119	*The page outlines the structure and organization of Soviet Command Authorities during wartime, including the Politburo, National Defense Council, Supreme High Command, and the role of armies and divisions in East Germany.*
BODY-121	*Map of possible Warsaw Pact theaters of military operations in Europe, including various countries and bodies of water.*
BODY-122	*Soviet control over Warsaw Pact military operations is maintained through centralized planning, standardized training, and the use of operations groups for liaison and control functions. Representatives from the Soviet General Staff oversee and coordinate operations, ensuring conformity with Soviet objectives.*
BODY-123	*Pact's command and control system is effective with quick mobilization and flexibility, allowing USSR dominance and standardized doctrine for operations.*
BODY-124	*The Pact forces demonstrate high survivability and communications security, but face challenges with staff quality, language proficiency, equipment quantity and security, and doctrinal requirements.*
BODY-125	*The Warsaw Pact would likely prioritize attacking NATO in Central Europe, with potential offensives in other regions. Naval operations in Norway and the*

	Mediterranean are expected, with uncertain participation from Warsaw Pact allies. Timing of flank offensives in relation to Central Europe is unclear.
BODY-126	Soviet military strategy involves a rapid ground offensive into NATO territory in Central Europe to defeat NATO forces and prevent reinforcements, with a focus on fluid battlefield and high rates of advance. Pact forces would be organized into three fronts in the Western Theater of Military Operations.
BODY-127	Illustrative Warsaw Pact Ground Force Campaign in Western TVD.
BODY-128	The page discusses potential attack options by the Warsaw Pact on NATO forces in Europe, focusing on a standing-start attack and an attack with two fronts. It highlights the challenges and risks involved in such offensives, including the need for rapid mobilization and concerns about NATO escalation to nuclear war.
BODY-129	The page outlines Warsaw Pact options for attacking NATO, including a three-front force with 50-60 divisions and an initial preparation time of eight days, and a two-front force with 40 divisions and a preparation time of four days. A five-front force with 80-90 divisions would take two weeks to prepare.
BODY-130	blank
BODY-131	The page discusses Soviet military options for attacking NATO, including scenarios with two, three, or five fronts. The Soviets would prefer a larger attack force to ensure superiority and sustainability, but might initiate hostilities with a two-front force in urgent circumstances.
BODY-132	Pact plans for multiple fronts in Central Europe, preferring to penetrate NATO defenses through gaps and weak points. Soviet views anticipate strong NATO reaction, with tank armies held in reserve for breakthroughs. Doctrine includes massing forces on narrow frontages and deploying tactical nuclear missiles quickly.
BODY-133	Soviet military doctrine emphasizes the use of motorized rifle divisions for breakthrough operations against NATO, anticipating NATO's use of nuclear weapons and focusing on tanks versus antitank weapons. Pact forces plan to reduce vulnerability during breakthrough efforts by dispersing units and converging rapidly near contact points.
BODY-134	The page discusses Soviet tactics for tank warfare, including jamming NATO communication and radar links, reducing tank vulnerability to ATGMs, and differences in replacement concepts between the Pact and the US. It also outlines potential operations in Central Europe in the event of a major breakthrough.
BODY-135	The reliability of NSWP forces in the USSR Pact is crucial for victory in a conflict with NATO. The Air Operation concept involves a large-scale coordinated effort by different air forces to achieve specific objectives, with the goal of destroying enemy air and nuclear forces.
BODY-136	Pact forces have a large number of tactical aircraft and air defense fighters available for use in Central Europe, with a focus on suppressing air defenses, providing fighter cover, and attacking NATO airfields. The number of aircraft available for an Air Operation would vary based on the Pact's mobilization efforts.
BODY-137	Illustrative allocation of Pact combat aircraft for use in the Western theater of military operations in January 1979, including deployment postures, total aircraft available, and allocation for various operations. Includes details on limited and full reinforcement options.
BODY-138	Pact air forces are prepared for a major offensive against NATO, with plans to deploy tactical aircraft closer to the West German border and suppress NATO air

	defenses in Central Europe. Intelligence gathering and combat operations are key components of their strategy.
BODY-139	Illustrative map of Warsaw Pact air operation corridors against NATO Central Region, including NATO airbases, HAWK missile belt, and penetration corridors through Poland, West Berlin, Netherlands, France, Germany, and Switzerland.
BODY-140	Pact tactical aircraft would use various weapons and jamming techniques to attack NATO air defense systems, airfields, and command facilities, with a focus on disrupting radar and communications. Reconnaissance would be conducted to gather intelligence for targeting.
BODY-141	The page discusses the potential effectiveness of a Pact Air Operation in NATO territory, focusing on surprise tactics, aircraft losses, and coordination challenges. It highlights the importance of reducing NATO's warning time and the advantage of attacking air defenses through a corridor approach.
BODY-142	Pact air forces face challenges in coordinating large numbers of aircraft for defense suppression assaults, with potential difficulties in command and control, reconnaissance capabilities, and navigation. Vulnerabilities include reliance on ground control stations, susceptibility to electronic countermeasures, and limited capability for airfield attacks against NATO.
BODY-143	Pact aircrews lack proficiency and training for effective combat missions, making a successful Air Operation against NATO unlikely. NATO's nuclear strike potential remains a concern, but Pact's deficiencies and weaknesses limit their effectiveness.
BODY-144	Warsaw Pact naval operations in the Baltic Sea aimed to gain control of the area, destroy NATO submarines and patrol boats, and facilitate amphibious operations against Denmark and West Germany. Coordination and timing were crucial for success.
BODY-145	Warsaw Pact naval forces available for Western theater operations in 1979 included submarines, combatants, amphibious ships, and aircraft. Challenges included dealing with West-German and Danish submarines and achieving air superiority. ASW operations in the Baltic were hindered by hydrological conditions.
BODY-146	Baltic amphibious operations by Pact forces involve coordination of air defense, amphibious landings, and support for ground offensives, with a focus on achieving air superiority and sea control to prevent NATO interference and secure strategic objectives in the region.
BODY-147	Pact planners recognize the need for air superiority and sea control in the Baltic Sea for successful amphibious operations, with a focus on mine warfare and anti-ship air operations. The Soviets plan to deploy submarines to the North Sea before hostilities.
BODY-148	The page discusses the importance of air superiority and various factors influencing the outcome of the Pact's Baltic campaign, including NATO threats and potential offensives in different regions.
BODY-149	The page discusses potential Soviet invasion plans for Austria, Italy, Yugoslavia, and Turkey, focusing on ground operations, amphibious assaults, and political considerations. It highlights the importance of securing the southern flank of the Western TVD and the challenges faced in executing these operations.
BODY-150	Illustrative Warsaw Pact operations in the Southwestern TVD involve mobilizing forces from Bulgaria to attack Greece, with difficulties in ground campaigns and competition for resources with operations in the Western TVD. NATO would receive warning from movements in this theater.

BODY-151　Potential Pact land operations in Greece and Turkey would focus on engaging Greek forces in Thrace and defending the western flank of the Maritime Front attacking Turkey. Seizing the Turkish Straits would offer strategic benefits, but Pact forces may face challenges in achieving air and sea superiority in the region.

BODY-152　Soviet naval forces in the Mediterranean would target Western SSBNs and aircraft carriers at the start of a war, with surface and submarine units operating from bases in the Soviet Union and possibly NSWP countries. They would intensify surveillance before hostilities and be prepared to attack immediately.

BODY-153　Warsaw Pact tactical aircraft available for use in the Southwestern Theater of Military Operations in January 1979, with details on fighters, fighter-bombers, light bombers, and reconnaissance/electronic warfare aircraft. Soviets could use aircraft and submarines to attack NATO naval forces in the Mediterranean.

BODY-154　Soviet submarines in the Mediterranean would only attack high-value targets, while surface ships would support submarines and conduct ASW operations. There is uncertainty about whether the Soviets would augment their surface forces in the Mediterranean before hostilities. NATO's air superiority would pose a challenge to Soviet forces.

BODY-155　Debate over the purpose and necessity of the Black Sea Fleet in relation to operations in the Mediterranean and against Turkey. Initial Soviet objectives in the Northwestern Theater focus on naval access and defense, with limited operations likely in northern Norway.

BODY-156　Soviet naval operations in Northwestern TVD would involve limited amphibious operations in Finnmark area, with focus on seizing Norwegian bases in Troms for flank security. Initial ground offensive would be deterred by strong NATO resistance and limited air coverage in Norwegian territory.

BODY-157　Soviet forces plan to use ground, naval, and air operations in northern Norway to counter NATO air defenses and establish control of the Norwegian and Barents Seas during conflict. They anticipate NATO carrier forces and amphibious landings, with a focus on anti-submarine warfare and naval engagements.

BODY-158　Soviet plans for controlling the Norwegian and Barents Seas involve deploying submarines, strike aircraft, and surface ships to weaken or defeat NATO naval forces. The Soviets may face challenges in coordinating their forces and adjusting their strategy based on NATO actions.

BODY-159　Soviets likely to allocate submarines for antisubmarine warfare and tactical support to SSBNs in North Atlantic. Disagreement on number and role of submarines south of Iceland. Potential deployment for reconnaissance, attacks, and mining near NATO bases. Uncertainty on specific allocations due to flexibility of naval warfare.

BODY-160　Soviet operating areas in North Atlantic for sea control and sea denial, with focus on interdicting US reinforcements to Europe. Submarine ASW operations likely restricted to Norwegian Sea due to vulnerability to Western air defenses. Naval reconnaissance forces include intelligence collection ships and long-range aircraft.

BODY-161　Soviets plan to use submarines and aircraft to target NATO forces in the G-I-UK gap, but face challenges from NATO air defenses and ASW forces. They may deploy submarines and LRA aircraft to strike carriers and bases in Norway, Great Britain, and Iceland.

BODY-163　Soviet naval forces in the central Norwegian Sea would aim for total sea control, deploying submarines and surface combatants for ASW and antiship attacks.

BODY-164 *Strikes by aircraft and submarines would be massive and coordinated, with potential for rapid transition to nuclear operations.*

BODY-164 *Soviet forces in the Barents Sea and Norwegian Sea would respond to perceived threats by deploying strike regiments, submarines, ASW aircraft, and helicopters. Submarines would face challenges in detecting Western submarines, and protection of SSBNs would be a key task for attack submarines.*

BODY-165 *Soviet naval forces face challenges in anti-carrier warfare due to weaknesses in surface ships and submarines, but could pose a threat with cruise missiles. Cooperation between ships, submarines, and aircraft is key for effectiveness in the Norwegian Sea.*

BODY-166 *Assessment of potential effectiveness of Soviet naval platforms and strike aircraft in tactical contexts is deemed unrealistic and lacking consideration of demonstrated Soviet naval effectiveness.*

BODY-167 *Soviet tactical nuclear operations against NATO in Europe would involve a mix of tactical ballistic missiles, aircraft, and strategic systems, with the primary objective being the destruction of military targets. The scope and targets would depend on campaign objectives and NATO's nuclear use.*

BODY-168 *Soviets would likely use tactical missiles and aircraft in initial strikes, focusing on air defense systems. They are unlikely to initiate nuclear strikes at sea during a conventional war with NATO in Europe. Strategic forces would target NATO surface ships, submarines, and land targets if authorized.*

BODY-169 *Soviet strategic forces target NATO nuclear sites, airfields, and command facilities in Europe, with Long Range Aviation bombers used for initial and follow-up strikes. Missile accuracy varies, with submarines targeting large ports. Coordination with tactical nuclear forces is key.*

BODY-170 *Continued modernization of Soviet theater forces facing NATO, with growth in manpower and hardware. NATO defense posture improving, especially in Central Europe. No major changes expected in near-term defense programs. Soviet leadership change inevitable, but unlikely to alter focus on theater forces. Soviet defense spending growing steadily.*

BODY-171 *No major technological advancements or demographic changes are expected to significantly alter the size or composition of Warsaw Pact forces in the next decade. Manpower shortages may be addressed through adjustments in recruitment and service terms. Military capabilities opposite NATO are expected to gradually increase.*

BODY-172 *Soviets are restructuring tank divisions with new weapons and support systems, including laser-guided munitions. Standardization issues persist with multiple tank models in production. Tank forces will be modernized with new equipment, emphasizing the tank as the backbone of ground assault forces. Advanced antiarmor countermeasures are lacking.*

BODY-173 *Expected increases in Pact artillery units with improved weapons and target acquisition capabilities, including the introduction of man-portable antitank systems. Deployment of new SP artillery weapons and armored personnel carriers, with advancements in ground force air defense systems. Soviets working on improved conventional munitions for tube artillery.*

BODY-174 *Soviet air force modernization includes integration of radar and missile launcher, production of MIG-23 Flogger and MIG-21 Fishbed variants, and testing of tactical ballistic missiles with conventional munitions. New ground attack aircraft SU-25 expected by 1980. No major changes in fixed-wing aircraft numbers expected.*

BODY-175 Soviets are developing advanced air-launched cruise missiles, precision-guided bombs, and improving reconnaissance and helicopter forces. Expect modernization in avionics, air ordnance, and air transport. Increased focus on electronic countermeasures and air-to-air combat training.

BODY-176 The Soviet Navy is expected to improve its capabilities in cargo delivery, air defense, and naval warfare over the next decade, with a focus on modernization and integration of new technologies to counter NATO forces.

BODY-177 Soviet Navy focused on increasing submarine output and capabilities, with plans for new classes of nuclear-powered submarines and improvements in SLOC interdiction. Surface combatants expected to decrease in number but increase in firepower. Diesel submarines to decrease, nuclear submarines to increase.

BODY-178 Soviet Navy is expanding with new carriers and cruisers, impacting naval warfare capabilities and missions, but proficiency and effectiveness remain uncertain.

BODY-179 Soviet Navy modernization includes new ships, aircraft, and amphibious capabilities, with a focus on missile technology and improved combatants. Plans for new classes of patrol boats, hydrofoils, and amphibious landing ships are in progress, with a shift towards antiship missile and ASW combatants.

BODY-180 Soviets testing new missile systems for naval defense, including ASW, antiship, and air defense. Improvements in sonar, detection systems, and ocean surveillance expected by mid-1980s. New ELINT satellite operational. Potential for new antiship ASM for Backfire aircraft.

BODY-181 Soviets are improving tactical nuclear forces with new weapons, increased missile forces, and more pilots trained in nuclear delivery. Plans to expand artillery brigades and deploy new missiles indicate growing flexibility in nuclear operations. Deployment of SS-21 and SS-22 missiles expected to increase firepower.

BODY-182 Projected Soviet peripheral strike forces opposite NATO in 1979, 1983, and 1988, including MRBMs, bombers, and ballistic missile submarines. Changes in deployment and capabilities are discussed, with a focus on modernization and potential limitations due to arms control agreements.

BODY-183 The Pact is improving its command structure and electronic warfare capabilities through the creation of a centralized command system and integrated communications system by 1990. Logistic support and mobile communications equipment are also being enhanced.

BODY-184 Soviet military operations outside Europe during a NATO-Warsaw Pact war would be limited by geography, logistics, and focus on quick victory in Europe. Concern with China is secondary, with potential for conflict only if Chinese forces mass on border.

BODY-185 Soviets could face challenges in supporting an attack on South Korea by North Korea, risking escalation with US and China. Unclear how they would manage a prolonged conflict with NATO or China. Soviet Pacific Fleet poses a threat in the region.

BODY-186 Soviets view US Pacific Fleet as threat, likely to strike carriers within 1,000-1,500 nm of USSR. Disagreement on extent of strategic considerations in naval actions during war in Europe. Concerns about US combat aircraft in Japan, potential airstrikes on Alaskan targets.

BODY-187 Soviet naval forces in the Indian Ocean and Middle East lack air cover and are not prepared for extended wartime operations. They may disrupt Western shipping but

	are unlikely to undertake major ground or airborne operations during a NATO-Pact war.
BODY-188	*Soviet naval presence in the South Atlantic and Caribbean is limited, with occasional deployments and use of port facilities in Cuba. Cuba lacks resources for significant military contribution. Introduction of Flogger aircraft in Cuba could signal potential for attacks in the Caribbean during a NATO-Pact war.*
BODY-189	*Disposition of Warsaw Pact general purpose forces as of January 1, 1979.*
BODY-190	*Blank.*
BODY-191	*Disposition of Warsaw Pact Ground Forces in January 1979, detailing divisions opposite NATO Central Region and on NATO flanks, as well as other Soviet divisions in Eastern USSR and Mongolia. Total of 227 Warsaw Pact divisions, including 76 on NATO flanks.*
BODY-195	*Table showing disposition of Warsaw Pact tactical helicopter forces in January 1979, including breakdown by type and region. Total of 3,160 helicopters, with primary missions of ground attack, transport, and support. NATO's flanks had 875 helicopters, other Soviet helicopters in Eastern USSR totaled 950.*
BODY-197	*The page provides a breakdown of Soviet general purpose submarines by fleet area and type, detailing the number of antiship missile tubes and torpedo attack submarines in each category, with a total of 257 submarines, including 87 nuclear-powered units.*
BODY-198	*The table lists selected Soviet surface combatants and carriers by fleet area in January 1979, totaling 272 principal surface combatants. It includes aircraft carriers, missile cruisers, cruisers, missile destroyers, destroyers, missile frigates, and frigates.*
BODY-199	*Soviet Naval Combat Aircraft breakdown by fleet area in January 1979, including reconnaissance, strike, tankers, fighters, ASW aircraft, and helicopters. Total of 1,039 aircraft, excluding training and transport roles. Various configurations and capabilities noted.*
BODY-200	*Document outlining dissemination procedures for classified information by the National Foreign Assessment Center to authorized officials in various government departments and agencies.*

NOTABLE PASSAGES

BODY-6   This National Intelligence Estimate was prepared primarily to satisfy the need expressed by US policymakers and planners for a reference document that would record current estimates of Warsaw Pact forces and intelligence judgments about the way these forces would be employed in a war with NATO.

BODY-15   "It is Soviet policy to acquire and maintain forces capable of successfully fighting either a conventional or nuclear war in Europe and to keep a clear numerical advantage over NATO in important military assets. Soviet leaders stress the need for large, combat-ready forces to be in place at the outset of hostilities. They intend any future European conflict to take place on Western, not Eastern, territory."

BODY-17   Improvements in the USSR's forward-based nuclear forces would permit the Soviets to fight a tactical nuclear war at relatively high levels of intensity without having to use USSR-based systems. Nonetheless, the Soviets' continued modernization of USSR-based peripheral strike systems argue that they still expect to have to resort to the use of these weapons at some stage of theater nuclear war.

BODY-18   "The Soviets are aware of the improved technology and growing numbers of NATO antitank weapons, but this awareness has not led to any diminution of their tank forces or any major change in the way they see these forces performing. Indeed, they have made even further increases to their tank strength and have begun producing new tank models."

BODY-19   Warsaw Pact Strategy for Initial Conventional Operations Against NATO

11. The USSR has developed contingency plans for military operations on all Pact land frontiers. The Soviets clearly expect Central Europe to be the decisive arena in a war with NATO and assign it the highest priority in the allocation of military manpower and equipment. The Soviets also have plans for offensive action in other NATO regions, but we have little direct evidence on the Pact's view of the timing of these flank offensives in relation to an offensive in Central Europe. We judge, however, that the Pact would be unlikely to start a war by mounting major ground offensives against all NATO sectors simultaneously. To do so would unnecessarily extend available Pact forces, airlift, and air and logistic support and

BODY-20   The ultimate authority for the direction of the Soviet military rests with the Politburo and the Soviet General Staff, but we believe that should a war occur between the Warsaw Pact and NATO, theater-level commands would be established and exercise direct operational control over fronts and fleets and at least some degree of control over those strategic assets allocated to support theater operations. Unlike NATO, the Warsaw Pact does not have theater headquarters in being in peacetime, although hardened command posts have been constructed for at least some Pact wartime headquarters. (III, 4-6)

BODY-21   "Except in extraordinarily urgent circumstances, the Pact would prefer to prepare at least a three-front force before initiating hostilities in Central Europe. We believe the Pact would begin to organize at least five fronts for use in Central Europe from the time of the decision to go to full readiness. There is virtually no chance the Soviets would attack from a standing start." (IV, 10-22)

BODY-22   "While the most immediate threat would come from Soviet ships and submarines already deployed in the Mediterranean, numerically the most sizable threat to NATO's naval forces there would come from missile-equipped Soviet strike aircraft, despite the fact that they would be operating without fighter escort." (IV, 135)

BODY-23   Soviet strategy in the North Atlantic calls for the early establishment of control of the Norwegian and Barents Seas and their approaches. Implementation of such a strategy probably would involve most of the Northern Fleet's submarines and virtually all of the surface forces and aircraft in an effort to exclude NATO forces from the area. The Soviets probably also plan some submarine operations farther into the North Atlantic to prevent transit of NATO carriers and amphibious task groups and to divert NATO naval strength. The Soviets would attempt to neutralize Western SSBNs near their bases and in the Norwegian Sea before they could launch their missiles. To this end they probably would initiate submarine and air operations against NATO naval forces as they exit their bases in Europe and possibly -against SSBNs from US

BODY-24   "New Soviet leaders will undoubtedly emerge from the ranks of the present group, which is responsible for creating current Pact forces and is committed to maintaining Soviet military strength in Europe. The new leaders will likely seek to avoid moves that would antagonize large segments of the military." (VI, 5)

BODY-25   "We foresee no development over the next several years which would appreciably alter the basic Pact strategy of an armor-heavy offensive against NATO in Central Europe." (VI, 17)

BODY-26   "We estimate that the centralized command structure could be complete by the early 1980s. The unified communications system could begin to improve the Pact's command capabilities by the mid-1980s, but it is not scheduled for completion until 1990." (VI, 101)

BODY-27   b. Number of Soviet Motorized Rifle Divisions (MRDs) That Have an Independent Tank Battalion (ITB). NSA, Army, and Air Force believe that all MRDs in Eastern Europe have an ITB. They base their position on COMINT and Soviet classified writings. Army and Air Force further believe that an ITB with an MRD would be standard in wartime. DIA and CIA estimate that two-thirds of the Soviet MRDs in Eastern Europe have ITBs but that few, if any, in the western USSR do. They base their view on COMINT, Pact exercises, and the fact that photography does not show independent tank battalions with other Soviet MRDs in Eastern Europe and the western USSR.

BODY-29   DIA and Army believe that the Pact would use both an individual and a unit replacement system and that the system used in a particular case would depend upon the situation. They further believe that individual replacement would be used primarily in cases of steady, attrition-type losses, while unit replacement would be used primarily in cases of large, sudden losses. (II, 231-232)

BODY-31   "Potential Effectiveness of Soviet Naval Operations in the North Atlantic. Paragraphs 191-197 of chapter IV consider that the evident technical limitations of the weapons and sensors on Soviet ships, submarines, and aircraft could impact significantly on Soviet efforts to control the Norwegian and Barents Seas, although the mutually supportive aspects of some operations may offset certain technical weaknesses. DIA and Navy believe that these paragraphs should convey a more balanced appraisal of potential effectiveness and that, as now phrased, they tend to overstress the weaknesses of Soviet platforms; they tend to give inadequate consideration of strengths, including the operation of these platforms as a mutually supportive force; and they tend to assess effectiveness in tactical contexts which are unrealistic." (IV, 191-200)

BODY-32   "constitutes a major watershed in the development of the Soviet Navy, has influenced the acquisition of other future ships, and has already exerted a significant influence on naval operations."

BODY-35 Soviet leaders believe that the initial stages of a conflict probably would be conventional, and they would prefer that a NATO-Pact conflict remain non-nuclear in order to avoid the catastrophic consequences of nuclear war and to take advantage of their superiority in conventional ground forces in Central Europe. Nevertheless, it is clear that the Soviets see a high probability that such a war would ultimately involve the use of nuclear weapons initiated either by the United States to avoid defeat in Europe or by the.

BODY-36 Estimate defined as the Soviets might view their defense effort Estimate defined for comparison with US accounts. Expenditures shown in charts B and C represent spending on investment for and-operation of general-purpose peripheral attack, strategic, and support forces. These expenditures are derived from our latest estimate of order-of-battle data on deployed forces and the costs associated with these forces.

BODY-37 Despite the Soviets' having adopted a policy for more flexible use of tactical nuclear weapons, and notwithstanding the impressive improvements they have made in forward-based tactical nuclear capabilities, they have not sought to match NATO's capacity for accurate and selective use of very-low-yield nuclear weapons.

BODY-38 Nonetheless, the Soviets continue modernization of USSR-based peripheral strike systems argues that they still expect to have to resort to the use of these weapons at some stage of theater nuclear war. Their uncertainty about their actual ability to deter the West from launching strategic nuclear strikes against Soviet territory in the face of a successful Soviet conventional assault-which is complicated by the existence of independent French and British nuclear systems targeted against the USSR-further argues against the likelihood that the Soviets would anticipate much success in achieving a decoupling strategy.

BODY-40 These agencies believe that in the final analysis the overriding factors governing first use of chemical weapons by the Soviets would be their assessment of NATO's chemical warfare capabilities and the advantages they expected to gain from such weapons.

BODY-42 They estimate that the United States could quickly augment the tactical air forces in Europe and deploy as many as four additional aircraft carriers to the European theater. They are extremely conservative in evaluating NATO's combat potential and sometimes ascribe exaggerated capabilities to NATO. The increase in conventional firepower in the ground and air forces has especially enhanced the Pact's ability to overcome organized NATO defenses in the absence of the nuclear strikes which formerly were relied upon to blast holes for the passage of armored striking forces in the opening phase of a European war.

BODY-43 Pact theater forces have emerged from a decade of change with their fundamental orientation on the tank intact, but with a more balanced structure for conventional war and with both conventional and nuclear firepower greatly increased.

BODY-44 "Pact forces opposite NATO are predominantly Soviet, but NSWP forces make a significant contribution and indeed are critical to Soviet strategy for conflict in Europe. Since the mid-1960s both Soviet and NSWP forces have been characterized by a growth in manpower and equipment and by modernization programs to improve their capabilities. Overall, the changes of the past decade or so have made these forces more balanced and operationally flexible, with improved capabilities for both nuclear and nonnuclear warfare."

BODY-45 "Armor has dominated Pact ground forces for the past several decades. During the decade before the mid-1960s, when Soviet military planners believed that war in

BODY-46 and earlier context:

> Europe could be nuclear from the outset, the survivability of armored forces underscored their value relative to other ground forces."

BODY-46   The mainstay of the Pact ground forces is the medium tank. In all, Pact forces opposite NATO have about 45,000 medium tanks at their disposal. Of these about 25,000 (10,500 Soviet, 14,500 NSWP) are located in Eastern Europe. Soviet forces are equipped with a mix of T-54/55, T-62, T-64, and T-72 models, while the NSWP armies rely almost exclusively on the T-54/55 series, with some T-34s still in the active forces. The T-55, which was first manufactured in 1958, is still in production; production of the T-62 ended in 1975.

BODY-51   'There is disagreement over whether the maximum range of the SA-4 is 50 or 80 kilometers.'

BODY-55   These divisions could probably mobilize reserve personnel and equipment and begin movement within about 48 hours, with selected elements moving even more rapidly. Their initial combat effectiveness would be lower than that of Category I divisions.

BODY-56   The training of Soviet soldiers begins before their induction into the armed forces. Compulsory preinduction training, which is prescribed by the Soviet 1967 Law on Universal Military Service, is believed to range from about 250 men to several times that figure. They are composed of a number of teams whose strength may vary from three to 15 men, given either in secondary schools, in the professional and technical education system, or at places of work. It includes a 140-hour basic training course designed to familiarize youths with the armed forces and provide psychological preparation for military service. Tactical field training is conducted in summer camps and includes weapons familiarization and live firing, marches, and tactical drills. Many specialists for the armed forces also receive some training

BODY-57   There is disagreement in the Intelligence Community regarding the success the Soviets have had in recruiting soldiers into their programs. According to one view, the Soviets have had little success, at least through the extended service program, in persuading conscript soldiers to remain in the service. The holders of this view note the harsh and demanding aspects of Soviet military service and point to the numerous reports from defectors, emigre of morale and disciplinary problems within the armed forces as the basis for this judgment.

BODY-58   The Soviet soldier is well drilled in his job. Units generally can carry out the basic maneuvers envisioned in tactical doctrine. Major weaknesses include the prevalence of rote, unrealistic, drill-type training at lower levels. The heavy use of simulators, subcaliber devices, and training equipment adds to this lack of realism. Army- and front-level staffs train primarily by command post exercises, often with extensive signal support and limited troop participation. While these exercises often involve realistic scenarios, staffs rarely have the opportunity actually to control and coordinate large numbers of troops in the field.

BODY-62   "Recent developments tend to indicate that the Warsaw Pact and particularly Soviet Frontal Aviation plan to conduct most wartime operations from main airfields where aircraft can be protected in hardened aircraft shelters. For more than 85 percent of the Soviet tactical aircraft in the NSWP countries, there now are facilities adequate to accommodate one armed, combat-ready aircraft per shelter. The sharing of shelters would provide protection for many more aircraft, although readiness would suffer because of engine starting restrictions and ground handling problems."

BODY-63 The combat capability of these units continues to be hampered by those pilots-25 to 35 percent of the total available-who are not qualified to conduct night or all-weather combat missions. Moreover, pilot proficiency has not progressed sufficiently to exploit fully the capabilities of the airframes and weapon systems of the third-generation aircraft currently in operation.

BODY-67 The Central Intelligence Agency believes that the operational assumptions basic to the NATO Mission Profile Hi-Lo-Hi definition are extremely optimistic and produce combat radius estimates which cannot be achieved under wartime conditions. CIA believes that the combat radii associated with the Lo-Lo-Hi definitions are much more in line with Warsaw Pact estimates of the combat radius capability of Pact aircraft and are in fact a more realistic reflection of Pact intentions concerning the use of these aircraft.

BODY-68 "In recent years the Soviets have introduced the MI-24 Hind, the first of their helicopters designed primarily for ordnance delivery. It offers such advantages over earlier helicopters as improved all-weather capabilities and versatility. The Hind also has an air-to-air capability against other helicopters and low, slow-flying fixed-wing aircraft."

BODY-70 With nearly all VTA airlift assets and Soviet airborne divisions deployed in the western USSR, VTA's airborne assault potential is clearly targeted toward Central Europe and NATO's flanks. Numerous airfields in nearby Warsaw Pact countries would be available for recovery and servicing, adequate fighter coverage is close at hand, and VTA crews are relatively familiar with the area.

BODY-71 For operations in the Mediterranean Sea, the Black Sea Fleet furnishes most of the surface ships and the Northern Fleet the submarines.

BODY-73 If the Soviets were not concerned with covert deployment of their ships to sea, they could probably get about half of their force opposite NATO under way with varying degrees of combat effectiveness within 48 hours. Those remaining units not undergoing major repairs or overhaul probably could put to sea in about four days, but would do so with reduced effectiveness. Naval air units normally maintain a low level of peacetime activity; most could reach full

BODY-75 The difficulties are brought out in reports concerning alcoholism, poor performance aboard ship, absences without leave, disciplinary infractions, and even a mutiny aboard a destroyer. These problems, which are reflections of Soviet society as a whole, could have an adverse impact upon peacetime training and materiel readiness programs and thus would explain the concern of senior naval authorities.

BODY-80 There is insufficient evidence to judge how the Soviets would use either of these aircraft against ships at sea or how effective they might be in wartime. Most Forger training thus far has been of the kind useful for attacks against ships at sea. The Fitters, however, all of which are based in the Baltic, are probably intended for ground attack in support of amphibious operations and antiship attacks.

BODY-82 The forces opposite NATO which are most capable of ASW operations beyond coastal waters include about 50 Soviet principal surface combatants, 30 nuclear-powered torpedo attack submarines, and about 45 fixed-wing ASW aircraft. The 16 ships with helicopters (those of the Kiev, Moskva, Kara, and Kresta-II classes) and the Krivak frigates are equipped with long-range (15 to 30 nm, or 28 to 56 km) ASW weapons. Only the Kiev- and Moskva-class units combine these features with a long-range (typically less than 10 nm) active sonar and more than one helicopter. Soviet ASW helicopters, however, are limited in their ASW operations at night

BODY-85   There is disagreement within the Intelligence Community concerning the extent, emphasis, and timing of the interdiction campaign. Some believe that the Soviets would commit some of their submarine fleet to an interdiction campaign, but not a large portion unless they had earlier defeated NATO carrier and amphibious forces without losing many of their submarines. Others believe that the Soviets would regard interdiction of US reinforcements to Europe to be of such significance and their submarine inventory of sufficient depth to warrant use of substantial numbers of attack submarines in this effort while still accomplishing their other missions.

BODY-87   Control of the airspace over an amphibious landing area in Europe would be a prerequisite for establishing a beachhead. Because the majority of likely Warsaw Pact amphibious objectives would be within the range of Soviet or East European airfields, land-based tactical aircraft could be made available to support the assault forces. The Soviet Fitter C/D regiment in the Baltic Fleet Air Force and some 50 MIG-17 Frescos of the Polish Navy probably would support Pact amphibious operations in the Baltic Sea.

BODY-88   "The Soviets have given their East European allies reason to believe that they will be provided nuclear weapons in wartime. The NSWP national commands, particularly the Polish and Czechoslovak commands, evidently train and plan for the eventuality that they will receive nuclear warheads in wartime."

BODY-89   "The circular error probable (CEP) of the SS-21 is estimated to be 200 to 300 meters at two-thirds the maximum range of 120 to 130 kilometers. This is a significant improvement in accuracy over the FROG-7, with a CEP of 400 meters at two-thirds the maximum range of 70 kilometers."

BODY-90   There is no reliable evidence that the Soviets have nuclear rounds for their 152-mm artillery pieces-the largest now in the forces in Central Europe.

BODY-92   The major portion of the land-based ballistic missile force that would be employed for peripheral attack consists of 416 SS-4 MRBM and 80 SS-5 IRBM launchers located at 54 complexes in the European and south-central USSR. This force includes 118 silo launchers and 378 aboveground launchers with fixed launch pads, a mode of deployment which makes them vulnerable to attack. Of these launchers, 445 are believed to be aimed against NATO and other targets on the western periphery of the USSR. The remaining 51 launchers probably are for use against targets in Asia and the Middle East.

BODY-97   There are only about 20 aircraft configured as tankers in the intermediate-range bomber force. In the past, the Soviets have made little use of this limited capability; in the case of the TU-22, aerial refueling has rarely been noted.

BODY-99   These assessments assume that the Backfire flies a straight-line unrefueled mission with bombs, is on an optimum high-altitude flight profile to and from the vicinity of the target area, but flies the last 200 nm to and from the target at a subsonic speed at low level.

BODY-100 According to one view, it is not possible with the evidence at hand to derive with confidence a single-figure capability for the maximum radius/range of the Backfire. The holders of this view are the Director, National Security Agency, and the Director of Naval Intelligence, Department of the Navy.

BODY-102 The nature of CW agent production is such that positive identification of production facilities within an industrial chemical complex is virtually impossible without knowledgeable human sources.

BODY-106 Pact logistic doctrine specifies that additional stocks are to be kept in the theater and in the national reserve to supply the fronts. In particular, responsibility for ensuring the flow of these supplies in wartime is assigned to the commander of the higher echelon from or through which they are to flow. In all cases of supply movement, ammunition has priority because it is critical to combat.

BODY-107 At this daily average rate of expenditure, and assuming no destruction of stocks, we calculate that there would be sufficient ammunition in the Central Region and the three western military districts of the USSR to sustain Pact forces for 40 to 50 days. It should be noted that this period could be lengthened considerably by drawing ammunition from the strategic reserve stocks in the USSR, particularly those located west of the Urals. Portions of these stocks, which total approximately 2.2 million tons, could be moved forward either in a buildup phase prior to the initiation of hostilities or during a subsequent reinforcement phase after hostilities had begun.

BODY-108 "In a war of short duration and high intensity the ability to sustain the momentum of an advance is determined not only by the availability of stocks but equally by the capability to move supplies, materiel, and personnel forward."

BODY-109 The major through-routes connecting Central Europe and the western USSR have a combined capacity of about 500,000 metric tons per day in each direction. In contrast to the well-established network in Central Europe, the rail networks on the flanks are not nearly as dense or well developed.

BODY-111 We believe that, rather than depend on stockpiles of war reserve equipment to replace losses in the early stages of a war, the Soviets would rely upon unit replacement by fully equipped units which exist in peacetime as low-strength or mobilization divisions. The large number of such units available are probably viewed by the Soviets as sufficient to sustain the forces until such time as production after M-day could build up new equipment reserves. The Soviets have modest stockpiles of older equipment not in units in the USSR, but our information on the serviceability and purpose of this equipment is scant. The stockpiles include some 1,400 tanks, approximately 7,000 artillery pieces, some 8,500 various air defense artillery pieces, about

BODY-112 "240. Total Pact air force consumption (not including air-to-surface missiles) during a campaign of 12 days would be about 40 percent of air ordnance stocks calculated to be stored in the East Germany, Poland, and Czechoslovakia, and the three western military districts. If there were no destruction of stocks, about 215,000 metric tons of ammunition would remain, sufficient to sustain air operations for an estimated additional 20 to 25 days. Air force consumption of POL for a campaign of 12 days would be about 640,000 metric tons. Approximately 1.9 million tons would remain available for an additional 40 to 45 days."

BODY-114 Merchant and naval distress communications traffic continues to indicate that a central authority is cognizant of the location of all merchant shipping on a near-real-time, 24-hour basis. The Soviets view naval command and control over merchant shipping as a routine measure which can be widely implemented in an emergency without the necessity of advanced notices and prior coordination.

BODY-115 There is very little information on the availability of spare parts at naval bases, ship repair yards, and supply depot complexes. Nonetheless we estimate that the fleet rear services organizations maintain sufficient stocks in dispersed locations to sustain combatants and submarines through at least 90 to 120 days of combat operations. During that time, defense industries could continue to produce replacements for high-usage items. Damaged ships could be selected for cannibalization, as necessary, in order to keep other units operational.

BODY-116　The ultimate authority for the direction of the Soviet military rests with the Politburo of the Communist Party of the Soviet Union. The Defense Council establishes military policy and makes fundamental decisions regarding the employment of military forces. Brezhnev, predesignated as Supreme Commander in Chief, would lead a Supreme High Command drawn from elements of the Ministry of Defense. This command would constitute the military-strategic leadership over all Pact military operations against NATO. The VGK probably includes at least the three first deputy ministers of defense and the commanders in chief of the five components of the Soviet armed forces.

BODY-118　In considering a future war with NATO, Soviet strategists envision widespread combat operations encompassing all of Europe and extending into the North Atlantic. Accordingly, they plan to divide the Western TV into three land TVDs in which they expect Pact and NATO forces to come in conflict. The Northwestern TVD, the Western TVD, and the Southwestern TVD are defined, each encompassing different regions and scenarios for military operations. The Soviets also expect major naval operations against NATO in the North Atlantic to occur in conjunction with a conflict in Europe. The complexity and strategic planning involved in these potential scenarios highlight the depth of Soviet military strategy.

BODY-124　"The Pact is demonstrating an increasing degree of interoperability in communications equipment."

BODY-125　We believe, however, that the need for unfettered naval operations from their Northern Fleet bases would almost certainly cause the Soviets to strike NATO facilities in northern Norway, and probably to attempt to occupy some territory there, and that the urgency of this need would lead them to do so concurrently with starting an attack in Central Europe.

BODY-128　The Soviets, considering their conservative view of NATO rapid mobilization capabilities, might well conclude that the attacking force could face an adverse situation before reinforcements could be committed. The attack would initially have to rely on incomplete lines of communication. The Soviets would not have time to establish a front-level command, control, and communications structure or to prepare the Soviet or East European populace or national economies for warfare-both basic requirements posed in Soviet military literature. Finally, the standing-start attack would leave other Pact strategic and general purpose forces-as well as the national economy-unprepared for expanded hostilities. In particular the Soviets would be concerned about the threat of NATO escalation to nuclear war.

BODY-129　"The smallest force the Pact might use to start theater offensive operations probably would consist of two fronts-a total of some 40 ground divisions plus support and tactical air units. In the most urgent circumstances, the Pact would need about four days to prepare this force. Attack with slightly less than four days is possible, but the complexity of the operation and the risks attending insufficient preparation would likely cause the Soviets to take more than four days to prepare this force."

BODY-131　Option III-Attack With Three Fronts. The third and fourth options are ones in which Soviet planners, under a less urgent need to defend or attack, would elect to bring the Pact to full readiness via a more efficient, phased buildup procedure and to attack when the force available for initial operations totaled three fronts (Option III) or five fronts (Option IV). The same evidence cited earlier on Pact buildup planning and procedures indicates that, in these circumstances, the Pact preference for a larger-than-two-front attack is well supported in Soviet writings and by analysis of Pact exercises. The phased buildup to three fronts-a total of some 50 to 60 divisions plus support and tactical air units-would offer a reasonable expectation of an orderly and efficient transition to an attack

BODY-132 The Pact would prefer to employ forces on multiple axes, moving in tactical march columns to penetrate defense positions through gaps; weak points, and open flanks, relying heavily on speed and maneuver. In areas where the Pact believed that it must penetrate strong, continuous NATO defenses it would mount breakthrough operations on each principal axis of advance. Depending on the importance of the axis of advance to the overall theater offensive plan and the strength of the defense, a breakthrough attempt might involve the major forces of either a front or an army.

BODY-133 The Soviets place considerable stress on efforts to anticipate NATO's intention to use nuclear weapons on a large scale and to anticipate it in time to launch a Pact preemptive attack. To this end, they expect to keep their own nuclear delivery systems in a high state of readiness and to conduct a vigorous reconnaissance and intelligence-collecting campaign against NATO's nuclear units and facilities, as well as its communications networks, to detect signs which might presage the imminent use of nuclear weapons.

BODY-135 The Pact would commit most of its tactical aircraft and a large number of its Long Range Aviation (LRA) bombers to a series of air assaults designed to achieve tactical surprise at the outset of hostilities and lasting for the first two to four days of combat.

BODY-136 Pact planners would regard attacks against NATO airfields as the principal way of gaining air superiority. They would intend such attacks to damage runways and other airfield facilities and thus degrade NATO's ability to operate its air forces effectively. They would also expect airfield attacks to account for most of the aircraft NATO would lose during the Air Operation. Pact fighter and ground-based air defenses would be expected, however, to contribute to the battle for air superiority by inflicting significant losses on NATO's air forces in the air.

BODY-137 "Allocation of tactical combat aircraft between ground forces support and the Air Operation is based on a 20-80 split after nuclear alert forces are withheld. This allocation is based on documentary evidence. Although we have no direct evidence, a 20-80 allocation between ground support and the Air Operation was also applied to tactical reconnaissance and electronic warfare aircraft."

BODY-141 Surprise would affect the Pact's chances of losses during the Air Operation. We believe, however, that the Pact probably would not measure the success of the Air Operation in these terms. Substantial Pact losses might be viewed as tolerable to Pact planners contemplating a short, decisive conflict, even if the Air Operation managed only to keep NATO's air forces preoccupied with fending for their own survival during the first few days of hostilities.

BODY-142 "Recent improvements in Pact reconnaissance capabilities should increase the speed with which strike aircraft could react to exploit intelligence giving the location of HAWK batteries. Soviet reconnaissance units in Central Europe, for example, now have aircraft equipped with television (Brewer D and Fishbed H). These aircraft types also have a real-time communications link to ground control stations that could direct strike aircraft to newly identified targets."

BODY-143 "By US standards, Pact tactical aircrews generally are not well trained for combat in the hostile environment they would likely encounter in executing the Air Operation. The training Pact aircrews receive is largely stereotyped, lacks realism, *and does not prepare them to exploit the full potential of their aircraft and its weapons systems."*

BODY-144 The broad objectives of Pact naval operations would be to gain complete control of the Baltic Sea and access to the North Sea to sever NATO's lines of communication in the North Sea, and deprive NATO of potential launch areas for carrier strikes against Pact air and ground forces in the Central Region. Control of the Baltic Sea would also facilitate subsequent amphibious operations against Denmark and West Germany, act as a defensive buffer for Pact territory, and defend Pact sea lines of communication from NATO attack.

BODY-145 "The Soviets probably would find it difficult to deal with West-German and Danish submarines in the Baltic, particularly if these forces were well coordinated. NATO boats have good shallow-water operating capabilities, are quiet, and have well-trained crews. Moreover, the Soviets would find it difficult to conduct antisubmarine warfare (ASW) operations without air superiority."

BODY-147 We conclude that failure to attain air superiority and sea control of the western Baltic, especially in conventional war, would almost certainly cause the Pact to reconsider the feasibility of its planned amphibious operations. If the amphibious assaults were canceled, Pact planners would also have to decide if any airborne operations could be conducted independently.

BODY-148 According to one view in the Intelligence Community, the allocation of most Pact tactical and LRA bomber aircraft to a large-scale Air Operation in West Germany and the Benelux countries would severely reduce the probability of the Pact's achieving air superiority over the Baltic in the initial stage of a war with NATO. Without air superiority, the Pact would have a low probability of sweeping NATO's mines or of successfully defending the amphibious force against NATO missile-armed fast patrol boats. It is further believed that Pact ASW forces probably would be unable to prevent NATO submarine attacks against the amphibious forces.

BODY-150 The ground campaign to seize the Straits would be difficult and time-consuming and would provide NATO time to obstruct the Straits and the mission of the Balkan Front is to break through Greek fortifications and to advance to the Aegean Sea and from there into.

BODY-152 An important initial mission of Pact tactical air forces would be to suppress NATO's forward air defenses in southern Europe, thus permitting the overflight of Long Range Aviation and naval aircraft heading for the Mediterranean. The Pact may also have plans to conduct a conventional air operation using tactical and LRA aircraft against NATO airfields in the Mediterranean area, but their ability to conduct such an operation would be constrained by the concurrent requirement for LRA bombers to conduct an air offensive in Central Europe and by the limited number of Pact fighter-bombers in the Southwestern TVD.

BODY-153 "whenever possible, the Soviets would use 20 to 40 aircraft to attack an important target such as an aircraft carrier task group. This number would be designed to overwhelm NATO air defenses and achieve the six to 10 hits which the Soviets believe are necessary to disable an aircraft carrier using conventional warheads."

BODY-156 During a period of tension before a war with NATO, the Soviet Northern Fleet would establish surface, submarine, and air patrols in the Norwegian and Barents Seas and attempt to detect and track Western forces in nearby waters. As the likelihood of a conflict increased, defensive minefields probably would be established along the sea approaches to the Soviet coast.

BODY-157 Soviet strategy calls for the early establishment of control of the Norwegian and Barents Seas and their approaches. Operations farther into the North Atlantic to prevent transit of NATO carriers and amphibious task groups and to divert NATO naval strength are probably also planned. The Soviets would attempt to.

BODY-161 If ships are important elements of Soviet ocean surveillance because they can monitor the disposition of NATO naval surface forces in distant areas without relying on NATO electronic emissions. Once hostilities began, however, these forces probably would suffer heavy attrition. TU-95 reconnaissance operations probably would then be restricted primarily to the Norwegian Sea, with occasional sorties into the North Atlantic.

BODY-163 It is unlikely that any Soviet surface combatant ships would be concentrated initially near the G-I-UK gap because they would be vulnerable to air attacks if NATO maintained air superiority in the area. In addition, fighter air cover for Soviet surface ships would be unavailable there because of the distances from Warsaw Pact airfields. YAK-36 V/STOL (vertical/short takeoff and landing) aircraft operating from the Kiev aircraft carrier probably would be unable to cope effectively with NATO high-performance fighters.

BODY-165 For anticarrier warfare, the Soviets' reliance on external targeting support could effectively restrict the operating areas of their long-range cruise missile submarines, such as the E-I and the J-class, to areas within range of the Bear D aircraft. In addition, these submarines must surface to launch their missiles and hence would be vulnerable. The more modern C-class would pose a more serious threat in distant waters, but these submarines probably would not be able to keep up with fast-moving carrier strike forces. Moreover, Soviet cruise-missile-armed submarines normally carry a mixed load of nuclear and conventionally armed missiles, thereby reducing the number available for conventional strikes.

BODY-166 Realistically, the potential effectiveness of Soviet strike aircraft should be measured in terms of radar coverage, as well as fighter coverage, that would have suffered some degradation in the early stages of hostilities.

BODY-167 Once the decision to use nuclear weapons was made, all tactical systems probably would come into play and the timing and targeting of tactical strikes would be planned to take advantage of the special characteristics of each system. The primary objective in Soviet tactical nuclear planning appears to be the assured destruction of military targets. Limiting collateral damage does not appear to be a main concern.

BODY-168 We believe that Soviet doctrine emphasizes counterforce rather than countervalue strikes. The prime objective of Soviet nuclear forces in wartime.

BODY-169 The Soviet Strategic Rocket Forces would have a key role during large-scale nuclear operations. Although the SRF's medium- and intermediate-range ballistic missiles would be assigned a variety of strategic targets, some sources have indicated they would be primarily used to destroy NATO airfields, air defenses, and command and control facilities beyond the reach of the Pact's forward-based tactical systems.

BODY-170 Nothing in NATO's current or near-term defense programs, however, is likely to precipitate any major change in the level of Pact efforts.

BODY-171 "In every Warsaw Pact country the military manpower procurement system depends on conscription. Conscripts provide up to 75 percent of the manpower assigned to the regular armed forces, the border guards, and some elements of the internal security forces. During the next decade, however, the number of young men reaching draft age each year will decline in most Pact countries, a trend that

BODY-174   *will complicate the allocation of manpower between the armed forces and industry."*

BODY-174   *The most interesting passage is: "New missiles such as the SS-21 have characteristics that give them a significant conventional capability. The SS-21, for example, could be used effectively with improved conventional munitions in an air defense suppression role. In such a role, tactical missiles offer the advantages of tactical surprise and assured penetrability, but they require timely and accurate reconnaissance data."*

BODY-176   *During the next decade, developments in the Soviet Navy will produce a force with improved capabilities to perform its peacetime and wartime missions. The Soviets will also press forward with programs to correct shortcomings in submarine detection, fleet air defense, logistic support, and communications. Indeed, developments over the past decade have been so rapid that a period of time may be required to integrate and consolidate advances and ensure that combat potentials are fully realized.*

BODY-177   *During the next decade we estimate that the number of diesel submarines will decrease from about 170 to about 85 as older units are replaced on a less than one-for-one basis; nuclear attack submarines will increase from 43 to about 75; nuclear cruise missile submarines will increase from 44 to about 55. Thus, the total number of general purpose submarines will decrease by about 15 percent - from 257 to about 215. Because a greater proportion of the force will be nuclear, however, there will be a significant increase in overall capabilities.*

BODY-178   *According to an alternative view, the acquisition of carriers with introduction of the Kiev clearly constitutes a major watershed in the development of the Soviet Navy. The holders of this view further believe that the Kiev already has influenced the acquisition of other future surface combatants, and enhances Soviet antiship, ASW, and other capabilities to an extent that could have significant influence on Pact naval operations in a NATO-Warsaw Pact war.*

BODY-179   *"The Backfire, using a variable flight profile and speeds near Mach 1.5 at high altitude, has a penetration capability against aircraft carrier defenses significantly superior to that of the Badger. The Backfire is currently being produced at a rate of between two and three per month, and to date deployment has been nearly equal between the Navy and Long Range Aviation. We project that production of the Backfire will continue into the 1980s."*

BODY-184   *"Despite increasing Soviet strategic concern with China and the major military buildup they have conducted in the Far Eastern USSR, the preponderance of evidence indicates that their main concern is still with the West."*

BODY-185   *A two-front war with China and NATO would represent the worst case situation for the Soviets. It would involve major ground and tactical air units in Asia and, depending on military developments, could require the Soviets to draw upon their strategic reserve force. Soviet reinforcements would be required to defeat a large Chinese conventional attack or to permit the Soviets any chance of overrunning all of northern China. If the Soviets were able to maintain their forward or defensive positions against China, the leadership probably would continue to give priority consideration to the Western theater. Major Chinese advances into Soviet territory during the early stages of a European war, as the Soviets have simulated in exercises, would be likely to cause Moscow to send some reserves to Asia.*

BODY-186   *The possibility of becoming embroiled in a two-front war against the United States, Japan, and China in the Far East while fighting NATO in Europe would weigh heavily in Moscow's decision whether to initiate combat operations in the Pacific. Nonetheless, the Soviets clearly regard the US Pacific Fleet as a dangerous adversary to be kept outside of striking distance of the USSR. Soviet sea control capabilities against US carrier and amphibious task groups are considerable in the area within about 1,000 to 1,500 nautical miles of the USSR.*

BODY-187   *The objective of these operations would be the securing of Middle East oil sources, rather than only interdicting the flow of oil to the West. Under these circumstances, Soviet forces in the Transcaucasus, North Caucasus, and Turkestan Military Districts, for example, might well be employed in ground and airborne operations through Iran into the Persian Gulf area.*

BODY-188   *"Operations in the Caribbean have to consider that offensive actions against the United States during the early stages of a NATO-Warsaw Pact war could result in decisive US retaliation."*

HR70-14

Warsaw Pact Forces Opposite NATO

National Intelligence Estimate
Volume II—The Estimate

Top Secret
NIE 11-14-79
31 January 1979
Copy 453

Warning Notice
Sensitive Intelligence Sources and Methods Involved
(WNINTEL)

NATIONAL SECURITY INFORMATION
Unauthorized Disclosure Subject to Criminal Sanctions

DISSEMINATION CONTROL ABBREVIATIONS

NOFORN–	Not Releasable to Foreign Nationals
NOCONTRACT–	Not Releasable to Contractors or Contractor/Consultants
PROPIN–	Caution—Proprietary Information Involved
NFIBONLY–	NFIB Departments Only
ORCON–	Dissemination and Extraction of Information Controlled by Originator
REL . . .–	This Information Has Been Authorized for Release to . . .

This publication is available on microfiche. To get a microfiche copy of this publication call ▢ (OCR/DSB); for future issuances in addition to or in lieu of hard copies, call ▢ (NFAC/Registry).

Top Secret

NIE 11-14-79

WARSAW PACT FORCES
OPPOSITE NATO

Volume II—The Estimate

SECRET

Top Secret

THIS ESTIMATE IS ISSUED BY THE DIRECTOR OF CENTRAL INTELLIGENCE.

THE NATIONAL FOREIGN INTELLIGENCE BOARD CONCURS, EXCEPT AS NOTED IN THE TEXT.

The following intelligence organizations participated in the preparation of the Estimate:

    The Central Intelligence Agency, the intelligence organizations of the Departments of State and Defense, and the National Security Agency

Also Participating:

    The Assistant Chief of Staff for Intelligence, Department of the Army

    The Director of Naval Intelligence, Department of the Navy

    The Assistant Chief of Staff, Intelligence, Department of the Air Force

PAGE LEFT BLANK INTENTIONALLY

PREFACE

This National Intelligence Estimate was prepared primarily to satisfy the need expressed by US policymakers and planners for a reference document that would record current estimates of Warsaw Pact forces and intelligence judgments about the way these forces would be employed in a war with NATO. It is intended to provide a baseline for any further studies comparing NATO and Pact forces.

This NIE is the first comprehensive estimate of Warsaw Pact forces opposite NATO since 1971. It is the first to attempt an analysis of Pact campaign plans for the European theaters of military operations and the first to integrate naval forces into these campaigns. It deals primarily with conventional forces and operations; it describes nuclear forces but provides only limited treatment of theater nuclear operations.

The NIE is in two volumes. This volume presents a detailed discussion of Pact doctrine, theater forces, and operational concepts for war in Europe. It also describes the main developments and trends in Pact theater forces and discusses those issues which bear most directly on the capabilities of Pact forces to perform their missions. Volume I is a summary of the Estimate.

The Estimate provides, particularly in its graphics, a great deal of information concerning the technical performance characteristics of Warsaw Pact weapon systems. This information is for general reference purposes only. More detailed data on characteristics of Pact weapons can be found in separate publications prepared by the various agencies within the Intelligence Community.

PAGE LEFT BLANK INTENTIONALLY

Top Secret

CONTENTS

	Page
PREFACE	iii
SCOPE NOTE	1
NOTE ON THE EVIDENCE	3
KEY JUDGMENTS	5
ISSUES	17

CHAPTER I. WARSAW PACT POLICY AND DOCTRINE FOR
THEATER WARFARE I-1

 A. General Considerations I-1
 B. Theater Nuclear Warfare I-3
 C. Chemical Warfare I-7
 D. Biological Warfare I-8
 E. Electronic Warfare I-9
 F. Soviet Views of NATO's Military Capabilities I-9
 G. Implications for Pact Forces I-10

CHAPTER II. WARSAW PACT FORCES FOR THEATER
WARFARE II-1

 A. Warsaw Pact Ground Forces II-1

  Manpower II-1
  Equipment II-1
  Warsaw Pact Ground Force Divisions II-10
  Airborne Forces II-12
  Special Operations Units II-13
  Personnel, Training, and Leadership II-13
  Ready Reserves II-15

 B. Warsaw Pact Air Forces II-15

  Tactical Air Forces II-16
  Military Transport Aviation II-27
  NSWP National Air Defense Forces II-27

 C. Warsaw Pact General Purpose Naval Forces II-27

  Force Composition and Readiness II-28
  Manpower, Personnel, and Training II-31
  Major Wartime Tasks II-32
  Antiwarship Capabilities II-32
  Antisubmarine Warfare Capabilities II-39
  Capabilities for Exercising Sea Control in the Sea Approaches to
   the Soviet Union II-41
  Capabilities for Exercising Sea Denial in NATO's Sea Lines of
   Communication II-41
  Amphibious Capabilities II-44

v

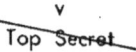

D.	Theater Nuclear Forces	II-44
	Tactical Nuclear Forces	II-44
	Soviet Peripheral Strike Forces	II-49
E.	Forces for Chemical Warfare	II-59
	Production	II-59
	Stockpile	II-59
	CBR Training and Equipment	II-60
F.	Forces for Electronic Warfare	II-61
	Forces	II-61
	Capabilities	II-62
G.	Warsaw Pact Logistics	II-63
	Ground Forces	II-63
	Air Forces	II-68
	Naval Forces	II-69

CHAPTER III. WARSAW PACT COMMAND AND CONTROL ... III-1

A.	The Wartime Command Structure	III-1
	Western Theater of War: The Warsaw Pact High Command	III-3
	Fronts	III-3
	Armies and Divisions	III-4
	Fleets	III-7
B.	Measures for Control of Combined Operations	III-7
	War Plans	III-7
	Standardization	III-7
	Representatives of Command	III-7
	Operations Groups	III-7
	Strategic Communications Support of Theater Forces	III-7
C.	Control Procedures for Nuclear Weapons	III-8
D.	Effectiveness of Pact Command and Control	III-8
E.	Vulnerability	III-8

CHAPTER IV. WARSAW PACT STRATEGY FOR INITIAL CONVENTIONAL OPERATIONS AGAINST NATO ... IV-1

A.	The Initial Campaign in the Western Theater of Military Operations	IV-2
	The Ground Offensive	IV-2
	The Air Offensive in Central Europe	IV-11
	Naval Operations in the Baltic	IV-20
B.	The Initial Campaign in the Southwestern Theater of Military Operations	IV-24
	Initial Ground Operations	IV-25
	Initial Naval Operations in the Black Sea	IV-27
	Initial Air and Naval Operations in the Mediterranean	IV-28

C. The Initial Campaign in the Northwestern Theater of Military
Operations IV-31
Naval Operations IV-32
Ground Operations in Northern Norway IV-32
Air Operations IV-33

D. Naval Operations in the North Atlantic IV-33
Strategy and Operations IV-34
Potential Effectiveness IV-40

CHAPTER V. THEATER NUCLEAR OPERATIONS V-1

A. Tactical Nuclear Operations V-1
B. Nuclear Strikes Against NATO by Soviet Strategic Forces V-3

CHAPTER VI. FUTURE FORCES VI-1

A. Factors Affecting Future Forces VI-1
Soviet Perceptions of NATO's Military Capabilities VI-1
Soviet Leadership VI-1
Economic Considerations VI-1
Demographic Factors VI-2
Technology VI-2
Sino-Soviet Relations VI-2

B. Trends in the Size and Composition of Future Forces VI-2
General VI-2
Ground Forces VI-3
Air Forces VI-5
General Purpose Naval Forces VI-7
Theater Nuclear Forces VI-11
Support Systems and Forces VI-13

ANNEX A. SOVIET MILITARY OPERATIONS OUTSIDE THE EUROPEAN THEATER DURING A NATO–WARSAW PACT WAR A-1

ANNEX B. DISPOSITION OF WARSAW PACT GENERAL PURPOSE FORCES, 1 JANUARY 1979 (tables) B-1

SCOPE NOTE

National Intelligence Estimate 11-14-79 is concerned with Warsaw Pact forces that are available for use against NATO.* It assesses the present and future capabilities of these forces for conventional, chemical, and theater nuclear warfare. It generally covers a period of five years in its future considerations but extends to 10 years where the information allows. This Estimate does not provide detailed treatment of Soviet forces along the Sino-Soviet border, the Soviet Pacific Fleet, or other forces in the Soviet Far East. Soviet military operations in distant areas during a NATO–Warsaw Pact war are considered in an annex.

The Estimate treats the following elements of the Pact's military forces:

— **Ground Forces.** The ground forces (including airborne and heliborne forces) of the USSR, East Germany, Poland, Czechoslovakia, Hungary, Romania, and Bulgaria and their organic air defense and tactical nuclear systems.

— **Air and Air Defense Forces.** Soviet Frontal (tactical) Aviation, Military Transport Aviation, and the bombers of Soviet Long Range Aviation, as well as the tactical air and national air defense forces (including ground-based systems) of the non-Soviet Warsaw Pact (NSWP) countries.

— **Naval Forces.** The general purpose submarines, surface ships, aircraft, auxiliaries, and amphibious forces of the three western Soviet fleets and the NSWP navies.

— **Soviet Ballistic Missile Forces for Peripheral Attack.** Those Soviet land-based (MRBMs, IRBMs, and ICBMs) and submarine-launched (SLBMs) ballistic missiles which are available for use against NATO in the European theater.

— **Support Functions.** Those activities and organizations which support and integrate Pact forces, such as command, control, and communications systems and logistic services.

---

*For the purpose of this Estimate, Pact general purpose ground and air forces available for early use against NATO include those located in the non-Soviet Warsaw Pact (NSWP) nations and in the USSR's Baltic, Belorussian, Carpathian, Leningrad, Odessa, Kiev, North Caucasus, and Transcaucasus Military Districts. Forces in the Moscow, Volga, Ural, and Turkestan Military Districts could be used against NATO or elsewhere. Also included in this Estimate are Pact general purpose naval forces in the three western Soviet fleets, including the Mediterranean Squadron, and the NSWP navies, as well as Soviet strategic forces which could be employed against European targets in a peripheral attack role.

Other recently completed National Intelligence Estimates and Interagency Intelligence Memorandums contain comprehensive assessments of some issues that are given summary treatment in this document.

- NIE 11-4-78, *Soviet Goals and Expectations in the Global Power Arena*, describes the broad strategic and political considerations which shape the Soviet defense posture.

- NIE 4-1-78, *Warsaw Pact Concepts and Capabilities for Going to War in Europe: Implications for NATO Warning of War*, assesses Pact attack options in Central Europe and the intelligence basis for our estimate of NATO's warning time there.

- NIE 11-3/8-78, *Soviet Capabilities for Strategic Nuclear Conflict Through the Late 1980s*, and NIE 11-6-78, *Soviet Strategic Forces for Peripheral Attack*, contain detailed estimates of Soviet strategic forces available for use against NATO.

- NIE 11-10-79, *Soviet Military Capabilities To Project Power and Influence in Distant Areas*.

- NI IIM 78-10018J, *Indications and Warning of Soviet Intentions To Use Chemical Weapons During a NATO-Warsaw Pact War*.

- NI IIM 78-10029, *Assessed Manpower of Warsaw Pact Forces in the NATO Guidelines Area*.

- NI IIM 78-10027J, *A Survey of Warsaw Pact Concealment, Deception, and Intelligence Denial Activity*.

NOTE ON THE EVIDENCE

KEY JUDGMENTS

Warsaw Pact Policy and Doctrine for Theater Warfare

1. It is Soviet policy to acquire and maintain forces capable of successfully fighting either a conventional or nuclear war in Europe and to keep a clear numerical advantage over NATO in important military assets. Soviet leaders stress the need for large, combat-ready forces to be in place at the outset of hostilities. They intend any future European conflict to take place on Western, not Eastern, territory. (I, 1-2)[1]

2. The Soviet Union views control of its East European allies as vital to its national interests. The East European members of the Pact provide sizable forces and a territorial buffer between NATO and the Soviet Union. (See figure 1.) The presence or proximity of large, well-equipped Soviet forces gives the Soviets considerable leverage in exerting control over these countries, thus safeguarding the integrity of the Warsaw Pact. The Soviets also value their military strength as a means of influencing European domestic and foreign policy decisions and deterring political or military developments which might alter the balance of power to their disadvantage. They do not, however, measure the military balance in Europe in isolation from the larger, global balance and, accordingly, are inclined to be very cautious in the use of military force in Europe. (I, 2-3)

3. Our analysis of Soviet nuclear policy and doctrine has led us to the following judgments:

— The Soviets believe that the initial stages of a conflict probably would be conventional, and they would prefer that a NATO-Pact conflict remain nonnuclear, but they expect that it would eventually involve the use of nuclear weapons. (I, 10)

— There is evidence that the Soviets now have a more flexible policy for the use of tactical nuclear weapons, but they apparently have not sought to match NATO's capacity for accurate and selective use of very low yield nuclear weapons, and they remain profoundly skeptical of the possiblity of controlling escalation. (I, 12)

— We cannot predict how the Soviets would respond to a limited and selective NATO use of nuclear weapons or the conditions under which the Soviets might initiate nuclear operations in a NATO-Pact war. (I, 13-14)

---

[1] References are to chapters (Roman numbers) and paragraphs (Arabic numbers) in this volume of the Estimate.

European NATO and the Warsaw Pact

Figure 1

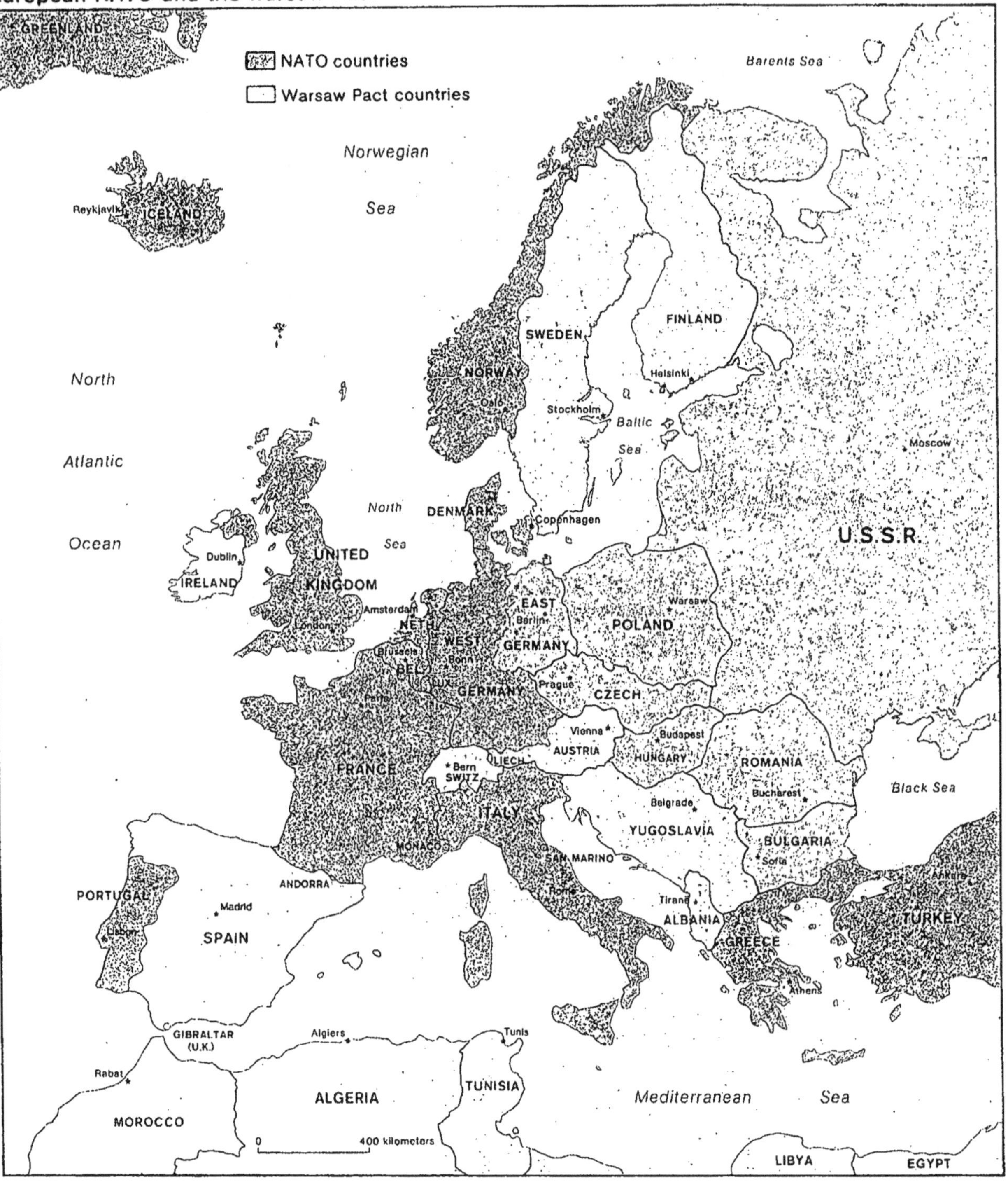

577644 1-79

— Preemption continues to be a feature of Soviet nuclear doctrine. (I, 15)

— Improvements in the USSR's forward-based nuclear forces would permit the Soviets to fight a tactical nuclear war at relatively high levels of intensity without having to use USSR-based systems. Nonetheless, the Soviets' continued modernization of USSR-based peripheral strike systems ▓▓▓▓▓▓▓▓ argue that they still expect to have to resort to the use of these weapons at some stage of theater nuclear war. (I, 16)

4. The Soviets are clearly planning against the contingency that chemical weapons might be used in a war between NATO and the Warsaw Pact. They have a continuing, vigorous program to equip and train Pact forces for operations in a toxic environment and have produced a variety of chemical agents and delivery systems. We are divided, however, on the question of Soviet policy for the first use of chemical weapons. Some believe [2] that it is unlikely that the Warsaw Pact would initiate offensive chemical warfare before the advent of nuclear war, but that the Pact's first use under these circumstances cannot be entirely excluded. Others believe [3] there is a strong possibility that the Soviets would initiate chemical warfare in a conventional conflict. Chapter I contains the rationale underlying these views. (I, 18-29)

Trends in Warsaw Pact Theater Forces

5. The past decade was marked by vigorous modernization of Soviet theater forces facing NATO. This modernization was accompanied by some increase in the manpower of the forces—especially in the late 1960s and early 1970s—as the number of weapons in units was increased and as support requirements grew to accommodate more, increasingly sophisticated hardware. Modernization of the Soviet theater forces is evidently continuing at much the same pace, along with modest, commensurate growth in manpower. The non-Soviet Warsaw Pact (NSWP) forces have shared in the Soviet buildup, although at a slower pace and with uneven results, especially in the more expensive tactical air and missile forces and in ground force armor replacement programs. (VI, 1)

6. Motivated by the prospect of a nonnuclear phase of hostilities and their recognition of a need for strong conventional forces even in the event of nuclear war, the Soviets have especially sought to improve

---

[2] *The holders of this view are the Central Intelligence Agency and the Director, Bureau of Intelligence and Research, Department of State.*

[3] *The holders of this view are the Director, Defense Intelligence Agency; the Director, National Security Agency; and the Senior Intelligence Officers of each of the military services.*

their conventional force capabilities. Since the late 1960s they have significantly increased manpower, tanks, artillery, armed helicopters, and air defense. They have been equipping their tactical air forces with aircraft having increased performance and load-carrying capacity. During this period the flexibility and conventional war potential of Soviet naval forces also have been improved by the acquisition of more capable ships, submarines, and aircraft. (I, 37)

7. At the same time, the Soviets have continued to increase the size of their theater nuclear forces and improve their flexibility. Since the early 1970s they have introduced nuclear-capable artillery systems, have increased their surface-to-surface tactical missile launchers in Central Europe, have assigned nuclear missions to additional tactical aviation units, and are deploying a new-generation intermediate-range ballistic missile and a new bomber. The Soviet Navy has also added systems which improve its capability to wage theater nuclear war. (I, 39)

8. Pact theater forces have emerged from a decade of change with their fundamental orientation on the tank intact, but with a more balanced structure for conventional war and with both conventional and nuclear firepower greatly increased. These changes, along with an infusion of more modern technology, have made Soviet theater forces competitive with leading Western armies in sophistication of organization and equipment. (I, 43)

9. Our analysis of these developments permits the following additional conclusions:

— The Soviets are aware of the improved technology and growing numbers of NATO antitank weapons, but this awareness has not led to any diminution of their tank forces or any major change in the way they see these forces performing. Indeed, they have made even further increases to their tank strength and have begun producing new tank models. (II, 7)

— The Soviets are pursuing a vigorous program to increase the effectiveness of their air munitions to exploit the enhanced capabilities of their newer aircraft. The role of Frontal Aviation for delivering tactical nuclear weapons clearly is expanding. (II, 89 and 158)

— The Soviet Navy in the past decade has significantly improved its capability to participate in a Pact-NATO war and now can undertake combat operations at greater distances from home waters. The introduction of new classes of submarines, Backfire bombers, and new missile systems has especially improved the Soviet Navy's strike capability against NATO surface forces. (II, 100)

— Since the late 1960s the Pact has adopted a unified command and control doctrine and has begun to modernize its command and control procedures and equipment. (I, 41)

— Pact ground force logistic capacity has also been improved, notably by large additions to motor transport and the development of improved support organizations and equipment. (I, 42)

10. We have also identified the following significant weaknesses which could adversely affect the performance of Pact theater forces:[4]

— Pact tactical air pilots are not as effectively trained—by US standards—as they should be to exploit fully the capabilities of the airframes and weapon systems of the third-generation aircraft currently in operation. (II, 69)

— Lack of automated equipment, or other means for timely and accurate location and reporting of mobile or semimobile targets, is believed to be a current weakness of Soviet aerial reconnaissance. (II, 86)

— The USSR's antisubmarine warfare (ASW) capabilities on the whole are such that its forces in most wartime situations would probably be unable to detect the presence of US and most other NATO submarines before attacks on Soviet surface ships. Crucial shortcomings are lack of long-range submarine detection devices, high radiated noise levels of Soviet submarines relative to those of the West, and lack of seaborne tactical air cover to protect deployed surface ship ASW forces. (II, 128)

Warsaw Pact Strategy for Initial Conventional Operations Against NATO

11. The USSR has developed contingency plans for military operations on all Pact land frontiers. The Soviets clearly expect Central Europe to be the decisive arena in a war with NATO and assign it the highest priority in the allocation of military manpower and equipment. The Soviets also have plans for offensive action in other NATO regions, but we have little direct evidence on the Pact's view of the timing of these flank offensives in relation to an offensive in Central Europe. We judge, however, that the Pact would be unlikely to start a war by mounting major ground offensives against all NATO sectors simultaneously. To do so would unnecessarily extend available Pact forces, airlift, and air and logistic support and would complicate command and control at the General Staff and Supreme High Command levels.

---

[4] Additional weaknesses which some agencies have identified can be found in the "Issues" section on pages 17-22 and in the discussions of those issues in the body of the Estimate.

Moreover, there would be political considerations that would lead the Soviets to defer attacks on some NATO countries in the hope of encouraging their nonbelligerence. (IV, 2-4)

12. We believe that the need for unfettered naval operations from their Northern Fleet bases would almost certainly cause the Soviets to strike NATO facilities in northern Norway, and probably to attempt to occupy some territory there, and that the urgency of this need would lead them to do so concurrently with starting an attack in Central Europe. We would also expect concurrent attacks on US naval forces in the Mediterranean. None of the other potential flank offensives appear to have that degree of urgency, although the Pact would be likely to move against the Turkish Straits early in a war. (IV, 5)

13. The Warsaw Pact's success in achieving its wartime objectives would depend on its ability to control and coordinate multinational, joint-service operations of great complexity. but our assessment of the system's strengths and weaknesses leads us to judge that it is adequate to alert forces and control mobilization, and to control combat operations. This assessment is discussed in detail in chapter III. (III, 1-31)

14. The ultimate authority for the direction of the Soviet military rests with the Politburo and the Soviet General Staff, but we believe that should a war occur between the Warsaw Pact and NATO, theater-level commands would be established and exercise direct operational control over fronts and fleets and at least some degree of control over those strategic assets allocated to support theater operations. Unlike NATO, the Warsaw Pact does not have theater headquarters in being in peacetime, although hardened command posts have been constructed for at least some Pact wartime headquarters. (III, 4-6)

15. Arrangements for exercising control of Pact forces within what the Soviets call the Western (or European) Theater of War have been evolving over the last few years. We now have evidence that indicates the commander in chief of the combined armed forces of the Warsaw Pact would control all Pact forces in this theater in wartime. The Soviets plan to divide the Western Theater of War into three land Theaters of Military Operations (TVDs) in which they expect Pact and NATO forces to come in conflict. These would include a Northwestern TVD (the Leningrad Military District and the Scandinavian Peninsula); a Western TVD (East Germany, Poland, Czechoslovakia, and the western USSR in the east and West Germany, the Benelux countries, Denmark, and possibly France in the west); and a Southwestern TVD (Greece, Turkey, and probably northern Italy and Austria). An area in the Norwegian Sea north of the Greenland-Iceland-United Kingdom

(G-I-UK) gap probably would be designated a Maritime TVD, and would include the Northern Fleet. The forces of the Baltic and Black Sea Combined Fleets initially would be under the control of the Western and Southwestern TVD headquarters—often called High Commands by the Soviets. The senior field command would be the front, an organization which is similar to a NATO army group in size, level of command, and function and which consists of three to five ground armies and an air army of 600 aircraft. (III, 7-10)

16. Our consideration of likely Pact operations in the Western TVD during the initial phase of a conventional war has resulted in the following key findings:

— Soviet military strategy calls for a massive and rapid ground offensive into NATO territory in Central Europe to defeat NATO forces, disrupt mobilization, and seize or destroy ports and airfields to prevent reinforcement. (IV, 7)

— Except in extraordinarily urgent circumstances, the Pact would prefer to prepare at least a three-front force before initiating hostilities in Central Europe. We believe the Pact would begin to organize at least five fronts for use in Central Europe from the time of the decision to go to full readiness. There is virtually no chance the Soviets would attack from a standing start.[5] (IV, 10-22)

— Pact planners regard early attainment of air superiority and destruction of much of NATO's tactical nuclear forces to be critical to the Pact's chances for victory in the theater. The Pact plans to achieve these objectives by conducting a large-scale, theaterwide conventional air offensive during the first several days of hostilities. (IV, 43-85)

— The broad objectives of Pact naval operations in the Baltic would be to gain complete control of the Baltic Sea and access to the North Sea to sever NATO's lines of communication in the North Sea, and deprive NATO of potential launch areas for carrier strikes against Pact air and ground forces in the Central Region. Failure to obtain air superiority and sea control probably would force the Pact to reconsider its planned amphibious operations in the western Baltic. (IV, 86-111)

17. As for operations in the Southwestern TVD, our conclusions are as follows:

— The Pact would confine its initial ground operations to the Turkish Straits area, Austria, and possibly eastern Turkey. In

---

[5] NIE 4-1-78, *Warsaw Pact Capabilities for Going to War in Europe: Implications for NATO Warning of War*, provides the detailed rationale for these conclusions.

addition, at the onset of a war, air and naval attacks would almost certainly be mounted against NATO forces in these areas and in the Mediterranean. (IV, 116-125)

— The Pact views early seizure of the Turkish Straits as crucial to the success of its maritime strategy in the Southwestern TVD. (IV, 113)

— While the Soviets might launch a limited offensive into eastern Turkey, we have no evidence that they would undertake operations against Iran during an initial phase. (IV, 123)

— Soviet naval operations in the Mediterranean would begin at the start of a war and would be aimed primarily at the destruction of Western ballistic missile submarines (SSBNs) and aircraft carriers. (IV, 131)

— While the most immediate threat would come from Soviet ships and submarines already deployed in the Mediterranean, numerically the most sizable threat to NATO's naval forces there would come from missile-equipped Soviet strike aircraft, despite the fact that they would be operating without fighter escort. (IV, 135)

18. We have good evidence that as part of the offensive by the Pact's Maritime Front, the Soviet Black Sea Fleet would attempt to secure control of the Black Sea, support the movement of Pact ground forces along the western littoral, and assist in seizing the Turkish Straits. To assist in the achievement of air and sea superiority and to protect the amphibious force, the Soviets probably would retain in the Black Sea at least some of their available larger combatants equipped for ASW and with surface-to-air missiles (SAMs)—such as Moskvas, Karas, Kashins, and Krivaks. There is disagreement in the Intelligence Community on the numbers of large surface combatants which would be retained in the Black Sea rather than deployed to the Mediterranean before the outbreak of hostilities. (IV, 126 and 142-144)

19. In the Northwestern TVD our information indicates that:

— Initial Soviet objectives in the Northwestern TVD center on ensuring freedom of action and uninhibited access to the open ocean for Soviet naval ships and aircraft and on maintaining the forward defense of the extensive complex of naval bases and strategic installations located on the Kola Peninsula. (IV, 145)

— Initial operations by Soviet land forces probably would be limited to northern Norway. We have no evidence indicating that the Soviets plan for a general offensive against Finland or Sweden early in a war. (IV, 150-153)

— Soviet amphibious ships carrying up to a regiment of Soviet naval infantry probably would attempt to seize limited objectives along the northern Norwegian coast. Initial amphibious operations probably would be confined to the coast of Finnmark, under conditions suitable for an early linkup with the ground forces. (IV, 148)

— The Soviets probably would not attempt a large-scale airborne assault in northern Norway, because the demands for air transport elsewhere against NATO probably would preclude early use of a formation as large as a complete airborne division. (IV, 154)

20. Soviet strategy in the North Atlantic calls for the early establishment of control of the Norwegian and Barents Seas and their approaches. Implementation of such a strategy probably would involve most of the Northern Fleet's submarines and virtually all of the surface forces and aircraft in an effort to exclude NATO forces from the area. The Soviets probably also plan some submarine operations farther into the North Atlantic to prevent transit of NATO carriers and amphibious task groups and to divert NATO naval strength. The Soviets would attempt to neutralize Western SSBNs near their bases and in the Norwegian Sea before they could launch their missiles. To this end they probably would initiate submarine and air operations against NATO naval forces as they exit their bases in Europe and possibly against SSBNs from US bases as well. In addition, at least some submarines would attack shipping engaged in resupply and reinforcement of Europe early in a war. There is disagreement in the Intelligence Community over the extent to which the Soviets would wage an interdiction campaign and over their capabilities for doing so. (IV, 157-200, and II, 142-149)

Theater Nuclear Operations

21. The primary objective in Soviet tactical nuclear planning appears to be the destruction of military targets, particularly NATO's means for waging nuclear war. Limiting collateral damage does not appear to be a main concern

Prospects for Warsaw Pact Theater Forces

22. In this Estimate we do not provide a detailed analysis of the factors that motivate the Soviets' military policy toward Europe and the development of their theater forces. These factors are discussed in detail

in NIE 11-4-78, *Soviet Goals and Expectations in the Global Power Arena*. We proceed from the premise that the developments we currently observe in Warsaw Pact theater forces opposite NATO represent the sorts of activities necessary to maintain and gradually improve the capabilities of these large standing forces. They are the activities necessary to replace obsolete or wornout equipment and to incorporate new weapons and tactics which flow from a vigorous Soviet research and development program. They portend no large, short-term change in the general size or character of these forces. (VI, 2)

23. Although we believe this to be a valid premise, we have examined a number of factors which conceivably could alter it:

— Nothing in NATO's current or foreseeable defense programs is likely to precipitate any major change in the level of Pact efforts. Over the longer term, however, a large-scale deployment by NATO of a new theater nuclear delivery system (such as a ground-launched cruise missile) could cause an upswing in Pact efforts, especially in air defense. (VI, 4)

— New Soviet leaders will undoubtedly emerge from the ranks of the present group, which is responsible for creating current Pact forces and is committed to maintaining Soviet military strength in Europe. The new leaders will likely seek to avoid moves that would antagonize large segments of the military. (VI, 5)

— Despite the decline in Soviet economic growth and the economic difficulties of such NSWP countries as Poland and Czechoslovakia, we find no evidence that suggests the Soviets will cut back resources for theater forces. Indeed, we have reliable evidence that some NSWP countries plan modest increases in defense spending. (VI, 7)

— During the next decade the number of young people reaching draft age each year will decline in most Pact countries, a trend that will complicate the allocation of manpower between the armed forces and industry, but this manpower squeeze is not expected to produce any decline in military personnel strength. (VI, 8-10)

— Despite continuing scientific advances we foresee no technological breakthrough that could lead to a major change in either the size or character of the Pact theater forces. (VI, 11)

24. Although the expansion in manpower which characterized Pact theater forces during the mid-1960s and early 1970s has slowed, we expect some gradual increase in manpower in Pact ground and air combat units opposite NATO over the next decade as ongoing programs are implemented. The overall number of ground and air combat units

opposite NATO is expected to remain at or near its current level, while a modest decline is anticipated in the number of general purpose naval ships and submarines. (VI, 14)

25. Warsaw Pact nations will continue to improve the weapons and equipment in their theater forces opposite NATO. Major weapon production and deployment programs which are clearly in midstream are expected to continue. In addition, the Soviets will no doubt seek to develop some entirely new weapons and support systems. Certain of these systems, such as laser or television-guided munitions, are already in testing. Still other Pact weapons—such as enhanced radiation weapons and advanced cruise missiles—may emerge in reaction to NATO weapons programs or force improvements. (VI, 15)

26. *Ground Forces.* Barring an agreement on mutual and balanced force reductions (MBFR), the number and disposition of Pact ground force divisions opposite NATO are likely to remain stable during the period of this Estimate, although expanded divisional organizations and the formation of new nondivisional units probably will account for moderate increases in manpower and equipment. We foresee no development over the next several years which would appreciably alter the basic Pact strategy of an armor-heavy offensive against NATO in Central Europe. Despite NATO's substantial and growing capability for antitank warfare, Pact planners will continue to regard the tank as the backbone of their ground assault forces. (VI, 17)

27. *Tactical Air Forces.* We believe that the number of fixed-wing aircraft in Soviet Frontal Aviation opposite NATO will remain essentially unchanged over the next decade. Efforts to improve the quality of Soviet tactical aircraft and munitions are likely to continue, although the rate of new aircraft deployment is expected to slow as the Soviets meet their current force objectives. Furthermore, we expect the Soviets to continue improving their support and subsidiary systems such as command and control, radioelectronic combat (REC), and reconnaissance data link systems. We expect in the next decade that several additional Soviet and NSWP combat helicopter regiments, primarily for ground attack, will be formed. No major changes are expected in the number of fixed-wing aircraft in the NSWP air forces. NSWP equipment modernization will continue to proceed gradually and be driven largely by economic considerations. (VI, 34)

28. *General Purpose Naval Forces.* During the next decade, developments in the Soviet Navy will produce a force with improved capabilities to perform its peacetime and wartime missions. The Soviets will have mixed success with programs to correct shortcomings in submarine detection, fleet air defense, logistic support, and communications. Developments over the past decade have been so rapid that a

period of time may be required to integrate and consolidate advances and ensure that combat potentials are fully realized. We expect a modest decline in the overall number of Soviet general purpose naval ships and submarines but newer and more capable units will be replacing older and less effective ones. (VI, 55)

29. *Theater Nuclear Forces.* Over the next decade the Soviets will continue their ongoing programs to improve their peripheral strategic strike forces and to eliminate the imbalance in battlefield nuclear capabilities they perceive in the European theater. Force improvement carried out to date and ongoing deployment of new systems are increasing the flexibility with which the Soviets can employ their theater nuclear forces. The introduction of nuclear-capable artillery will provide low-yield tactical nuclear weapons and delivery systems with sufficient accuracy to permit employment in close proximity to Pact forces. (VI, 90)

30. *Command, Control, and Communications.* We estimate that about one week currently would be required before the Pact's wartime communications links could be established to theater-level headquarters and to supporting strategic commands. Communications, between Moscow and the fronts and within the fronts, to control combat operations by divisions and armies could be effectively established within a few days. However, the Pact has two programs under way— the creation of a centralized command structure and the establishment of a unified communications system—which, during the period of this Estimate, could shorten the time required by the Pact to get its command and control system prepared for war. The two programs are intended to establish in peacetime the theater-level (High Command) resources needed to control Pact forces once they are released from national control. We estimate that the centralized command structure could be complete by the early 1980s. The unified communications system could begin to improve the Pact's command capabilities by the mid-1980s, but it is not scheduled for completion until 1990. (VI, 101)

ISSUES

During the preparation of this Estimate disagreements among NFIB agencies arose on a number of issues—some key, most secondary—gists of which are contained in this section. Parenthetical references at the end of each gist are to chapters (Roman numbers) and paragraphs (Arabic numbers) in this volume of the Estimate.

a. Likelihood of Soviet Initiation of Chemical Warfare in a Conventional War. All agencies are agreed that, once widespread nuclear war began, the Warsaw Pact would not be constrained in its use of chemical weapons. With respect to the question of Soviet policy on the first use of chemical weapons before the advent of nuclear war, there are two views. CIA and State judge that it is unlikely the Pact would initiate such use, although the possibility cannot be entirely excluded. DIA, NSA, Army, Navy, and Air Force believe that there is a strong possibility of such use. (I, 24-29)

b. Number of Soviet Motorized Rifle Divisions (MRDs) That Have an Independent Tank Battalion (ITB). NSA, Army, and Air Force believe that all MRDs in Eastern Europe have an ITB. They base their position on COMINT and Soviet classified writings. Army and Air Force further believe that an ITB with an MRD would be standard in wartime. DIA and CIA estimate that two-thirds of the Soviet MRDs in Eastern Europe have ITBs but that few, if any, in the western USSR do. They base their view on COMINT, Pact exercises, and the fact that photography does not show independent tank battalions with other Soviet MRDs in Eastern Europe and the western USSR. (II, 12)

c. Success of Soviet Career Noncommissioned Personnel Programs. All agencies agree that the Soviets are seeking to induce conscripts to serve as career noncommissioned personnel upon completion of their mandatory service. CIA, NSA, and State conclude that the Soviets have had little success because of the harsh conditions of military service. DIA, Army, and Air Force believe that there is insufficient evidence to support conclusions about the planned scope of the Soviets' recruiting programs or their success in implementing them. They also believe that, with a combination of incentives on the one hand and pressure from the political organization on the other, the Soviets should be able to overcome any difficulties in recruiting career enlisted personnel. (II, 44-45)

d. Amount of Combat-Related Training in Soviet Air Units Stationed in East Germany.

e. **Soviet Capability To Activate Reserve Submarines.** CIA estimates that no reserve submarines with their crews could be brought to combat readiness in less than 90 days. DIA and Navy estimate that six to 10 reserve submarines could be brought to operational status in 30 days and a total of 25 to 30 submarines in 90 days. (II, 106)

f. **Soviet Long-Range Airborne Antisubmarine Warfare (ASW) Capability.** CIA and NSA estimate that the TU-142 Bear-F aircraft has an operational radius of about 2,050 nautical miles with three hours of on-station time and about 2,500 nm with no on-station time. DIA, Navy, and Air Force hold that the maximum radius with three hours of on-station time is 3,150 nm. (II, 131-132)

g. **Extent, Emphasis, and Timing of the Soviet Interdiction Campaign Against NATO Sea Lines of Communications (SLOC).** CIA, NSA, and State judge that the Soviets would not likely attempt a serious SLOC interdiction campaign unless they had previously defeated NATO carrier and amphibious forces without losing their submarines. NSA further believes that the extent and degree of an anti-SLOC campaign is largely scenario dependent and that in a prolonged crisis, where the outcome is in serious doubt, the attractiveness of SLOC interdiction in advance of a conflict goes up. DIA and Navy conclude that the Soviets consider SLOC interdiction of such significance, and their submarine inventory of sufficient size, as to warrant use of substantial numbers of attack submarines in this effort while accomplishing their other missions. (II, 142-146)

h. **Soviet Capabilities To Execute a SLOC Interdiction Campaign.** CIA and State estimate that the USSR's ability to attack merchant ships in the open ocean would be significantly constrained by submarine torpedo loads, lack of replenishment opportunities, turn-around time, long transits, combat attrition, and limited target information. DIA and Navy judge that these limitations are sensitive to the timing, manner, and level at which hostilities begin, but in any event are not sufficient to prevent the Soviets from mounting a significant SLOC threat. (II, 147)

i. **Torpedo Capacities of Soviet Attack Submarines.** In support of its position that Soviet SLOC interdiction capabilities are constrained by submarine torpedo capacities, CIA has produced a table (table II-9) which assumes that all submarines carry torpedoes 53 centimeters in diameter (7.8 meters long). DIA believes that two 40-cm torpedoes (4.5 m long) probably could be substituted for each of up to six of the longer torpedos in most classes, thereby substantially increasing wartime torpedo loads. (II, 147)

j. Role of the Backfire Bomber. CIA, State, NSA, and Navy estimate that the performance characteristics, deployment patterns, training programs, and exercise participation of the Backfire, as well as Soviet statements concerning this aircraft, point to peripheral strike as its primary mission. DIA, Army, and Air Force estimate that the Backfire is a long-range bomber with the capability to strike US targets on unrefueled range and radius missions. They agree that it will have significant peripheral missions but note that the Soviets have the option to use the Backfire's intercontinental capabilities. Thus, in their view, the Backfire poses a significant threat to the contiguous United States as well as to areas on the Soviet periphery. The reader is referred to NIE 11-3/8-78 for information on performance data. (II, 178-179)

k. Capabilities of Soviet Motor Transport in Wartime. CIA and State believe that the peacetime shortage of cargo vehicles in Category II and III divisions and in army- and front-level motor transport units and the heavy reliance in wartime on mobilized civilian trucks and reservist drivers point to potential weaknesses in the wartime logistic system, particularly in the early stages of a conflict. DIA and Army believe that the Estimate understates the capability of wartime Soviet motor transport. In support of this position they point out that the mobilization system provides for filling out lower category units with vehicles and drivers for war, that civilian trucks are often identical to those in military service, that Soviet vehicles designated for mobilization are inspected by military teams, that reservist drivers would be performing duties related to their civilian occupation, and that the Group of Soviet Forces in Germany already has a lift capability that exceeds its requirements. (II, 220-221)

l. Warsaw Pact Personnel Replacement System in Wartime. CIA, State, and NSA judge that unit replacement is the Warsaw Pact's preferred system for replacing combat personnel. DIA and Army believe that the Pact would use both an individual and a unit replacement system and that the system used in a particular case would depend upon the situation. They further believe that individual replacement would be used primarily in cases of steady, attrition-type losses, while unit replacement would be used primarily in cases of large, sudden losses. (II, 231-232)

m. Pact Initiation of War From a Two-Front Posture After Four Days of Preparation. All agencies agree that, because four days would allow only minimal preparations, which would entail serious risks, the

Pact would initiate war from this posture only in extraordinarily time-urgent circumstances. CIA and State believe that the Pact would take such action only if it perceived the threat of an imminent NATO attack. DIA, NSA, Army, Navy, and Air Force hold that the Soviets might choose to attack with the two-front force in a variety of urgent contingencies. A broader treatment of this issue is given in NIE 4-1-78. (IV, 13-18)

n. **Likely Effectiveness of a Warsaw Pact Air Offensive (the "Air Operation") in Central Europe.** CIA and State conclude that a massive Pact air offensive at the outset of a war would do considerable damage to NATO's air and air defense forces, but probably would not be so effective as to prevent NATO's air forces from being able to deliver nuclear weapons on a large scale. DIA and Air Force believe that no judgment with any useful level of confidence on the effectiveness of an air operation is possible at this time because we lack adequate analysis of the factors involved which apply to both NATO and the Pact and of the interaction of the forces of both sides. (IV, 85)

o. **Likely Effectiveness of Pact Operations To Achieve Air Superiority and Sea Control in the Baltic Sea.** CIA, NSA, and State conclude that the allocation of most Pact tactical and LRA bomber aircraft to a large-scale Air Operation in West Germany and the Benelux countries would severely reduce the probability of the Pact's achieving air superiority over the Baltic in the initial stage of a war. Also, Pact ASW forces would be unable to prevent NATO submarine attacks against Pact amphibious forces. DIA and Air Force believe that there has been insufficient analysis of the factors and assumptions which would support such a conclusion. Navy believes that the achievement of air superiority is but one of a number of factors which, taken together, will determine the outcome of the Pact's Baltic campaign. (IV, 109-111)

p. **Augmentation of Soviet Naval Forces in the Mediterranean by Black Sea Surface Combatants During a Period of Tension Prior to Hostilities.** CIA and State estimate that the Soviets would deploy few, if any, combatants to augment their Mediterranean Squadron because the ships are needed more in the Black Sea for fleet air defense and ASW in support of Pact operations against the Turkish Straits. DIA, NSA, and Navy conclude that the Soviets would augment with at least a few, and possibly up to 12, modern Black Sea surface units because they would be of greater value in the Mediterranean than in the Black Sea. (IV, 142-144)

q. **Number of Submarines Soviets Would Employ in the North Atlantic SLOC Interdiction Role.** CIA, NSA, and State judge that about 10 submarines would be dispersed in North Atlantic shipping lanes for reconnaissance and attacks against shipping and naval targets of opportunity. Some of these submarines might alternatively have missions of minelaying near NATO naval bases or patrolling off major NATO naval bases to report on NATO movements and attack major warships. DIA and Navy believe that, in a typical initial wartime deployment, some 20 submarines would be positioned astride NATO's sea lines of communication to attack warships and ships carrying critical materiel to Europe in the initial phase of a war. The number of Soviet submarines dedicated to this effort would be scenario dependent. (IV, 168-169)

r. **Potential Effectiveness of Soviet Naval Operations in the North Atlantic.** Paragraphs 191-197 of chapter IV consider that the evident technical limitations of the weapons and sensors on Soviet ships, submarines, and aircraft could impact significantly on Soviet efforts to control the Norwegian and Barents Seas, although the mutually supportive aspects of some operations may offset certain technical weaknesses. DIA and Navy believe that these paragraphs should convey a more balanced appraisal of potential effectiveness and that, as now phrased, they tend to overstress the weaknesses of Soviet platforms; they tend to give inadequate consideration of strengths, including the operation of these platforms as a mutually supportive force; and they tend to assess effectiveness in tactical contexts which are unrealistic. (IV, 191-200)

s. **Likelihood of Soviet Use of Nuclear Weapons at Sea Before Their Use on Land.** Navy judges that, under certain circumstances, nuclear operations at sea would not await employment of nuclear weapons on land. All other agencies estimate that the USSR would be unlikely to initiate the use of nuclear weapons at sea while a war was being fought with only conventional weapons against NATO in Europe. (V, 10-11)

t. **Speed of New Soviet Nuclear-Powered Attack (SSN) and Nuclear-Powered Guided Missile (SSGN) Submarines.** DIA and Navy estimate that the maximum speeds for some of the new SSN and SSGN classes could reach 37 knots. CIA estimates that these submarines will be capable of speeds up to 33 knots. (VI, 63)

u. **Effectiveness of the Soviet Aircraft Carrier Kiev and Its Impact Upon the Evolution of Soviet Naval Missions.** CIA and State believe that a few ships of this class do not represent a significant improvement in Soviet capabilities to fight a war with NATO. They, and NSA, believe that, although it may constitute a major turning point in the development of the Soviet Navy, it is premature to judge the impact of the acquisition of carriers upon the evolution of naval missions. DIA and Navy hold that the introduction of the Kiev constitutes a major watershed in the development of the Soviet Navy, has influenced the acquisition of other future ships, and has already exerted a significant influence on naval operations. (VI, 69-70)

    v. Propulsion of Large Combatant Being Fitted Out in Leningrad. CIA believes that the evidence is too ambiguous to classify the ship as to propulsion. DIA and Navy hold that this ship probably is nuclear powered. (VI, 71)

CHAPTER I

WARSAW PACT POLICY AND DOCTRINE FOR THEATER WARFARE

A. General Considerations

1. It is Soviet policy to acquire and maintain forces capable of successfully fighting either a nuclear or conventional war in Europe.[1] The Soviets take a conservative view of NATO's military capabilities and of the risks of instability in Eastern Europe. These concerns and their evident conviction that military power is a key element of a successful foreign policy have led the Soviets, together with their Warsaw Pact allies, to keep a clear numerical edge over NATO, especially in Central Europe, in important military assets such as tanks, artillery, and combat aircraft, and to strive continually to close the technological gap.

2. The Soviets intend any future European conflict to take place on Western, not Eastern, territory and stress the need for large, combat-ready forces to be in place at the outset of hostilities. The Soviets also conclude that the initial stages of a conflict probably would be fought with conventional weapons and that even in the event of massive nuclear exchanges, large general purpose ground, air, and naval forces would be needed to defeat surviving NATO forces and occupy Western Europe.

3. The Soviet Union views control of its East European allies as vital to its national interests. The East European members of the Pact provide sizable forces and a territorial buffer between NATO and the Soviet Union. (See figure I-1.) The presence of or proximity of large, well-equipped Soviet forces gives the Soviets considerable leverage in exerting control over these countries, thus safeguarding the integrity of the Pact. The Soviets also value their military strength as a means of influencing European domestic and foreign policy decisions and deterring political or military developments which might alter the balance of power to their disadvantage. They do not, however, measure the military balance in Europe in isolation from the larger, global balance and, accordingly, are inclined to be very cautious in the use of military force in Europe.

4. Soviet expenditures for general purpose ground, air, and naval forces, as well as for those strategic attack forces directed primarily at Eurasian targets, are an important indicator of the USSR's emphasis on developing and maintaining its theater force capabilities. The Central Intelligence Agency estimates that of total Soviet defense spending during the period 1967-77, almost 40 percent was devoted to procurement and operation of theater forces. (See figure I-2.) Roughly three-fourths of these outlays can in turn be directly attributed to those theater forces arrayed opposite NATO. During this period, procurement of weapons, equipment, and spare parts accounted for more than three quarters of the USSR's outlays for theater forces.

5. Warsaw Pact military policy is synonymous with Soviet policy. Soviet military policy is formulated at the highest military and political levels and derives from Moscow's policies with regard to its national security requirements, its conception of the nature of a possible future war in Europe, and a desire to be the predominant military force on the Eurasian continent. In the Soviet view, Pact forces must be organized and prepared for any mission, from defending against a NATO attack to launching a theater offensive.

6. A strong, in-depth defense of the homeland is basic to Soviet military doctrine. Moscow's war-fighting strategy also dictates that Warsaw Pact forces protect the Soviet homeland and lines of communication so that an offensive or counteroffensive could be successfully carried out. We find no evidence of an intent on the part of the Soviets merely to defend territory. On the contrary, the hallmark of Soviet military doctrine is offensive action. It provides the motive force behind the Soviet emphasis on high combat readiness, the desire to seize the initiative, and the requirement for substantial numerical superiority in the main battle areas, backed by strong reserves, to ensure the momentum of the attack. Pact theater force developments over the past decade reflect a systematic

---

[1] For an expanded discussion of Soviet military policy in Europe, see NIE 11-4-78, *Soviet Goals and Expectations in the Global Power Arena*.

Peacetime Structure of the Warsaw Pact

Figure I-1a

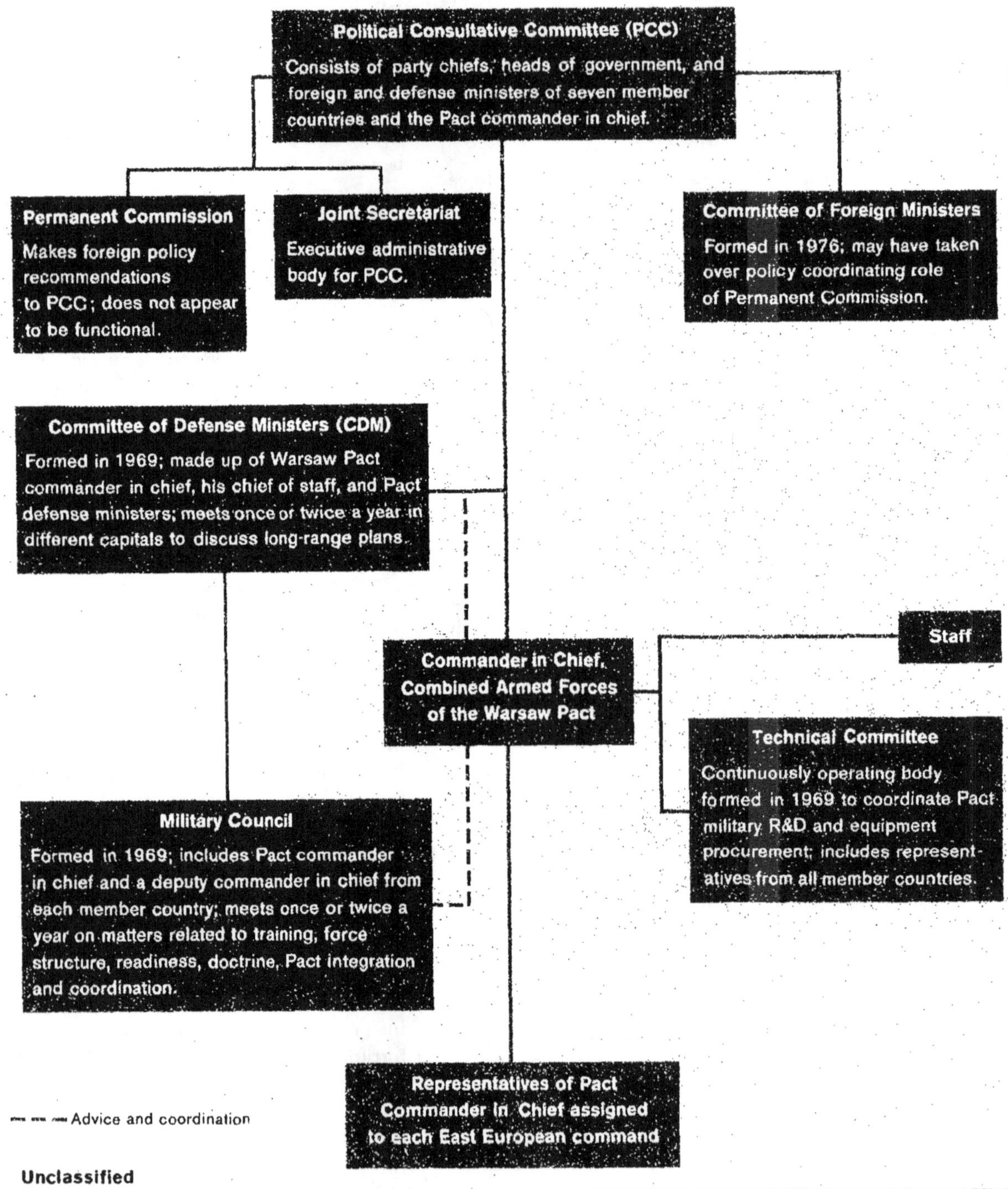

Political Consultative Committee (PCC)
Consists of party chiefs, heads of government, and foreign and defense ministers of seven member countries and the Pact commander in chief.

Permanent Commission
Makes foreign policy recommendations to PCC; does not appear to be functional.

Joint Secretariat
Executive administrative body for PCC.

Committee of Foreign Ministers
Formed in 1976; may have taken over policy coordinating role of Permanent Commission.

Committee of Defense Ministers (CDM)
Formed in 1969; made up of Warsaw Pact commander in chief, his chief of staff, and Pact defense ministers; meets once or twice a year in different capitals to discuss long-range plans.

Commander in Chief, Combined Armed Forces of the Warsaw Pact

Staff

Technical Committee
Continuously operating body formed in 1969 to coordinate Pact military R&D and equipment procurement; includes representatives from all member countries.

Military Council
Formed in 1969; includes Pact commander in chief and a deputy commander in chief from each member country; meets once or twice a year on matters related to training, force structure, readiness, doctrine, Pact integration and coordination.

Representatives of Pact Commander in Chief assigned to each East European command

— — — Advice and coordination

Unclassified

Figure I-1b

Membership: Soviet Union, Bulgaria, Czechoslovakia, East Germany, Hungary, Poland, and Romania. Albania ceased participation in 1961; formally withdrew in 1968.

Obligations of Membership: Mutual defense of European territories of member states. Action in Europe against one member to be considered attack on all.

Agreements Signed: Multilateral alliance formed by Treaty of Friendship, Mutual Assistance, and Cooperation signed by eight original members at Warsaw in 1955. All remaining members also have bilateral mutual assistance treaties with each other.

Soviet Forces in Eastern Europe: Presence governed by bilateral status-of-forces agreements as well as, in the case of East Germany and Poland, by the Potsdam Agreement of 1945. Strengths of Soviet forces (ground and air) are:

East Germany 406,000 Hungary 69,000
Czechoslovakia 75,000 Poland 48,000

Romania engineered the withdrawal of Soviet troops (an estimated 35,000) in 1958. Bulgaria allows a Soviet Warsaw Pact element comprising only 100 to 150 senior staff officers, under an unpublished agreement the details of which are not known.

Administrative Structure: Headquartered in Moscow, but including various bodies which meet on occasion in other Pact capitals. Soviet officers dominate all components, but other six Pact members are represented in all administrative and policymaking components.

Peacetime Control: The Soviet commander in chief of the Warsaw Pact does not directly control Pact forces in peacetime, but his membership in all important bodies gives him considerable influence. He also exerts influence through written Pact directives and personal dealings with East European Defense Ministers and General Staffs. As members of Soviet high command and as a first deputy minister of defense, he also has leverage with the Soviet General Staff, which prepared Pact operational war plans. The Pact chief of staff, moreover, is one of two first deputy chiefs of the Soviet General Staff.

Wartime Control: In wartime the Pact's command structure would be under the control of the Soviet High Command. See chapter III for a detailed assessment of the Pact's wartime command structure.

effort to meet these doctrinal requirements for conducting conventional and nuclear offensives in the European theater.

7. Also among the key tactical concepts which determine how the USSR would fight a war in Europe are force superiority, combined arms, and surprise. Force superiority is something all military strategists hope to achieve, but the concept takes on exceptional importance in current Soviet military thinking and practice. Its continuing role in Soviet planning is demonstrated not only by repeated doctrinal statements, but also by Pact peacetime dispositions, by exercises, and by the size of the forces fielded for the intervention in Czechoslovakia.

8. Joint action by all components of the military forces is closely associated with that of force superiority. The Soviets reckon that successful conduct of a war with NATO will require the combined efforts of their entire military establishment. Planning and preparations for joint operations are manifest in the Pact's current force posture and training programs.

9. Finally, Soviet doctrine stresses surprise as a means to increase the likelihood of success of either tactical or strategic military operations. Surprise in the Soviet view can be achieved through many means—cover, concealment, camouflage, deception, and unexpected tactics, the main objective being to achieve force superiority on the battlefield. While surprise and force superiority need not conflict, Soviet planners recognize a potential trade-off between the two, as when the chances of surprise are improved by limiting force size or the size of the force is increased at the risk of lessening surprise. While they would make every effort to maximize both, the Soviets are likely to favor force superiority: superiority in forces is real and affords advantages that are certain; surprise is a less tangible advantage and always runs some risk of being compromised.

B. Theater Nuclear Warfare

10. Soviet leaders believe that the initial stages of a conflict probably would be conventional, and they would prefer that a NATO-Pact conflict remain non-nuclear in order to avoid the catastrophic consequences of nuclear war and to take advantage of their superiority in conventional ground forces in Central Europe. Nevertheless, it is clear that the Soviets see a high probability that such a war would ultimately involve the use of nuclear weapons initiated either by the United States to avoid defeat in Europe or by the

Estimated Soviet Expenditures for Defense, 1967-77

Figure I-2

A. Estimated Total Expenditures
Billion 1970 Rubles

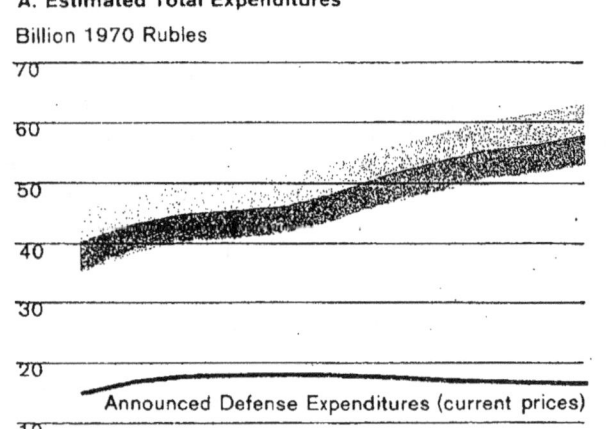

Estimate defined as the Soviets might view their defense effort

Estimate defined for comparison with US accounts.

B. Index of Growth of Estimated Total Expenditures for Procurement and Operation of Peripheral Attack and General Purpose Forces
Calculated in 1970 Rubles
1967=100

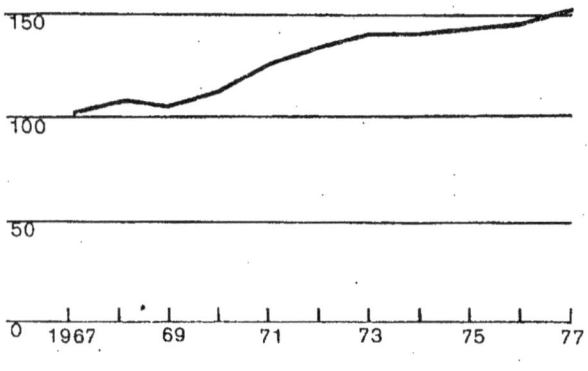

C. Percentage Distribution of Estimated Total Expenditures, 1967-77
Calculated in 1970 Rubles

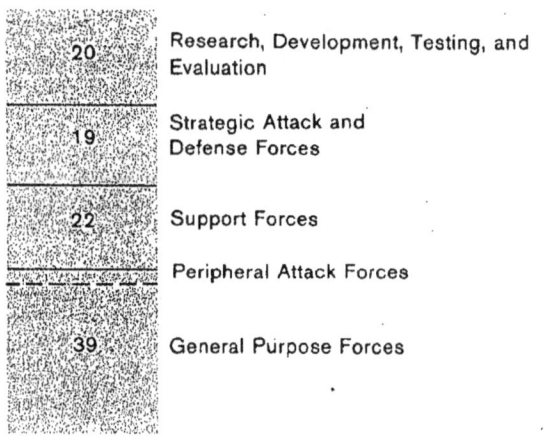

- 20 Research, Development, Testing, and Evaluation
- 19 Strategic Attack and Defense Forces
- 22 Support Forces
- Peripheral Attack Forces
- 39 General Purpose Forces

Expenditures shown in charts B and C represent spending on investment for and operation of general purpose, peripheral attack, strategic, and support forces. These expenditures are derived from our latest estimate of order-of-battle data on deployed forces and the costs associated with these forces. The expenditures shown here differ from the breakdown given in NIE 11-3/8-78, which includes expenditures for peripheral attack forces within expenditures for strategic forces. Not included in expenditures for general purpose and peripheral attack forces shown in charts B and C are:

- Outlays for military research, development, testing, and evaluation relating to general purpose or peripheral attack force weapon systems.

- Costs of nuclear weapons allocated to general purpose and peripheral attack forces. Because most of the nuclear weapons are utilized by the strategic forces, all nuclear weapons costs have been included with those forces. Nuclear weapons total about 2 percent of estimated Soviet expenditures.

- Costs of support forces associated with general purpose and peripheral attack forces.

577619 1-79 CIA

USSR if the war were going badly for the Pact. Accordingly, it is Soviet military policy to acquire and maintain forces capable of successfully fighting a nuclear war in Europe, to establish the command relationships necessary to control these forces, and to formulate a doctrine for the use of nuclear weapons against NATO in a European conflict.

11. In the 1960s it was Soviet policy to retaliate against any NATO nuclear initiative with a theaterwide strike. By 1970, however, the Soviets had adopted a policy for <u>more flexible use of nuclear weapons against NATO.</u> the qualitative and numerical advances in their forward-based tactical nuclear forces since 1970, reflect a concerted program to improve the Pact's nuclear flexibility and develop alternatives to the single option of a theaterwide response to even a small-scale NATO use of nuclear weapons. Alternative responses that have at least been examined include.

— **Delayed responses to NATO's first, small-scale use of nuclear weapons.** Soviet planners may have begun to regard the limited, selective use of nuclear weapons by NATO as a distinctive, if transitional, phase of conflict that would not necessarily require an immediate nuclear response.

— **Responses at the lower end of the nuclear spectrum with small-scale strikes by forward-based systems rather than with theaterwide strikes involving USSR-based systems.** We have reliable evidence that in 1970 the Soviets decided that NATO's selective use of tactical nuclear strikes may, in certain circumstances, make it necessary for the Soviets to make corresponding strikes and that certain missile units must be kept ready for selective strikes.

— **Escalation of the intensity of nuclear strikes over time.** the Soviets have at least considered the possibility of graduated escalation, either at their own discretion or in response to NATO.

12. Despite the Soviets' having adopted a policy for more flexible use of tactical nuclear weapons, and notwithstanding the impressive improvements they have made in forward-based tactical nuclear capabilities, they have not sought to match NATO's capacity for accurate and selective use of very-low-yield nuclear weapons. Although they have evidently been working on nuclear artillery for at least 20 years and have nuclear-capable artillery units in the western USSR, they do not appear to have given high priority to fielding it in Central Europe. Also, their armory of tactical nuclear warheads has shown a strong trend toward higher rather than lower yields.

Although the Soviets now have the necessary forces and employment doctrines to conduct limited nuclear war in Central Europe, we believe that they remain skeptical of the possibility of controlling escalation.

13. In sum, we cannot predict how the Soviets might respond to a limited and selective NATO first use of nuclear weapons or to their perception of NATO's preparations for the imminent use of nuclear weapons. They might conceivably continue purely nonnuclear operations, or they might respond with small-scale nuclear strikes of their own. They might also launch a theaterwide nuclear strike.

14. Neither can we be certain of the circumstances under which the Soviets might initiate nuclear operations in a NATO–Warsaw Pact war.

Summary of Soviet Nuclear Responses as Reflected in Exercises Since the Mid-1960s

Figure I-3

NATO First Nuclear Use	Soviet Responses In the 1960s	In the 1970s
• Small-scale use (limited and selective) — Not seen in Pact exercises since 1975	• Theaterwide strikes — Preemption if possible	• Continuation of nonnuclear operations • Small-scale strikes (forward-based systems) • Graduated escalation • Theaterwide strikes
• Large-scale use (theaterwide strikes)	• Theaterwide strikes — Preemption if possible	• Theaterwide strikes — Preemption if possible

16. We have considered whether the Soviets have adopted a strategy of "decoupling" nuclear war in Central Europe from the employment of peripheral systems. We have found no direct evidence of such a strategy in recent Soviet military writings or information from other human sources. However, the substantial increases in the number and quality of Pact tactical nuclear systems in Central Europe have provided the Pact with a capacity to conduct nuclear war there at relatively high intensities without having to resort to USSR-based systems.

Nonetheless, the Soviets' continued modernization of USSR-based peripheral strike systems argues that they still expect to have to resort to the use of these weapons at some stage of theater nuclear war. Their uncertainty about their actual ability to deter the West from launching strategic nuclear strikes against Soviet territory in the face of a successful Soviet conventional assault—which is complicated by the existence of independent French and British nuclear systems targeted against the USSR—further argues against the likelihood that the Soviets would anticipate much success in achieving a decoupling strategy.

17. In writings, Soviet military theorists still warn that escalation to the intercontinental level would be likely and could occur at any point during a theater conflict, conventional or nuclear, although restriction to the theater level is not ruled out. The Soviets probably see an advantage in limiting the use of nuclear weapons to the theater level, but they continue to plan and prepare against the likelihood that theater nuclear war would involve strikes on the USSR and escalate to intercontinental conflict.[2]

---

[2] The potential effect of improvements in USSR-based strategic systems for peripheral attack, in concert with improvements in Soviet intercontinental strike systems, on the possibility of decoupling theater nuclear war from intercontinental conflict is treated in NIE 11-3/8-78, *Soviet Capabilities for Strategic Nuclear Conflict Through the Late 1980s.*

C. Chemical Warfare

18. The Soviets are clearly planning for the contingency that toxic chemical agents might be used in a war between NATO and the Warsaw Pact. They have a continuing, vigorous program to equip and train Pact forces for operations in a chemical, biological, or radiological (CBR) environment. In addition, they have produced a variety of modern nerve agents and have the delivery systems and tactics necessary for the large-scale offensive use of these agents, but we do not know the size or the composition of the Soviet stockpile of chemical agents and filled munitions.

19. The Soviets are signatories of the 1925 Geneva Protocol which prohibits the use of chemical weapons, although they, like most other signatories, have reserved the right of retaliation. Beyond that we have no direct information on the Soviets' policy for use of chemical weapons and must infer their intentions about the circumstances in which they might use chemical weapons from their writings about the likely nature of a future war in Europe.

20. The Soviets categorize chemical weapons—as they do nuclear and biological weapons—as "weapons of mass destruction" whose initial use must be authorized at the highest political level. All of the Pact's operational stocks of chemical weapons and agents are believed to be under Soviet control in peacetime. Some are stored in Central Europe. The control and release procedures for chemical weapons are not necessarily the same as for nuclear weapons, and there is some evidence that, once released, chemical weapons would be subject to fewer restrictions on subsequent use than nuclear weapons. In addition, peacetime security over chemical weapons appears less rigorous than for nuclear weapons and is believed to be as much to prevent hazardous exposure as to prevent unauthorized use.

21. In the extensive body of available Pact writings dealing with the likely nature of a future war in Europe and addressing the broad strategic and operational considerations for conducting conventional, nuclear, and chemical warfare, there is no discussion of Pact intentions or plans to initiate chemical warfare during a nonnuclear conflict. In other writings which deal with tactical and technical problems of combat without explicit reference to the overall situation, Pact writers do treat the use of chemical weapons extensively.

22. Whatever the circumstances of initial use, once offensive chemical warfare had been authorized, the Pact's employment doctrine would lead it to attempt to achieve surprise and to employ chemical weapons on a large scale in the hope of catching NATO troops unprotected. Prime objectives, for example, would be to disable airfields, nuclear and logistic depots, and command and control facilities. Other important objectives might include reduction of NATO's antiarmor capabilities and air defenses or stopping amphibious landings.

23. Once widespread nuclear warfare had begun, the question of whether to use chemical weapons would be largely tactical. Pact writings on theater nuclear war usually assume that chemical weapons would be used also. In such circumstances, chemical weapons are thought to be a valuable complement to conventional and nuclear weapons, because their effects can be more widespread than conventional weapons and they present fewer troop safety problems and produce fewer obstacles to friendly troop maneuver than do nuclear weapons.

24. With respect to the question of Soviet policy on the first use of chemical weapons, there are two views within the Intelligence Community. According to one view,[3] it is unlikely that the Warsaw Pact would initiate offensive chemical warfare (CW) before the advent of nuclear warfare, but the Pact's first use under these circumstances cannot be entirely excluded. According to an alternative view,[4] there is a strong possibility that the Pact would initiate CW in a conventional conflict.

25. The agencies holding the first view base their judgment on the evidence cited above and on their assessment of the risks and benefits which the Soviets would consider in deciding whether to use chemical

---

[3] *The holders of this view are the Central Intelligence Agency and the Director, Bureau of Intelligence and Research, Department of State.*

[4] *The holders of this view are the Director, Defense Intelligence Agency; the Director, National Security Agency; and the Senior Intelligence Officers of each of the military services.*

weapons

26. These agencies recognize, however, that the Pact's first use of chemicals before the onset of nuclear war cannot be entirely excluded. They believe that the circumstance most likely to cause the Pact to initiate chemical warfare during a conventional conflict would be one in which the Soviets saw little possibility of a successful Pact outcome without chemicals and were prepared to risk having the conflict escalate to nuclear war. In deciding, the Soviets would consider the potential value of employing their superior chemical warfare capability and the possible benefits to be derived from the surprise, shock effect, and destructive impact of its use against NATO troops. These factors would be weighed against their assessment of the likelihood and consequences of NATO retaliation with nuclear weapons. These agencies judge that, under the present military circumstances, the Soviets would rate this likelihood as high and would expect large-scale nuclear war to be the eventual outcome.

27. They believe that, in the future, the Soviets' appreciation of the risks and rewards of introducing chemical weapons into a conventional conflict in Europe is likely to be affected by their perception of the trends in the balance of their own and NATO's nuclear and chemical warfare capabilities. For example, should they conclude that NATO's ability and resolve to retaliate with nuclear weapons were significantly diminished, they might feel less constrained against introducing chemical warfare. By the same token, they would be less inclined to initiate chemical warfare—during either conventional or nuclear conflict—if they believed NATO had a well-developed capability to defend against chemical attack and to retaliate effectively with its own chemical weapons.

28. The agencies holding the second view judge that Pact forces possess the resources to wage offensive CW on a large scale. They recognize that the infrequency with which Pact staffs apparently practice CW in large-scale field training exercises   could impact adversely on their efficiency in conducting CW operations. However, tactical employment of CW in divisional and lower field training exercises and simulating the use of chemical weapons by NATO in Pact field training exercises provide opportunities to practice the skills necessary for effective CW employment. These agencies also note that Pact forces are well prepared to operate in a CW environment. They engage in extensive training which routinely includes such realistic measures as conducting artillery practice and small unit exercises in full protective suits. Pact forces have large numbers of organic CBR defense personnel, and they are well equipped with modern protective and decontaminated equipment. These unprecedently large-scale preparations for operating in a CW environment are especially significant in that they have been made in the absence of any serious CW threat from NATO.

29. These agencies believe that the following considerations would be likely to influence a Soviet decision on first use of chemical weapons in a conventional conflict:

— The Soviets might view the risk of NATO nuclear retaliation to be less significant because of their own nuclear capability, or they might conclude that NATO would not respond with nuclear weapons to Pact first use of chemical weapons.

— The Soviets probably appreciate that mass employment of chemical weapons at the outset of a conventional war could facilitate penetration of NATO defenses and permit the high rates of advance which they believed necessary for victory in a short war.

— They probably recognize that, as in nuclear warfare, the element of surprise would offer distinct advantages to the first user.

— They might see their extensive capability in chemical warfare as providing them a decisive advantage in an area in which NATO could not catch up during a short war.

These agencies believe that in the final analysis the overriding factors governing first use of chemical weapons by the Soviets would be their assessment of NATO's chemical warfare capabilities and the operational advantages they expected to gain from such use.

D. Biological Warfare

30. All Warsaw Pact countries have signed the Biological Warfare Convention prohibiting the production, storage, and use of biological weapons. There is no evidence that any of them have violated the

treaty. The Convention permits defensively oriented BW programs which the Soviets are known to have. ▢ available evidence do not treat offensive use of biological weapons. We assume, however, that the Soviets are continuing research on biological agents, and that they have facilities which could be used to produce biological weapons if a decision were made to do so.

E. Electronic Warfare

31. The Soviets have a broad-based policy concerning electronic warfare—"radioelectronic combat" in the Soviet lexicon—and have made it a fundamental part of their battle planning at the tactical and strategic level. The Soviet concept of radioelectronic combat is considerably broader than the US concept of electronic warfare. It encompasses jamming, camouflage, concealment and deception, and operations to destroy NATO's intelligence and electronic control systems, especially those for nuclear forces, while protecting the USSR's own systems and forces. It also includes reconnaissance and signal intelligence efforts to identify and locate NATO's electronic control systems and to determine their vulnerabilities. In the Soviet view, radioelectronic combat is to be integrated into all phases of warfare, and we expect that NATO's intelligence and electronic control systems at all levels would be subject to concerted electronic and physical attack.

F. Soviet Views of NATO's Military Capabilities

32. The Soviets respect the capabilities of NATO's armed forces and are keenly aware of NATO's economic potential and its ability, given time, to mobilize additional forces. (See figure I-4.) In measuring the magnitude of the threat in Europe, they probably include France, inasmuch as France is still a member of NATO, continues to participate in some joint planning with NATO commanders, and maintains some 50,000 troops in West Germany. The Soviets probably also weigh the potential contribution of non-NATO countries such as Sweden and Spain.

Selected Indexes of NATO and Warsaw Pact Military Potential — Figure I-4

	Population (Millions)	Labor Force (Millions)	GNP (Billion US$)	Total Armed Forces (Thousands)
NATO	565 (Other 347, US 218)	235 (138, 97)	3,509 (1,818, 1,691)	4,911 (2,828, 2,083)
Pact	374 (Other 113, USSR 261)	189 (52, 137)	1,290 (330, 960)	5,606 (1,206, 4,400)

33. The Soviets have accurate information on NATO order of battle, command and control arrangements, alert procedures, and readiness categories. They have knowledge of Western mobilization plans and plans to transfer combat forces from the United States to Europe. They know the nature of the forces earmarked for such deployment, the scheduling of the transfer, and the mission of these forces in the early phases of a war. They estimate that the United States could quickly augment the tactical air forces in Europe and deploy as many as four additional aircraft carriers to the European theater. They are extremely conservative in evaluating NATO's combat potential and sometimes ascribe exaggerated capabilities to NATO.

34. The Soviets view NATO's nuclear arsenal as the primary threat to Warsaw Pact forces. They credit NATO with a large inventory of nuclear weapons and delivery systems which include various types of aircraft, artillery, and tactical surface-to-surface missiles. They appreciate that the mobility, survivability, and flexibility of these systems make them difficult to combat effectively. They see a continuing trend toward the modernization and improvement of these weapon systems. They have grave concerns about development of the cruise missile with its potential for significantly increasing NATO's nuclear strike capability. They are also concerned about the enhanced radiation warhead which they contend will lower the nuclear threshold in Europe.

35. Areas in which the Soviets consider NATO conventional capabilities to be especially significant include the impressive and improving capabilities of NATO's antitank defenses and the continuing modernization of NATO's tactical air forces. These factors are assessed by the Soviets as having substantially improved NATO's conventional forces, although they still believe that Soviet and other Warsaw Pact forces have made relatively more progress in improving their overall conventional capabilities.

36. The Soviets recognize the formidable strength of NATO's navies, particularly the carrier strike forces, ballistic missile and antisubmarine submarines, and amphibious assault forces. They see geography as favoring NATO's naval power. The USSR attributes a broad range of missions and capabilities to NATO's fleets in either a conventional or nuclear war, the most threatening being their ability to attack rear area and coastal targets and to counter Pact naval forces.

G. Implications for Pact Forces

37. Motivated by the prospect of a nonnuclear phase of hostilities and their recognition of a need for strong conventional forces even in the event of nuclear war, the Soviets have sought to improve their conventional force capabilities. Since the late 1960s they have significantly increased manpower, tanks, artillery, armed helicopters, and air defenses. They have been equipping their tactical air forces with aircraft possessing increased performance and load-carrying capacity. During this period the flexibility and conventional war potential of Soviet naval forces also have been markedly improved by the acquistition of more capable surface combatants, submarines, amphibious ships, replenishment ships, and aircraft.

38. The increase in conventional firepower in the ground and air forces has especially enhanced the Pact's ability to overcome organized NATO defenses in the absence of the nuclear strikes which formerly were relied upon to blast holes for the passage of armored striking forces in the opening phase of a European war. Pact stress the special importance of artillery in the breakthrough phase when a nuclear strike is not employed initially. The added firepower also increases the Pact's capability to destroy NATO's nuclear delivery systems and warhead stockpiles during a conventional phase, which is emphasized in Soviet tactical doctrine.

39. At the same time, the Soviets have continued to increase the size of their theater nuclear forces and improve their flexibility. Since the early 1970s they have introduced nuclear artillery systems, increased their surface-to-surface tactical missile launchers in Central Europe, assigned nuclear missions to additional tactical aviation units, and are deploying a new generation of intermediate-range ballistic missiles and a new bomber. The Soviet Navy has also added systems which improve its capability to wage theater nuclear war.

40. At sea the establishment and maintenance of Soviet naval forces on NATO's flanks in the Mediterranean and elsewhere since the late 1960s also have implications for the Pact's potential strategies for conflict in the European theater. Those Soviet naval units which are continuously deployed forward on the littoral of Europe have significant capabilities in either a conventional or theater nuclear context, especially at the outset of hostilities.

41. Since the late 1960s the Pact has adopted a standardized command and control doctrine and has begun to modernize its command and control procedures and equipment. Providing impetus to Pact efforts to improve command and control are the technological improvements in communication systems and the growing complexity of future combat caused by the proliferation of modern weapon systems.

42. Pact ground force logistic capacity has also been improved, notably by large additions to motor transport and the development of improved support organizations and equipment. These improvements have been made partly to support the increased demands for ammunition and fuel imposed by changed tactical organization and doctrine and partly to increase the combat endurance of the forces in either nuclear or conventional war.

43. Pact theater forces have emerged from a decade of change with their fundamental orientation on the tank intact, but with a more balanced structure for conventional war and with both conventional and nuclear firepower greatly increased. These changes, along with an infusion of more modern technology, have made Soviet theater forces competitive with leading Western armies in sophistication of organization and equipment.

CHAPTER II

WARSAW PACT FORCES FOR THEATER WARFARE

1. Warsaw Pact forces for operations against NATO can best be described in terms of major groupings:

— Ground, tactical air, and air defense forces in Eastern Europe and in the military districts of the USSR opposite NATO, and possibly these types of forces in the Moscow, Volga, Ural, and Turkestan Military Districts.

— Naval forces of the three Soviet European fleets and the non-Soviet Warsaw Pact (NSWP) countries.

— Most medium- and intermediate-range and some intercontinental ballistic missiles of the Soviet Strategic Rocket Forces.

— Most intermediate-range and some long-range bombers of Soviet Long Range Aviation.

2. Pact forces opposite NATO are predominantly Soviet, but NSWP forces make a significant contribution and indeed are critical to Soviet strategy for conflict in Europe. Since the mid-1960s both Soviet and NSWP forces have been characterized by a growth in manpower and equipment and by modernization programs to improve their capabilities. Overall, the changes of the past decade or so have made these forces more balanced and operationally flexible, with improved capabilities for both nuclear and nonnuclear warfare.

A. Warsaw Pact Ground Forces

Manpower

3. Warsaw Pact ground forces opposite NATO number about 1.9 million men. The Soviet Union accounts for roughly half of the total or just over 1 million men. About half of these Soviet forces are stationed in Eastern Europe and half in the military districts of the USSR that are opposite NATO. The size and distribution of these forces are shown in table II-1.

Table II-1

Warsaw Pact Ground Force Manpower Opposite NATO *
January 1979

	Soviet	NSWP	Total
East Germany	365,000	106,000	471,000
Poland	35,000	232,000	267,000
Czechoslovakia	68,000	143,000	211,000
Hungary	59,000	72,000	131,000
Bulgaria	—	105,000	105,000
Romania	—	140,000	140,000
USSR	553,000	—	553,000
Total	1,080,000	798,000	1,878,000

* Includes Soviet and East European forces in the non-Soviet Warsaw Pact countries (East Germany, Poland, Czechoslovakia, Hungary, Romania, and Bulgaria) and Soviet forces in the Baltic, Belorussian, Carpathian, Leningrad, Odessa, Kiev, North Caucasus, and Transcaucasus Military Districts of the USSR. This note applies to all the tables in chapter II.

SECRET

4. Since the late 1960s, overall Pact ground force manpower has increased substantially. Pact forces in Central Europe—where our information is best—have increased more than the forces opposite NATO's flanks. Ground force manpower in the Soviet Groups of Forces in Central Europe, for example, has expanded by some 75,000 men since the late 1960s, while the East German, Polish, and Czechoslovak ground forces have registered an increase of 65,000 men.[1] About three-fourths of this increase took place before 1973. Figure II-1 depicts several important trends in Warsaw Pact ground forces in Central Europe.

Equipment

5. Pact ground forces are well equipped with weapons either of Soviet origin or patterned after Soviet models. The equipment inventory is being continually modernized with the introduction of new, improved

---
[1] The transfer of some Polish territorial forces to the active ground forces accounts for a portion of this increase.

Trends in Warsaw Pact Ground Forces in Central Europe, 1969 and 1979

Figure II-1

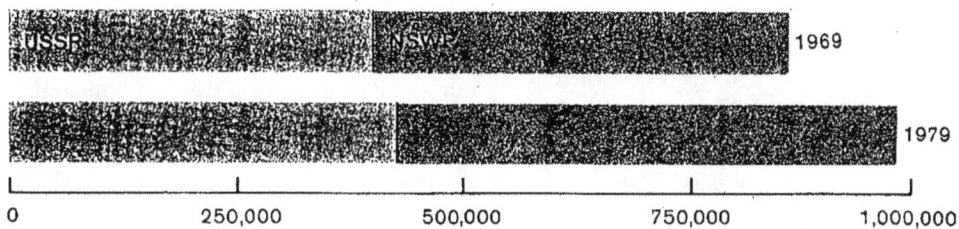
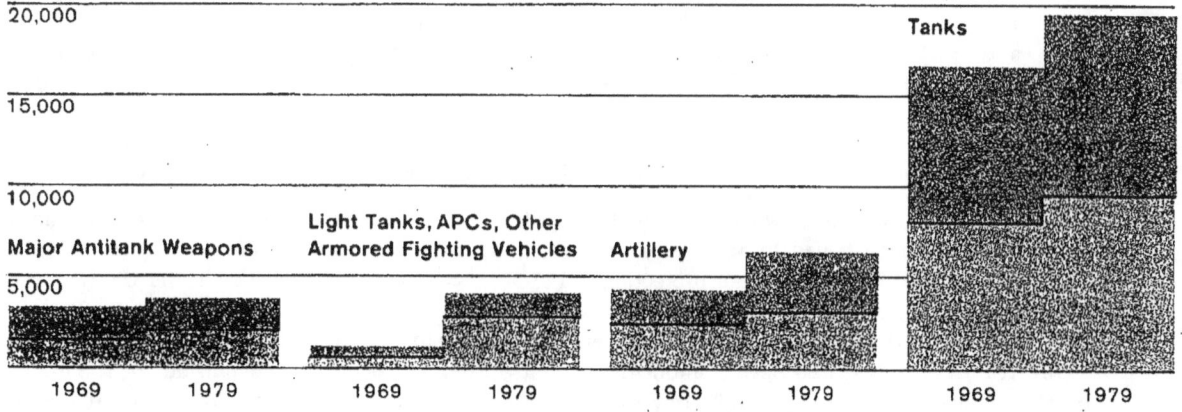

Includes all ATGMs, and all antitank guns and recoilless rifles with maximum effective ranges greater than 500 meters. Does not include BMP-mounted weapons.

Includes the PT-76 and the BMP.

Includes all artillery pieces and multiple rocket launchers greater than 100 mm.

Includes medium and heavy tanks.

577620 1-79 CIA

combat vehicles, support equipment, and weapons designed to increase mobility and provide greater, more accurate firepower. Despite impressive modernization programs, however, Pact ground forces retain a mixture of old and new equipment. Although Pact forces are considerably more standardized than NATO's, items such as T-34 and T-54/55 tanks, the BTR-152 and earlier models of BTR-60 armored personnel carriers, and various older models of field artillery and antiaircraft guns, are still operational and contribute to a growing diversity within the Pact weapons inventory. Although most Pact equipment is of Soviet production and design, the share produced by the NSWP countries is increasing.

6. **Tanks.** Armor has dominated Pact ground forces for the past several decades. During the decade before the mid-1960s, when Soviet military planners believed that war in Europe could be nuclear from the outset, the survivability of armored forces underscored their value relative to other ground forces. In the late 1960s, when these planners were forced to contend with the possibility of both a conventional and a nuclear conflict, armored forces were still believed to offer maximum flexibility.

7. The Soviets are aware of the improved technology and growing numbers of NATO antitank weapons and have demonstrated this awareness by modifying their forces and tactics to counter the antitank threat. As in earlier Soviet responses to changing perceptions of battlefield conditions, such adjustments have not led to any diminution of the tank forces, or any major change in the way the Soviets see these tank forces performing. Indeed, they have made even further increases to their tank strength and have begun producing new tank models.

8. The mainstay of the Pact ground forces is the medium tank. In all, Pact forces opposite NATO have about 45,000 medium tanks at their disposal. Of these about 25,000 (10,500 Soviet, 14,500 NSWP) are located in Eastern Europe. Soviet forces are equipped with a mix of T-54/55, T-62, T-64, and T-72 models, while the NSWP armies rely almost exclusively on the T-54/55 series, with some T-34s still in the active forces. The T-55, which was first manufactured in 1958, is still in production; production of the T-62 ended in 1975.

9. In the last few years, two new tanks, the T-64 and T-72, have been issued to Soviet ground forces. Both tanks incorporate better armor protection, a 125-mm smoothbore gun, an automatic loading system, and an electro-optic, possibly laser, rangefinder. (See figure II-2.) Both tanks also have a stabilizing system on the main gun enabling the tank crew to aim and fire on the move.

10. The T-64 is assigned both to Soviet units in the USSR and to those in Eastern Europe. Some 4,500 to 6,000 T-64 tanks have been produced, of which about 2,600 are in Eastern Europe. Some 6,000 T-72s have been produced thus far. All have been assigned to Soviet units in the USSR. Thus far, however, only about 1,200 T-72s have been confirmed with Soviet units in the military districts of the USSR opposite NATO.

11. The T-72, or an improved version, probably will be the main production tank well into the 1980s. The T-72 is heavier than its predecessors but is faster and quieter, and has a lower silhouette than the T-54/55 or T-62. It also has an improved suspension system, a more advanced and more powerful diesel engine, and composite or laminated armor designed to provide increased protection against high-explosive antitank (HEAT) warheads.

12. Since the late 1960s the number of medium tanks in Soviet tank divisions has increased from 313 to 322 and in Soviet motorized rifle divisions from 188 to 214. Those Soviet motorized rifle divisions opposite NATO which have independent tank battalions have as many as 265 tanks.[2]

13. *Artillery.* In all, the Pact has assigned about 18,200 artillery pieces of 122-mm or larger to its ground forces opposite NATO. Of these, some 8,800 (3,600 Soviet, 5,200 NSWP) are located in Eastern Europe. Pact artillery is still predominantly towed but is being improved by the addition of four new self-propelled models and a new multiple rocket launcher. The Soviets are continuing to replace the towed 122-mm howitzers with self-propelled models in their motorized rifle regiments. The new 152-mm self-propelled howitzer also is continuing to enter the inventory. Thus far, it has replaced older towed pieces in the artillery regiments of several Soviet motorized rifle and tank divisions and at least one artillery division. Because the self-propelled weapons provide superior cross-country mobility and protection for their crews, they are better suited to support fast-moving armored attacks. (See figure II-3.)

14. A new 203-mm self-propelled gun and a new 240-mm self-propelled mortar are being deployed in heavy artillery brigades in the USSR as replacements for their older towed predecessors. Both systems are capable of firing nuclear rounds and, although neither has yet been sighted outside the USSR, we estimate that they will be deployed eventually with Soviet forces in Eastern Europe.[3]

15. A 16-tube multiple rocket launcher of about 240-mm caliber has been fielded with the Soviet artillery division in East Germany. We have identified 36 launchers thus far. If fielded in quantity, this weapon would increase Pact capabilities for massed fire support during conventional operations. Soviet

---

[2] *There are varying estimates of the number of Soviet motorized rifle divisions which currently have independent tank battalions (ITBs). According to one estimate, about two-thirds of Soviet motorized rifle divisions in Eastern Europe have ITBs but few, if any, divisions in the western USSR do. This is the view of the Central Intelligence Agency; the Director, Defense Intelligence Agency; and the Director, Bureau of Intelligence and Research, Department of State. Another view is that all Soviet motorized rifle divisions in Eastern Europe currently have ITBs. The holders of this view are the Director, National Security Agency; the Assistant Chief of Staff for Intelligence, Department of the Army; and the Assistant Chief of Staff, Intelligence, Department of the Air Force. The latter two further believe that, for planning purposes, all Soviet motorized rifle divisions in the USSR also would, when committed to combat, have ITBs.*

[3] For a more detailed discussion of Soviet nuclear artillery, see paragraphs 161 and 162 in this chapter.

Principal Warsaw Pact Medium Tanks

Figure II-2

	T-72	T-64	T-62	T-54/55
	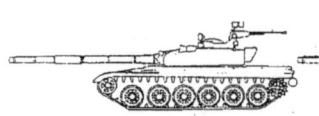		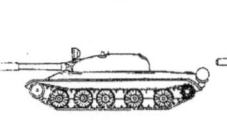	
Main armament	125-mm smoothbore gun	125-mm smoothbore gun	115-mm smoothbore gun	100-mm rifled gun
Onboard ammunition (rounds)	40	40	40	34/43
Weight (metric tons)	41	38	37	36
Speed (km/h)	60+	60+	50	50
Cruising range (km)				
Without auxiliary tanks	500	500	450	400/500
With auxiliary tanks	650	650	650	600/715
Length/height (m)	6.9/2.3	6.3/2.3	6.6/2.4	6.2/2.3
Year operational	1974	1968	1961	1949/58

Secret

Warsaw Pact Self-Propelled Artillery

Figure II-3

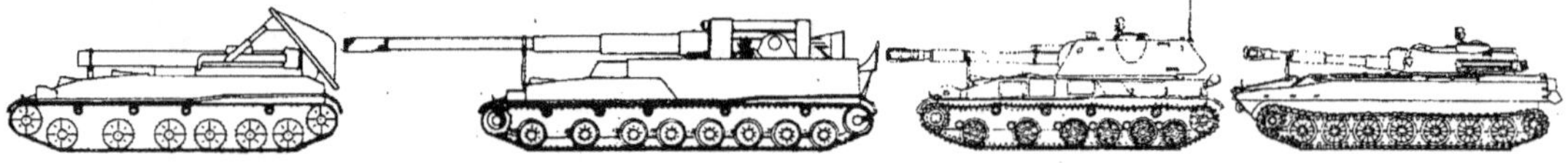

	240-mm SP Mortar, M-1975*	203-mm SP Gun, M-1975*	152-mm SP Howitzer, M-1973	122-mm SP Howitzer, M-1974
Onboard ammunition (rounds)	Unknown	Unknown	40	40
Maximum range (m)	12,000	28,000–30,000	17,300	15,300
Weight (metric tons)	25	30	27	17
Length (m)	7.4	10.0	8.4	7.4
Cruising range (km)	500	500	500	500
Year operational	1977	1975	1973	1974

*Artists' concepts based on limited information. These weapons are believed to be nuclear capable.

Secret

artillery units in both tank and motorized rifle divisions also are being expanded. For example, six-piece, 122-mm howitzer batteries in the motorized rifle regiments in Soviet motorized rifle divisions have grown to 18-piece battalions.

16. In addition to artillery weapon systems, the Soviets are deploying a number of new artillery support vehicles to improve their artillery fire direction, control, and target acquisition capabilities. Laser rangefinders, fire-control computers, and fire-control data transmission systems have been issued to some artillery units. There is also evidence that the Soviets now are producing and training with proximity fuses, which will make their artillery considerably more effective against unarmored vehicles and troops without overhead protection.

17. Modernization and some expansion are under way in NSWP artillery units but at a much slower pace than in Soviet units. East Germany is replacing its BM-21 multiple rocket launchers with the Czechoslovak RM-70 system, which can rapidly reload a second salvo carried on board. Poland and Czechoslovakia now have a few 122-mm self-propelled howitzers, and Czechoslovakia has added a new artillery division.

18. *Armored Personnel Carriers and Other Combat Vehicles.* Soviet divisions in Eastern Europe are equipped with a full complement of APCs. Shortages remain in Soviet divisions in the western USSR, however, with some divisions lacking as much as two-thirds of their APCs. One-half to two-thirds of the 20,500 Soviet APCs opposite NATO are now modern amphibious models. (See figure II-4). The rest are older models with relatively poor cross-country mobility. The Soviets continue to replace these APCs with improved models—the BTR-60PB and the BMP. The BTR-60PB is an amphibious, wheeled APC which provides good mobility and armor protection from small arms and shell fragments. The BMP is an amphibious, tracked vehicle designed to operate closely with tanks and has greater armor protection than the BTR-60PB. It is equipped with a machinegun, a 73-mm gun, and the Sagger antitank guided missile launcher. It also has a CBR (chemical, biologi-

Modern Warsaw Pact Armored Fighting Vehicles and APCs

Figure II-4

	BMP	BTR-60PB	BMD (Airborne)
		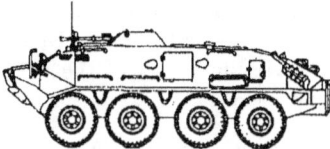	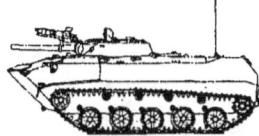
Armament	73-mm gun 7.62-mm machinegun Mount for antitank guided missile	14.5-mm and 7.62-mm machineguns	73-mm gun Three 7.62-mm machineguns Mount for antitank guided missile
Weight (metric tons)	13.6	10.3	8.0
Length/height (m)	6.7/1.9	7.2/2.3	5.4/1.7
Speed (km/h)	70	80	80
Cruising range (km)	500	500	320
Crew	3	3	2
Number of passengers	8	14	6

cal, radiological) protective system to allow operations in a toxic or radioactive environment.

19. Variants of the BMP are also entering the Soviet ground forces in increasing numbers. These include the M-1974 command vehicle, the M-1975 surveillance vehicle, and the M-1976 reconnaissance vehicle, which is replacing the PT-76, the only light tank in service. The BMD, a lightly armored, airdroppable, assault vehicle is assigned to Soviet airborne divisions. It is amphibious and has the same weapons as the larger BMP, plus two additional machineguns.

20. The NSWP ground forces are on the whole still predominantly equipped with older APCs. The East German, Czechoslovak, and Polish ground forces, however, have large numbers of the more modern APCs, including some 1,600 BMPs and several thousand BTR-60s or a Czechoslovak/Polish-manufactured equivalent. Hungary, Romania, and Bulgaria are largely equipped with older APCs. Overall, the NSWP ground forces have about 11,000 APCs.

21. *Ground Force Air Defense Systems*. Pact ground forces opposite NATO are equipped with a variety of tactical surface-to-air missile (SAM) and antiaircraft (AA) gun systems. A program to replace gun systems and older SAMs with more mobile SAM systems was begun in the late 1960s and continues, with Soviet units in Eastern Europe and along the Sino-Soviet border receiving highest priority. Upgrading of the remaining Soviet units and of the NSWP forces is proceeding more slowly.

22. The SA-4 Ganef, a long-range, medium-to-high-altitude SAM system (see figure II-5), has replaced the older, less mobile SA-2 Guideline in Soviet front- and army-level organizations. The SA-4 system represents a major improvement over the SA-2 because it has twice the range and each launcher has two missiles available for refire. It has begun to appear in the inventories of Czechoslovak, East German, and Polish forces as well, but in fewer numbers. Each of these forces has deployed only one SA-4 brigade. The SA-3 Goa is still fielded with Soviet ground forces in the forward area for point defense of airfields.

23. The SA-6 Gainful and SA-8 Gecko systems are designed to replace the S-60 57-mm AA gun as division-level air defense weapons. The SA-6 is a mobile, medium-range, low-to-medium altitude system. The SA-8 is a highly mobile, low-altitude system with approximately one-half the maximum missile range of the SA-6. The SA-8 is unique among Pact SAM systems in that it carries both its radar and missiles on the same vehicle—a characteristic which provides greater operational flexibility.

24. Replacement of the S-60 gun system with SA-6s and SA-8s has proceeded much more rapidly in Soviet forces in Eastern Europe than in those in the USSR or NSWP forces. Two-thirds of Soviet tank and motorized rifle divisions in Eastern Europe have been equipped with one or another of these systems. (See table II-2.) Only about 10 percent of Soviet divisions in the USSR and four NSWP divisions have SA-6s, however, and no SA-8s have been fielded yet with non-Soviet forces. SA-6 regiments have been deployed at army level, however, in most NSWP countries. S-60 guns replaced by mobile SAMs may be reorganized into AA units for additional air defense of fronts or armies.

25. Pact ground forces are also equipped with the SA-7 Grail and SA-9 Gaskin missile systems. The SA-7 is fielded at the company level. It is a man-portable system with an infrared homing missile and is de-

Table II-2

Status of Air Defense Modernization in Warsaw Pact Ground Force Divisions Opposite NATO [a]
January 1979

	Divisions [b]	Equipped With [c]		
		SA-6	SA-8	AA
Soviet				
In Eastern Europe	31	19	5	7
In the USSR	72	7	1	64
Total	103	26	6	71
NSWP [d]				
East Germany	6	3	—	3
Poland	13	—	—	13
Czechoslovakia	10	—	—	10
Hungary	6	1	—	5
Romania	10	—	—	10
Bulgaria	6	—	—	6
Total	51	4	—	47
Grand Total	154	30	6	118

[a] See footnote to table II-1, following paragraph 3.
[b] Does not include airborne divisions or the Polish Sea Landing Division.
[c] Most combat-ready and some reduced-strength or cadre divisions are also equipped with SA-9s and the ZSU-23-4 gun systems. All Pact divisions probably have the man-portable SA-7.
[d] Does not include nine army-level SA-6 regiments in Polish, Czechoslovak, Hungarian, Romanian, and Bulgarian ground forces.

Selected Mobile Air Defense Systems in Warsaw Pact Ground Forces

Figure II-5

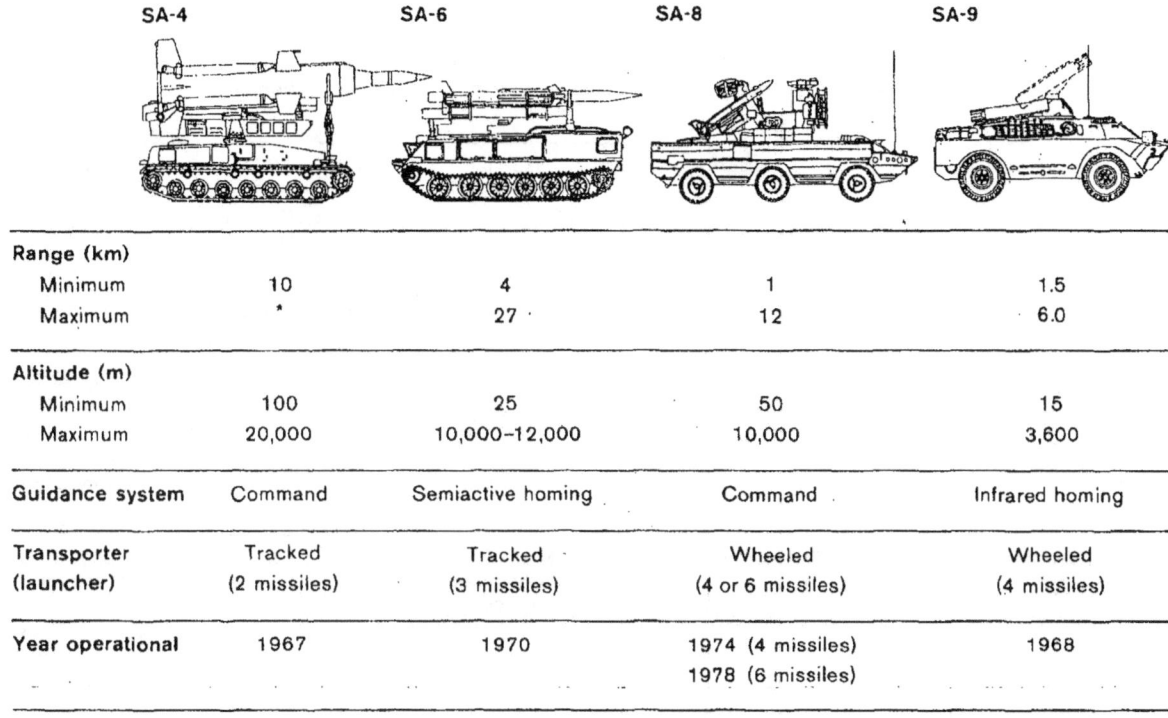

	SA-4	SA-6	SA-8	SA-9
Range (km)				
Minimum	10	4	1	1.5
Maximum	*	27	12	6.0
Altitude (m)				
Minimum	100	25	50	15
Maximum	20,000	10,000–12,000	10,000	3,600
Guidance system	Command	Semiactive homing	Command	Infrared homing
Transporter (launcher)	Tracked (2 missiles)	Tracked (3 missiles)	Wheeled (4 or 6 missiles)	Wheeled (4 missiles)
Year operational	1967	1970	1974 (4 missiles) 1978 (6 missiles)	1968

*There is disagreement over whether the maximum range of the SA-4 is 50 or 80 kilometers.

signed for use against helicopters and other slow-flying aircraft. The SA-9 missile is also an infrared system but has a greater range than the SA-7 and is carried aboard a modified amphibious scout car. It is deployed along with the ZSU-23-4 AA system as part of a regimental air defense battery. The extent to which these systems have been deployed as replacements for older AA systems is difficult to determine. We assume that all Pact forces have been equipped with the SA-7. The SA-9 and ZSU-23-4 are probably with the regiments of all combat-ready tank and motorized rifle divisions and with approximately 30 percent of reduced-strength or cadre divisions.

26. The Soviets recently began forming antiaircraft divisions in the USSR which may be similar to their AA units of the World War II type. At least one of these units has been identified in COMINT, and additional units have been reported by human sources. A minimum of 200 pieces of antiaircraft artillery has been observed at each of eight installations in the USSR, suggesting that additional divisions may be formed. Considering the relative ineffectiveness of these AA systems, we are as yet unable to determine the mission of the divisions.

27. *Antitank Weapons.* The Soviet arsenal of antitank weapons includes both guided missiles and artillery. (See figure II-6.) Antitank guided missiles (ATGMs) are heliborne, vehicle mounted, and man portable. Improved models of the radio-controlled AT-2 Swatter and wire-guided AT-3 Sagger with semiautomatic guidance are mounted on modified scout cars and helicopters. The Sagger can also be mounted on the BMP and BMD and is available in a manpack version. Some first-generation Swatters and Saggers are still in service. Three new ATGM systems are also being deployed with Soviet forces. The AT-4 Spigot man-portable ATGM, the AT-5 Spandrel vehicle-mounted system, and the AT-6 Spiral heliborne system have all been observed recently with the Soviet forces in East Germany. The vehicle-mounted system, suitable also for helicopter mounts, has a nonretractable launch rack with five launching

Warsaw Pact Antitank Guilded Missiles

Figure II-6

	Takeoff weight (kg)	Range (km) Minimum	Range (km) Maximum	Guidance system	Ground mount	Carrier/launch vehicles	Helicopter mount	Year operational
AT-1 Snapper	24	600	2,300	Manual wire-guided	No	BRDM (3 mounts) GAZ-69 (4 mounts)	No	1958
AT-2a Swatter	29	500	2,500	Manual radio-guided	No	BRDM (4 mounts)	No	1960
AT-2b Swatter	29	500	3,500	Manual radio-guided	No	BRDM (4 mounts)	Hind (4 mounts) Hip (4 mounts)	1965
AT-2c Uprated Swatter	29	300	3,500	Manual radio-guided, infrared terminal homing	No	BRDM (3 mounts)	Hind (4 mounts) Hip (6 mounts)	Mid-1970s
AT-3 Sagger	11	500	3,000	Manual wire-guided	Yes	BRDM (6 mounts) BMP and BMD (1 mount)	Hoplite (4 mounts)	1961
AT-3c Uprated Sagger	11	300	3,000	Semiautomatic (optical target tracking infrared missile tracking) wire-guided	Yes	BRDM (6 mounts) BMP and BMD (1 mount)	Hoplite (4 mounts) Hip (6 mounts)	1968–70
AT-4 Spigot	Unknown	70	2,000	Semiautomatic wire-guided	Yes	Unknown	Unknown	1973–75
AT-5 Spandrel	Unknown	100	4,000	Semiautomatic wire or radio command link	Yes	BRDM (5 mounts)	Possible	1974–76
AT-6 Spiral	Unknown	100	5,000	Semiautomatic radio command link	No	Unknown	Hind D (4 mounts)	1974–76

tubes mounted on a rotating pedestal similar to the SA-9. It was first observed in 1977 mounted on a BRDM-2 scout car. The AT-6 Spiral was first observed during a firing exercise in East Germany in 1978 being launched from modified Hind D helicopters. Antitank (AT) guns and recoilless guns have not received the priority in development and deployment that the ATGM has in recent years. The 100-mm AT gun is standard in Soviet units, but 85-mm antitank guns are retained in some divisional and nondivisional AT units.

28. NSWP forces have a wide variety of antitank weapons including recoilless guns, AT guns from 57-mm to 100-mm, and AT guided missiles. Except for a few Czechoslovak-produced weapons, all are of Soviet origin. The East Germans are equipped with the latest Soviet 100-mm antitank gun, the T-12/T-12A, but the other forces retain older weapons of various calibers, which are inferior to the better Soviet weapons. NSWP forces are gradually improving their antiarmor capabilities by acquiring more ATGM launcher vehicles and manpack ATGM sets. The East Germans, Poles, and Romanians, for example, have received the AT-4 Spigot. Only the East Germans are currently equipped to Soviet standards with Sagger ATGM launcher vehicles, but the Czechoslovaks are increasing the numbers of ATGM launcher vehicles in their forces.

29. *Engineering Equipment.* The principal support task for the engineers is to help sustain the mobility of Pact offensive forces. The Pact has developed modern engineer and river-crossing equipment. With the PMP ribbon bridge, the Soviets have spanned a river the size of the Rhine in approximately half an hour during exercises. The Pact also has a large stock of ferries and tracked amphibious transporters, and a variety of mine-clearing vehicles which fire rocket-propelled, explosive line charges to clear gaps in minefields. In addition, the Pact has vehicles fitted with mine-clearing plows, light dozer blades, and other mechanical devices. Vehicles such as these also could be used to clear rubble and obstacles.

30. *Surface-to-Surface Missiles and Rockets.*[4] The Pact arsenal of rockets and surface-to-surface missiles includes free rockets over ground (FROGs) and short-range ballistic missiles. All Pact ground forces are equipped with FROGs and SS-1 Scuds, which are capable of delivering conventional, as well as chemical, and nuclear warheads. The poor accuracy of these systems would make them relatively ineffective in a conventional role against point targets. Soviet forces also have the SS-12 Scaleboard and its follow-on, the SS-22. A new missile, the SS-21, is being deployed to Soviet units as a replacement for the FROG. The FROG, the SS-21, and possibly the SS-22 also can carry a cluster-munition warhead.

Warsaw Pact Ground Force Divisions

31. Tank and motorized rifle divisions are the basic tactical units of Pact ground forces.[5] The Pact maintains a grand total of 217 active tank and motorized rifle divisions (166 Soviet and 51 East European) at varying strengths in its peacetime ground forces. The number of such divisions opposite NATO stands at 154. (See table II-3 and figure II-7). The Soviets have an additional 16 tank and motorized rifle divisions in the Moscow, Ural, Volga, and Turkestan Military Districts which could be used against NATO or elsewhere.

32. In peacetime, Pact divisions are maintained in various states of readiness suitable for the conduct of limited combat operations on short notice and for generating large forces through rapid mobilization. We classify Pact ground force divisions according to our estimates of their peacetime manning and equipment levels:

— **Category I:** These divisions are estimated to have a full complement of combat equipment and more than three-fourths of their authorized wartime personnel. All divisions in the Soviet Groups of Forces and eight East European divisions are manned closer to wartime strength. All Category I divisions could be brought up to strength and ready to move within 24 hours.

Table II-3

Warsaw Pact Tank and Motorized Rifle Divisions Opposite NATO.*
January 1979

| | In Eastern Europe | | In the | |
	Soviet	NSWP	USSR	Total
Divisions	31	51	72	154
Tank	16	15	22	53
Motorized Rifle	15	36	50	101

* See footnote to table II-1, following paragraph 3. See table B-1 in annex B for detailed order of battle of Pact ground force divisions.

SECRET

[4] For a more detailed discussion of Pact tactical rockets and missiles, see paragraphs 159 and 160 in this chapter.

[5] Pact airborne divisions are discussed in paragraphs 36 and 37.

Peacetime Location of Warsaw Pact Ground Force Divisions Opposite NATO

Figure II-7

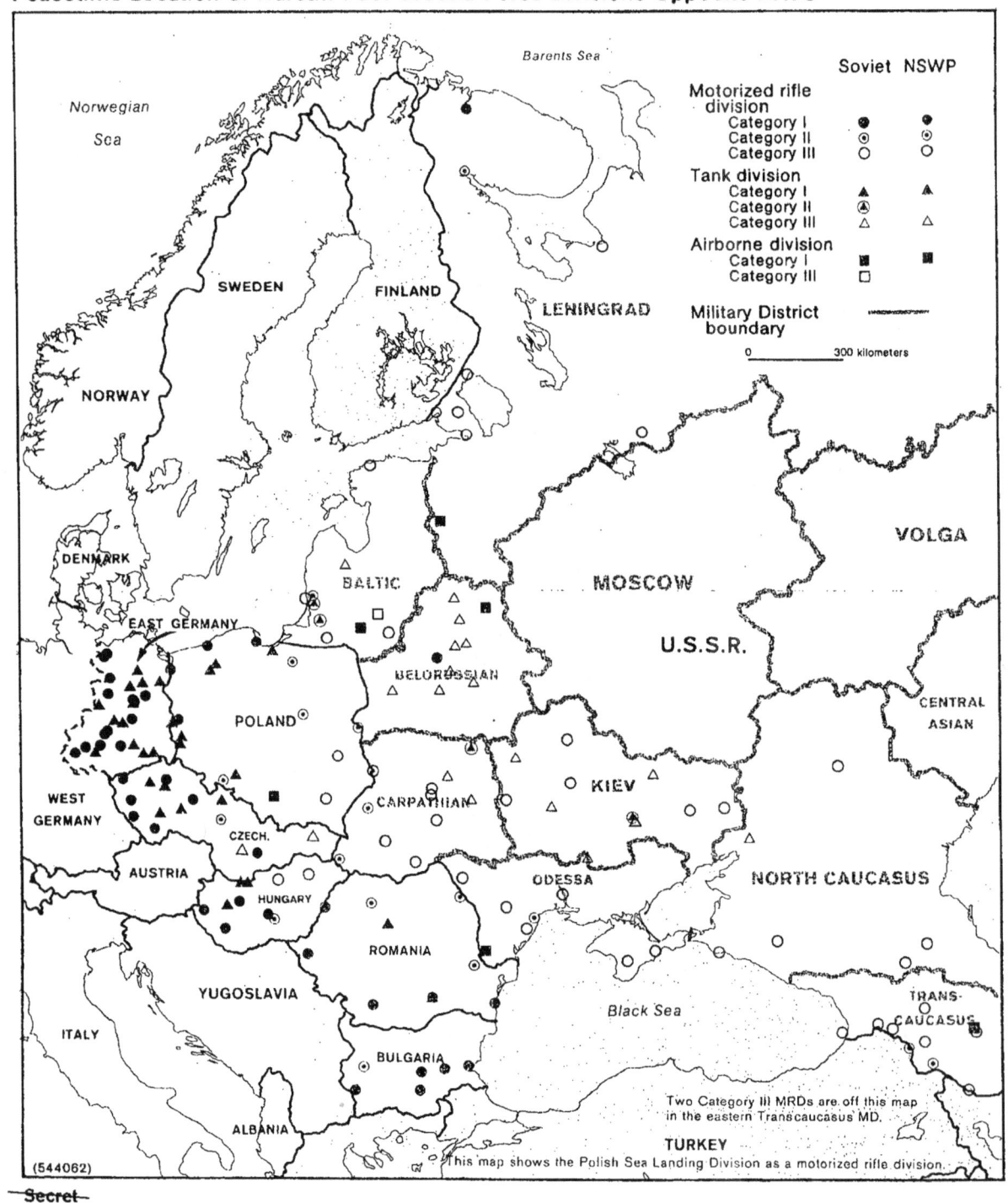

— **Category II:** These divisions also have a full complement of combat equipment, but frequently lack some support equipment. Assigned personnel strengths vary from about one-third of authorized wartime strength in some NSWP divisions to about two-thirds in Soviet divisions. These divisions could probably mobilize reserve personnel and equipment and begin movement within about 48 hours, with selected elements moving even more rapidly. Their initial combat effectiveness would be lower than that of Category I divisions.

— **Category III:** These divisions are manned at cadre strength with manpower levels ranging from about one-tenth to one-third of authorized wartime personnel. They apparently have most of their essential combat equipment, except APCs, but have less support equipment than Category II divisions. Category III divisions generally would require 72 hours or more to mobilize reserve personnel and equipment and begin movement. Their initial combat effectiveness would be lower than Category II divisions.

— **Mobilization Divisions:** In addition to the above categories of active divisions, the Soviets have a number of mobilization divisions. In peacetime these divisions consist only of small staff and cadre elements. They would be equipped during mobilization from equipment stockpiled in divisional sets and manned from pools of reservists or designated personnel. We estimate that these divisions would require several weeks of preparation before they would be ready for service, possibly in a rear area security role or as replenishments for the general reserve. The Soviets maintain a total of 15 such divisions in the USSR opposite NATO, and the NSWP countries have 10 or 11.

33. All Pact countries have well-organized mobilization systems that can rapidly fill understrength ground units with personnel and equipment from the civilian economy. These systems are built around a network of local committees which maintain lists of reservists and civilian equipment and which are intended to contact, assemble, and deliver these resources rapidly to the local military units. The system has not been tested on a broad scale, although local tests occur often.

34. The base of personnel and equipment in the Pact economies is adequate to support Pact mobilization plans. During the past five years, about 5 million Soviet and 2 million NSWP military personnel were released from active duty and constitute a ready reserve to flesh out understrength units upon mobilization. In addition, the Pact countries have earmarked a large number of civilian trucking entities for wartime use by the military. Similar arrangements exist for medical units that would be formed from civilian hospitals. An unknown number of Soviet civilian reservists employed within the Soviet Groups of Forces are also reservists earmarked for such mobilization fill. If available in large numbers they could permit the Soviets to meet their most immediate manpower requirements in a matter of hours. In an exercise in the Group of Soviet Forces in Germany (GSFG) in 1974, the time required for these reservists to report to their designated units was from four to six hours.

35. Organizations and elements at army and front level, particularly rear service units, require longer to mobilize than the combat units which they support. In addition, significant portions of the Soviet and other Pact rear services required for wartime operations do not exist in peacetime. Major elements, such as medical and transport units, would have to be mobilized from the civilian economy.

Airborne Forces

36. In addition to tank and motorized rifle units intended for theater war, the Pact also maintains large airborne forces. These forces, which have remained relatively constant in numbers over the past decade, include eight Soviet divisions (one is a training division), one Polish division, and smaller units in each of the other non-Soviet countries. Soviet airborne divisions are centrally controlled by Airborne Troops Headquarters in Moscow and are considered strategic reserves of the Supreme High Command (VGK). Soviet airborne divisions could be used in a variety of wartime situations ranging from operations under the direct control of the VGK to tactical-level missions. The Soviet divisions also have important potential uses other than war in Europe, such as intervention in Third World areas.[6]

37. Soviet airborne division command and control, ground mobility, and antitank capabilities have been improved with the introduction of new equipment, although this additional equipment has placed an added burden on the Soviets' limited airlift resources. If all the current assets of Soviet Military Transport

---

[6] See National Intelligence Estimate 11-10-79 for details of Soviet capabilities for projecting military power and influence in distant areas.

Aviation (VTA) were used simultaneously, only one fully equipped Soviet airborne division (7,300 men), or the combat assault elements of two divisions, could be lifted. NSWP airborne units have virtually no lift capabilities of their own, and depend almost entirely on Soviet VTA for this purpose.

Special Operations Units

38. The Soviets have units which they refer to as special operations brigades. These are tasked to carry out long-range reconnaissance and sabotage against such targets as nuclear weapons facilities, airfields, depots, air defense installations, and command and control facilities. Peacetime strengths of the units are believed to range from about 250 men to several times that figure. They are composed of a number of teams whose strength may vary from three to 15 men, depending on the assigned mission.

39. We have identified one of these units in East Germany and several in the western military districts of the USSR. Similar units also exist in all NSWP countries. Virtually all members of these units receive parachute training and some instruction in demolition and foreign language. Some are known to be trained as frogmen. There are reports indicating that the teams may wear civilian clothes or the uniforms of NATO member countries.

Personnel, Training, and Leadership

40. Pact armed forces depend heavily on universal conscription to meet military manpower requirements. In the USSR, conscripts make up roughly 75 percent of total active strength. Terms of service vary by nation and branch of service but generally are two or three years in length. The Soviets induct their conscripts semiannually, usually for a two-year term of service. The induction of new Soviet conscripts, the release of those whose terms of service have expired, and the assignment to units of the graduates of noncommissioned officer (NCO) and specialist training courses all occur during the semiannual induction periods in May and November. This massive turnover, at times as much as one-third of unit strength, causes considerable disruption. There is a major reduction in training and exercise activity while troop rotation is under way. Approximately 125,000 troops are rotated every six months in the Groups of Forces in Eastern Europe.

41. The Soviets have upgraded their ground force training in recent years as a result of two factors. The increasing amount of complex equipment entering the inventory usually requires a more highly trained soldier to operate or maintain it. Because the conscript's term of service is now two years, the Soviets are faced with the requirement to provide more training in less time for their largely conscript army. This has prompted the Soviets to modify their training system to include increased emphasis on preinduction training, individual specialist training, and intensified unit training.

42. The training of Soviet soldiers begins before their induction into the armed forces. Compulsory preinduction training, which is prescribed by the Soviet 1967 Law on Universal Military Service, is given either in secondary schools, in the professional and technical education system, or at places of work. It includes a 140-hour basic training course designed to familiarize youths with the armed forces and provide psychological preparation for military service. Tactical field training is conducted in summer camps and includes weapons familiarization and live firing, marches, and tactical drills. Many specialists for the armed forces also receive some training by the Voluntary Society for Assistance to the Army, Navy, and Air Force (DOSAAF), the Soviet preinduction training organization. These specialists, who have completed their compulsory preinduction training, receive additional training in such fields as aviation, scuba diving, parachuting, vehicle operation and maintenance, radio/radar operation, and electronics. A recent Soviet article stated that a third of the conscripts received specialized military-technical training in the DOSAAF.

43. After induction into the armed forces, approximately one-fourth to one-half of all conscripts are sent to training units or schools for six months of NCO or specialist training in such areas as tank gunnery and radio operation. On completion of their courses, soldiers join their units during the next troop rotation. Conscripts not assigned to training units or schools are sent directly to their unit, where they receive approximately four weeks of basic training, after which they participate in regular unit training. In addition, the Soviets are making an effort to retain skilled enlisted specialists. In 1972 the rank of warrant officer (*praporshchik*) was introduced into the ground forces and strong efforts were made to recruit enlisted men as warrant officers. The program for extended service NCOs (*sverkhsrochnik*) was dropped in 1972 when the rank of warrant officer was introduced, but was reinstated a year later in order to retain highly trained soldiers.

44. There is disagreement in the Intelligence Community regarding the success the Soviets have had in recruiting soldiers into their programs. According to one view,[7] the Soviets have had little success, at least through the extended service program, in persuading conscript soldiers to remain in the service. The holders of this view note the harsh and demanding aspects of Soviet military service and point to the numerous reports from defectors, emigres [   ] of morale and disciplinary problems within the armed forces as the basis for this judgment. They further note that there are few extended servicemen listed on the available rosters of Soviet ground force units and they do not see any decline in the number of conscripts required as a result of increased numbers of career servicemen.

45. According to an alternative view,[8] there is not sufficient evidence to support conclusions about the planned scope of the warrant officer and extended service personnel programs or Soviet success in implementing them. The holders of this view believe that, by increasing the proportion of career personnel in the Soviet ground forces, these programs have the potential for significantly raising the level of their combat readiness and capabilities. They do not believe that there is reliable evidence on Soviet requirements for conscript personnel or changes in these requirements and they do not believe that defectors and emigres are a reliable basis for judging Soviet morale and discipline. They believe that available rosters of Soviet ground force units are not a good indicator of the current status of Soviet career noncommissioned personnel programs because these programs were instituted or revitalized only in 1972 and may not yet have reached their full projected scope. They note that the conditions of service for career noncommissioned personnel are radically different from those for conscripts and are similar to those for officers with respect to pay, housing, leave, travel, shopping, and other benefits. With a combination of incentives on the one hand and pressure from the political organization on the other, the Soviets should be able to overcome any difficulties in recruiting personnel for these programs.

46. Unit training is conducted during winter and summer periods scheduled around the semiannual troop rotation. Training is rigorous and intensive. Heavy emphasis is placed on political indoctrination and rote, drill-type training. Weapons training involves heavy use of simulators and firing subcaliber ammunition. Allocations of ammunition are low and live firing is infrequent. For routine, low-level training, units use a small amount of training equipment which they have at their disposal in addition to their TO&E (table of organization and equipment) allocations. Night training is given emphasis and includes road marches, night firing, and tactical exercises. Other areas emphasized include frequent river crossing, rapid movement and maneuver, and operations in a CBR environment, including decontamination and negotiation of contaminated areas. Field training is frequent. Full-strength Soviet units carry out at least two field training exercises per year at battalion level, one or two at regimental level, and one at division level. Division-level exercises are often provided with tactical aviation support.

47. The training in NSWP forces is generally patterned after the Soviet model with semiannual troop inductions driving the training cycle. Comparable preinduction training organizations also exist in the NSWP countries. The quality of training of the northern tier NSWP forces is generally higher than that of their southern counterparts. In some respects, the quality of training of East German and Czechoslovak forces surpasses that of the Soviets. Combined exercises with the Soviets occurs frequently in the northern NSWP countries, occasionally in Hungary, but rarely in Bulgaria and Romania.

48. The Soviet officer and his East European counterpart are selected and promoted on the basis of professional qualifications and political loyalty. Pact officers are well educated in military and civil institutions; we judge them to be technically and militarily competent as a group. Officers generally serve longer tours of duty in one job than their Western counterparts, allowing them to acquire thorough knowledge of their jobs. The Soviets are attempting to provide quick advancement and increased responsibility for outstanding officers.

49. There appear to be some problems with lower level leadership in the Soviet ground forces. The Soviet military press is replete with criticism of junior officers who do not exert sufficient initiative in training and exercises to provide varied, realistic, and challenging training. In addition, most noncommissioned officers are conscripts only 18 to 20 years old. However, these problems in lower level leadership should be

---

[7] *The holders of this view are the Central Intelligence Agency; the Director, Bureau of Intelligence and Research, Department of State; and the Director, National Security Agency.*

[8] *The holders of this view are the Defense Intelligence Agency; the Assistant Chief of Staff for Intelligence, Department of the Army; and the Assistant Chief of Staff, Intelligence, Department of the Air Force.*

interpreted in light of the way the Soviet command system is supposed to work. Little detailed planning, coordination, or initiative is expected of squad, platoon, company, and battalion commanders. These commanders are expected to be closely supervised executors of detailed plans drawn up at regimental and higher levels. This system could discourage independent small-unit actions, but would probably cause Soviet forces to be rapidly responsive to the commands of regiment and division commanders.

50. The Soviet soldier is well drilled in his job. Units generally can carry out the basic maneuvers envisioned in tactical doctrine. Major weaknesses include the prevalence of rote, unrealistic, drill-type training at lower levels. The heavy use of simulators, subcaliber devices, and training equipment adds to this lack of realism. Army- and front-level staffs train primarily by command post exercises, often with extensive signal support and limited troop participation. While these exercises often involve realistic scenarios, staffs rarely have the opportunity actually to control and coordinate large numbers of troops in the field.

51. The Warsaw Pact military structure is predicated on a harsh and demanding disciplinary system which exacts unquestioning obedience and adherence to regulations. In practice, however, it is evident that Pact forces suffer from the same breaches of discipline that are found in other armies. These include alcoholism, desertion and AWOL, misappropriation of military equipment, and black-market activities. Statistics pertaining to these breaches of discipline are impossible to obtain, but Soviet military authorities appear to be concerned about them, and we receive reports of their occurrence, particularly in the Soviet armed forces, often enough to indicate that the problem is persistent.

52. Morale problems are also prevalent. Certain problems, such as alcoholism and ethnic hostility, are common to Soviet and East European societies in general. Others, such as desertion and suicide, probably are a reflection of the harshness of military life. The soldier receives extremely low pay, his housing and food are barely adequate, he is subject to constant abuse or harassment by NCOs and officers, and his training is repetitive and boring. In addition, he is often a victim of prejudice and hostility if he is a member of a minority group. Soviet troops are usually isolated from the civilian populace, as is the particular case of the Soviet soldier in Eastern Europe.

53. These morale and disciplinary problems probably do not impair overall combat or unit effectiveness for several reasons: many problems are endemic to a peacetime military force and probably would disappear in time of war; the Soviet system and authorities have pervasive control over the soldier's activities and time; and a basic feeling of respect for authority and patriotism, continually exploited by authorities, provides an underlying motivation to the Soviet soldier for honorable service and obedience.

Ready Reserves

54. According to the Soviet Law on Universal Military Service, Soviet soldiers have a reserve obligation after discharge from active duty. Enlisted men must remain in the reserves until age 50, with refresher training scheduled according to the age of the reservist. Officers under 35 years old are subject to annual recall for periods as long as three months, until a maximum of 30 months of reserve training has been completed. Reserve officers under 30 years of age may be recalled to active duty for two to three years during peacetime, but this is rarely done. NSWP countries have similar laws but they vary in some details.

55. Training for Pact reservists is uneven. Although many reservists would probably fill mobilization positions that require little military expertise or require skills similar to those of their civilian occupations, most apparently do not receive periodic refresher training. By contrast, a small group of reservists who are to be mobilized for the operation or maintenance of complex equipment are called up frequently for training. Reserve training would not be a significant factor in the combat effectiveness of those divisions in which most key positions are already filled by active-duty personnel. In cadre divisions, however, where reservists must assume a large portion of the responsibility, training deficiencies would reduce unit effectiveness. The initial effectiveness of recalled reservists, in any case, would depend upon the length of time since release from active duty. In most cases, priority of recall would be directed toward those most recently released, thereby reducing refresher training burdens and minimizing reservist handicaps stemming from a lack of updated training.

B. Warsaw Pact Air Forces

56. The Soviet Air Forces are divided into three functional components: Long Range Aviation (LRA), Frontal (tactical) Aviation, and Military Transport Aviation (VTA).[9] The primary missions of LRA are

---

[9] Details of the role and capabilities of LRA in theater war are discussed in section D of this chapter (beginning at paragraph 153) and in chapters IV and V. Soviet Naval Aviation is treated in section C of this chapter (beginning of paragraph 100) and in chapter IV. Soviet strategic air defense forces are discussed in NIE 11-3/8-78.

intercontinental nuclear strikes and conventional or nuclear strikes in support of theater forces. Frontal Aviation missions include counterair, ground attack, reconnaissance, electronic warfare (EW), and helicopter ground attack and troop lift. The primary mission of VTA is the transport of airborne assault forces.

57. All NSWP countries have air forces for national air defense. In addition, Poland, Czechoslovakia, and Bulgaria have tactical air forces. East Germany has one ground attack unit and Romania has two. None of the NSWP air forces have sufficient transport aircraft to support other than small-scale airlift operations. The current personnel strength of the Soviet air forces opposite NATO is estimated to be about 500,000 and that of the NSWP air forces stands at about 200,000. Figure II-8 shows the geographic disposition of Pact air forces opposite NATO.

Tactical Air Forces

58. **Fixed-Wing Aircraft.** There are about 4,600 fixed-wing combat aircraft in Soviet Frontal Aviation and another 1,175 in NSWP tactical air units. Although there was sizable growth in Soviet Frontal Aviation during the late 1960s, primarily because of the buildup against China, the size of Pact tactical air forces opposite NATO has been relatively stable at approximately 4,200 fixed-wing combat aircraft. We have evidence that the Soviets have resubordinated at least several strategic air defense regiments to Frontal Aviation. The full extent of these changes is unclear, however, and their impact on the structure and size of Soviet Frontal Aviation has not yet been determined. Accordingly, these resubordinated aircraft are not reflected in our tabulations of the strength of Frontal Aviation shown in this Estimate. (See table II-4.)

59. These forces are divided into air armies or tactical air elements. Soviet Frontal Aviation is organized into 16 air armies, most of which are located along the periphery of the USSR in areas adjoining potential combat areas or in Eastern Europe. Non-Soviet Warsaw Pact tactical air forces include air armies in Czechoslovakia and Poland, an air corps in Bulgaria, and some independent fighter-bomber and reconnaissance units in East Germany and Romania. The size and composition of the air armies vary greatly depending on location and assigned missions. The Soviet 16th Tactical Air Army in East Germany is the largest and best equipped. In wartime, combat operations by individual air armies would usually be controlled by the various Pact front commanders. However, the Pact has plans for the use of tactical air forces in operations that would be temporarily controlled by a command at a higher level than the front, such as at the theater or Moscow level.

Table II-4

Warsaw Pact Fixed-Wing Tactical Aircraft Opposite NATO [a] January 1979

	In Eastern Europe Soviet	NSWP	In the USSR	Total [b]
Fighter	765	295	675	1,735
Fighter-Bomber	450	630	650	1,730
Light Bomber	30	—	30	60
Reconnaissance/EW	175	245	245	665
Total	1,420	1,170	1,600	4,190

[a] See footnote to table II-1, following paragraph 3. Also see table B-2 in annex B for a more detailed order of battle of Pact tactical aircraft.
[b] These totals do not include about 1,210 fighters assigned to the NSWP national air defense commands or trainers and combat reserve aircraft.

60. The basic combat unit of Pact tactical air forces is the regiment (or wing in the East German Air Force), each of which is assigned a primary mission. There are essentially four types of regiments: fighter regiments, which would be used primarily in air-to-air combat; fighter-bomber and light bomber regiments, which would be used to attack ground targets; and reconnaissance regiments, which would provide photographic and electronic reconnaissance. Each regiment normally consists of three flight squadrons, and headquarters, flightline maintenance, and general maintenance elements. Fighter and fighter-bomber squadrons generally have 12 aircraft; and light bomber squadrons, 10 aircraft. Most fighter and fighter-bomber regiments also have six to 10 additional combat aircraft for maintenance float, four to six combat-capable trainers, and three to four non-combat-capable trainers for training and administrative purposes. A typical regiment may number about 500 personnel, including some 60 pilots in flight status. Supporting each regiment are an independent base maintenance battalion and a signals battalion manned with as many as 700 additional personnel.

61. Those Warsaw Pact air forces in Central Europe for which we have good evidence are manned at varying levels below their intended wartime personnel strengths. Evidence relating to two of the five Soviet air divisions in East Germany, for example, indicates that they are manned at 80 percent of their planned

Figure II-8. Peacetime Location of Warsaw Pact Air Forces Opposite NATO

wartime strength. In light of this evidence we estimate the other Soviet air divisions in Central Europe are similarly manned. We have good evidence on personnel strengths for only one NSWP air force. This evidence indicates that the total force is manned at 60 percent of wartime strength and combat air units at 70 percent. We estimate that the other NSWP air forces are also manned below their intended wartime strengths. We have no good evidence, however, on the extent of this undermanning. Pact air units could initiate combat operations utilizing existing peacetime strengths; however, mobilization of additional personnel would be required before the Pact could conduct a sustained large-scale air offensive.

62. *Helicopter Forces.* Warsaw Pact helicopter forces have two primary missions: combat and combat support. Combat helicopters include those assigned to units responsible for attacking ground targets or transporting assault troops. Opposite NATO the Pact has assigned some 1,700 combat helicopters to this mission. (See table II-5.) Of these, about 300 helicopters have as their primary mission the attack of ground targets; and the remaining 1,400 helicopters have a primary mission of transporting assault forces. An additional 900 helicopters are assigned to Pact units opposite NATO for various combat support roles including rescue, communications, relay, airborne command posts, artillery spotting, electronic warfare, and liaison. A significant development in recent years has been the introduction of heavily armed helicopters. Figure II-9 shows the increase in the number of Pact helicopters opposite NATO since the early 1970s.

63. Soviet combat helicopters (ground attack and assault transport) are organized into regiments which

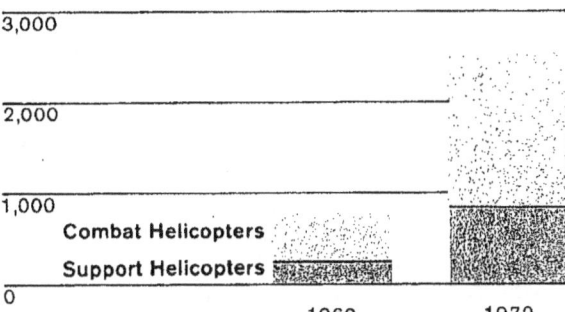

Figure II-9

Increase in Warsaw Pact Helicopters Opposite NATO, 1969 and 1979

vary in size from 50 to more than 100 helicopters. NSWP helicopter regiments generally are smaller than Soviet regiments. If used to transport troops, each Soviet ground attack helicopter regiment probably could lift simultaneously one or two reinforced motorized rifle battalions without their vehicles. Soviet assault transport regiments using only MI-8 Hip helicopters could conduct the simultaneous lift of two to three reinforced motorized rifle battalions without their vehicles. Using both Hip and MI-6 Hook helicopters, these assault transport regiments could lift a force of the same size along with heavier equipment and light armored vehicles. The largest ground force unit transported by helicopters would probably be of regimental size.

64. *Base Structure.* The Warsaw Pact has an extensive airfield network from which to launch and sustain military air operations. In the USSR west of the Urals there are some 230 active military airfields; the Soviets also operate 40 military airfields in the NSWP countries. Eighty-four airfields operated by the NSWP air forces complement the Soviet base structure. There are hundreds of other airfields—civil, factory flyaway, and unoccupied (including dispersal) fields, highway strips, and fields with temporary surfaces—which could be used by military aircraft.

65. Since 1970, the Pact nations have completed construction of at least 11 new military airfields, started construction of at least nine others, and signifi-

Table II-5

Warsaw Pact Helicopters Opposite NATO *
January 1979

Primary Mission	In Eastern Europe Soviet	NSWP	In the USSR	Total
Combat Helicopters				
Ground Attack	175	25	110	310
Assault Transport	275	555	555	1,385
Total Combat	450	580	665	1,695
Support Helicopters	370	125	425	920
Grand Total	820	705	1,090	2,615

* See footnote to table II-1, following paragraph 3. See table B-3 in annex B for a detailed order of battle of Pact helicopter forces opposite NATO.

cantly improved the runway capability at 62 military airfields in the NSWP countries and the USSR west of the Urals. All major military and most civil airfields in the Pact countries have been, or are being, equipped with modern lighting, improved navigational aid equipment, more adequate and improved refueling systems, and other ancillary support facilities. Installations for the storage, testing, and handling of air-to-air (AAM) and air-to-surface (ASM) guided missiles have been identified at most military airfields which have aircraft equipped with these weapons. Approximately 3,400 shelters (hangarettes) have been built since the late 1960s to protect aircraft at main operating bases in the USSR west of the Urals and in the NSWP countries. Other defensive improvements include hardening and increasing POL and ammunition storage facilities, hardening command and control facilities, and establishing pipeline systems to service aircraft in shelters.

66. This airfield development program has achieved four specific objectives. First, the Soviets have expanded their pilot and navigator training capability by building new training airfields and improving existing ones. Second, they have improved their airfield capability within the Soviet Union to support their new, longer range, higher performance ground attack fighter aircraft and the Backfire bomber. Third, all Pact nations have increased the survivability and sustainability of their combat air forces. Fourth, they have increased their capability to conceal and protect large numbers of aircraft in bunkers. The overall net effect of the Pact military airfield development since 1968 is a greater capability to conduct both offensive and defensive air operations.

67. Recent developments tend to indicate that the Warsaw Pact and particularly Soviet Frontal Aviation plan to conduct most wartime operations from main airfields where aircraft can be protected in hardened aircraft shelters. For more than 85 percent of the Soviet tactical aircraft in the NSWP countries, there now are facilities adequate to accommodate one armed, combat-ready aircraft per shelter. The sharing of shelters would provide protection for many more aircraft, although readiness would suffer because of engine starting restrictions and ground handling problems. About half of the 1,200 or so shelters on Soviet main bases could be used to shelter more than one aircraft; this would provide protection for over 600 additional reinforcement aircraft. Still more aircraft could be given some protection by on-base dispersal and use of revetments.

68. Dispersal airfields with natural surfaces continue to be maintained in an operational condition in the forward areas. Teams of personnel to operate these airfields appear to be available at the main operating bases. There is uncertainty, however, about the availability of sufficient ground support equipment to sustain operations from these bases concurrently with main base operations. Some storage facilities, with sufficient POL and ammunition for a limited number of sorties, are located near the natural-surface airfields. These cannot be used, however, by some of the more modern aircraft. On balance, supply stocks in depots, pipeline, and transport organizations appear adequate to support reinforcement aircraft from the western USSR or other intratheater redeployments.

69. *Pilot Training and Proficiency.* By US standards the Soviet Frontal Aviation flight training program is more conducive to perfecting a pilot's basic flying skills than to preparing him for combat. A typical Soviet pilot spends four years in a flying school and an additional three to four years training in an operational combat unit before he is considered qualified, by Soviet standards, to carry out the full range of combat missions assigned to his unit. In conducting operational training, a Soviet tactical pilot flies approximately the same number of sorties per year as his US counterpart, but the sorties are less than half as long in duration and involve far fewer combat-related training events.

70. In recent years, activity specifically identified as combat-related training has amounted to approximately 25 percent of the total number of flights by Frontal Aviation pilots in East Germany. The purpose of some other flight activity, which in the United States is termed "mission in zone" training, is the subject of some disagreement within the Intelligence Community. According to one view,[10] this activity is largely aerobatic and not combat related. At least 80 percent involves a single aircraft that does not practice engaging aerial or ground targets. An alternative view [11] holds that because little is known about the specifics of this activity, and because more than one aircraft are known to have engaged in this activity simultaneously in the same general area, some additional combat training may be involved.

71. Despite increases in the number of pilots assigned to Soviet units in the forward area, the overall

---

[10] *The holder of this view is the Central Intelligence Agency.*
[11] *The holders of this view are the Director, Defense Intelligence Agency; the Director, National Security Agency; and the Assistant Chief of Staff, Intelligence, Department of the Air Force.*

combat capability of these units continues to be hampered by those pilots—25 to 35 percent of the total available—who are not qualified to conduct night or all-weather combat missions. Moreover, pilot proficiency has not progressed sufficiently to exploit fully the capabilities of the airframes and weapon systems of the third-generation aircraft currently in operation. The Soviets acknowledge that their combat pilots are not trained as effectively as they should be, but for reasons that are not clear to us they do not appear to be taking major corrective measures to enhance the quality of training significantly. Such steps would include devoting a greater share of training time to the performance of combat-related tasks and introducing more realism by exposing these pilots to enemy tactics and simulated hostile air defense environments.

72. *Combat Capabilities.* One of the most significant developments in Warsaw Pact tactical air forces in recent years has been their modernization through the introduction of new aircraft. The new aircraft have greater ranges, can carry greater payloads, are equipped with better, more advanced avionics, and are armed with better, more effective munitions. These attributes combine to give the Pact's air forces the capacity to deliver more effective firepower under a greater variety of conditions. Another significant development in recent years has been the development of heavily armed helicopters.

73. The Pact began reequipping its air forces in the late 1960s with fighter units receiving initial priority. Late-model MIG-21 Fishbed and MIG-23 Flogger B aircraft were introduced to replace earlier model Fishbeds in these units. Modernization of the fighter-bomber forces began four to five years later with SU-17 Fitter C/D, MIG-27 Flogger D, and some late-model Fishbeds replacing the MIG-17 Fresco and SU-7 Fitter A. Light-bomber units also began reequipping in the mid-1970s by acquiring the SU-24 Fencer A as a replacement for the YAK-28 Brewer B/C. Modernization has progressed more rapidly in Soviet than in the NSWP air forces. Newer aircraft now account for about 80 percent of the Soviet force, 20 percent of the NSWP force, and two-thirds of total Pact tactical air force opposite NATO. (See figure II-10.)

74. In 1969 some 30 percent of the Pact's tactical fighters were unable to conduct aerial engagements under adverse weather conditions; all attacks had to be performed from the real hemisphere, and the fighters had virtually no capability to intercept low-flying aircraft. (See figure II-11.) Today, nearly 95 percent of Pact fighters are able to operate in adverse weather,

and 40 percent of the force is equipped with the Flogger B, which has an all-aspect intercept and limited lookdown/shootdown capability. In 1969 all Pact fighter-bombers relied on ground-based navigation aids or dead reckoning to navigate over NATO territory, forcing them to operate at vulnerable medium altitudes. Beagle and Brewer light bombers provided the Pact's only autonomous adverse weather bombing/navigation capability. Today there are about 45 percent fewer aircraft (Brewers and Fencers) pos-

Modernization Trends in Warsaw Pact Tactical Air Forces Opposite NATO, 1969–1979

Figure II-10

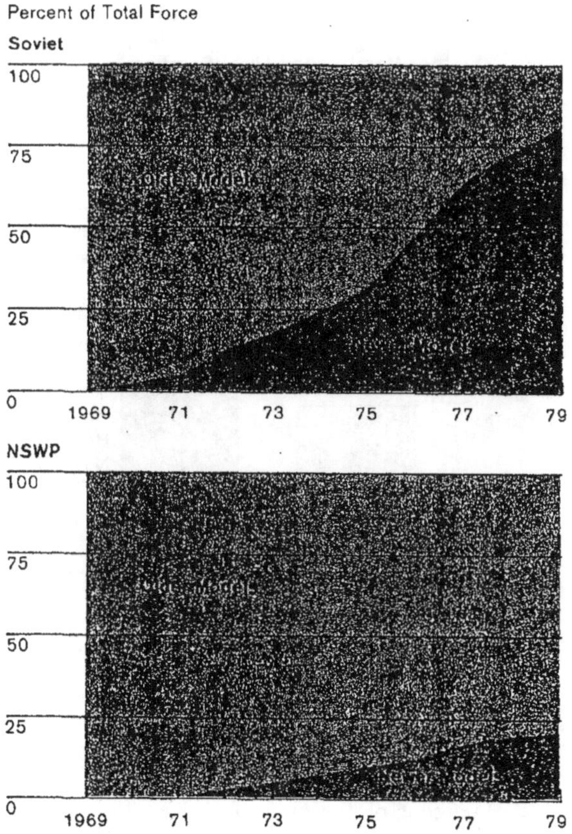

Avionics Trends in Warsaw Pact Tactical Aircraft Opposite NATO, 1969 and 1979

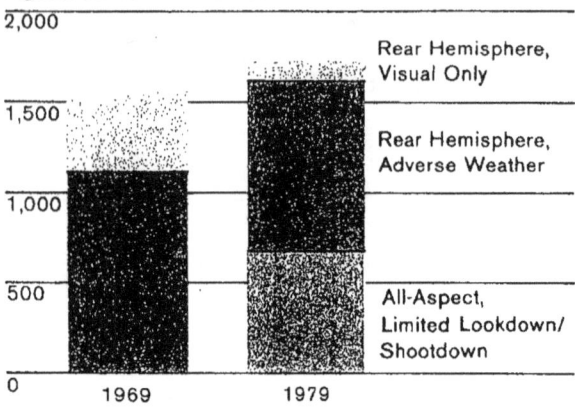

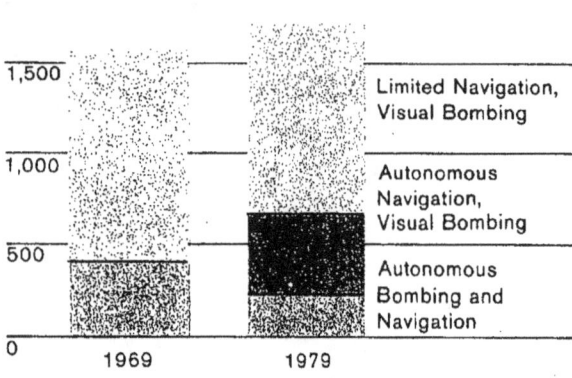

Figure II-11

sessing this capability. The fewer numbers, however, have been more than offset by an increase in the number of fighter-bomber units. Now also, some 30 percent of the aircraft in Pact fighter-bomber units can navigate accurately at lower altitudes in adverse weather using only onboard avionics, although they still have to acquire their targets visually for precise weapons delivery.

75. In 1969 the Pact, with its short-range, low-payload aircraft, had only a few tactical aircraft capable of conducting combat operations past the Rhine. Today, large numbers of Pact tactical aircraft can operate well into France and the Benelux countries, illustrating the progress made by the Pact over the past decade in the combat capabilities of its tactical air forces. Figure II-12 depicts the payload and operations radius of selected Pact tactical aircraft.

76. Although recent improvements have significantly enhanced the capability of the Pact's tactical air forces to conduct long-range offensive operations, the basic role of these forces remains unchanged. The Pact's tactical air forces continue to have two primary missions—air defense and ground attack support of the Pact's ground armies. The continuing emphasis on air defense is indicated by the high priority in equipment modernization accorded fighter units.

77. *Air-to-Air Combat.* The primary mission of the Warsaw Pact's tactical fighter forces is to engage NATO's aircraft, preferably over NATO territory. All Soviet Frontal Aviation fighter units are equipped with all-weather MIG-21 or MIG-23 aircraft. (See figure II-13.) About two-thirds of the fighters in the NSWP tactical air forces are all-weather models. The majority of the MIG-21s are the latest variants, which, compared with earlier MIG-21s, have a greater fuel and payload capability, an integral gun, and improved electronic equipment. MIG-23s now are in the inventories of all Soviet Groups of Forces opposite NATO and in the western USSR. These aircraft are equipped with new air-to-air missiles. They have a 360-degree attack capability, but at low altitudes this capability is likely to be restricted to engagements from the rear. They have a limited capability to engage targets flying below them at target altitudes of 500 meters over land or 300 meters over water, although in such engagements only a small altitude separation is possible.

78. Other Warsaw Pact all-weather fighters are limited by their radar equipment and armaments to attacks from the rear against most aircraft targets. Against slow-moving targets like helicopters flying at about 500 meters, they would be capable of head-on attacks. Most Warsaw Pact fighters would experience considerable difficulty against low-flying targets because of limitations both in their radar equipment and in air battle management capabilities. At low altitude, gun-armed fighters could engage a visually acquired target. Fighters using semiactive radar homing, beam-riding, or infrared missiles would generally require favorable conditions for completing successful missile attacks against low-flying aircraft. Some air-to-air missiles are infrared homing versions which would be

Radius and Payload Capabilities of Selected Pact Tactical Aircraft*

Figure II-12

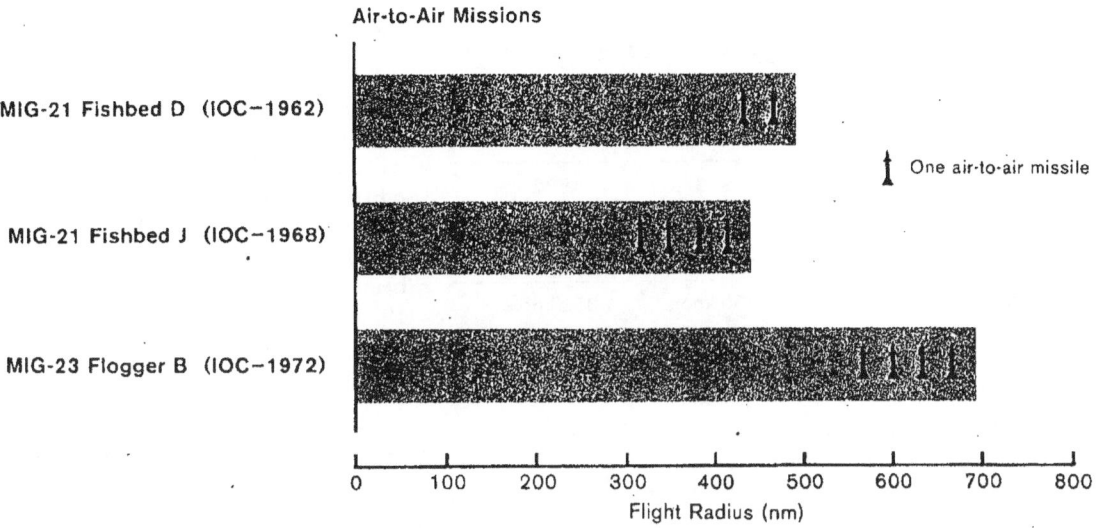

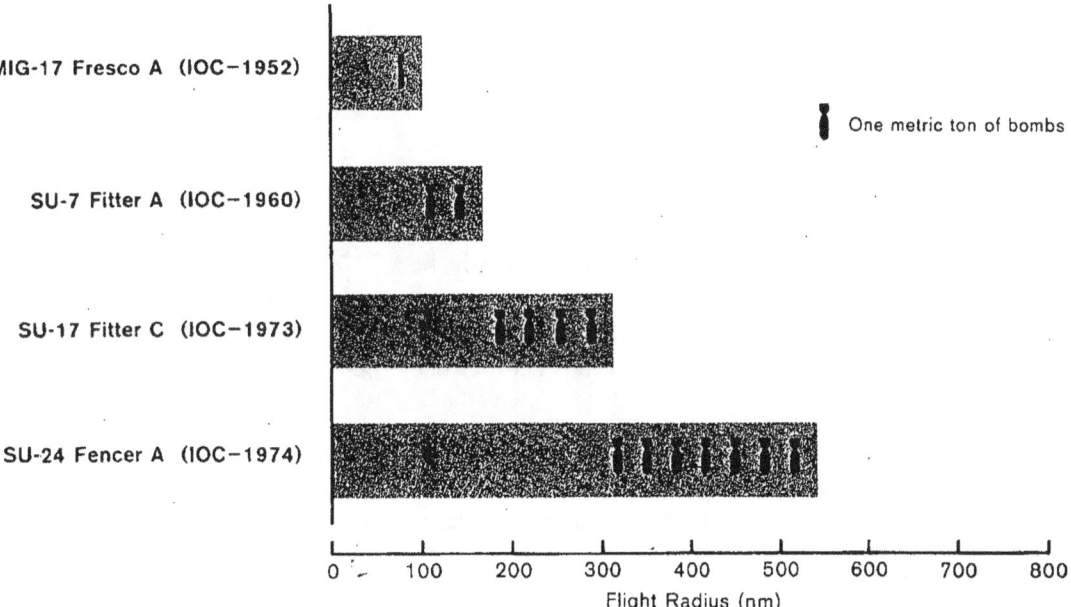

*Flight radii shown for air-to-air missions were calculated using maximum missile loads and external fuel tanks. Flight radii shown for ground attack missions were calculated using maximum bomb loads which do not permit use of external fuel tanks.

Selected Warsaw Pact Fighter Aircraft

Figure II-13

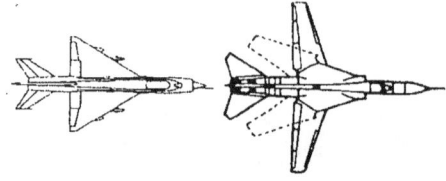

	MIG-21 Fishbed J	MIG-23 Flogger B
Year operational	1968	1972
Length (m)	16	18
Maximum speed	1,260 knots Mach 2.2	1,350 knots Mach 2.35
Combat radius (nm):		
Subsonic area intercept with 4 air-to-air missiles and 1 external fuel tank	385	610
Supersonic area intercept with 4 air-to-air missiles and 1 external fuel tank	195	415

relatively ineffective in clouds. The latest fighter variants carry semiactive radar homing missiles which alleviate this problem.

79. Pact fighter units have a secondary mission of attacking ground targets but have recently cut back on the amount of time their pilots devote to ground attack training. Flight activity in Soviet fighter units over the past two years has shown a 50-percent decrease in ground attack training, which previously amounted to 15 percent of total combat training. Training no longer allocated to this secondary mission is devoted instead to air-intercept missions.

80. **Conventional Ground Attack.**[12] Frontal Aviation has the mission of conducting ground attack operations against supply lines and rear area installations which support these forces. Soviet doctrine and capability favor preplanned attacks to destroy, neutralize, or delay NATO's forces before they can be brought to bear against Warsaw Pact forces. These attacks are generally planned at such distances from Warsaw Pact ground forces that close coordination of each strike mission with the fire and movement of friendly forces is not required.

81. The Warsaw Pact has established a joint ground-air control system which is designed to provide the coordination necessary to conduct close-in missions when required. It consists of a series of joint air control parties which are attached to the various ground force echelons, radar-equipped control teams, and ground-based forward air controllers. This system, which has been observed in training exercises since the early 1970s, may also be used to coordinate aircraft and ground-based air defenses, although how it would function in such an operation is not fully understood.

82. The introduction of new ground attack aircraft has improved the Pact's capabilities in several respects. For example, the newer fighter-bombers—the Fencer, Flogger, and Fitter C/D—can carry at least twice the bomb payload of the older Fitter A and can deliver this payload with approximately three to four times greater accuracy. (See figure II-14.) The net effect of the greater payload and delivery accuracy is that the Pact's newer ground attack aircraft are significantly more effective than the earlier aircraft in ground attack missions.

83. The Pact's new aircraft can also be used under a greater variety of conditions. The new fighter-bombers, for example, are more capable of striking ground targets in conditions of poor visibility. This capability is provided by an integrated weapons delivery and navigation system which allows the aircraft to arrive over large target areas such as airbases. However, the pilot must still visually acquire individual small targets to ensure accurate weapons delivery. Tactically, such a capability would be most useful in conventional bombing against targets occupying large areas or in delivering nuclear weapons. The SU-24 Fencer has a newer bomb navigation radar which should give it the capability to deliver weapons with an error of 150 meters in low visibility conditions against well-defined targets. This is substantially better than the blind bombing capability of Fitter C/D and Flogger D aircraft.

84. Warsaw Pact aircrews rely largely on some form of control or direction from their ground-based command posts for all offensive support operations. This control often involves the use of airborne relay communications. Ground-based radar equipment with

---

[12] The nuclear strike capabilities of Pact tactical air forces are discussed in paragraphs 157 and 158 of this chapter.

Top Secret

Selected Warsaw Pact Fighter-Bomber Aircraft

Figure II-14

	Year operational	Maximum speed (knots)	Representative fuel/weapons/payloads			NATO* mission profile (radius in nm)		
			Fuel (kg)	Fuel tanks	Bomb, rocket or TASM loads	Hi-Lo-Hi	Lo-Lo-Hi	Lo-Lo-Lo
SU-17 Fitter D	1976	1,205 Mach 2.1	3,730	0	8x500-kg bombs	300	175	135
			3,730	0	20x100-kg bombs	330	180	135
			5,060	2	6x500-kg bombs	530	290	210
			5,060	2	ECM pod and 96x57-mm rockets	595	320	225
			5,060	2	4xAS-10 TASMs	580	300	215
MIG-27 Flogger D	1975	975 Mach 1.7	4,365	0	4x500-kg bombs	380	225	170
			6,360	3	4x500-kg bombs	620	350	250
SU-24 Fencer A	1974	1,435 Mach 2.5	9,080	0	7x1,000-kg bombs	540	285	205
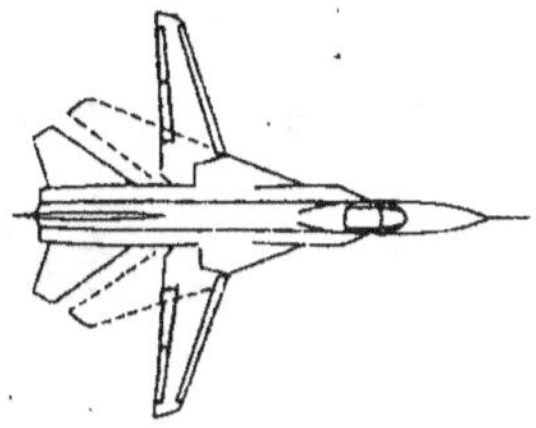			14,925	2	10x250-kg bombs	980	515	340
			9,980	0	4xAS-10 TASMs	685	325	225
			14,925	2	4xAS-10 TASMs	1,075	530	400
			13,290	2	2xAS-9 TASMs	935	460	315

*The Central Intelligence Agency believes that the operational assumptions basic to the NATO Mission Profile Hi-Lo-Hi definition are extremely optimistic and produce combat radius estimates which cannot be achieved under wartime conditions. CIA believes that the combat radii associated with the Lo-Lo-Hi definitions are much more in line with Warsaw Pact estimates of the combat radius capability of Pact aircraft and are in fact a more realistic reflection of Pact intentions concerning the use of these aircraft.

Secret

major ground formations is used by tactical controllers for radar vectoring of attack aircraft toward the target area, after which pilots are responsible for navigation to specific targets and their visual identification. Along the frontline, tactical controllers can hand over control to ground-based forward air controllers, who would then provide target-recognition guidance and, if necessary, target marking.

85. *Reconnaissance.* In the Soviet view, the most important function of tactical reconnaissance is to detect enemy nuclear delivery means to enable accurate and timely execution of combat operations against them. Large numbers of reconnaissance aircraft are considered necessary to give proper support to offensive operations. To provide this support, air reconnaissance is conducted both as an integral part of other basic air tasks and as a specified mission by special fighter-reconnaissance and bomber-reconnaissance units. The Soviets believe that a variety of ground and airborne sensors, together with visual observation, must be used to provide a multiple-source data base. Improved sensors, including side-looking airborne radar (SLAR) and real-time television data link systems, have been installed in some reconnaissance aircraft.

86. Aerial reconnaissance capabilities range from those provided by visual observation to the supersonic, high-altitude MIG-25 Foxbat B/D. Reconnaissance missions are a constant feature of Warsaw Pact exercises; every Warsaw Pact aircrew has the responsibility to report visual sightings. Specialized intelligence collection aircraft are configured for photographic, active radar, communications, and electronic intelligence-gathering missions. Mobile photo-processing units are available at most Soviet reconnaissance units in Eastern Europe. Although the total number of aircraft with the primary mission of reconnaissance is known, our knowledge of their actual reconnaissance capabilities, especially their timeliness and quality, is poor. The lack of automated equipment or other means for timely and accurate location and reporting of mobile or semimobile targets, is believed to be a current weakness.

87. Most Soviet reconnaissance units have secondary missions and additional combat responsibilities. For example, MIG-21 Fishbed H units normally devote part of their training to ground attack, and one such unit may also be tasked with air defense. Some MIG-25 Foxbat B/D aircraft are known to have practiced supersonic, high-altitude runs which could be interpreted as simulating weapons delivery, but as yet this aircraft is not known to carry either nuclear or conventional weapons or to have an operational weapons delivery role.

88. *Helicopters.* In recent years the Soviets have introduced the MI-24 Hind, the first of their helicopters designed primarily for ordnance delivery. (See figure II-15.) It offers such advantages over earlier helicopters as improved all-weather capabilities and versatility. The Hind also has an air-to-air capability against other helicopters and low, slow-flying fixed-wing aircraft. A variant of the MI-8, the Hip E, has been equipped with rocket pods, machineguns, and antitank guided missiles.

89. *Air Munitions.* The Soviets are pursuing a vigorous program to increase the effectiveness of their air munitions to exploit the enhanced capabilities of their newer aircraft. They apparently believe that the increased maintenance and training requirements generated by new, advanced air munitions are justified to correct the deficiencies of the older, simpler munitions. The net effect of these air munition improvement programs should be to reduce the number of aircraft required for effective target destruction. The improved guidance systems and delivery techniques also should increase the survivability of Pact aircraft in an air conflict.

Warsaw Pact Ground Attack Helicopters — Figure II-15

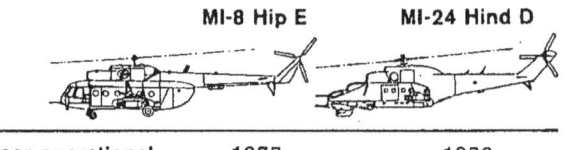

	MI-8 Hip E	MI-24 Hind D
Year operational	1977	1976
Length (m)	18.2	17.3
Maximum useful load (kilograms, fuel and payload)*	4,500	5,300
Maximum combat radius* (nm)	95	120

*Maximum useful load and combat radius calculated with a maximum payload at maximum gross weight using a rolling takeoff.

90. A new medium-range air-to-air missile, the AA-7 Apex, evidently is being fielded in both infrared seeking and semiactive versions. (See figure II-16.) The missile probably has a limited shootdown capability to match the limited lookdown, search-and-track features of the airborne intercept radar on the Flogger B. In addition, a new short-range, infrared-seeking air-to-air missile, the AA-8 Aphid, is in service. This missile is smaller than earlier missiles, probably is more maneuverable, and is estimated to have a launch range of 0.25 to 5 nautical miles (about 450 to 9,000 meters). The Soviets also have fielded the AA-2d (Atoll D), an infrared homing air-to-air missile which may have an improved infrared seeker, improved motors, and possibly better maneuverability. Both the AA-8 and AA-2d can be used on the Fishbed and Flogger.

91. All Pact ground attack aircraft can carry a wide range of ground attack weapons, including pods of 57-mm rockets, large unguided rockets, conventional bombs of up to 500 kilograms, and cluster weapons. In addition, many carry guns and cannons. Three different tactical air-to-surface missiles (TASMs) have also been developed in recent years. One of these, the AS-7 Kerry, was developed some years ago as a short-range, beam-riding missile for use on earlier model MIG-21s. We have evidence, however, that the Fitter C and Flogger D are also capable of using a command-guided variant of the Kerry missile. The other two TASMs, the AS-9 and AS-10, are completely new missiles. The AS-9 is an antiradiation missile with an estimated maximum range of 60 nm (10 km). The AS-10 is a semiactive laser-guided missile with a maximum range of approximately 6 nm (11 km).

92. The Soviets have made some advances in streamlining their bomb shapes, and in developing retardation devices which allow ordnance to be delivered in high-speed, low-level flight. A runway-cratering bomb was issued in 1974 and is probably able to penetrate about half a meter of reinforced concrete in low-altitude delivery. The standard Soviet 250-kg fragmentation bomb has been modified with a telescoping fuse to increase shrapnel effect. The Soviets

Selected Warsaw Pact Air-to-Air and Air-to-Surface Missiles for Tactical Aircraft

Figure II-16

	Year operational	Guidance	Range (nm)	Carrier aircraft
Atoll AAM				
AA-2b	1960	Infrared	3–4	Fishbed, Flogger B/C/E
AA-2c	1970	Semiactive radar	3–4	Fishbed J/K/L/N, Flogger E
AA-2d	1973	Infrared	4–6	Fishbed L/N, Flogger B
Apex AAM				
AA-7a	1974	Semiactive radar	10	Flogger B
AA-7b	1974	Infrared	10	Flogger B
Aphid AAM				
AA-8	1975	Infrared	2–3	Fishbed L/N, Flogger B
AS-7 Kerry TASM	1971	Command or beam rider	6	Fishbed F, Fitter C/D, Flogger B/D, Fencer A
AS-9 TASM	1975	Antiradiation homing	27–30	Fitter C/D, Fencer A
AS-10 TASM	1976	Semiactive laser	6–8	Fitter C/D, Flogger D, Fencer A

may also have recently introduced an improved series of cluster bombs and are believed to be developing precision guided bombs.

Military Transport Aviation

93. The primary mission of VTA is to lift Soviet airborne forces but other missions include the movement of troops, equipment, supplies, and nuclear weapons. A mission which has been expanded recently is the delivery of economic and military assistance materiel to Soviet client states in the Third World. VTA operates some 665 medium and heavy transport aircraft, of which approximately 555 are the medium-range AN-12 Cub. About 50 AN-22 Cock long-range transports (which can carry all ground force divisional equipment) and 60 of the new IL-76 Candid long-range transports are also in the inventory. (See figure II-17.) Most of these aircraft are based in the western USSR.[13]

94. Civil aircraft from Aeroflot provide supplemental support to VTA and include about 1,300 medium- and long-range transports. These aircraft are configured primarily for personnel or light cargo airlift, but Aeroflot's 160 AN-12s could be used to lift heavy equipment. Aeroflot aircraft transport some 100,000 personnel over a period of about three to four weeks during the semiannual rotation of troops for the Soviet Groups of Forces in Eastern Europe.

95. Military Transport Aviation devotes considerable training time to its primary mission of transporting airborne assault troops, including night drops, close formation flying, and low-level navigation. We believe that VTA exercises and training activities demonstrate an adequate level of competence to transport airborne assault troops but that the success of this mission would depend upon a favorable air environment.

96. The movement of all unit equipment and the 7,300 personnel assigned to an airborne division would require the entire lift capacity of VTA. Assuming an aircraft serviceability rate of about 85 percent, VTA's total serviceable fleet probably would prove inadequate for a full division lift. In combat operations, however, airborne units would probably leave behind their administrative personnel and some equipment such as trucks. We calculate that VTA could lift the assault elements of two airborne divisions simultaneously, including combat and combat support equipment with some transport, supplies, and support elements. With its large force of cargo-configured transport aircraft, VTA is well equipped to transport equipment and supplies, especially the types of equipment found in Pact airborne units. A factor which limits Soviet air transport capabilities is the low ratio of aircrews to operational aircraft (1.3 to 1). With such a ratio, crew fatigue becomes a critical factor during sustained operations.

97. With nearly all VTA airlift assets and Soviet airborne divisions deployed in the western USSR, VTA's airborne assault potential is clearly targeted toward Central Europe and NATO's flanks. Numerous airfields in nearby Warsaw Pact countries would be available for recovery and servicing, adequate fighter coverage is close at hand, and VTA crews are relatively familiar with the area.

98. Forty additional AN-12 Cubs, which are assigned to a VTA special purpose regiment, have been modified as electronic warfare platforms. These aircraft are assigned the mission of EW support of paradrop operations of the airborne forces as well as standoff EW support for fighter and bomber aircraft. During peacetime, these Cubs are used to provide an EW environment for training activities of Soviet and Warsaw Pact air defense forces.

NSWP National Air Defense Forces [14]

99. Each of the NSWP countries maintains a national air defense force consisting of fighter-interceptor units, surface-to-air missile units, and a radar network. (See table II-6.) In effect, these forces constitute a forward extension of Soviet strategic air defenses. The SAM units are predominantly equipped with SA-2s, but some countries also have SA-3s. The interceptor components number about 1,200 fighter aircraft, which, in addition to their primary mission of defense of the national airspace, could provide limited support to ground forces.

C. Warsaw Pact General Purpose Naval Forces

100. The Soviet Navy has in the past decade or so significantly improved its capability to participate in a Pact-NATO war. In addition to providing support to the Pact's ground forces and defending the Pact's maritime frontiers, the Soviet Navy can now undertake combat operations at greater distances from home waters. Soviet general purpose naval forces opposite

---

[13] We also have noted, albeit infrequently, AN-12 Cubs and IL-76 Candids of VTA training in radar-assisted, free-fall bombing, but do not ascribe major capabilities or wartime missions to VTA in this role.

[14] For a discussion of Soviet strategic air defense capabilities, see NIE 11-3/8-78.

Selected Warsaw Pact Transport Aircraft

Figure II-17

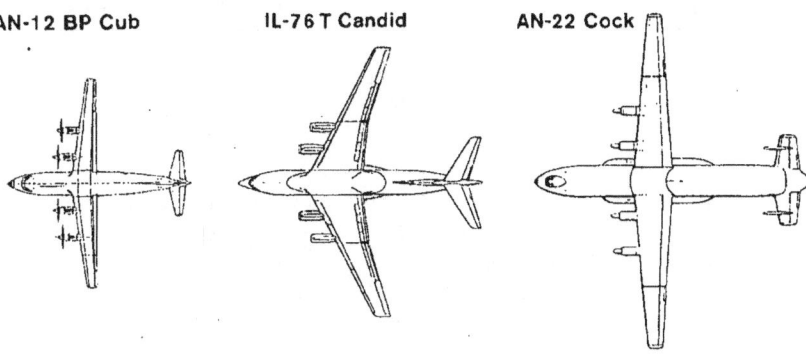

	AN-12 BP Cub	IL-76 T Candid	AN-22 Cock
Year operational	1959	1974	1967
Maximum payload (kg)	20,000	40,000	80,000
Cruise speed (knots)	320	415	355
Range with maximum payload (nm)	750	3,420	2,250

Table II-6

NSWP National Air Defense Forces January 1979

	SA-2 Sites	SA-3 Sites	Fighter-Interceptors
East Germany	24	4	270
Poland	36	12	330
Czechoslovakia	23	4	175
Hungary	12	3	145
Romania	17	—	225
Bulgaria	18	7	65
Total	130	30	1,210

NATO are from the Northern, Baltic, and Black Sea Fleets. (See figure II-18.) The Northern Fleet carries the major burden of operations in the Barents and Norwegian Seas and in the Atlantic. The fleets in the Baltic and Black Seas, together with navies of four NSWP countries, are tailored primarily for control of those two seas and for the support of land operations against NATO along the shores of and at the entrances to these seas. For operations in the Mediterranean Sea, the Black Sea Fleet furnishes most of the surface ships and the Northern Fleet the submarines.

Force Composition and Readiness

101. Warsaw Pact general purpose naval forces include submarines, surface ships, and aircraft. The general purpose submarine force consists of cruise missile and torpedo attack submarines. The principal surface combatants are about equally divided between frigates and larger ships of missile frigate, destroyer, and cruiser size. The role of sea-based aircraft is clearly emerging in the Soviet Navy with the construction of three Kiev-class aircraft carriers, following the two Moskva-class helicopter ships which entered the inventory in the late 1960s. Smaller surface combatants include mine warfare ships, submarine chasers, and missile-armed patrol craft. Soviet Naval Aviation (SNA) has three principal combat components distinguished by missions: antiship strike, reconnaissance and electronic warfare, and antisubmarine warfare

Operating Bases of the Three Western Fleets of the USSR

Figure II-18

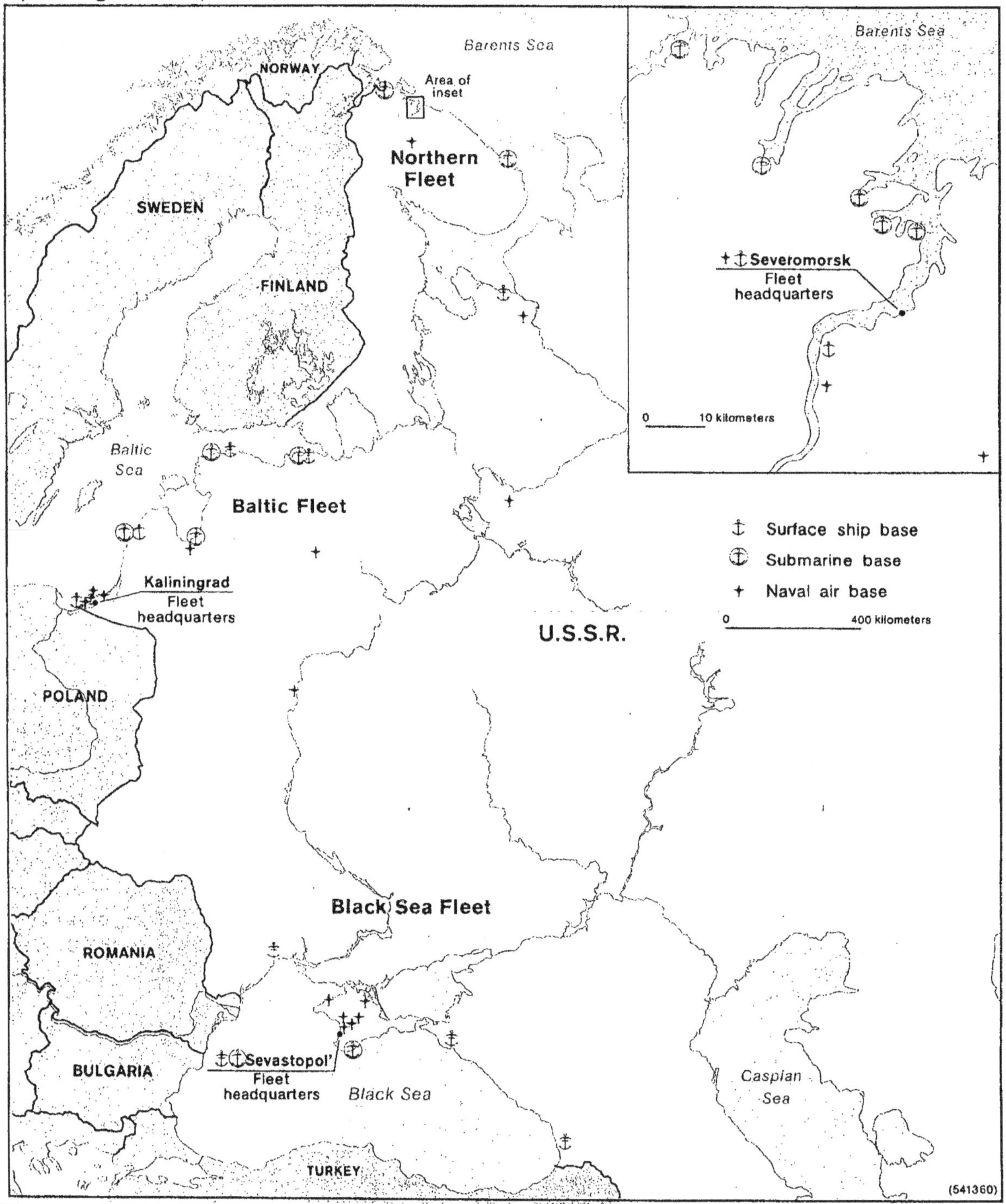

Secret

577629 1-79 CIA

(ASW). Table II-7 and figure II-19 show the current size, composition, and trends in Pact general purpose naval forces.

102. If the Soviets were not concerned with covert deployment of their ships to sea, they could probably get about half of their force opposite NATO under way with varying degrees of combat effectiveness within 48 hours. Those remaining units not undergoing major repairs or overhaul probably could put to sea in about four days, but would do so with reduced effectiveness. Naval air units normally maintain a low level of peacetime activity; most could reach full

Table II-7

Warsaw Pact General Purpose Naval Forces Opposite NATO [a]
January 1979

	Soviet [b]	NSWP	Total
General Purpose Submarines			
Cruise Missile Units	43	—	43
Torpedo Attack Units	135	8	143
Principal Surface Combatants			
Aircraft Carriers	1 [c]	—	1
Helicopter Ships	2	—	2
Cruisers	26	—	26
Destroyers	49	1	50
Missile Frigates	19	—	19
Frigates	102	4	106
Selected Minor Surface Combatants [d]	278	85	363
Amphibious Ships	66	34	100
Selected Support Ships [e]	85	4	89
Naval Aircraft [f]			
Reconnaissance/EW Aircraft	84	10	94
Strike Aircraft	254	—	254
Tankers	56	—	56
Fighters/Fighter-Bombers	71	52	123
ASW Fixed-Wing Aircraft	105	—	105
ASW/Reconnaissance Helicopters	164	48	212

[a] The NSWP navies and the Soviet forces assigned to the Northern, Baltic, and Black Sea Fleets. Detailed order-of-battle data for these and Soviet Pacific Fleet naval forces are contained in tables B-4, B-5, and B-6 in annex B.

[b] Figures exclude some 100 attack submarines and 30 principal surface combatants kept in reserve status.

[c] A second Kiev-class aircraft carrier is operational in the Black Sea, but we believe it will deploy to the Pacific Fleet.

[d] Patrol combatants, mine-warfare ships, and missile-equipped coastal patrol craft.

[e] Oilers, replenishment oilers, missile tenders, repair ships, and submarine tenders.

[f] In addition, these are about 120 transport aircraft and 105 transport helicopters which support Soviet Naval Aviation.

Soviet Naval Forces Opposite NATO, 1969 and 1979
Figure II-19

Three Soviet Western Fleets [a]

Cruise Missile and Torpedo Attack Submarines

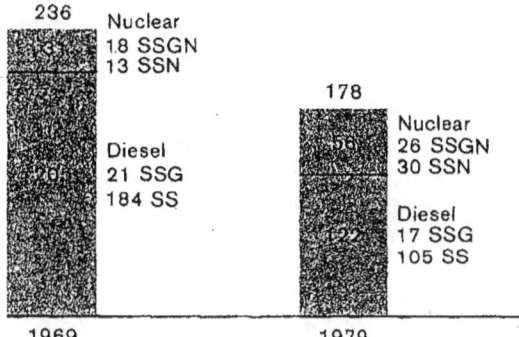

1969: 236 — Nuclear: 18 SSGN, 13 SSN; Diesel: 21 SSG, 184 SS
1979: 178 — Nuclear: 26 SSGN, 30 SSN; Diesel: 17 SSG, 105 SS

Major Surface Combatants [b]

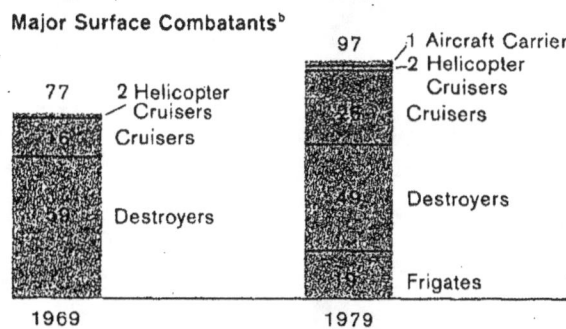

1969: 77 — 2 Helicopter Cruisers, Cruisers, Destroyers
1979: 97 — 1 Aircraft Carrier, 2 Helicopter Cruisers, Cruisers, Destroyers, Frigates

Tonnage of Major Surface Combatants [b]

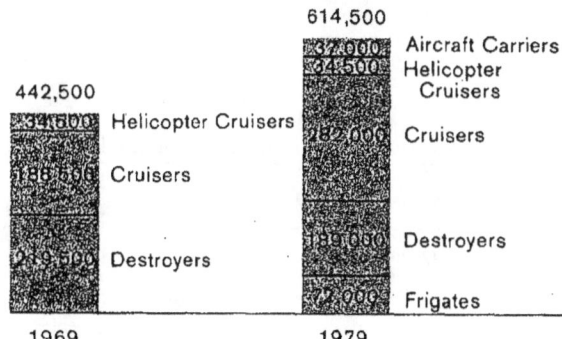

1969: 442,500 — Helicopter Cruisers, Cruisers, Destroyers
1979: 614,500 — Aircraft Carriers, Helicopter Cruisers, Cruisers, Destroyers, Frigates

[a] Excludes reserve units.
[b] Combatants over 3,000 tons, excluding reserve units.

577630 1-79 CIA

combat readiness in several hours and a few alert aircraft could react in 30 to 40 minutes.

103. Table II-8 reflects the normal peacetime status of the Soviet naval units. During an extended period of tension, the number of ships able to put to sea on short notice would be increased, while training and maintenance probably would be accelerated to improve combat effectiveness. Many of the combatants undergoing minor repair or in refresher training following repairs probably could regain an acceptable level of combat readiness within a week or two and most could be made combat ready within two months. The rest of the foreign long-term overhaul or modification would be unavailable for combat operations even with several months' preparation.

which a covert transition would occur, this information reflects Soviet expectations of achieving full combat readiness for the Soviet fleets.

105. In addition to the active forces, the Soviets have some 30 principal surface combatants and 100 submarines in a reserve status in the western fleet areas. These units differ widely in levels of maintenance and readiness, ranging from complete preservation and storage to at least external maintenance and upkeep. Some units receive periodic checks of systems, including propulsion systems, and a few W-class submarines and Skoryy-class destroyers are rotated in and out of the active force.

106. We have little information concerning the overall readiness of this reserve fleet. The apparent wide disparity of maintenance status, however, indicates that the time required to place these units in combat operation would vary. One view [15] in the Intelligence Community holds that six to 10 submarines could be brought to operational status in 30 days and a total of 25 to 30 submarines in 90 days. Another view [16] is that virtually no reserve submarines with their crews could be brought to combat readiness in less than 90 days. As for the reserve surface combatants, all agree that a significant number of these probably could not be brought to sufficient combat readiness rapidly enough to have an active role in the course of combat operations.

107. The Soviet Navy draws information on surface ship locations from a large and comprehensive ocean surveillance system, including HF/DF (high-frequency/direction-finding) stations, ELINT (electronic intelligence) and radar satellites, reconnaissance aircraft, intelligence collection ships, and civilian maritime assets. It provides intelligence on naval movements and deployments worldwide. Command and control systems and procedures have been expanded and improved to allow control of operating forces from Naval Headquarters in Moscow, from fleet headquarters, or by command authorities afloat.

Manpower, Personnel, and Training

108. Current Soviet naval personnel strengths are adequate to meet peacetime requirements. Upon mobilization, fewer than 50,000 reservists would be needed to provide full complements for all ships, both active and reserve. The Soviets can easily mobilize this

Table II-8

Normal Peacetime Status of Soviet Naval Forces

Activity	Percent of Force*	Status
Attack Submarines:		
Major Overhaul	20	Unavailable
Minor Repair	20	Reduced Readiness
Home Waters	40	Operable
Deployed	20	At Sea
Principal Surface Combatants		
Major Overhaul	20-25	Unavailable
Minor Repair or Refresher Training	25-30	Reduced Readiness
Home Waters	35-40	Operable
Deployed	10-15	At Sea

* Percentages are approximate, based on varying amounts of data for respective force components. Available data are more extensive for the submarine force than for the surface fleet and therefore probably more accurate.

---

[15] *The holders of this view are Director, Defense Intelligence Agency, and the Director of Naval Intelligence, Department of the Navy.*

[16] *The holder of this view is the Central Intelligence Agency.*

number from a pool of 300,000 reservists released from active duty within the previous five years. Other reservists would be called up to fill out the naval support establishment but we do not know the gross number required or the functional skills needed by type and number.

109. The growing complexity of naval weapon systems demands greater technical expertise in operation and maintenance. The Soviets, to a much greater extent than is normal in Western navies, rely on officers and warrant officers to operate, maintain, and repair their complex equipment. Soviet naval officers have a strong technical background, acquired during the five years they spend at officer training schools, most of which provide engineering degrees. Major shortcomings of the Soviet Navy's training system, however, include its overemphasis on narrow specialization and its apparent failure to instill the qualities of initiative and adaptability essential to effective leadership at sea. These weaknesses could constitute a disadvantage under combat conditions.

110. The Soviets apparently lack sufficient enlisted personnel technically qualified to handle their increasingly complex equipment. A low reenlistment rate has tended to exacerbate this deficiency. The recent extension of shipboard duty from 18 months to two years for those enlisted personnel with higher education appears to be an attempt to reduce shortages of technically skilled personnel. In an effort to compensate for these shortages, the Soviet Navy periodically has engaged in concentrated campaigns to encourage and promote cross-training of enlisted personnel and officers in a second specialty. There is little evidence that such campaigns have had a lasting effect.

111. Shipboard training of new sailors revolves around the semiannual conscription cycles, each of which appears to account for about a 15-percent turnover of personnel. This training is based on an annual cycle, much of which is aimed at developing individual ship proficiency and readiness. The high turnover of enlisted conscripts is partially offset by the long tenure of career personnel. It is not uncommon, for example, for the latter to spend five to 10 years aboard the same ship. Although shipboard training has been improving, it continues to be excessively structured and stereotyped. We are uncertain whether these factors would seriously degrade combat performance.

112. There is evidence of morale and disciplinary problems among Soviet naval personnel. As with the ground forces, statistics pertaining to the scope of these problems are unavailable, but Soviet naval authorities appear to be concerned. These problems are most evident among enlisted noncareerists—who account for about 95 percent of enlisted personnel—but are found among only a relatively small proportion of officers and enlisted career personnel. The difficulties are brought out in reports concerning alcoholism, poor performance aboard ship, absences without leave, disciplinary infractions, and even a mutiny aboard a destroyer. These problems, which are reflections of Soviet society as a whole, could have an adverse impact upon peacetime training and materiel readiness programs and thus would explain the concern of senior naval authorities. We doubt, however, that these problems would prevail during wartime to an extent which would affect ship operations or crew performance, because in wartime most of the motivational and disciplinary problems would disappear.

Major Wartime Tasks

113. The wartime missions of the Warsaw Pact's general purpose naval forces are to exercise sea control in waters from which NATO's sea-based air and ballistic missile strike and amphibious projection forces can reach the Soviet Union, to support and protect Soviet ballistic missile submarines, to exercise sea denial in the sea lanes necessary for resupply and reinforcement of Europe from the United States, and to project power ashore in support of Pact ground forces. Although the relative emphasis that would be placed on each of these missions in a conflict would depend upon the way hostilities were initiated and the course of the war, the Soviets in their major exercises have focused on ASW and attacks on carriers, cruisers, and amphibious task forces.

Antiwarship Capabilities

114. Soviet Navy resources capable of acting to counter NATO's surface naval forces include missile-equipped bombers, submarines, and surface combatants which are supported by ocean surveillance systems, including ELINT and radar satellites and aircraft, for detecting, identifying, and tracking potential surface targets. These surveillance systems are centrally controlled from Navy and General Staff headquarters in Moscow, and information derived from these systems is made available to the fleets.

115. Major exercises since 1970 have demonstrated the Soviet approach to, and capabilities for, a large ocean surveillance operation coordinated with strike activities in various areas. They indicate that the detection and tracking of NATO carriers and amphib-

ious task forces would be accomplished primarily by land-based electronic surveillance of the task force's high-frequency radio transmissions supported by satellites for electronic intercept and radar reconnaissance. This type of surveillance would be supplemented by aircraft, submarine, and surface ship reconnaissance for both detection and positive identification.

116. The major weakness of the Soviet ocean surveillance system is its heavy reliance on electronic emissions from potential targets. When NATO forces implement emission control (EMCON) conditions, which occur during NATO exercises, Soviet surveillance capabilities are impaired, sometimes drastically. If EMCON conditions were imposed in wartime, Soviet naval and civilian maritime assets and radar satellites probably would be able to provide adequate data only on Western surface forces previously located or those within striking range of Warsaw Pact countries. Elsewhere, large NATO ships would probably be less vulnerable to detection because of the limitations of the radar satellites and the nearly impossible task of providing surveillance by surface ships and aircraft in areas of NATO air superiority. A pair of radar satellites could, under optimum conditions, provide coverage of 60 to 80 percent of the likely carrier and amphibious task force transit lanes in the Atlantic in a day, but another four days would be needed to provide full coverage. Soviet capabilities to estimate the disposition of NATO surface forces could be progressively degraded by the use of deception techniques against radar satellites, combined with EMCON.

117. The Soviets have some 43 antiship cruise missile submarines (see figure II-20) in their western fleets for deployment in the Atlantic and European theater area. Four submarine-launched antiship cruise missile (ASCM) systems (see figure II-21), are operational, each capable of delivering either conventional or nuclear warheads. Deployed units probably carry an equal mix of high-explosive and nuclear warheads. They probably also carry at least two nuclear torpedoes. The ASCM-equipped submarines include:

— Seven C-I and three C-II-class nuclear-powered units, each of which can fire eight antiship

Selected Newer Soviet General Purpose Submarines

Figure II-20

	Year operational	Propulsion/max. submerged speed (knots)	Armament
C-II cruise missile submarine 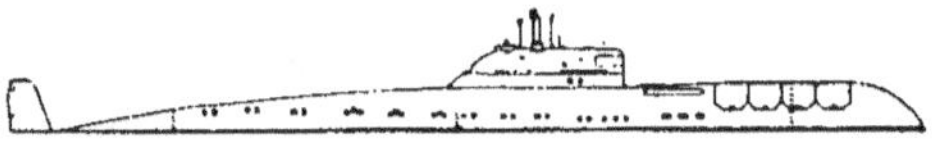	1974	Nuclear/23	SS-N-9 antiship cruise missile Torpedoes: ASW and antiship
V-II attack submarine 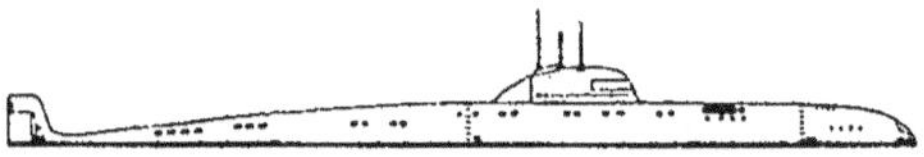	1973	Nuclear/31	SS-N-15 ASW missile Torpedoes: ASW and antiship
A attack submarine 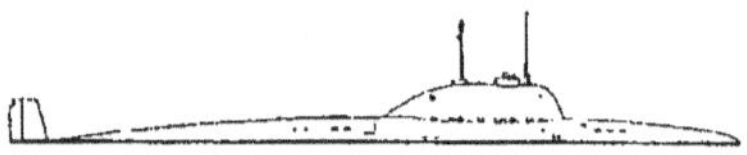	1978	Nuclear/27+	Possible ASW missile Torpedoes
T attack submarine 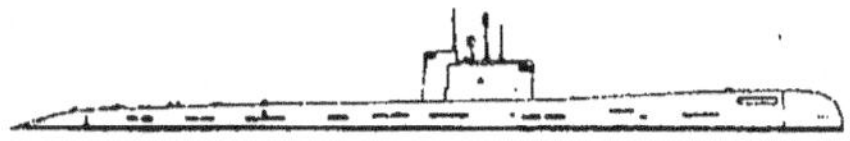	1973	Diesel/16	Possible ASW missile Torpedoes

Top Secret

Selected Soviet Sea-Launched Cruise Missiles

Figure II-21a

	Payload (kg)	Speed	Maximum system range (km)*	Guidance	Launch platform	IOC
SS-N-2a	515 HE	Mach 0.9	35–40	Radar or IR	Osa and Komar PTG	1959
SS-N-2b	515 HE	Mach 0.9	35–40	Radar or IR	Osa PTG	1964
SS-N-2c	330 HE	Mach 0.9	83	Radar or IR	Osa PTG Mod Kildin DD Mod Kashin DDG	1975
SS-N-3a	1,000 HE or nuclear	Mach 1.4	410	Radar	J SSG E-II SSGN	1962
SS-N-3b Mod 1 The coastal defense version of this missile is called the SS-C-1b.	1,000 HE or nuclear	Mach 1.5	410	Radar	Kynda CG Kresta I CG	1962
SS-N-3b Mod 2	1,000 HE or nuclear	Mach 1.5	410	Radar	Kresta I CG	1977
SS-N-3c	Nuclear	Mach 1.2	830	Autopilot/inertial	W SSG E-II SSGN (poss) J SSG (poss)	1962
SS-N-7	500 HE or nuclear	Mach 0.9	65	Radar	C-I SSGN C-II SSGN	1968
SS-N-9	500 HE or nuclear	Mach 0.9	110	Radar and IR	Nanuchka PGG Sarancha PGGH C-II SSGN P SSGN	1971
SS-N-12	1,000 HE or nuclear	Mach 2.4	550	Radar	E-II SSGN Kiev CVSG	1976
SS-N-14 Data insufficient for drawing.	E45-70A or E45-75A Torpedo	Mach 0.9	55	Active/passive acoustic	Krivak FFG Kresta II CG Kara CG	1974

*This is the maximum distance that the missile can travel and still effectively engage a target. In many cases, the missiles have a greater propulsion range but are not considered effective in an antiship role.

Secret

579024 4-79 CIA

Nominal Flight Profiles of Selected Soviet Sea-Launched Cruise Missiles

Figure II-21b

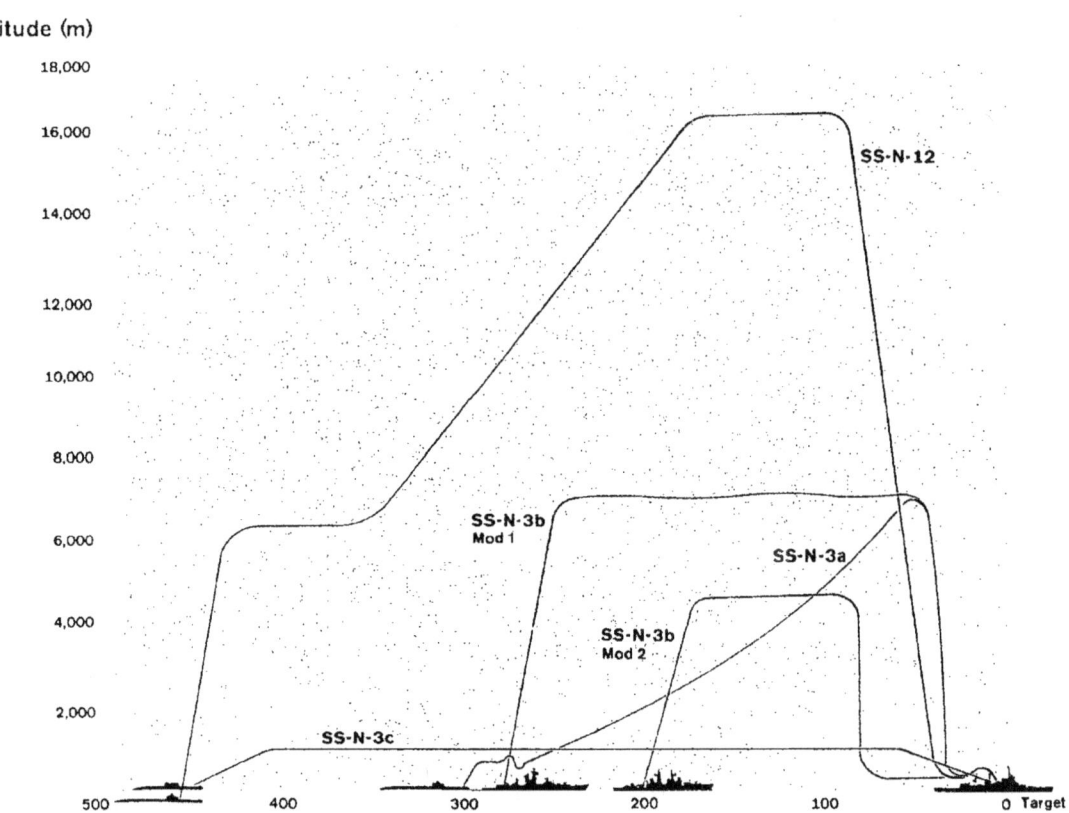

missiles while submerged. The C-I fires the SS-N-7 missile to a maximum range of 35 nautical miles (65 km). The C-II probably fires the SS-N-9 missile to a maximum range of 60 nm (110 km). Both missiles are guided by a preset autopilot. The SS-N-7 uses active radar terminal homing and the SS-N-9 uses a dual mode seeker, with active radar and infrared (IR) terminal homing.

— Fifteen E-II-class nuclear-powered submarines, each carrying eight, surface-launched, long-range missiles. Most E-IIs carry the 220-nm (410-km) SS-N-3a missile. To date at least two of these submarines have been converted to fire the 300-nm (555-km) SS-N-12. Both missiles use active radar terminal homing and midcourse targeting information to enhance accuracy. Those submarines with the SS-N-12 system also can receive initial target data directly from ELINT and radar satellites. Additional E-IIs are being modified, presumably to carry the SS-N-12.

— Twelve J-class diesel-powered submarines, each with four SS-N-3a missiles. Like the E-IIs, the J-class submarines require external targeting support and must surface to fire their missiles.

— A single P-class nuclear-powered submarine probably was designed to fire 10 missiles while submerged, but we are uncertain whether the P-class has been equipped with missiles. The missile system for the P-class has not been identified, although it may be the SS-N-9.

In addition to antiship cruise missile submarines there are also five obsolescent W-class submarines equipped with the inertially guided SS-N-3c missile which was

II-35

designed primarily for use against large-area targets, such as ports, and which has a range of 450 nm (830 km).

118. In addition to cruise-missile submarines, the Soviet western fleets include 30 nuclear-powered and some 59 long-range F-, Z-, and T-class diesel-powered attack submarines. Most Soviet nuclear attack submarines are fast—27 to 32 knots—and, despite relatively high noise radiation, could be effective in antiship operations. Soviet long-range diesel submarines are much slower than the nuclear units. They are particularly susceptible to detection when snorkeling, but can remain submerged for extended periods. In addition there are medium- and short-range diesel units which would likely be employed in areas closer to the Soviet Union.

119. The Soviet Navy has some 215 missile-equipped bomber aircraft opposite NATO for antiship attacks. (See figure II-22.) They include about 175 TU-16 Badgers and some 40 Backfires. These aircraft carry four types of missiles with various flight profiles and speeds and maximum ranges of from 80 to about 200 nm (145 to 360 km). There are also about 40 TU-22 Blinder A's which could be used for bombing and mining. The naval Badgers, which first entered service in 1957, are relatively large and slow moving by current standards. They are highly vulnerable to modern air defenses such as those of well-defended aircraft carrier task groups. Improvements in their missile and electronic warfare systems, however, have maintained them as firstline strike aircraft.

120. The introduction of some 40 Backfire bombers into the Baltic and Black Sea Fleet air forces to date has significantly improved the strike capability of the Soviet Navy against NATO surface forces.[17] Because of the modern, higher speed air-to-surface missile it carries, its variable flight profiles, its maneuverability, and its high-speed capabilities, the Backfire has a higher probability of penetrating NATO naval air

---

[17] See NIE 11-3/8-78 and section D of this chapter (paragraph 179 and figure II-30) for details of the differing agency estimates of the Backfire's capabilities.

Soviet Naval Strike Aircraft

Figure II-22a

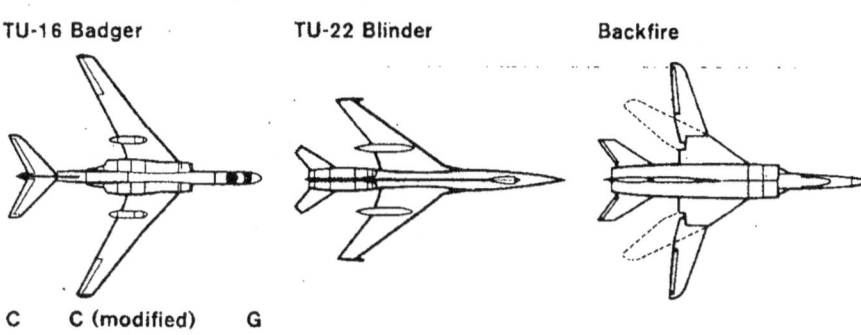

	TU-16 Badger			TU-22 Blinder	Backfire
	C	C (modified)	G		
Year operational	1960	1971	1965	1962	1974
Payload	One AS-2	Two AS-5 or two AS-6	Two AS-5 or two AS-6	3,000 kilograms (bombs)	
Maximum unrefueled radius (nm)	1,450	1,150	1,150	1,740	See figure II-30b for differing agency assessments of the Backfire's performance characteristics.
Maximum radius with prestrike refueling (nm)	2,050	1,850	1,850	2,350	

defenses and attacking targets in the open ocean than does the Badger. Also, it is far more capable than the Badger of crossing potentially hostile land areas, such as Turkey and Greece, and operating over the Mediterranean.

121. In the antiship role, wartime operational considerations probably would tend to dictate the use of Backfires for strikes against important NATO warships in certain key areas. These areas would include the North Atlantic at least as far south as the Greenland–Iceland–United Kingdom (G-I-UK) gap, the North Sea, and the Mediterranean. The operational constraints tending to limit the use of Backfires include mission planning allowances for combat maneuvering, and requirements for routing around and penetrating NATO air defenses. Aerial refueling could add flexibility for the employment of Backfires, however.

122. The Soviet naval air forces opposite NATO have in the past few years added some 40 shore-based SU-17 Fitter C/D and some 35 carrier-based YAK-36 Forger V/STOL (vertical/short takeoff and landing) aircraft, which improve their overall capabilities against NATO naval surface forces. There is insufficient evidence to judge how the Soviets would use either of these aircraft against ships at sea or how effective they might be in wartime. Most Forger training thus far has been of the kind useful for attacks against ships at sea. The Fitters, however, all of which are based in the Baltic, are probably intended for ground attack in support of amphibious operations and antiship attacks.

123. The three Soviet western fleets have 14 principal surface combatant ships armed with antiship cruise missiles. (See figure II-23.) Six of these ships have long-range (160 to 300 nm, or 300 to 555 km) missiles, including the Kiev aircraft carrier, with an estimated 24 SS-N-12s; two Kynda cruisers, with 16 SS-N-3b's each; and three Kresta-I cruisers, with four SS-N-3b's each. To fire these missiles accurately to their maximum range requires that these ships obtain external targeting support. For this purpose, the Kiev and the Kresta-Is carry reconnaissance helicopters and,

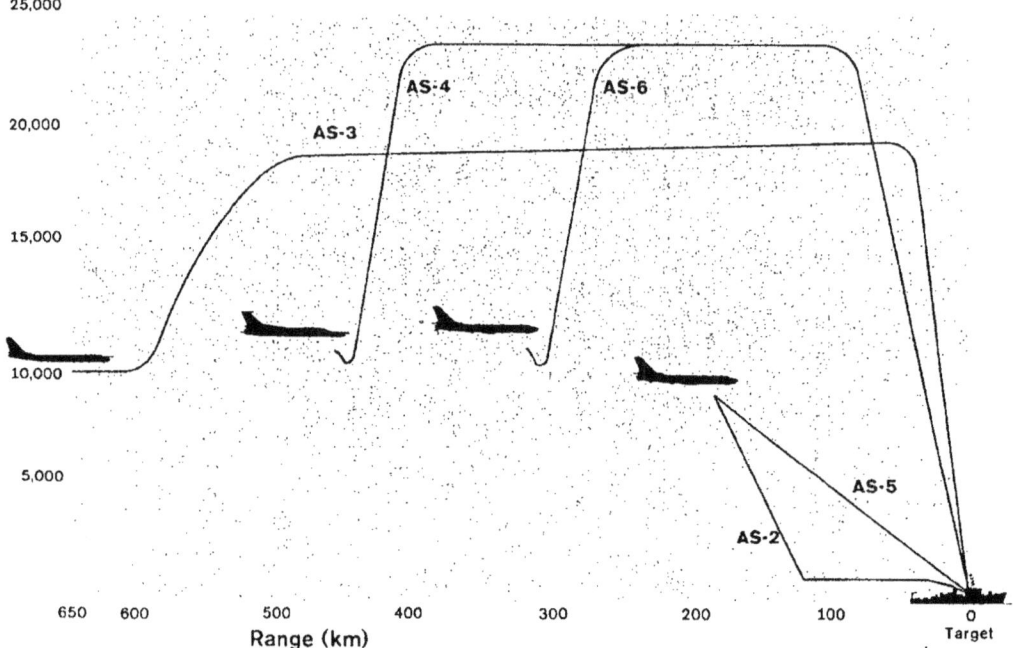

Figure II-22b

Nominal Flight Profiles of Soviet Air-Launched Cruise Missiles

Selected Soviet Major Surface Combatants

Figure II-23

	Year operational	Propulsion	Armament
Kiev Aircraft carrier 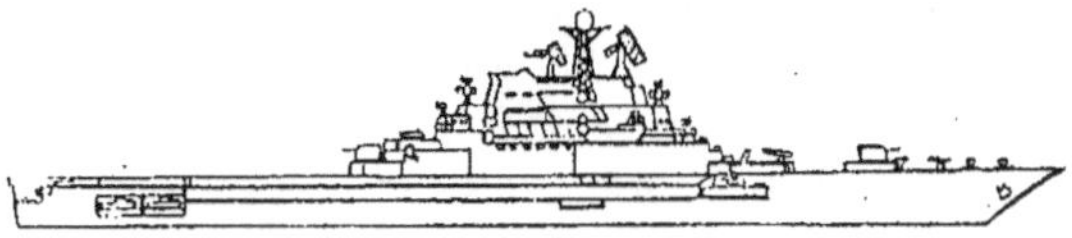	1976	Steam	32–50 ASW/helicopters and V/STOL fighters SS-N-12 antiship cruise missiles SA-N-3 SAMs SA-N-4 SAMs SUW-N-1 ASW rockets 76-mm guns Gatling guns Probable torpedoes RBU-6000 ASW rockets
Moskva Helicopter ship 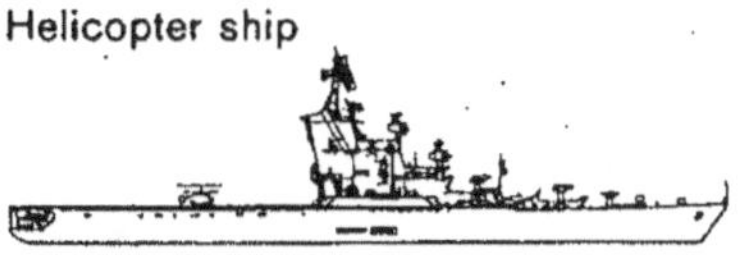	1968	Steam	16–24 ASW helicopters SA-N-3 SAMs SUW-N-1 ASW rockets 57–mm guns Torpedoes RBU-6000 ASW rockets
Kara Cruiser 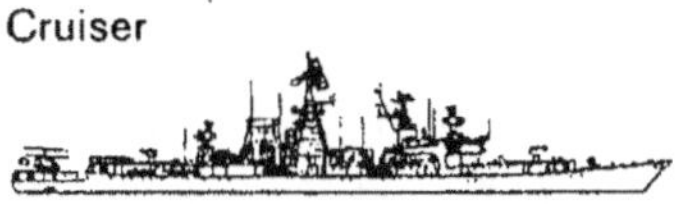	1972	Gas turbine	SA-N-3 SAMs SA-N-4 SAMs SS-N-14 ASW missiles u/i SAMs on 1 ship 76–mm guns Gatling guns Torpedoes RBU-1000 and RBU-6000 ASW rockets
Kresta II Cruiser 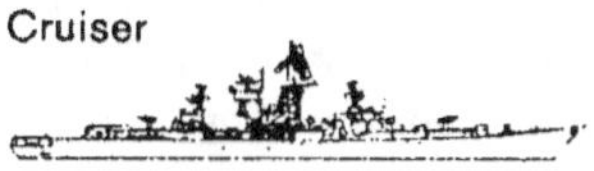	1970	Steam	SA-N-3 SAMs SS-N-14 ASW missiles 57-mm guns Torpedoes RBU-1000 and RBU-6000 ASW rockets
Krivak Frigate 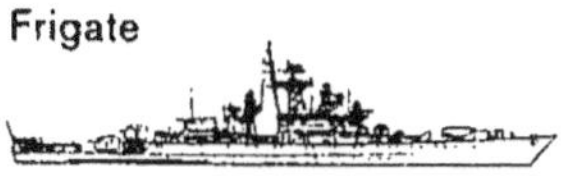	1970	Gas turbine	SA-N-4 SAMs SS-N-14 ASW missiles 76–mm, 100–mm guns Torpedoes RBU-6000 ASW rockets

Secret

579028 4-79 CIA

along with the Kyndas, can receive target data from Bear D aircraft. The Kiev can also receive targeting data directly from radar and electronic intelligence satellites and possibly could use its V/STOL aircraft for targeting assistance. The remaining eight missile-equipped ships are destroyers, each armed with four missiles that can be fired to a maximum range of about 45 nm (80 km).

124. Other Soviet surface combatants opposite NATO which are equipped with antiship cruise missiles include 14 Nanuchka-class and about 75 Osa-class missile patrol boats. The former are fitted with six 60-nm (110-km) SS-N-9 missiles, while the Osa units have four 19-nm (35-km) SS-N-2b or 45-nm (83-km) SS-N-2c missiles each. Except for the SS-N-2 series, all current Soviet antiship cruise missiles are believed capable of carrying a nuclear or a conventional warhead.

125. Although the Soviets have a large inventory of ships, submarines, and aircraft capable of conducting attacks on NATO ships, the successful accomplishment of such strikes under wartime situations depends on a variety of factors. Among the most significant are: the effectiveness of Soviet ocean surveillance and electronic warfare, the number of launch platforms available for antiship use, the achievement of strategic or tactical surprise, and whether nuclear weapons are used by the Soviets or NATO. With accurate targeting and the use of nuclear weapons in surprise attacks, the Soviet naval forces normally deployed in peacetime would constitute a severe threat to NATO carriers and amphibious task groups in European waters. Timely warning of a Soviet attack, however, would allow NATO task forces to take action which could enhance their survivability.

126. The surface-to-air missile systems aboard some 75 Soviet principal surface combatants can also be used against surface ships. The most capable of these systems is the SA-N-3, which has an operational range of 10 to 20 nm (18 to 37 km) in an antiship mode and may have a nuclear as well as a conventional warhead. This system is installed in the Soviet western fleets' 16 units of the Kiev, Moskva, Kara, and Kresta-II classes, probably with magazine capacities of either 48 or 72 missiles. In addition, the ASW homing torpedo payload of the SS-N-14 cruise missile could be used against surface ships, but we consider this unlikely.

Antisubmarine Warfare Capabilities

127. In a NATO–Warsaw Pact conflict, the Pact's antisubmarine warfare tasks would be varied and extremely difficult. The Pact navies must seek out Western ballistic missile submarines (SSBNs) and counter Western attack submarines. Attacks on Western SSBNs would have to be undertaken in their worldwide patrol and base areas. The task of countering attack submarines would be markedly different for protecting Pact forces in the approaches to the USSR, on the one hand, and for the protection of Soviet naval operations in more distant waters, on the other.

128. Pact ASW capabilities on the whole are extremely limited. The crucial Soviet shortcomings are lack of long-range submarine detection devices, the high radiated noise levels of Soviet submarines relative to those of the West, and the lack of seaborne tactical air cover to protect deployed surface ship ASW forces. Nonetheless, virtually all modern Soviet surface combatants carry ASW weapons and sensors, and large numbers of Soviet aircraft and helicopters are fitted for ASW operations.

129. The forces opposite NATO which are most capable of ASW operations beyond coastal waters include about 50 Soviet principal surface combatants,[18] 30 nuclear-powered torpedo attack submarines, and about 45 fixed-wing ASW aircraft. The 16 ships with helicopters (those of the Kiev, Moskva, Kara, and Kresta-II classes) and the Krivak frigates are equipped with long-range (15 to 30 nm, or 28 to 56 km) ASW weapons. Only the Kiev- and Moskva-class units combine these features with a long-range (typically less than 10 nm) active sonar and more than one helicopter. Soviet ASW helicopters, however, are limited in their ASW operations at night and in bad weather.

130. The V-class nuclear-powered attack submarines, of which 19 are in the Northern Fleet, are the most capable Soviet submarines for ASW.

131. The Soviet medium- and long-range airborne ASW capability consists of IL-38 May and TU-142 Bear F aircraft, which are equipped with sonobuoys

---
[18] Ships of the Kiev, Moskva, Kresta-II, Kara, Kashin, Mod-Kashin, and Krivak classes.

and surface search radars. (See figure II-24.)

[19] *The holders of this view are the Central Intelligence Agency and the Director, National Security Agency.*

Selected Soviet Aircraft for Antisubmarine Warfare

Figure II-24

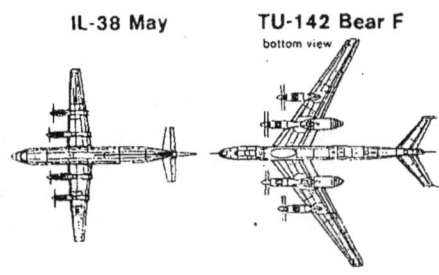

	IL-38 May	TU-142 Bear F bottom view
Year operational	1968	1971
Payload (kg)	Sonobuoys, torpedoes, and depth charges[b] (5,400)	Sonobuoys, torpedoes, and depth charges[b] (8,500)
Maximum radius[a] (nm)	1,350	2,050 or 3,150[c]

a. Radius values include allowance for three hours of loiter time on station.

c. See paragraphs 131 and 132 of chapter II for differing agency views on the radius of the Bear F.

133. Other Soviet forces opposite NATO—designated primarily for coastal ASW—are much more numerous, but their individual capabilities are generally poorer. These include about 155 minor surface combatants with sonars, about 45 short- and medium-range diesel submarines, nearly 60 short-range fixed-wing ASW aircraft, and about 100 shore-based ASW helicopters. In addition, the Polish, East German, and to a lesser degree the Bulgarian and Romanian Navies have a variety of units which are trained for coastal ASW defense and are being integrated into the combined Pact fleets in the Baltic and Black Seas.

135. Effective ASW depends in part on Pact surveillance capabilities, which, outside coastal waters, are extremely limited. This limitation is primarily caused by Soviet failure to develop long-range undersea surveillance systems. Soviet efforts to achieve such a capability would, in any event, be constrained because the Pact lacks sites from which major Western naval operating areas could be monitored. Furthermore, if the Soviets were to emplace an underwater surveillance system on Pact territory, its effectiveness would be limited because the waters along Pact shores are for the most part shallow and therefore unsuitable for carrying sounds over long distances.

[20] *The holders of this view are the Director, Defense Intelligence Agency; the Director of Naval Intelligence, Department of the Navy; and the Assistant Chief of Staff, Intelligence, Department of the Air Force.*

136. Although the undersea surveillance capabilities of the Pact navies are only fair in coastal waters, they are better there than in more distant areas because the Pact countries can concentrate ASW forces and use antisubmarine sensors emplaced near their own coasts. Among the surveillance systems in these coastal waters are individual and field arrangements of tethered, short-range acoustic buoys; various ships and submarines on picket duty; shore-based surface-search radars; and HF/DF intercept sites.

137. In sum, the quietness of Western submarines, the technical characteristics of the Pact equipment, and Pact signal processing capabilities combine in most cases to restrict severely the range at which Western submarines can be detected. Locating data could be provided at greater ranges through detection of periscopes or other masts with surface search radars (especially in low sea states) or through HF/DF of radio transmissions in the cases in which they occur.

138. In waters beyond the Pact's coastal regions, Soviet ships and submarines, including those best equipped for ASW, are vulnerable to attack by NATO submarines.

139. Nevertheless, there are situations, particularly in their own coastal waters and ocean areas over which they have temporary control, in which Pact ASW forces might be able to prevent NATO submarines from disrupting key maritime operations. Soviet and combined Pact amphibious and convoy exercises often include substantial numbers of units employed as ASW screening forces, and in wartime such tactics could well be effective—especially in areas accessible to Soviet air forces, or in operations against the less capable NATO submarine forces.

Capabilities for Exercising Sea Control in the Sea Approaches to the Soviet Union

140. In theater hostilities in Europe, a high-priority task of the Pact navies would be to ensure that their sea approaches were secure and open to Pact use. Pact strategy calls for establishing sea control in the Barents Sea and in the closed seas—the Baltic and Black Seas—thus denying these waters to the enemy. The Pact navies maintain the bulk of their naval forces in these areas, including some principal combatants, and large numbers of smaller combatants, submarines, and ASW aircraft. These forces continue to receive new ships with the latest attack and air defense missiles, sonars, torpedoes, and mine-warfare equipment. They can be supported by fighter and attack aircraft of the Soviet Air Defense Forces and Frontal Aviation. The Pact has also concentrated coastal defense missile and artillery batteries to defend ports, bases, and other critical facilities.

141. In addition to using the forces described above to attack approaching NATO naval forces, the Pact would probably lay defensive minefields, particularly in key areas. Although there is little specific evidence the large number of ships for mining—as well as the submarines and aircraft capable of laying mines—suggests that the Soviets probably plan to conduct mine warfare on a considerable scale. Additionally, naval exercises indicate that the Pact expects to conduct countermine operations against NATO mining in approaches to Pact countries.

Capabilities for Exercising Sea Denial in NATO Sea Lines of Communication

142. In wartime, the Soviets probably would attempt sea denial operations in NATO's sea lines of communication by attacking noncombatant ships—merchant vessels and naval auxiliaries—on the high seas, striking ports and harbors, and mining heavily traveled waters. The extent of the commitment of forces to an interdiction effort would depend on a number of factors such as the emphasis on operations against carriers, amphibious ships and SSBNs, the course of the conflict, the level at which it is initiated, Soviet expectations as to the degree and pace of escalation, and the extent of Pact and NATO mobilization.

143. Successful attacks on noncombatant ships at sea would depend primarily on the availability and capability of Soviet attack submarines for this mission. The combat radii of Soviet ASM-equipped naval aircraft would rule out their use—if operating out of Soviet bases—over most of the length of the more southerly sea lanes to Great Britain and France. They have some capability near Great Britain, but unless air defenses there were destroyed, such strikes could be more costly than the expected results might warrant.

144. The Soviets currently maintain an active inventory of about 180 cruise-missile and torpedo attack submarines in their western fleets. Of these, the some 115 long-range units based in the Northern Fleet, the only fleet in the western USSR with largely unrestricted access to the North Atlantic sea lanes, form a potential strike force for interdiction. The demands placed on resources by the Soviet Navy's other missions would limit the number of submarines available for interdiction because large numbers of Soviet naval forces would have to be devoted to controlling the Baltic Sea, the Black Sea, and much of the Norwegian Sea, as well as their approaches, against incursion by Western carriers, amphibious forces and submarines, and because a portion of the Soviet attack submarine force probably would be committed to operations against NATO naval bases and in the open ocean.

145. There is disagreement within the Intelligence Community concerning the extent, emphasis, and timing of the interdiction campaign. Some believe [21] that the Soviets would commit some of their submarine fleet to an interdiction campaign, but not a large portion unless they had earlier defeated NATO carrier and amphibious forces without losing many of their submarines. Others believe [22] that the Soviets would regard interdiction of US reinforcements to Europe to be of such significance and their submarine inventory of sufficient depth to warrant use of substantial numbers of attack submarines in this effort while still accomplishing their other missions.

146. Those holding the former view believe that the Soviets would be deterred from seriously trying to exploit the West's dependence on long sea lines of communication unless attrition—or Western strategy—reduced the threat from NATO's nuclear strike and projection forces. According to this view, the presence of NATO carriers in or near areas like the Norwegian and Mediterranean Seas would cause the Soviets to commit large forces in counteraction, heavy losses would result, and the Soviets would lack the submarines to engage simultaneously in strong antifleet and antishipping operations. Those holding the latter view believe that the timing and extent of Soviet interdiction operations depend more upon the disposition and tactics of NATO naval forces and upon Soviet intentions and expectations as to the course of the conflict, than upon the prior achievement of other naval tasks. According to this view, circumstances such as an early stalemate in Central Europe or a NATO decision not to deploy carrier and amphibious forces immediately into the Norwegian Sea would lead the Soviets to mount a substantial interdiction effort during the early phase of a conflict when NATO would be convoying critical war material, including elements of US divisions and their equipment, to Europe.

147. There are also disagreements over Soviet capabilities to execute an interdiction campaign, irrespective of the Soviet committment to interdiction. These disagreements stem from different judgments and interpretations of evidence regarding: torpedo loads, replenishment opportunities, turnaround time, transit distance, combat attrition, and target information.

— **Torpedo Loads.** According to the first view, Soviet naval strategy stresses the likelihood of a short nuclear war and the importance of striking a few high-value targets. The torpedo capacities of Soviet submarines are consistent with this strategy, but would severely limit the number of attacks against merchant ships the submarines could make while on station during an interdiction campaign (see table II-9). Soviet cruise missile submarines, which constitute nearly one-third of the USSR's fleet of long-range general purpose submarines, carry few (the C-class) or no (the E-II and the J-class) torpedo reloads. Soviet long-range torpedo attack submarines can carry 16 to 22 torpedoes, but in practice many of these would not be used against merchant ships because recent evidence shows that combat-ready Soviet submarines are loaded with ASW and nuclear torpedoes, as well as antiship weapons. The second view holds that the Soviet long-range attack submarines most likely to participate in such a campaign (principally the N-class, F-class, and T-class) clearly carry sufficient torpedoes to conduct a significant number of attacks on Western shipping. Additionally, the loading of individual submarines would be contingent on assigned missions; submarines would not necessarily have a mix of different weapon types in wartime as is customary in peacetime.

---

[21] *The holders of the first view are the Central Intelligence Agency; the Director, Bureau of Intelligence and Research, Department of State; and the Director, National Security Agency. The Director of NSA further believes that the extent and degree of a campaign against the sea lines of communication is largely scenario dependent and that, in a prolonged crisis, where the outcome is in serious doubt, the attractiveness of interdiction in advance of a conflict goes up.*

[22] *The holders of the second view are the Director, Defense Intelligence Agency, and the Director of Naval Intelligence, Department of the Navy.*

Table II-9

Estimated Torpedo Capacity for Soviet Attack Submarines [a]

Long-Range Submarine Class	Number of Torpedoes [b]
V	16–18
C	12
N	18–20
E-II	8
J	6
T	22
F	22
Z	22
Medium-Range Submarine Class	
W	12
R	14

[a] Assumes each submarine carries a full load of 53-centimeter (7.8 meters long) antishipping torpedoes.

[b] The Director, Defense Intelligence Agency, points out that the "full wartime load" of these submarines is unknown and that these estimates are predicated on a loading under peacetime operating conditions of weapons of 53-cm diameter (7.8 meters long). His agency estimates that two 40-cm torpedoes (4.5 meters long) probably could be substituted for each of up to six 53-cm torpedoes in most classes. The Director of DIA notes, therefore, that the wartime torpedo loads of these classes could be substantially greater than shown.

SECRET

— **Replenishment Opportunities.** The first view holds that Soviet submarines would have to return to home waters for resupply, that Soviet naval support ships probably would not operate outside Soviet-controlled waters because they would be vulnerable to attack, and that any Soviet merchant ships at sea when war began probably would not be available by the time the submarines exhausted their torpedoes. According to the second view, Soviet long-range attack submarines can operate for periods of weeks without having to refuel and, conceivably, could take on fuel from Pact merchant ships, and an individual submarine would probably have sufficient time to attack its targets before having to return to base for torpedo reloading.

— **Turnaround Time.** All agree that Soviet submarines would have to spend some time in port between patrols. The first group believes it might be as long as 25 days, which was the German experience in World War II. The second believes the time could be compressed to less than 25 days, especially in a period of intense conflict.

— **Transit Distance.** Holders of the first view believe that the effectiveness of Soviet submarines would be impaired by the distance between the Northern Fleet submarine bases and the North Atlantic sea lanes. They point out that if NATO convoys were routed southward to reduce the danger from Pact aircraft, Soviet submarines would have to travel 2,500 to 3,500 nm; nuclear-powered submarines traveling at 12 knots would spend about 22 days in a round trip (6,000 nm) to the sea lanes, while diesels averaging 5 knots would spend 54 days in transit. The others note that despite the long transit distances, Soviet long-range attack submarines have the range to undertake patrols in the North Atlantic sea lanes of sufficient duration to have ample opportunity to attack a number of Western ships.

— **Combat Attrition.** All agree that Soviet submarines based in the Northern Fleet would have to travel through the Norwegian Sea and the G-I-UK gap, areas which favor NATO ASW efforts, and that even on station, operating areas would be continuously within range of NATO's land-based ASW aircraft, as well as other ASW platforms. The first view is that the resultant combat attrition would be prohibitive. The second is that, although Soviet submarines would be particularly open to attack by Western ASW forces at several points, this threat would be reduced by attacks against NATO ASW aircraft and bases, on SIGINT facilities, and on facilities of the US sound surveillance system (SOSUS).

— **Target Information.** The first group believes that it would be difficult for attack submarines to identify high-value ships in ocean traffic containing many ships of low value. They note that under North Atlantic combat and weather conditions, attacks on merchant ships would be likely to result in little more than random success at destroying ships loaded with military cargoes instead of ships loaded with civilian industrial or other goods. The second group judges that the Soviets probably would have clandestine reporting, including detailed information on cargoes and ship departure times, as well as locating data from technical collection, including radar and ELINT ocean reconnaissance satellites and long-range HF/DF. According to this view, the combination of these assets would likely provide the intelligence necessary to direct attacks on the more valuable convoys and—with greater difficulty—individual ships.

148. All agree that, in a conventional war, the Soviets could attempt to disrupt port operations in

Western Europe by a bombing offensive. The large and repetitive bombing attacks necessary for such an offensive would reduce the availability of aircraft for other missions. Most bombers would be required for the battle for air superiority and the destruction of NATO nuclear delivery systems. Thus the Pact would probably commit few bombers against port facilities early in a war. If the Pact achieved air superiority in Western Europe, and if a large part of its bomber force remained, a systematic bombing campaign against ports could be initiated. In a theater nuclear war, the Soviets also would interdict shipping by missile and air strikes on ports in Western Europe and, in an intercontinental war, those in North America as well.

149. Pact intentions for using mines to interdict merchant shipping are not clear. While some Soviet submarines may have a wartime mission to lay mines in restricted water such as in the approaches to a few key NATO ports, they would not have the capability to mine large areas of the North Atlantic littoral densely and still perform other missions. Soviet surface ships and aircraft would be unable to lay and replenish minefields effectively in areas of NATO air superiority.

Amphibious Capabilities

150. The Soviets have some 6,000 men in their Naval Infantry forces opposite NATO. The basic unit is the naval rifle regiment, totaling about 1,900 men in three infantry battalions, a tank battalion, and supporting units. Three regiments have been identified, one in each western fleet area. The Naval Infantry depends heavily on its tanks and armored vehicles, but is constituted primarily for mobility rather than for firepower. Its tasks are to spearhead amphibious assaults against mainland and island beachheads and to attack in the rear of enemy formations—in both cases in support of the ground campaign. In some cases, Naval Infantry units would be immediately reinforced from the sea by ground forces trained for follow-up amphibious landings.

151. The amphibious elements of NSWP countries would be available to augment the Soviet Naval Infantry forces. In the Black Sea area, the combined strength of the Soviet, Bulgarian, and Romanian amphibious forces total some 4,400 men. However, the Bulgarian and Romanian elements are not nearly as well trained as their Soviet counterparts and do not have sufficient lift capacity to carry all of their men and equipment in a single assault operation. These countries do not usually engage in combined amphibious exercises with the Soviets. In the Baltic, however, where large combined operations recently have occurred, the Soviets, Poles, and East Germans have the equivalent of four naval infantry regiments totaling some 8,000 men. Although the Polish and East German Navies are capable of transporting less than half of their assault troops in a single lift, turnaround time for subsequent lifts could be rapid.

152. Control of the airspace over an amphibious landing area in Europe would be a prerequisite for establishing a beachhead. Because the majority of likely Warsaw Pact amphibious objectives would be within the range of Soviet or East European airfields, land-based tactical aircraft could be made available to support the assault forces. The Soviet Fitter C/D regiment in the Baltic Fleet Air Force and some 50 MIG-17 Frescos of the Polish Navy probably would support Pact amphibious operations in the Baltic Sea.

D. Theater Nuclear Forces

153. Pact nuclear weapons which could be employed in a theater war against NATO are of two distinct types: tactical nuclear weapons in the hands of Soviet general purpose forces and Soviet strategic nuclear weapons.

Tactical Nuclear Forces

154. Since the late 1960s the tactical forces have especially experienced important changes in both size and capabilities. (See figure II-25.) These changes have included:

— Significant increases in the inventory of tactical nuclear delivery systems in Europe. The expansion has already included about a one-third increase in the number of tactical surface-to-surface missile launchers and a tripling of nuclear delivery aircraft in Central Europe since 1970.

— Increases in the number of tactical nuclear weapons the Soviets plan to use in Central Europe. Nuclear weapons allocations that we have noted in exercises conducted by the critical Central Front have tripled.

— Increases in the warhead yields of tactical surface-to-surface missiles. The motivation for the larger yields is unclear, but the Soviets may perceive a requirement for greater areas of destruction to compensate for the relatively poor

Warsaw Pact Tactical Nuclear Forces Opposite NATO, 1969 and 1979

Figure II-25

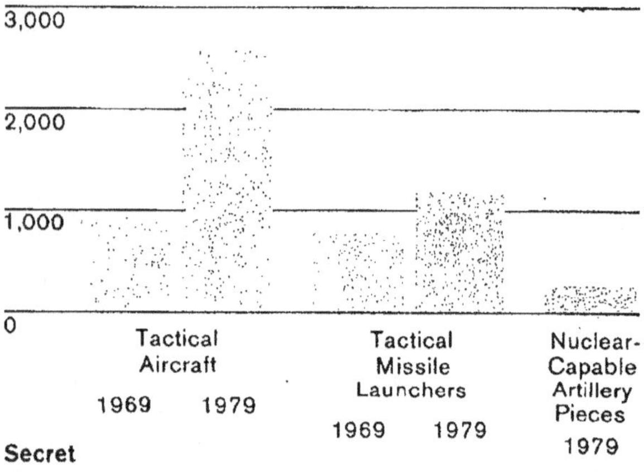

[Bar chart showing Tactical Aircraft, Tactical Missile Launchers (1969 and 1979), and Nuclear-Capable Artillery Pieces (1979)]

Secret

577633 1-79 CIA

Table II-10

Warsaw Pact Tactical Nuclear Forces Opposite NATO*
January 1979

	In Eastern Europe Soviet	In Eastern Europe NSWP	In the USSR	Total
Tactical Aircraft				
Fighters	765	—	580	1,345
Fighter-Bombers	450	135	650	1,235
Light Bombers	30	—	30	60
Total	1,245	135	1,260	2,640
Tactical Missile Launchers				
FROG	125	185	260	570
SS-1/Scud	150	125	240	515
SS-12/Scaleboard (includes SS-22)	—	—	72	72
SS-21	—	—	6	6
Total	275	310	578	1,163
Nuclear Artillery				
203-mm SP Guns/Towed Gun-Howitzers	—	—	144	144
240-mm SP Mortars/Towed Mortars	—	—	144	144
Total	—	—	288	288

* See footnote to table II-1, following paragraph 3.

accuracy of their current missile systems and the lack of timely, accurate reconnaissance data on small, mobile targets.

— Development and deployment of a new generation of tactical nuclear delivery systems with characteristics superior to those of their predecessors. Newer models of Soviet tactical aircraft have greatly improved range and payload capabilities, and more effective tactical surface-to-surface missiles are being deployed.

155. The Soviets have a variety of tactical nuclear delivery systems in their ground and tactical air forces deployed opposite NATO. (See table II-10.) Nuclear weapons are also carried by many of the Soviet Navy's general purpose ships, submarines, and aircraft.

156. The Soviets have given their East European allies reason to believe that they will be provided nuclear weapons in wartime. The NSWP national commands, particularly the Polish and Czechoslovak commands, evidently train and plan for the eventuality that they will receive nuclear warheads in wartime. Fronts commanded by non-Soviets have also been notionally allocated nuclear weapons in recent Pact exercises. In addition, we have information that NSWP war plans may include procedures for the transfer of Soviet nuclear warheads to NSWP missile units. Thus, while we have no direct evidence regarding Soviet intentions, we judge that NSWP tactical aircraft and missiles, as shown in table II-10, are likely to be used for nuclear operations in Europe.

157. *Tactical Aircraft.* Numerically, the most important nuclear delivery systems in Eastern Europe are Soviet tactical aircraft. Virtually all Soviet fighter and fighter-bomber units in Eastern Europe conduct training and exercise activities which indicate a mission of delivering nuclear bombs. As of 1975, however, only about one-third of the pilots in these Soviet units were qualified by Soviet standards to drop nuclear bombs. We expect that the number of Soviet tactical air units in the USSR which have nuclear missions will increase as the Soviets continue to reequip units with new, nuclear-capable aircraft.

158. The role of Frontal Aviation for delivering tactical nuclear weapons is expanding.

159. *Tactical Missiles.* Ground force nuclear delivery systems consist mainly of the FROG, Scud, and Scaleboard missiles. (See figure II-26.) The Soviets have 31 FROG battalions with some 125 launchers and 11 Scud brigades with 150 launchers in Eastern Europe. They have another 65 FROG battalions (260 launchers) and 20 Scud brigades (240 launchers) in their military districts opposite NATO. The Scud has a range of about 300 km and the FROG about 70 km. No Scaleboard launchers (900-km range) are believed to be located in Eastern Europe, but we estimate that six Scaleboard units with 72 launchers are part of the forces in the USSR earmarked for use against NATO. NSWP forces have 310 FROG and Scud launchers.

160. The Soviets are improving the quality of their tactical ballistic missile forces. The SS-21, a new missile (range of 120 to 130 km) roughly comparable to the US Lance, is now with at least one division in the western USSR. It offers major improvements in range and accuracy over the FROG, which it is replacing.[23] The SS-21 evidently has a cluster-munition warhead in addition to the usual nuclear, chemical, and conventional warheads. A cluster-munition warhead would significantly improve the SS-21's utility during conventional warfare against soft targets such as personnel and equipment in the open or NATO air defense and electronics installations. The SS-22, a replacement missile for the Scaleboard, became operational in 1977 and probably has already been issued to some Scaleboard units in the USSR. It is

---

[23] The circular error probable (CEP) of the SS-21 is estimated to be 200 to 300 meters at two-thirds the maximum range of 120 to 130 kilometers. This is a significant improvement in accuracy over the FROG-7, with a CEP of 400 meters at two-thirds the maximum range of 70 kilometers. CEP is a conventional index of accuracy defined as the radius of the circle centered on the intended target within which there is a 50-percent probability that an arriving missile warhead will fall.

Selected Warsaw Pact Tactical Surface-to-Surface Missiles

Figure II-26

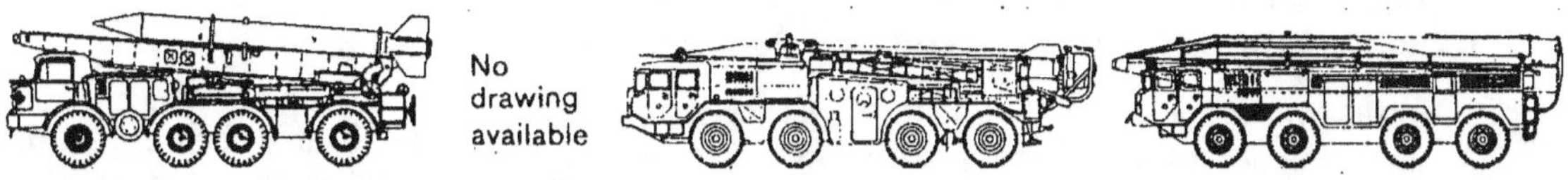

	FROG-7	SS-21	Scud B	SS-12/22 Scaleboard
Year operational	1965	1976	1961	1965/1977
Range (km)				
Minimum	12	10-15	50	200
Maximum	70	120	300	925
Warhead yield (kt)	10	0.5	10	10
	200	10	300	300
		200		500
CEP (m) at two-thirds range*	400	200-300	500-900	700-800/300-400
Propulsion	Single stage-solid	Single stage-solid	Single stage-liquid	Two stage-solid

*CEP (circular error probable) is a conventional index of accuracy defined as the radius of a circle centered on the intended target within which there is a 50-percent probability that an arriving missile warhead will fall.

similar to the Scaleboard missile in range capability but probably has improved accuracy and warheads.

161. *Nuclear Artillery.* The Soviets have 250 to 300 nuclear-capable artillery pieces in their forces in the western USSR. Nuclear-capable 203-mm self-propelled guns and 240-mm self-propelled mortars have been identified in two heavy artillery units there. Five other heavy artillery units there are equipped with obsolete 203-mm and 240-mm weapons. No Soviet heavy artillery units have been identified outside the USSR. There is no reliable evidence that the Soviets have nuclear rounds for their 152-mm artillery pieces—the largest now in the forces in Central Europe.

162. Soviet nuclear artillery developments suggest that the expanded use of Frontal Aviation is regarded as only a partial solution to the problems of providing close-in nuclear support to Pact ground forces. Soviet writings have long acknowledged that, because NATO's nuclear-capable artillery would be deployed close to the battleline, Pact artillery fire would be the most effective and responsive means for destroying it.

163. *Naval Forces.* All fleets in the Soviet Navy are also equipped with nuclear-capable weapon systems for use in theater warfare. Virtually all of the USSR's operational submarines carry [   ] nuclear torpedoes, and at least half of the missiles on board Soviet cruise-missile submarines are equipped with nuclear warheads. This loading reflects the Soviet belief that, although war could begin conventionally in Europe, it would be fought under constant threat of escalation to the use of nuclear weapons.

164. During the conventional phase of hostilities, about a third of the Navy's strike aircraft probably would be held in reserve for nuclear operations. Several Soviet writers also have indicated that a "large" reserve of submarines and nuclear-capable surface ships might be withheld until the transition to nuclear war. The Soviets evidently see the risk of escalation to nuclear war to be so high that they are willing to sacrifice a substantial degree of their nonnuclear capabilities to be prepared for the more serious nuclear war contingency.

165. *Soviet Nuclear Weapons Storage Sites in Eastern Europe.* There are 23 Soviet storage sites in Eastern Europe, at least some of which almost certainly contain nuclear weapons. Eleven of them are located at Soviet tactical airfields, and 12 are isolated installations for the storage of warheads for tactical missiles and rockets. (See figure II-27.) it is also believed unlikely that these installations, with their extensive security, high-quality support facilities, and in most instances apparently continuous occupation by Soviet troops, would be maintained simply as future staging points for warheads moved from the USSR in time of tension or after a conflict began. We do not believe that the NSWP countries operate or control any of the nuclear storage sites in Eastern Europe.

166. There is no firm evidence regarding the mix of weapons stored in these bunkers, the portion of the interior space used for storage, or that reserved for warhead assembly, maintenance, and checkout.

167. Depending on the type stored and storage practice, the storage sites in Eastern Europe could hold a total of 370 to 1,070 tactical nuclear bombs, and 1,700 to 2,900 FROG and Scud warheads. Table II-11 contains the range of estimates of storage capacity.

168. There is no firm evidence on Pact requirements for tactical nuclear warheads and bombs in Central Europe. It seems clear, however, that the Soviets currently consider their requirements to be higher than those envisioned by Pact planners as late

as 1969 or 1970.

169. Missile warhead storage capacity in Central Europe appears adequate, provided the higher estimates of capacity are correct, but bomb storage capacity appears to be insufficient to satisfy the requirements for tactical nuclear operations
Soviets are estimated to have storage capacity for only 200 to 605 bombs in East Germany, 70 to 185 in Poland, and 30 to 95 in Czechoslovakia. They probably plan to move additional bombs and warheads into the forward area from the numerous tactical nuclear weapons storage sites in the western USSR before or during hostilities.

Soviet Peripheral Strike Forces [24]

170. For strategic forces the most significant developments have been the deployment of the Backfire bomber and the SS-20 intermediate-range ballistic missile. The Backfire is well suited for the peripheral strike mission and greatly improves the payload and penetration capabilities of Soviet bomber forces targeted against NATO. The mobile SS-20 force, when fully deployed, will have greater survivability and destructive power than the present peripheral missile force.

171. Elements of all the Soviet strategic attack forces—the Strategic Rocket Forces (SRF), Long Range Aviation (LRA), and the Soviet Navy—have the mission of carrying out nuclear strikes against NATO targets. (See table II-12.) These include medium- and intermediate-range ballistic missiles (SS-4 MRBMs, SS-5 and SS-20 IRBMs), LRA bombers (Badger, Blinder, Backfire), and ballistic missile submarines (G-class and H-class). Only a relatively small portion of the USSR's ICBMs and modern ballistic missile submarines would be likely to be used to strike targets in NATO Europe, and the 150 strike-configured Bear and Bison bombers in LRA are intended mainly for intercontinental missions.

172. *Medium- and Intermediate-Range Ballistic Missiles.* The major portion of the land-based ballistic missile force that would be employed for peripheral attack consists of 416 SS-4 MRBM and 80 SS-5 IRBM launchers located at 54 complexes in the European and south-central USSR. (See figure II-28.) This force includes 118 silo launchers and 378 aboveground launchers with fixed launch pads, a mode of deployment which makes them vulnerable to attack. Of these launchers, 445 are believed to be aimed against NATO and other targets on the western periphery of the USSR. The remaining 51 launchers probably are for use against targets in Asia and the Middle East.

[24] This section summarizes the current status of Soviet peripheral strategic forces intended for use against NATO. A more detailed description of the deployment patterns and technical characterisitics of these systems is contained in NIE 11-6-78, *Soviet Strategic Forces for Peripheral Attack.*

Top Secret

Potential Target Coverage of SS-20

Figure II-28b

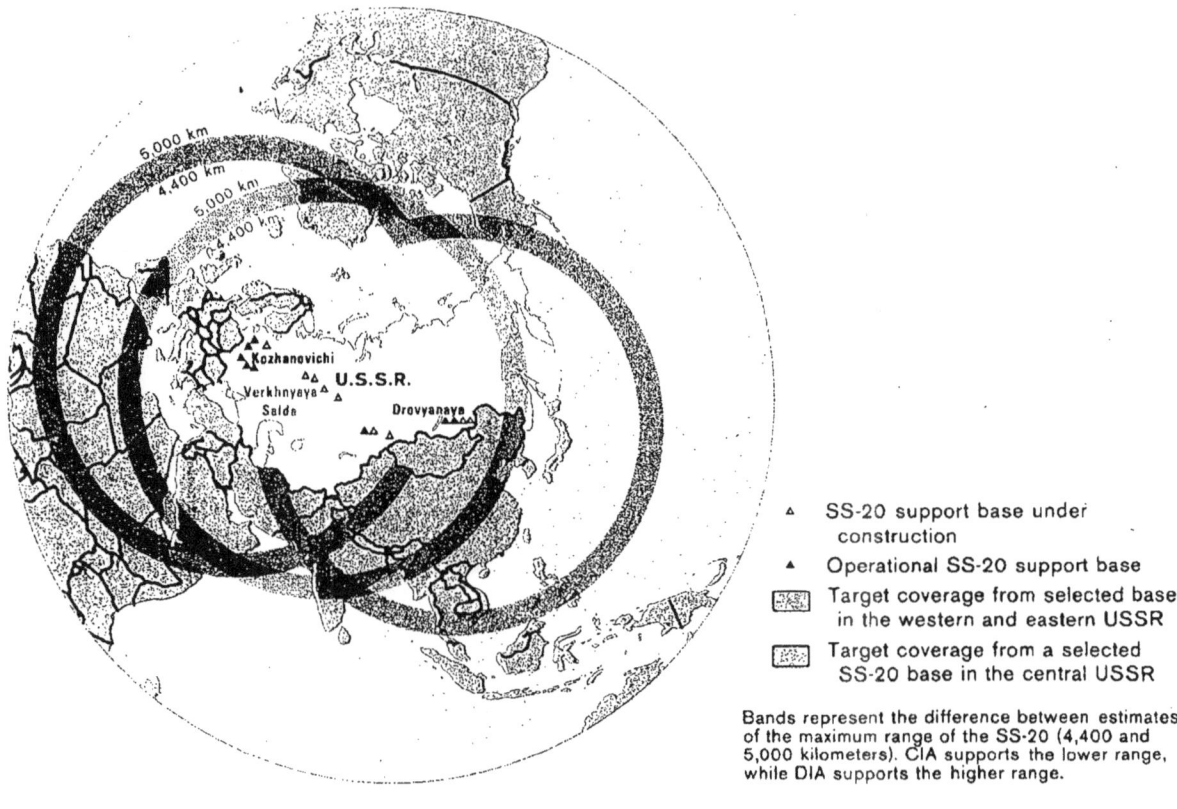

- △ SS-20 support base under construction
- ▲ Operational SS-20 support base
- ▨ Target coverage from selected bases in the western and eastern USSR
- ▨ Target coverage from a selected SS-20 base in the central USSR

Bands represent the difference between estimates of the maximum range of the SS-20 (4,400 and 5,000 kilometers). CIA supports the lower range, while DIA supports the higher range.

Estimated Characteristics of Soviet MRBMs and IRBMs

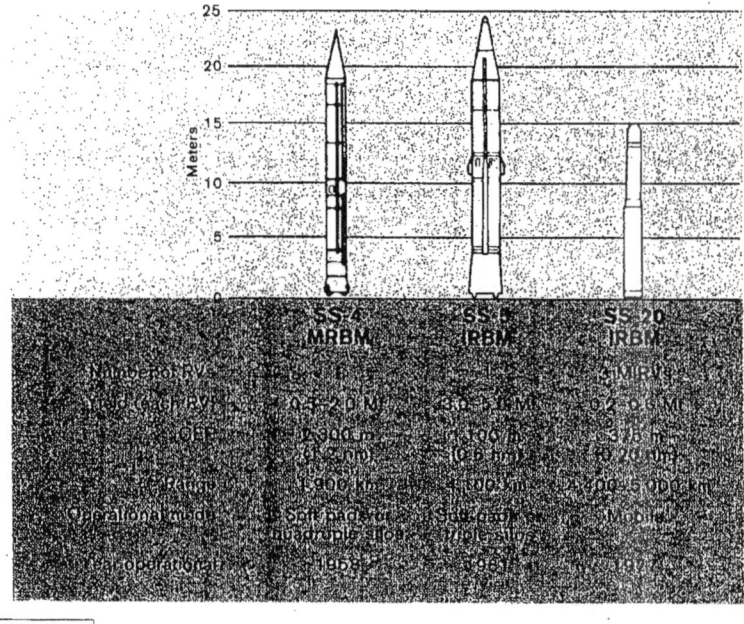

II-51

Top Secret

Table II-12

Soviet Strategic Attack Forces Intended Chiefly for Use Against NATO
January 1979

Land-Based Missiles (Launchers)	
SS-4 MRBM	384
SS-5 IRBM	61
SS-20 IRBM	45-63 *
Total	490-508
Long Range Aviation Bombers	
TU-16 Badger	325
TU-22 Blinder	155
Backfire	45
Total	525
Submarine-Launched Ballistic Missiles (Submarines/Launchers)	
G-I SSB	1/3
G-II SSB	6/18
H-II SSBN	4/12
Total	11/33

* Range reflects uncertainty about the operational status of two SS-20 bases.

173. The latest land-based ballistic missile to be deployed for theater use is the SS-20 IRBM system. This system is mobile, a characterisitic that significantly reduces its vulnerability. It carries three multiple, independently targetable reentry vehicles (MIRVs), a payload that allows more targets to be attacked with fewer missiles. It uses solid propellants and has better accuracy, reaction time, and refire capabilities than the SS-4 and SS-5. The better survivability and refire capability of the SS-20 system as compared with the SS-4 and SS-5 will significantly increase the firepower and flexibility of the Soviet peripheral strike forces. The reduced vulnerability of the SS-20 missiles could also lessen the Soviet incentive to launch them preemptively to prevent their destruction by a NATO first strike.

174. We expect that eventually the SS-20 will replace the SS-4s and SS-5s and that, by the early 1980s, it will be the mainstay of the land-based ballistic missile force for peripheral use.

175. *Intercontinental Ballistic Missiles.* The Soviets have about 1,400 ICBM launchers, some of which could be brought to bear against peripheral targets if necessary. In the late 1960s, they built 120 SS-11 launchers which were oriented so as to provide better coverage of West European and Middle Eastern targets. Although these missiles have since been replaced with newer systems, the Soviets may continue to allocate some of the ICBM force to peripheral targets. All the USSR's new ICBMs have the capability to be launched in nearly any direction and probably can be retargeted rapidly. In addition, all but the SS-18 ICBM have been tested at reduced ranges.

176. *Intermediate-Range Bombers.* The LRA intermediate-range bombers can perform a variety of missions in peripheral areas, including delivery of conventional and nuclear weapons, reconnaissance, and electronic warfare. These aircraft provide the Soviets with a mission flexibility that is not available with either land- or sea-based missile forces. The LRA intermediate-range bomber force based opposite NATO now consists of about 155 Blinders and 325 Badgers. This represents about 75 percent of the total Soviet intermediate-range bomber force. About 65 of the Blinders carry the AS-4 air-to-surface missile and do not have a bombing capability. About 15 of the remaining 90 Blinders are specially configured for reconnaissance and have no capability for weapons delivery, and another 15 are used as trainers. About 170 Badgers opposite NATO are equipped with AS-5 or AS-6 missiles but can also be used as free-fall bombers. (See figure II-29.) The rest of the Badgers opposite NATO, with the exception of about 10 that are configured as tankers, have only a free-fall bombing capability or are configured for electronic support or reconnaissance missions.

177. Since the late 1960s, the Soviets have been working to improve the capabilities of the air-to-surface missiles carried by their bombers. In 1970 they deployed the AS-6, a missile superior to the older AS-5 in both range and speed. All Badger units have since been equipped with the AS-6, although some AS-5s remain in service. The Soviets have also developed a guidance system that permits their AS-4, AS-5, and AS-6 missiles to home on radar signals and thus suppress enemy air defenses. The Badger, which accounts for about two-thirds of the force, entered service some 25 years ago and has not been produced since 1959. The Blinder, a design of the late 1950s, began to enter the force in 1962 and went out of production in 1969. Nevertheless, the Soviets are seeking to extend the useful life of those aircraft by equipping them with improved missiles and converting some to conduct electronic warfare. They clearly

178. *Backfire.* Late in 1974 the Soviets began deployment of the Backfire to both Long Range Aviation and Soviet Naval Aviation units in the western USSR. This latest Soviet bomber has a combat radius and payload capacity that exceeds existing Soviet intermediate-range bombers. It is well suited for strikes against strategic targets on the periphery of the USSR. It has swingwings which enable it to cruise at supersonic speeds a higher altitudes and at high subsonic speeds at low altitudes. It is equipped with ECM equipment to facilitate penetration of modern air defenses. On a high-speed, low-level penetration mission, the Backfire would be able to take off from a base in the interior of the USSR with the flexibility to strike a greater number of more distant targets in Europe, Asia, and Africa than either the Badger or Blinder. The Backfire can carry either conventional or nuclear bombs or AS-4 ASMs. There are about 45 Backfires operational within LRA in the western USSR, and another 40 are operational in SNA. Backfires are being produced at a rate of between two and three per month.

179. According to one view in the Intelligence Community, the performance characteristics, deployment patterns, training programs, and exercise participation of the Backfire, as well as Soviet statements concerning it, point to peripheral strike as its primary mission.[25] According to another view, the Backfire is a long-range bomber with the capability to strike US targets on unrefueled range and radius missions. The holders of this view agree that the aircraft will have significant peripheral missions, but they would note that the Soviets have the option to use the Backfire's intercontinental capabilities at their own initiative. Thus, in their view, the Backfire poses a significant threat to the contiguous United States as well as to areas on the Soviet periphery.[26] (For differing views of the Backfire's unrefueled combat radius and of the areas it could strike on unrefueled radius missions from current deployment bases, see figure II-30.)

---

[25] *The holders of this view are the Central Intelligence Agency; the Director, Bureau of Intelligence and Research, Department of State; the Director, National Security Agency; and the Director of Naval Intelligence, Department of the Navy.*

[26] *The holders of this view are the Director, Defense Intelligence Agency; the Assistant Chief of Staff for Intelligence, Department of the Army; and the Assistant Chief of Staff, Intelligence, Department of the Air Force. The performance of the Backfire is addressed at greater length in NIE 11-3/8-78, Soviet Capabilities for Strategic Nuclear Conflict Through the Late 1980s.*

180. *Long-Range Bombers.* The Soviets could strike peripheral targets with their Bear and Bison bombers even though they are intended primarily for intercontinental operations. Use of these aircraft would enable the Soviets to attack distant targets, particularly naval task forces at sea. During exercises, LRA Bears have simulated such antiship strikes. About 70 of the 105 Bears assigned to LRA are armed with air-to-surface missiles and most of the remainder with free-fall bombs. Of the 82 Bisons in LRA, about 30 are equipped as tanker aircraft, while the rest are free-fall bombers. We also have evidence that a development program is under way to equip Bears to carry bombs or two AS-4s or AS-6s instead of a single AS-3.

181. *Ballistic Missile Submarines.* The peripheral strike forces of the Soviet Navy consist of 22 G- and H-class ballistic missile submarines, of which 11 are probably targeted against NATO. (See figure II-31.) The G- and H-class submarines initially served as part of the Soviet intercontinental attack force, but by the mid-1970s the availability of newer, more modern submarines allowed the Soviets to begin relieving these older units of their intercontinental mission. Recent patrol patterns suggest that almost all operational G- and H-class ballistic missile submarines have shifted to peripheral attack missions.

182. In 1976, the Soviets transferred six G-II class submarines from the Northern Fleet to the Liepaja Naval Base on the Baltic Sea—the first deployment of ballistic missile submarines to that operating area. From Liepaja, G-II class submarines fitted with their 800-nm SS-N-5 missiles could cover targets in West Germany, the Benelux countries, and Scandinavia without leaving local waters. By moving to the area off the coast of Poland, they could extend missile coverage to include much of the United Kingdom, France, and Italy. Operations in the Baltic would be more secure than in the Norwegian Sea, inasmuch as NATO countries have only a few ASW forces in the Baltic, and Soviet naval and air forces could offer protection for the submarines. There are four H-class SSBNs based in the Soviet Northern Fleet. It would take these units four days to deploy to a position where their SS-N-5 missiles would be within range of West European targets. For this purpose, however, they would have to transit around Norway and would be vulnerable to detection by Western ASW forces.

183. The G- and H-class submarines add a degree of flexibility to the strategic forces for peripheral strike and their mobility makes them considerably less vulnerable than the fixed, land-based missile systems.

Characteristics of Soviet Intermediate-Range Bombers

Figure II-29a

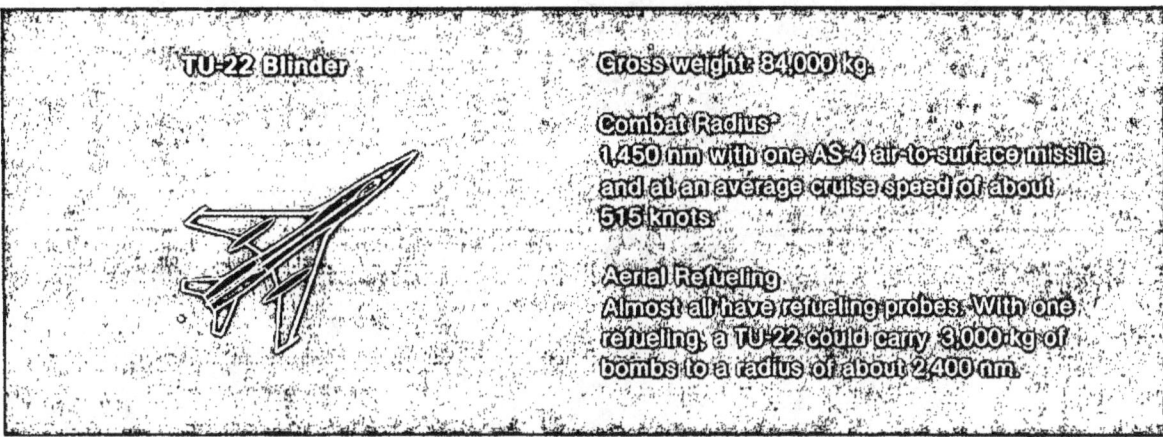

TU-16 Badger

Gross weight: 76,000 kg.

Combat Radius*
1,200 nm with two AS-5 or 900 nm with two AS-6 air-to-surface missiles and at an average cruise speed of about 445 knots.

Aerial Refueling
About 100 are capable of being refueled in flight. With one refueling, a TU-16 could carry 3,000 kg of bombs to a radius of about 2,300 nm.

TU-22 Blinder

Gross weight: 84,000 kg.

Combat Radius*
1,450 nm with one AS-4 air-to-surface missile and at an average cruise speed of about 515 knots.

Aerial Refueling
Almost all have refueling probes. With one refueling, a TU-22 could carry 3,000 kg of bombs to a radius of about 2,400 nm.

There are only about 20 aircraft configured as tankers in the intermediate-range bomber force. In the past, the Soviets have made little use of this limited capability; in the case of the TU-22, aerial refueling has rarely been noted.

*Based on subsonic flight at optimum cruise altitude. For jet aircraft, a general rule is that each mile flown at altitudes of 300 meters or less reduces combat radius by about 2 miles. For example an aircraft with a combat radius of 1,000 nm could fly only 600 nm if required to fly at an altitude of 100 meters for 200 nm (1,000−[2x200]=600); the first 400 nm would be flown at high-altitude cruise and the remaining 200 nm at low level.

Characteristics of Selected Soviet Air-to-Surface Missiles for Use Against Land Targets

Figure II-29b

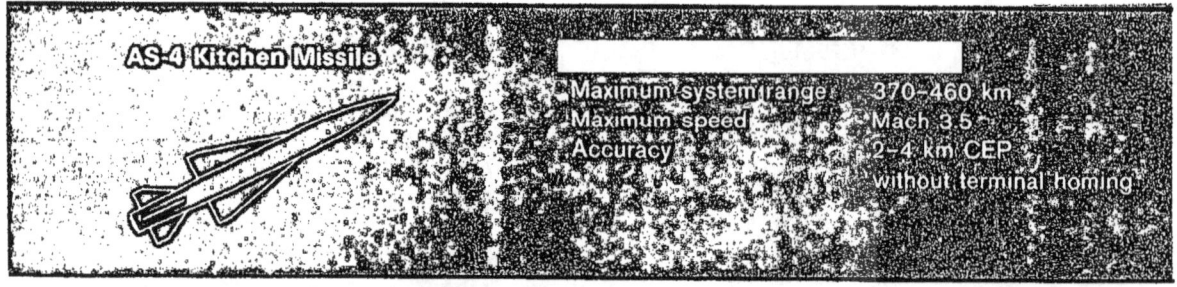

AS-4 Kitchen Missile
- Maximum system range: 370–460 km
- Maximum speed: Mach 3.5
- Accuracy: 2–4 km CEP without terminal homing

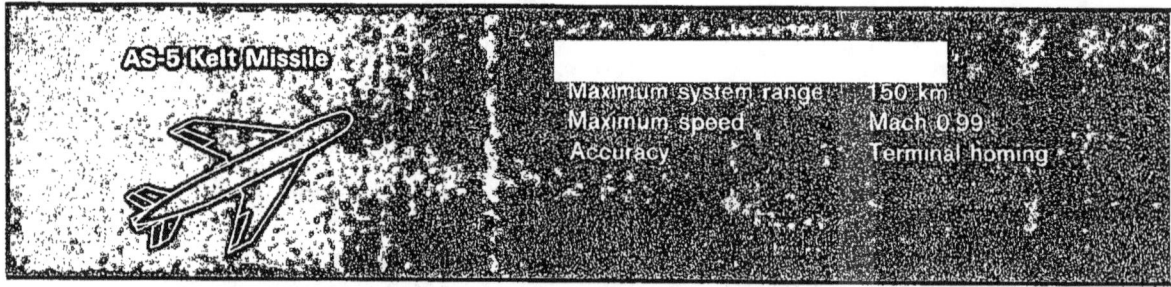

AS-5 Kelt Missile
- Maximum system range: 150 km
- Maximum speed: Mach 0.99
- Accuracy: Terminal homing

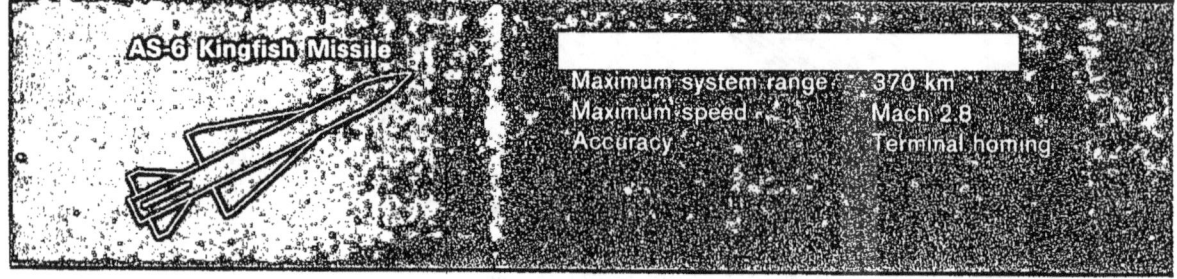

AS-6 Kingfish Missile
- Maximum system range: 370 km
- Maximum speed: Mach 2.8
- Accuracy: Terminal homing

Assessments of Backfire's Capability Against Peripheral Targets

Figure II-30a

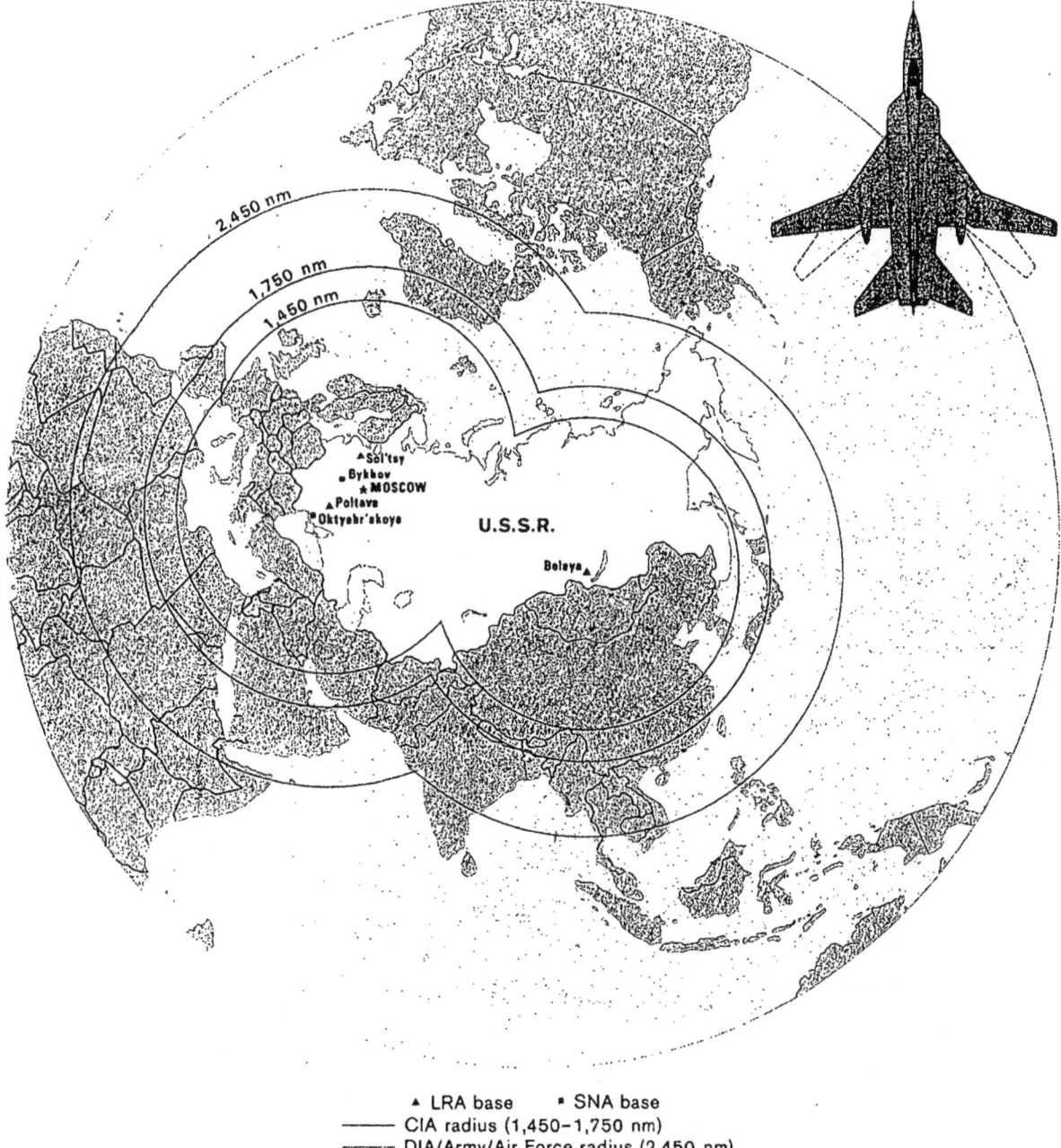

▲ LRA base   ■ SNA base
—— CIA radius (1,450–1,750 nm)
- - - DIA/Army/Air Force radius (2,450 nm)

Note: These assessments assume that the Backfire flies a straight-line unrefueled mission with bombs, is on an optimum high-altitude flight profile to and from the vicinity of the target area, but flies the last 200 nm to and from the target at a subsonic speed at low level. The figures cited here are different from those representing the subsonic, high-altitude missions depicted in figure II-30b.

Differing Agency Assessments of the Backfire

Figure II-30b

Estimated Characteristics [a][b]	DIA/Army/Air Force		CIA	
Weights—kg (lb$_m$)				
Structural Weight	33,500	(73,800)	33,700	(74,270)
Operational Empty Weight	52,400	(115,500)	50,800	(112,000)
Fuel Weight, Bombing Mission	68,000	(150,000)	51,700	(114,000)
Payload Weight, Bombing Mission	9,400	(20,800)	4,500	(10,000)
Takeoff Gross Weight	130,900	(288,500)	107,000	(236,000)
Propulsion				
Installed Intermediate Sea-Level Thrust—kN (lb$_f$)	120	(27,000)	105	(23,500)
Installed Maximum Afterburner Sea-Level Thrust—kN (lb$_f$)	210	(47,000)	145	(32,500)
Cruise Specific Fuel Consumption (lb$_m$/lb$_f$-hr)	0.93		1.04	

	DIA/Army/Air Force	CIA Optimized Aerodynamic Design [c]	CIA Compromised Aerodynamic Design [c]
Aerodynamics			
Cruise Lift-to-Drag Ratio	16.6	16.3	13.9
Cruise Speed—Mach	0.79	0.80	0.80
Mission Performance Unrefueled—nm [d]			
All-High, Bomber, Radius/Range	2,900/5,400 [e]	2,150/4,150	1,825/3,525
All-High, 2 ASMs, Radius/Range	2,600/4,500	1,650/2,900	1,400/2,425
200 nm Sea-Level Dash, Bomber, Radius/Range [f]	2,450/4,950	1,750/3,750	1,450/3,125
200 nm Sea-Level Dash, 2 ASMs, Radius/Range [f]	2,200/4,000	1,275/2,525	1,050/2,100
200 nm Supersonic Dash, Bomber, Radius/Range [g]	1,750/3,950	950/3,050	825/2,600
Mission Performance Refueled—nm [d]			
All-High, Bomber, Radius/Range	4,000/7,500 [e]	3,200/6,225	2,825/5,475
All-High, 2 ASMs, Radius/Range	3,750/6,450	2,800/4,950	2,500/4,350
200 nm Sea-Level Dash, Bomber, Radius/Range [f]	3,650/7,050	2,875/5,775	2,525/5,080
200 nm Sea-Level Dash, 2 ASMs, Radius/Range [f]	3,400/6,000	2,500/4,550	2,200/4,000
200 nm Supersonic Dash, Bomber, Radius/Range [g]	2,900/6,050	2,025/5,100	1,825/4,550

[a] This table gives assessments of performance for the Backfire as it is currently configured.

[b] According to one view, it is not possible with the evidence at hand to derive with confidence a single-figure capability for the maximum radius/range of the Backfire. The holders of this view are the Director, National Security Agency, and the Director of Naval Intelligence, Department of the Navy.

[c] The longer range and radius values in the assessment of the Backfire by the Central Intelligence Agency are based on an assumed aerodynamic design which is optimized for subsonic performance, while the shorter range and radius values are based on an assumed compromised design. CIA has considered both designs because they represent reasonable upper and lower bounds of the Backfire's subsonic cruise efficiency.

[d] The uncertainties in these estimates of the Backfire's performance are as follows: CIA range ±300 nm, radius ±160 nm; DIA/Army/Air Force range +162 nm, −486 nm, radius +87 nm, −261 nm.

[e] The radius/range values of the DIA/Army/Air Force assessment, with a 4,500-kg (10,000-lb) payload, comparable to that used by the CIA assessment, are 2,950/5,750 nm unrefueled.

[f] These radius/range values are for a high-altitude, optimum-cruise profile except for a 200-nm subsonic dash at sea level into the target area. The radius value also includes a 200-nm subsonic dash for egress (400 nm total).

[g] The radius value includes 200 nm for ingress and 200 nm for egress at supersonic speed (400 nm total); the range value includes 200 nm for ingress only.

Characteristics of G-and H-Class Submarines and Their Missiles

Figure II-31

Submarines

G-II-Class

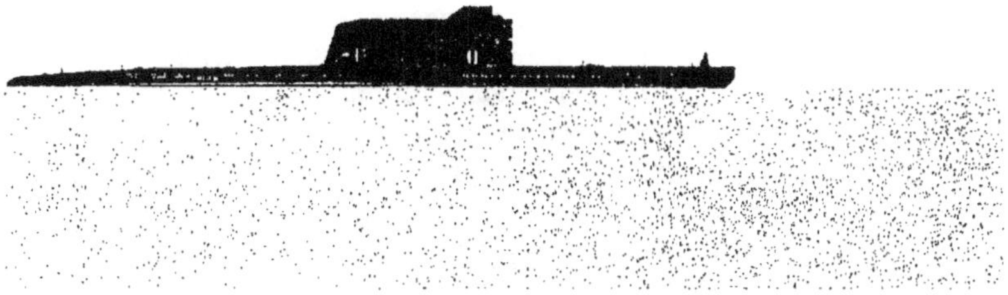

Length	98 meters
Displacement	2,300/2,800 tons
Propulsion	Diesel
Maximum submerged speed	14 knots
Normal transit speed	5 knots
Launch tubes	3
Missile	SS-N-5

H-II-Class

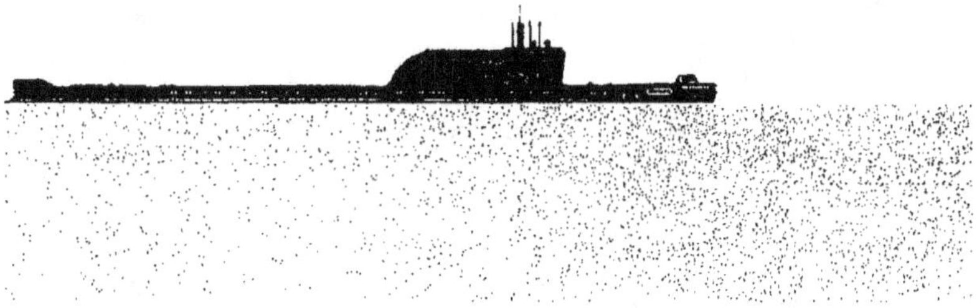

Length	116 meters
Displacement	4,900/5,900 tons
Propulsion	Nuclear
Maximum submerged speed	26 knots
Normal transit speed	12-14 knots
Launch tubes	3
Missile	SS-N-5

Missiles

SS-N-4*

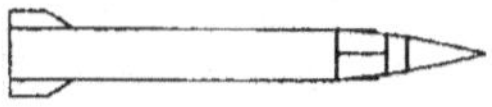

Launch	Surface
Range	550 km
RVs	1
CEP	1,900-3,700 m (1-2 nm)
Platform	G-I

*Only three units of the G-I-class submarines carry the SS-N-4.

SS-N-5

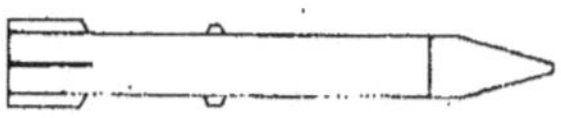

Launch	Submerged
Range	1,300-1,600 km
RVs	1
CEP	1,900-3,700 m (1-2 nm)
Platform	G-II and H-II

Despite these advantages the G- and H-class submarines have several limitations. Both classes are about 20 years old. The patrols of the diesel-powered G-class submarine are limited by fuel requirements. The nuclear-powered H-class submarines are relatively noisy and thus more vulnerable to detection, and their nuclear power plants are not as reliable as those on more modern nuclear submarines.

184. The SLBMs of D- and Y-class submarines could also be used to attack peripheral targets. The Soviets almost certainly have developed contingency plans for use of the SS-N-6 on some Y-class submarines against targets on the periphery of the USSR. The relative importance of the peripheral attack role for these modern SSBNs would probably depend largely upon the circumstances leading up to a conflict and the scenario for its initiation. We cannot, therefore, predict the number of units that might be employed for such missions. We continue to believe, however, that the D- and Y-class force as a whole is dedicated primarily to missions against US targets.

E. Forces for Chemical Warfare

185. The Soviets have had a broad-based R&D program for chemical warfare (CW) since World War II, and they remain in the forefront in CW technical knowledge. Pact forces generally are well equipped and trained to operate in a CBR (chemical, biological, radiological) environment. Pact ground forces have a variety of systems capable of delivering chemical agents which would enable them to cover large areas of the combat zone from the forward edge of the battle area to at least 300 kilometers beyond. Air-dropped munitions provide the potential for large-scale strikes against NATO, especially against enemy nuclear delivery targets. Naval weapon systems also provide a theater chemical warfare capability against ships at sea, points of embarkation, forward storage sites, and amphibious landing operations.

Production

186. No facilities in Warsaw Pact countries have been positively identified as currently producing toxic CW agents in militarily significant quantities, although several in the USSR and in some of the other NSWP countries have historical associations with CW agent production and may still be engaged in this activity. The nature of CW agent production is such that positive identification of production facilities within an industrial chemical complex is virtually impossible without knowledgeable human sources.

187. There is no question that the Soviets and some East Europeans either have produced or are capable of producing toxic agents, inasmuch as their chemical plants are already handling most of the raw materials required to produce these agents. We believe that the Soviet chemical industry can easily handle production sufficient to maintain current Soviet reserves of bulk chemical agents, plus whatever additional quantities are required to replace agents consumed by training and deterioration. The quantities involved are relatively small, and large-scale production of agents would not be necessary.

Stockpile

188. At the present time there are 10 major installations in the USSR believed to be associated with the storage of CW toxic agents, filled munitions, or both. A lack of evidence precludes determining the size or composition of the Soviet CW agent stockpile, however. Because we know that the Soviets have developed a range of toxic agents and delivery systems, and tactical doctrine for their use, and because we have fragmentary evidence on some field depots for chemical storage, we do not doubt that they have operational stocks, including some in Eastern Europe. We believe these include nerve agents such as GB (sarin) and GD (thickened and unthickened soman), as well as older types of agents such as hydrogen cyanide, mustard, and the mustard-lewisite mixture. Research relating to incapacitating agents, such as the hallucinogen BZ and agents closely related to it, is also continuing, but there is no evidence that any agents of this type are stockpiled.

189. Soviet systems for the dissemination of toxic CW agents provide a capability to attack designated targets in almost any tactical or weather situation. The means of delivery include bulk-fill artillery and mortar shells; multiple rail- and tube-launched rockets, chemical mines; warheads for free rockets over ground (FROGs), tactical ballistic missiles, and possibly cruise missiles; aerial bombs and possibly spray tanks; and naval chemical munitions. (See table II-13.)

190. The variety of Soviet chemical agents provides a capability for attacking protected and unprotected troops in the open and for producing a residual contamination on equipment and terrain. Targets in

Table II-13

Selected Warsaw Pact CW Agents and Weapon Systems

Agent	Artillery Munitions (size in millimeters)	Free-Fall Bombs (weight in kilograms)	Rocket Warheads	Missle Warheads
(entry indicates availability of delivery system for agent specified)				
Nerve				
Thickened Soman	—	100	FROG	Scud
Sarin	122, 152	100, 250	BM-21, BM-24	—
Vesicant (Blister)				
Mustard	122, 152	—	—	—
Thickened Mustard	122, 152	—	—	—
Thickened Lewisite	122, 152	—	—	—
Mustard/Lewisite Mixture	—	100, 250, 500, 1,000, 1,500	—	—
Thickened/Mustard/Lewisite Mixture	—	250, 1,000	—	—
Systemic				
Hydrogen Cyanide	—	250, 500	BM-21, BM-24	—

the immediate path of a Soviet advance probably would be attacked with nonpersistent CW agents delivered by tube and rocket artillery and aerial bombs. Some Soviet chemical bombs are fitted with a fuse designed to provide optimum area coverage.

191. Warsaw Pact military writings indicate that fragmentation-chemical shells, which disseminate the liquid agent fill almost entirely as vapor and aerosol in order to cause casualties quickly through inhalation, are to be used with unthickened GB, mustard, and probably GD. Thickened GD is also probably filled in aerial airburst bombs and missile warheads to produce casualties from the toxic "rain" effect. Warheads for the FROG and Scud filled with thickened GD and fused to burst at high altitude are planned to achieve a casualty rate of up to 80 percent among unprotected personnel. The casualties would be caused primarily by skin penetration of the toxic, thickened GD "rain."

192. Rocket artillery would be used to blanket large areas with the nonpersistent agents GB and hydrogen cyanide, the latter where immediate occupation of the area after the attack was desired. The blister agents, mustard and mustard-lewisite mixtures, are contained in aerial and ground munitions fused to airburst for maximum area contamination with the toxic liquid. They would be used against personnel in the open and to contaminate materiel and selected areas of terrain, especially on the axes of defensive operations. Groundbursts of thickened blister agent munitions would be used to achieve very heavy contamination of smaller areas. Chemical mines are usually filled with blister agents and would be used alone or interspersed with antitank or antipersonnel mines.

CBR Training and Equipment

193. Soviet research in chemical, biological, and radiological warfare has been extensive. The Soviets possess large quantities of a wide range of equipment, much of which is of recent design, for use in a toxic environment. Extensive training in its use is integral to military exercises for all Soviet and NSWP ground, naval, and air forces. These same training procedures and protective equipment would enable the Soviets to operate on the offensive as well as on the defensive within the toxic areas of combat. Equipment and training for chemical protection are combined with that for biological or radiological protection, and the special CBR troops are responsible for these three types of activity. At present there are about 60,000 personnel and 8,000 decontamination and 4,000 reconnaissance vehicles assigned to specialized Pact CBR defense units. If all current, active Pact ground, air, and naval units were brought up to full strength, the number of Pact CBR personnel would double.

194. CBR protective equipment supplied to the individual soldier is judged to be adequate to protect him in a toxic environment for a matter of hours or even days, depending on the nature and concentration of the contaminant. The Soviets have developed field protective shelters equipped with ventilation systems providing air from which both toxic particulate matter and toxic vapors have been removed. Air purification systems (filter and positive pressure) are being installed on armored personnel carriers, tanks, and some trucks. The Soviets have several types of decontamination trucks that can be used for decontamination of men, terrain, and equipment, including clothing and weapons. Agent detector kits and automatic alarms are available in adequate quantities and are capable of rapidly detecting all standard lethal Western and Soviet CW agents. As with other nations, a critical weakness for the USSR is the problem of timely detection of the presence of nerve agents.

195. The Pact has formed CBR defense stations at most of its air regiments to help these forces operate in a contaminated environment. Individual protective equipment and several types of decontamination stations and vehicles for personnel, equipment, and aircraft have also been deployed at most major airbases. Routine training is conducted in CBR defense—training which includes alerts and exercises.

196. Some classes of Soviet naval ships have been equipped with positive-pressure citadels and filtered ventilation systems to permit them to operate in a CBR environment. Soviet naval ships have wash-down systems to enable them to remove CBR contamination. Some classes of merchant vessels and landing ships have also been constructed with CBR protective systems.

F. Forces for Electronic Warfare

197. In the Soviet concept, electronic warfare is a fundamental part of overall planning and must be integrated into all phases of combat operations. In the early 1970s, a radioelectronic combat (REC) department was created within the Staff of the Combined Armed Forces of the Pact to promote electronic warfare and to ensure standardization of equipment and procedures among the Pact armies.

Forces

200. Over the past decade the Soviets have initiated a broad series of programs to modernize and expand their already significant offensive and defensive capabilities for REC in the European theater. Some of these programs are still at an early stage of development, however, and will not be completed before the mid-to-late 1980s. In addition, the Pact is seeking to improve its organization, procedures, and performance of REC units, and the abilities of Pact ground, air, and naval forces to operate under jamming conditions.

Capabilities

206. We are unable to determine the extent to which the equipment of Pact jamming units meets Soviet standards, but the Soviets have stated that production of newer systems is lagging. The bulk of the jamming equipment currently deployed represents

technology of the 1950s and the early 1960s. More modern equipment first appeared in the early 1970s, but representative models of this more advanced equipment are only now appearing in the Pact, primarily in Soviet units. Several types of new equipment will not be deployed fully until the mid-1980s.

this regard dates from the early 1970s. We have no way to judge the soundness of these Pact planning factors in a future war as they relate to the attrition rates for equipment and the consumption rates of expendables such as ammunition.

Our estimates of the levels of supplies are based on calculations of the capacities of identified storage facilities, adjusted to take loading factors into account.

Ground Forces

210. ***Doctrine.*** Pact logistic doctrine, based almost exclusively on Soviet principles, specifies stock levels to be maintained at each echelon. (See table II-15.) The adequacy of supplies for a given period of time would depend on the intensity and duration of combat as well as Pact capabilities to begin replenishment.

211. Pact logistic doctrine specifies that additional stocks are to be kept in the theater and in the national reserve to supply the fronts. In particular, responsibility for ensuring the flow of these supplies in wartime is assigned to the commander of the higher echelon from or through which they are to flow. In all cases of supply movement, ammunition has priority because it is critical to combat.

212. ***Ammunition Stocks.*** We believe ammunition stocks are maintained at the various echelons within the Pact as shown in table II-15. Some 600 ground force ammunition depots have been identified in Eastern Europe and in the USSR west of the Urals. We have calculated Pact ground force ammunition stocks in these depots

G. Warsaw Pact Logistics

209. Warsaw Pact exercises, classified writings, and other evidence indicate that the Pact is planning logistic support for a series of short campaigns of high intensity, involving the rapid achievement of a breakthrough and advance to strategic objectives in the NATO rear. Warsaw Pact logistic planning factors are evidently based on Soviet World War II experience, and updated in accordance with changes in tactics, force structure, and equipment. Our information in

Table II-15

Days of Supply for Warsaw Pact Ground Force Echelons

Division	3-5 days
Army	2 days
Front Forward	4 days
Front Rear	10 days
Total	19-21 days

SECRET

Table II-16

Calculations of Warsaw Pact Ammunition Stocks Based on Depot Capacities
January 1979

	Ammunition (metric tons)
Czechoslovakia	420,000
East Germany	435,000
Poland	460,000
Total	1,315,000
Baltic Military District	100,000
Belorussian Military District	140,000
Carpathian Military District	115,000
Total	355,000
Hungary	220,000
Bulgaria	130,000
Romania	300,000
Total	650,000
Opposite NATO Flanks [a]	810,000
Strategic Reserves [b] (West of Urals)	2,200,000

[a] Includes stocks in the Leningrad, Odessa, Kiev, North Caucasus, and Transcaucasus Military Districts.
[b] Includes stocks in the Moscow, Ural, and Volga Military Districts.

SECRET

213. The Soviets estimate that a front would require 120,000 to 150,000 metric tons of ammunition in a nonnuclear offensive operation lasting 12 to 15 days.[28] These amounts are intended to allow not only for expenditures, but also for reestablishing the required reserves and replacing combat losses in preparation for subsequent operations. In such a 12- to 15-day operation, for example, ammunition requirements for a three-front operation against NATO's Central Region would range from 360,000 to 450,000 tons.

214. Calculated ammunition stocks in the forward area exceed the requirements for a single three-front operation and thus would support subsequent operations. The stocks in the three western military districts are probably sufficient to support the reinforcing effort of two second-echelon fronts, consisting of as many as 29 divisions. Additional ammunition for operations against NATO could be made available from strategic reserves located west of the Ural Mountains.

215. There is little information on Warsaw Pact ammunition estimates for a protracted conflict in which the Pact fails to make a breakthrough and NATO maintains a cohesive defense. Ammunition expenditures would probably be greater than in a successful Warsaw Pact attack, at least initially, and could surge to 50,000 tons a day during periods of high-intensity combat or reach a daily average of 35,000 to 40,000 tons over a more prolonged period. At this daily average rate of expenditure, and assuming no destruction of stocks, we calculate that there would be sufficient ammunition in the Central Region and the three western military districts of the USSR to sustain Pact forces for 40 to 50 days. It should be noted that this period could be lengthened considerably by drawing ammunition from the strategic reserve stocks in the USSR, particularly those located west of the Urals. Portions of these stocks, which total approximately 2.2 million tons, could be moved forward either in a buildup phase prior to the initiation of hostilities or during a subsequent reinforcement phase after hostilities had begun.

216. **POL.** Our calculations of the levels of Pact POL stocks for military use are less critical to judgments of Pact sustainability than ammunition because the margin of supply over requirements appears to be greater than that for ammunition, and POL production more closely approaches projected consumption. In addition, the use of supplemental civilian POL stocks would almost double available military supplies. Calculated Pact POL stocks opposite Central Europe, based on an assumed 80 percent of estimated capacity, are shown in table II-17.

217. On the basis of Soviet POL consumption factors, we have calculated that five fronts opposite Central Europe consisting of 87 divisions would consume approximately 400,000 tons of POL in an offensive operation lasting 12 to 15 days, well below the estimate of available supplies. Calculated POL stocks

Table II-17

Calculations of Warsaw Pact POL Stocks Opposite Central Europe Based on Depot Capacities
January 1979

	POL (metric tons)
Czechoslovakia	426,000
East Germany	555,000
Poland	514,000
Total	1,495,000
Baltic, Belorussian, and Carpathian Military Districts	2,200,000

SECRET

---
[28] All tonnages in this section are in metric tons.

would probably sustain a force of this size for a period up to three months.

218. *Transportation and Movement.* In a war of short duration and high intensity the ability to sustain the momentum of an advance is determined not only by the availability of stocks but equally by the capability to move supplies, materiel, and personnel forward. The Soviets estimate that in the course of a front operation, as much as 350,000 tons of supplies would be delivered to the front, or an average of about 30,000 tons daily. Deliveries from front to committed armies would amount to about 20,000 tons daily.

219. Soviet plans call for 16,000 of the 20,000 metric tons to be moved by front motor transport. The numbers of trucks available in the Group of Soviet Forces in Germany (GSFG) has been substantially increased in recent years (see figure II-32) and we estimate that, by itself, the GSFG motor transport brigade could lift about 18,000 tons simultaneously. This estimate, however, does not take into account daily losses due to combat attrition, mechanical and human failures, and accidents that would occur in a combat situation. Presumably, the GSFG could acquire additional trucks in an emergency, either by commandeering East German civilian trucks or by bringing mobilized civilian trucks from the USSR.

220. NSWP forces and Soviet forces in the USSR would require large-scale augmentation with civilian trucks in wartime. Category II and III divisions and army- and front-level motor transport units would get most of their trucks this way. All Warsaw Pact countries have plans to call up civilian trucks and drivers on a large scale to reach war footing. Considerable preparations for this are made in peacetime, including prior designation of trucks to be mobilized and military inspections for serviceability. The Soviets evidently have the most elaborate system and have established paramilitary truck units in civilian motor transport establishments to meet their highest priority truck requirements in wartime. Partial tests of the Warsaw Pact truck callup system are conducted in peacetime.

Cargo and POL Lift Capacities of Soviet Divisions, 1969 and 1979

Figure II-32

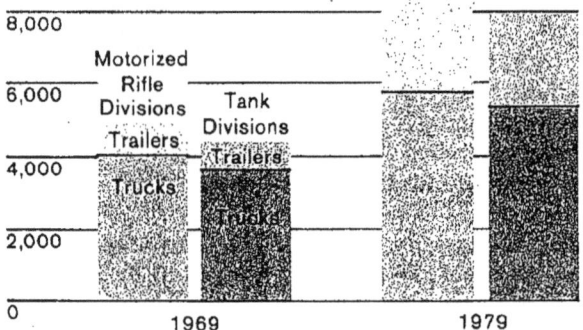

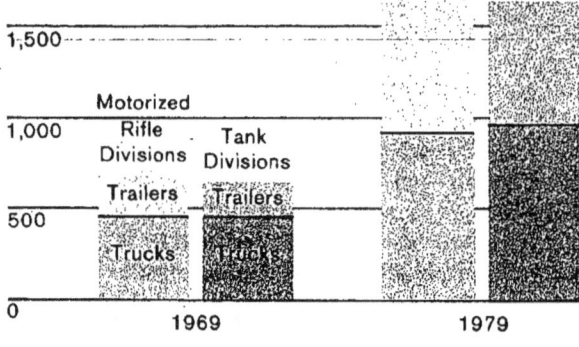

577621 1-79 CIA

We judge, however, that despite weaknesses in the transport system, the Pact would be able to assemble sufficient motor transport to meet its wartime requirements.

221. According to an alternate view,[29] paragraph 220 implies erroneously that there are serious weaknesses in the Pact's wartime motor transport system which are due primarily to the system's reliance on

---

[29] *The holders of this view are the Director, Defense Intelligence Agency, and the Assistant Chief of Staff for Intelligence, Department of the Army.*

mobilization. The holders of this view point out that the fact that Category II and III divisions and nondivisional motor transport units do not have all their cargo vehicles or drivers in peacetime is not unique; all lower category units rely on mobilization. Trucks used in the civilian sector are similar and often identical to their military counterparts. Since the bulk of those vehicles in the USSR designated for mobilization are organized into paramilitary units (*avtokolonnas*), there would be little difficulty in integrating this equipment into military units. Upon mobilization, reservist drivers of these vehicles would be performing duties closely related to their civilian occupation and, in the case of paramilitary transport organizations, for the same supervisors. Thus, the integration of these reservists into motor transport units would be easier than for most other reservists, whose civilian occupations have no corresponding military duties. The holders of this view further point out that analyses of the performance of Soviet motor transport conducted after the 1968 invasion of Czechoslovakia do not support the conclusion that there were serious weaknesses in the system. On the contrary, these analyses concluded that the Soviet invasion of Czechoslovakia demonstrated the adequacy of rear service elements to support large-scale ground force deployments, and that vehicle reliability and maintenance appeared satisfactory. In any event, the number of *avtokolonnas* has increased greatly since 1968 and currently numbers more than 400 in the USSR. Moreover, the quality of trucks assigned has shown a substantial improvement over the same period. The holders of this view agree that there have been some reports of vehicle breakdowns in truck pools in East Germany, Czechoslovakia, and Poland, but would not characterize these reports as widespread. Finally, the holders of this view point out that the implication in paragraph 219 that the GSFG would require commandeered or mobilized trucks is not supported by fact. They point out that since the simultaneous lift capability of the GSFG motor transport brigade exceeds anticipated daily requirements, the lift capability of this organization in normal resupply operations would be adequate to compensate for normal wartime attrition.

222. The Soviets are increasing the lift capabilities of their motor transport units by introducing a new truck, the KamAZ-5320. This vehicle, with an estimated capacity of 8 metric tons, has a 60-percent greater lift capacity than the Ural-375, which it is augmenting in some motor transport units in the forward area.

223. The Soviets also have developed a number of heavy lift regiments using the MAZ-537 prime mover and low-bed semitrailer, the standard tank transporter of the Soviet ground forces. Six heavy lift regiments have been identified in the USSR opposite NATO: four in the western USSR and one each in the Moscow and Odessa Military Districts. These units are capable of transporting all the tanks of five or six tank divisions. They provide a significant capability for the strategic movement of armor by road. The concept, developed at least as early as 1967, was used in the 1968 invasion of Czechoslovakia. Heavy lift regiments increase the alternatives available to Soviet planners, and would add flexibility and speed to any reinforcement of Soviet forces in Eastern Europe.

224. *Transportation Network.* Railroads are the primary means of transportation during mobilization, for long-distance movements. The Pact rail network in Central Europe is dense, totaling about 51,000 kilometers, and, conveniently for military operations, it generally runs east to west. Its centralized control facilitates responsiveness to military requirements. The major through-routes connecting Central Europe and the western USSR have a combined capacity of about 500,000 metric tons per day in each direction. In contrast to the well-established network in Central Europe, the rail networks on the flanks are not nearly as dense or well developed.

225. The highway system in East Germany, Poland, and Czechoslovakia exceeds 430,000 km, and major routes have the capacity to handle nearly 120,000 tons per day. Movement of materiel to a distance less than 300 km probably would be made by road. For movement over greater distances, both rail and road are likely to be used. Movement along the road and rail nets could be substantially reduced if refined petroleum were moved by the pipeline of the Communist European economic community (CEMA). Conversion of the pipeline from crude to refined products would take about one week; thereafter the system would be capable of delivering 55,000 tons of petroleum daily to both East Germany and Czechoslovakia. There is some evidence that Pact logistic planners intend to convert the pipeline in time of war, and it appears to be a feasible contingency measure to supplement existing petroleum supply methods.

226. Pact movement plans are not available to us but, according to a study by the Defense Intelligence Agency, 29 divisons, plus support and supplies, could be moved over the rail and highway system from the western USSR to Central Europe in some 11 to 14 days. These findings are consistent with the judgment elsewhere in this Estimate (chapter IV, paragraph 21)

that the Soviets could have these 29 divisions available for combat in Central Europe in 14 days.

227. *Maintenance.* Pact maintenance support in wartime would be heavily concentrated in front and army units. Although maintenance units exist at division and below, they are austere by Western standards and divisions would be dependent on army and front organizations for much of their maintenance support. Field maintenance units at front and army levels are capable of making extensive repairs. Soviet drivers, especially those assigned to armored vehicles, receive mechanical training and mobile repair teams are available to frontline units. While these resources would enable combat units to make minor repairs in wartime, the concentration of maintenance support above division level would require that most heavily damaged equipment be evacuated to the rear for repair.

228. The Soviets plan their maintenance requirements in wartime according to their assumed combat attrition rates. These rates are calculated on a daily basis for an army engaged in a conventional offensive in which a breakthrough is achieved. Thereafter, the attrition rates are expected to fall sharply. According to classified Soviet writings, the daily rates for an army are approximately as follows:

Artillery and missile launchers	2-3 percent
Tanks	12-15 percent
Armored combat vehicles	6-8 percent
Motor transport vehicles	5-6 percent

229. Within these projected combat losses, the Soviets believe 40 to 50 percent would require light repair, 20 to 25 percent medium repair, and 10 to 15 percent major repair; 20 to 25 percent would be total losses. The Soviets plan to make only light repairs in combat at unit levels below division. Division maintenance facilities would make both light and medium repairs but the bulk of the medium repair work would be accomplished at front-level repair facilities. Major repair work would not be done in the field during combat but would probably be assigned to rear repair facilities in the USSR.

230. Thus, for a tank army in the GSFG with approximately 1,300 medium tanks, the Soviets would expect to lose some 700 tanks in the initial four days of a breakthrough operation. Of this number, they would expect about 370 tanks to be repaired and eventually restored to service. We are unable to judge whether these Soviet estimates reflect a realistic picture of Pact maintenance capabilities. The Pact concept for replacing major items of equipment is based on the assumption that, during an operation, large numbers of active units will be deployed forward from rear echelons as unit replacements. Individual equipment replacement will be limited principally to out-of-action situations for divisional units.

231. *Personnel Replacement and War Reserves.* As with equipment, some in the Intelligence Community believe that unit replacement represents the preferred replacement system within the Warsaw Pact for combat personnel.[30] Based on initial strength, Pact estimates of daily casualty rates during a conventional offensive operation are about 1 percent for the front, 0.6 to 1.2 percent for an army, 3 to 6 percent for committed divisions, and 10 to 16 percent for regiments.

232. An alternative view[31] holds that the Soviets would use both an individual and a unit replacement system, depending on the situation. The holders of this view believe that the Soviets would implement an individual replacement system to feed ongoing replacements into Warsaw Pact units to replace relatively small, steady attrition-type losses that would result primarily from the use of conventional weapons. Unit replacement would be used to supplement this system in situations where large sudden losses, caused primarily by nuclear weapons, occurred or in instances where the individual replacement system proved unable to replace cumulative losses.

233. A pool of men and equipment which would be immediately available for replacement purposes is present in training units in the Groups of Forces. In the GSFG, there are approximately 500 tanks and 7,000 men in one motorized rifle and five tank

---

[30] *The holders of this view are the Central Intelligence Agency; the Director, Bureau of Intelligence and Research, Department of State; and the Director, National Security Agency.*

[31] *The holders of this view are the Director, Defense Intelligence Agency, and the Assistant Chief of Staff for Intelligence, Department of the Army.*

training regiments. Replacement personnel would also be available from the large pool of reservists in the USSR. NSWP countries similarly have large reservist pools and well-organized mobilization systems.

234. We believe that, rather than depend on stockpiles of war reserve equipment to replace losses in the early stages of a war, the Soviets would rely upon unit replacement by fully equipped units which exist in peacetime as low-strength or mobilization divisions. The large number of such units available are probably viewed by the Soviets as sufficient to sustain the forces until such time as production after M-day could build up new equipment reserves. The Soviets have modest stockpiles of older equipment not in units in the USSR, but our information on the serviceability and purpose of this equipment is scant. The stockpiles include some 1,400 tanks, approximately 7,000 artillery pieces, some 8,500 various air defense artillery pieces, about 600 armored personnel carriers, and miscellaneous equipment, all in the military districts west of the Urals.

235. **Production.** Production factors and surge rates would not have a significant impact on the outcome of a short war in Europe. The logistic capability of the Pact to support a protracted conflict would depend largely on whether production rates could keep pace with expenditure and attrition rates. For the most critical supply category, ammunition, the estimated monthly capacity of plants producing conventional small arms, tank, and artillery ammunition in East Germany, Poland, Czechoslovakia, and the USSR are shown in table II-18.

Air Forces

236. **Doctrine.** Warsaw Pact air force logistic doctrine calls for the distribution of supplies to air units in two ways: air force channels provide the logistics requirements which are unique to air operations, such as aviation POL; and the military district (within the USSR) or the front-level rear service organizations supply common-use items. The front is responsible for storing and delivering common-use items to all military units within its organization. It is also required to supplement the motor transport resources of an air army.

237. **Stockpiles.** In addition to airfield stocks, there are stocks of POL, ammunition, and technical and common supplies stored at centrally located depots throughout the Warsaw Pact. Air units would normally be expected to replenish their airfield stocks from these off-base depots. Air units usually draw their technical supplies from centrally located air force supply depots and draw their common supplies from centrally located supply depots under the operational control of front rear service elements. There are some air force depots which support air units with both technical and common supplies.

238. Pact air forces are calculated to have 290,600 metric tons of ammunition, bombs, and rockets stockpiled in the Central Region—East Germany, Czechoslovakia, and Poland—and an additional 130,000 tons in the USSR west of the Urals.[32] POL storage facilities associated with Pact air forces have a calculated total of 2.5 million metric tons in storage immediately opposite the NATO Central Region: 1.3 million in the East Germany, Poland and Czechoslovakia, and 1.2 million in the three western military districts of the USSR. This does not include a substantial amount of POL stored in airfield facilities.

239. **Consumption.** We calculate that, during a three-front operation lasting 12 days, Warsaw Pact air forces would expend approximately 143,000 tons of

Table II-18

Estimated Monthly Ammunition Production Capability of the USSR, East Germany, Poland, and Czechoslovakia
January 1979
(metric tons)

	M-Day	M+30	M+60	M+90	M+120
Small arms, tank, and artillery ammunition	50,000 to 60,000	50,000 to 60,000	105,000 to 110,000	125,000 to 130,00	125,000 to 130,000

ammunition, bombs, and rockets and some 23,700 tons of air-to-surface missiles. These quantities would support a surge period of one day for Backfire, Badger, and Blinder aircraft of Long Range Aviation and a three-day surge period for Soviet and NSWP tactical air forces and NSWP air defense fighters. These calculations are based upon the assumption that, during the surge period, LRA aircraft would generate a maximum of two sorties a day, and aircraft of the other forces, from three to five sorties a day. Subsequently, the number of daily sorties would decline as a result of aircraft attrition. As the sortie rate declined, the expenditure rate would decline accordingly.

240. Total Pact air force consumption (not including air-to-surface missiles) during a campaign of 12 days would be about 40 percent of air ordnance stocks calculated to be stored in the East Germany, Poland, and Czechoslovakia, and the three western military districts. If there were no destruction of stocks, about 215,000 metric tons of ammunition would remain, sufficient to sustain air operations for an estimated additional 20 to 25 days. Air force consumption of POL for a campaign of 12 days would be about 640,000 metric tons. Approximately 1.9 million tons would remain available for an additional 40 to 45 days.[33]

241. *Maintenance.* For Pact air forces the goal of the maintenance system in peacetime is to maintain 85 percent of all aircraft assigned to a regiment in an operationally ready status. To attain this goal, the Soviets and their allies have established a maintenance system involving a series of scheduled inspections and servicings. Responsibility for this program rests with the regimental maintenance specialists of the Soviet Aviation Engineering Services. These specialists, who include engineers, mechanics, and technicians, are assigned to flight branches, squadron maintenance units, and to the primary servicing element of the regiment, the technical maintenance unit. Maintenance personnel probably have the technical competence to meet peacetime requirements but evidently are in short supply, thus requiring augmentation from the civilian labor pool. A shortage of technicians would probably not affect the outcome of a conflict of short duration, but could affect the outcome of a prolonged conflict by reducing the combat sortie sustainability rate.

242. Two other factors will have an effect on sortie rate, even in a short conflict. First, the Pact follows the concept of evacuating to the rear those regimental aircraft that require extensive repairs. This eliminates the possibility of rapid turnaround provided by on-site repairs and reduces the number of aircraft available for regimental operations. Second, the growing sophistication of the Pact aircraft requires increasing maintenance and service time. Recent reports indicate that the ratio of maintenance to flying time of newer aircraft is increasing. Servicing time, which includes refueling and rearming these advanced aircraft, is also increasing because improvements of servicing facilities have not kept pace with aircraft improvements.

243. In sum, we believe the older Frontal Aviation aircraft could meet the projected three-sortie-per-day rate for an initial three-day period but probably would be reduced to one sortie per day thereafter. The newer aircraft, requiring more maintenance and service time, probably could not make more than two sorties per day during the surge period and one per day thereafter.

Naval Forces

244. Just as the Pact's air and ground logistics would be crucial to operations against NATO, naval logistics would also be key to Pact naval operations in support of European ground and air campaigns. The success of the Pact's initial naval operations would be dependent on the Soviets' ability to maximize the availability of combatants and timely deployment to key areas. In a protracted war, the success of sustained combat operations would depend on the Soviet capabilities to replenish and maintain units at sea.

245. The critical items of supply are munitions and fuel. Assuming maximum readiness and deployment of naval forces in their normal operating areas, we believe the principal surface combatants supported by oilers from their home fleets could operate at sea for about 30 to 40 days. Subsequently, fuel would be required from reserves in home fleets or replenishment rendezvous areas. Estimated patrol duration before replenishment is at least 40 days for diesel submarines of medium range and 60 days for those of long range.

246. Of the 39 oilers in the three western fleets, only six are considered modern underway replenishment ships by Western standards. These six, plus six

---

[33] These estimates are based on the maximum numbers of aircraft available (excluding combat trainers) and thus represent a minimum period for Pact sustained operations. Additional ammunition and POL stocks located in the military districts west of the Urals, as well as civilian POL stocks in East Germany, Poland, and Czechoslovakia, would increase the available supplies for combat operations. Factors such as a lower sortie rate, aircraft attrition, and aircraft withhold missions would also contribute to a longer period of sustained operations.

older ships, are the only ones capable of underway refueling alongside. The remaining smaller oilers are restricted to using the bow-to-stern method where only one ship is serviced, either by replenishment under way at slow speed, by lying dead in the water, or at anchor. The Soviets continue to practice the bow-to-stern method more frequently than alongside refueling. Diesel submarines are fueled at anchor. We believe these limitations would constrain Soviet ability to sustain operations at sea.

247. A major constraint on extended combat operations by Soviet missile armed ships and submarines is their generally small supply of onboard weapons reloads.

248. The amount of provisions carried aboard principal Soviet surface combatants and submarines varies with the age and type of unit. Ships of the Kiev and Moskva class, nuclear submarines, and long-range diesel submarines are believed to carry at least 60 days of supplies, while Kara and Kresta-II units and medium-range diesel submarines carry an estimated 40-day load. The older cruisers and newer destroyers hold sufficient provisions for 30 days of operation, while older destroyers and frigates are self-sufficient for about 20 days.

249. The Soviet Navy has the capability for dead-in-the-water munitions replenishment but only a marginal capability for underway transfer of munitions. There have been examples of underway munitions resupply at sea, but, on the whole, the Soviets have thus far preferred to handle munitions transfer at anchorages and ports. The lack of training in at-sea munitions resupply, like that of refueling, places a limitation on the Soviet Navy's ability to maintain combat-capable forces at sea for extended periods, particularly in those sea and ocean areas where transit times to sources of supply are long.

250. Soviet combatants are deficient in their capability to make fresh water. The Navy requires fresh water for crews and for boilers of steam-driven ships, which make up the majority of Soviet principal surface combatants. Although Soviet ships usually have evaporators to distill seawater for shipboard requirements, these generally have not been adequate. Resupply of fresh water remains a major requirement.

251. The Soviet Navy is also deficient in its ability to replenish dry cargo while under way. Soviet stores and refrigerator ships are not capable of underway transfer, but the six replenishment oilers in the Soviet western fleets can carry dry cargo and have a limited capability to transfer while under way. The Soviets rarely have been observed practicing this, however, and instead conduct almost all reprovisioning while dead in the water, at anchor, or in port.

252. *Shipboard Maintenance and Damage Control.* The sustainability of individual ships in combat is directly related to the availability of onboard spare parts and the ability of crews to maintain equipment under the rigors of combat and to repair battle damage at sea quickly and effectively. Most modern combatants and submarines in the Soviet Navy probably have sufficient spares to permit them to accomplish their initial wartime tasks before resorting to resupply. Although Soviet naval crews probably would be capable of handling most routine repairs, they are by and large still poorly equipped and trained for damage control.

253. Because of their heavy reliance on depot maintenance and repair, the Soviets have not developed an extensive capability to maintain and repair ships at sea. Soviet shipboard maintenance and repair practices, therefore, are not optimized for sustaining combat operations at sea and, in our judgment, would constitute a constraint on sustained operations. Aboard ship the Soviets currently use a scheduled inspection and maintenance system which requires maintenance to be performed periodically. Much shipboard maintenance and most repairs are accomplished by officers and warrant officers rather than by enlisted personnel because of the low technical proficiency of the latter. The officers are extensively trained in their fields of specialization and are able to repair most routine equipment and machinery malfunctions.

254. Although we have limited information on Soviet damage control procedures and effectiveness, there is ample evidence that damage control requires improvement. Four major incidents at sea, between 1968 and 1974 resulted in substantial casualties and may have been aggravated by the lack of an effective damage control organization.

255. In the past, damage control in the Soviet Navy has been grossly deficient. Over the past two years, however, the Soviets have placed new emphasis on improved damage control readiness. Recent evidence indicates that the fleet leadership is paying increased attention to this critical aspect of seamanship. For example, emergency action drills at sea are being reported to fleet headquarters, a practice we did not observe until about two years ago.

256. *Other Maritime Assets.* The foregoing estimates of sustainability were derived on the assumption that only naval auxiliary support ships would be available during the initial stages of conflict. The merchant fleet, however, is routinely employed to augment the naval auxiliary force, and we expect this support to continue in wartime. Merchant tankers currently provide more than half the fuel delivered to deployed naval ships, although with the gradually increasing availability of improved naval oilers, that portion will diminish. The Navy has an effective command and control relationship with the merchant and fishing fleets and directs those merchant and fishing ship operations which may affect naval readiness.

257. Many officers in these fleets are also reserve officers in the Soviet Navy, and occasionally active-duty naval officers are assigned to merchant ships with appropriate cover. Merchant tankers under charter to the naval auxiliary tanker fleet to support naval operations regularly use naval communications circuits. Many merchant ships are drilled in or have onboard instructions for the use of naval communications, and it appears that all merchant ships are at least nominally prepared for being placed rapidly under naval control in a crisis. In addition, the Navy has the option of using merchant communications circuits for command and control, an option it occasionally exercises. Merchant and naval distress communications traffic continues to indicate that a central authority is cognizant of the location of all merchant shipping on a near-real-time, 24-hour basis. The Soviets view naval command and control over merchant shipping as a routine measure which can be widely implemented in an emergency without the necessity of advanced notices and prior coordination. Thus, before the beginning of hostilities and subsequently, selected merchant marine ships which are not already under Navy control and perhaps a few fishing fleet assets probably would be directed to relatively safe locales where they could service combatants or naval auxiliaries and become part of the logistic force.

258. In view of the limitations of most Soviet naval auxiliaries for conducting underway replenishment, we believe that only those naval oilers capable of underway refueling would operate in the general area of combat operations. All other support ships, both naval and civilian, probably would seek to minimize their presence in combat areas.

259. *Forward Basing.* To support their worldwide naval operations the Soviets continue to seek access to foreign shore facilities for logistic purposes, major repairs, communications, and support of aircraft deployments. They receive POL products in a small number of selected ports. Various levels of repair support are available at shore facilities in Yugoslavia, Syria, Tunisia, and Cuba, and from Soviet Navy repair ships in protected anchorages or in port in Angola and the People's Democratic Republic of Yemen (PDRY). Communications facilities for fleet support have been established in Syria, Cuba, Angola, and the PDRY, and airfields in the first three countries are used by Soviet Naval Aviation aircraft to stage reconnaissance flights. But the Soviets no longer have the use of port facilities and airfields in Egypt and Somalia, and the Guinean Government recently halted Soviet air operations from Conakry. These developments will obviously force the Soviet leadership to continue its search for the use of port and airfield facilities in Africa and the Indian Ocean littoral from which the Soviets can stage aircraft and carry out fleet maintenance during peacetime operations.

260. To be effective in wartime, these forward bases would require stockpiles of nonperishable foodstuffs, ammunition (including missiles and torpedoes, with both conventional and nuclear warheads), POL, spare parts, and some form of repair capability. Much of this could be made available by pre-positioning naval auxiliaries or merchant ships. In a prolonged war, these bases and auxiliaries would themselves require resupply. We have no evidence of stockpiling, however, certainly not in quantities sufficient to sustain combat operations. Nor do we believe the Soviet Union is capable of replenishing such bases and auxiliaries in time of war, primarily because of the difficulty in establishing effective air cover over supporting lines of communication. In sum, in terms of wartime sustainability, Soviet forward facilities in Africa, the Caribbean, and Indian Ocean littoral are, for the foreseeable future, of marginal value.

261. *Logistic Support Afloat.* To provide direct support of combat operations we believe modern naval replenishment oilers will operate in the combat zone to satisfy fuel requirements through underway replenishment. In addition, the Soviet Navy could station an afloat logistics group—comprising naval or merchant and fishing fleet oilers, ammunition ships, missile support ships, repair ships or tenders, combat stores ships, and merchant fleet cargo ships—at a point in the Greenland Sea between Jan Mayen Island and North Cape. They in turn would be supplied by naval auxiliaries or ships of the merchant and fishing fleets shuttling back and forth to Northern Fleet bases. This concept has the advantage of greatly reducing transit time between the combat zone and rear services support bases and increasing the availability of ships for combat operations. We estimate the Soviets would deploy modern replenishment oilers to operate in close proximity to combatants, but we do not believe they would establish an afloat logistic group in an open-ocean area.

262. *Support in Fleet Areas.* Analysis of fleet fuel stocks and combatant availability shows that sufficient naval fuel reserves are held in the Black Sea, Baltic and Northern Fleets to sustain wartime operations for at least 90, 150, and 80 days, respectively. Commercial marine fuel stocks are not included in this assessment; if included, they would more than double the supply for each fleet. We lack precise data on inventories of naval ordnance stored ashore. We believe, however, that sufficient munitions are stored in each fleet area to rearm individual combatants and submarines at least several times.

263. There is very little information on the availability of spare parts at naval bases, ship repair yards, and supply depot complexes. Nonetheless we estimate that the fleet rear services organizations maintain sufficient stocks in dispersed locations to sustain combatants and submarines through at least 90 to 120 days of combat operations. During that time, defense industries could continue to produce replacements for high-usage items. Damaged ships could be selected for cannibalization, as necessary, in order to keep other units operational.

264. The railroad and highway networks south of Leningrad and west of the Urals are sufficiently well developed to permit the Baltic and Black Sea Fleets to be supported in wartime from the industrial and agricultural heartland. The Northern Fleet, however, has no highway connecting it with points south. It is served only by the inland waterway system and single rail lines to Arkhangel'sk and to Murmansk; from there, railroads and poor-quality highways extend to bases farther north. Naval airbases of the Northern Fleet are similarly isolated. Since the Northern Fleet probably would be the most active of the fleets in wartime, it would place greater demands upon the rear services system than the others. We estimate that stockpiles of POL, munitions and spares, and supplies of foodstuffs in all three fleet areas could be replenished as required, as long as the overland lines of communication remain serviceable.

265. We have not identified any maintenance or logistic problems in Soviet Naval Aviation which would significantly inhibit sustained combat operations from its main airfields. Adequate fuel for extended operations is apparently available and the Soviets produce large numbers of expendable combat items such as sonobuoys and cruise missiles, many of which are stored at or near the main naval airfields. Intensive and continuous combat operations at maximum effort for more than a week at a time could severely strain aircrews and the maintenance system, and temporarily reduce aircraft availability. Moreover, SNA's capability for sustained operations probably would be reduced sharply if it were forced to use its reserve airfields for long periods of time because these airfields seem to have only a limited amount of combat stores and minimum maintenance facilities.

CHAPTER III

WARSAW PACT COMMAND AND CONTROL

1. The Pact's success in achieving its wartime objectives would depend on its ability to control and coordinate multinational, joint-service operations of great complexity. [ ] individual member nations have the command and control elements necessary to form the Pact's wartime control structure, [ ]

2. In peacetime, the Warsaw Pact headquarters does not control the armed forces of member states. Each state controls its armed forces through its national command authority, which is made up of key party, government, and military leaders. (See figure III-1.) Operational control of national forces is exercised by each country's general staff. Overall Pact defense planning is coordinated among Pact members, but the process is clearly Soviet dominated.

3. Establishment of the Pact wartime command system is not automatic. It entails authoritative release of forces from national control and their subordination to the Pact's high command.[1] Political and military consultations between senior Pact leaders would be necessary to coordinate preparations for war. These consultations could be made in person or by telephone. There are telecommunication systems connecting East European capitals and Moscow which can provide secure communications for telephone consultations. East European and Soviet national command authorities also have special secure communications at their disposal.

---
[1] For a detailed treatment of the alert and mobilization procedures and the peacetime readiness and Pact forces, see NIE 4-1-78, *Warsaw Pact Concepts and Capabilities for Going to War in Europe: Implications for NATO Warning of War.*

A. The Wartime Command Structure

4. The ultimate authority for the direction of the Soviet military rests with the Politburo of the Communist Party of the Soviet Union. The wartime role of the Politburo is unclear, but its involvement as a group would probably be limited to only the most crucial decisions. A subset of the Politburo, the Defense Council, establishes military policy and makes fundamental decisions regarding the employment of military forces. We believe that the Defense Council would form the nucleus of a largely civilian national defense command organ. [ ] This body would consider all defense issues and provide broad guidelines for the conduct of military operations.

5. Brezhnev, predesignated as Supreme Commander in Chief, would lead a Supreme High Command (*Verkhovnoye Glavnokomandovaniye*—VGK) drawn from elements of the Ministry of Defense. (See figure III-3.) This command would constitute the military-strategic leadership over all Pact military operations against NATO. The VGK probably includes at least the three first deputy ministers of defense and the commanders in chief of the five components of the Soviet armed forces. One of the Soviet first deputy ministers of defense (currently, Marshal Kulikov) is the commander in chief of the combined armed forces of the Warsaw Pact member states. The Soviet General Staff is the executive agent of the VGK and, as such, is the focal point for operational control of Soviet armed forces and those of the Pact in wartime.

6. We believe that, should a war occur between the Warsaw Pact and NATO, theater commands (see inset) would be established and exercise direct operational control over fronts and fleets and at least some degree of control over those strategic assets allocated to support theater operations. The Soviets refer to these commands as High Commands of troops in a Theater of War (TV) or Theater of Military Operations (TVD).

National Control of Warsaw Pact Forces in Peacetime

Figure III-1

East European Country

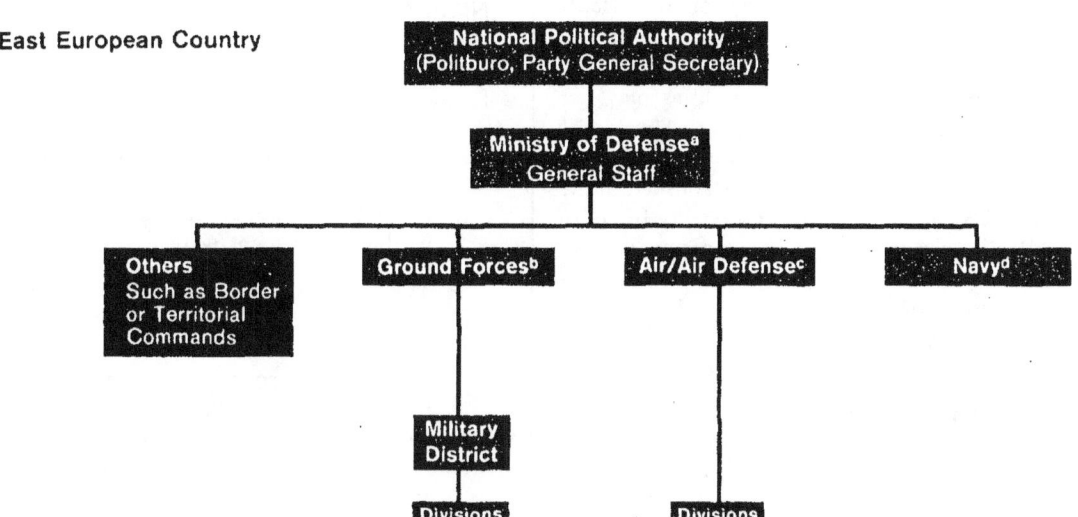

USSR

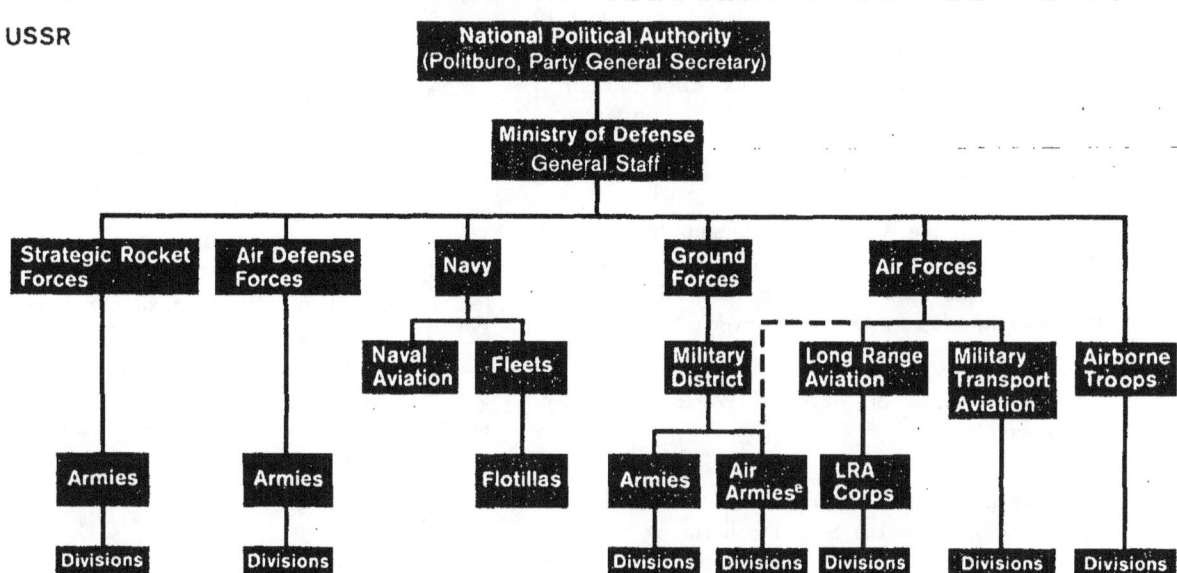

a. There are considerable differences in how East European defense ministries are organized.

b. Some do not have Ground Forces headquarters; some have Military Districts or Regions that became armies; some have armies subordinate to a Military District.

c. Some have separate air and air defense commands; some have air armies or corps.

d. Not all have naval commands.

e. The Soviet Air Force (SAF) sometimes exercises centralized control of tactical air armies from SAF headquarters or from SAF operations groups deployed to theater commands.

> ### THEATER COMMANDS
>
> The Soviets define a theater of war (*teatr voyny*—TV) as the territory of any one continent, together with the sea areas adjoining it and the airspace above it, on which hostilities may develop—for example, the European Theater of War. A TV usually includes several TVDs. Another TV presumably would be established in the eastern USSR against China and enemy forces in the Pacific region. Not all of the national forces would be detached from national control. Residual forces would be retained under national control as territorial defense forces for rear area security and as strategic national reserves.
>
> A theater of military operations (*teatr voyennykh deystviy*—TVD) is defined as a particular territory, together with the associated airspace and sea areas, including islands (archipelagos), within whose limits a known part of the armed forces of the country (or coalition) operates in wartime, engaged in strategic missions which ensue from the war plan. A TVD may be ground, maritime, or intercontinental. According to their military-political and economic importance, TVDs are classified as main or secondary.

Unlike NATO, the Warsaw Pact does not have theater headquarters in being in peacetime. Hardened command posts have been constructed for at least some Pact wartime headquarters, however.

Western Theater of War: The Warsaw Pact High Command

7. Arrangements for exercising control of Pact forces within what the Soviets call the Western (or European) Theater of War have been evolving over the last few years. Although ultimate control of all Pact operations continues to be the VGK and the Soviet General Staff, we now have evidence that indicates the commander in chief of the combined armed forces of the Warsaw Pact would control all Pact forces in this theater in wartime. We are less certain of how he would do this—whether the High Command of the Warsaw Pact would become a component of the Soviet High Command with the responsibility for operational control over forces within the Western Theater or whether it would form a separate command entity.

8. In considering a future war with NATO, Soviet strategists envision widespread combat operations encompassing all of Europe and extending into the North Atlantic. Accordingly, they plan to divide the Western TV into three land TVDs in which they expect Pact and NATO forces to come in conflict. (See figure III-4.)

— **The Northwestern TVD.** Based on the Soviet Leningrad Military District, this theater would encompass the Scandinavian Peninsula and immediately adjacent waters.

— **The Western TVD.** This theater would include, on the Pact side, Soviet and East European forces in East Germany, Poland, and Czechoslovakia and Soviet forces in the western USSR; and, on the NATO side, West Germany, the Benelux nations, Denmark, and possibly France and northern Spain. Pact operations in the western Baltic Sea also would be included in this TVD.

— **The Southwestern TVD.** Soviet planners envision military operations against Greece and Turkey and probably northern Italy and Austria. This theater would also include the Black and Mediterranean Seas.

9. The Soviets also expect major naval operations against NATO in the North Atlantic to occur in conjunction with a conflict in Europe. The equivalent of the TVD in Soviet maritime strategy is the MTVD, the Maritime Theater of Military Operations. We are less certain about the approximate boundaries of MTVDs than we are about those of TVDs. Operations, exercises, and documentary evidence suggest that the Soviets would regard an area in the Norwegian Sea north of the Greenland–Iceland–United Kingdom (G-I-UK) gap as an MTVD.

Fronts

10. Regardless of what echelons of command are created to integrate wartime theater-level and strategic operations, the senior tactical command would be the front. Although not directly comparable to any Western organization, the front would be similar to the NATO army group in size, level of command, and function. A front would usually consist of three to five ground armies, each including three to five tank or motorized rifle divisions, and an air army of as many as several hundred tactical aircraft. A front operating in a maritime sector might also control any naval elements which were chiefly devoted to that front's mission. The ground forces of the front would also

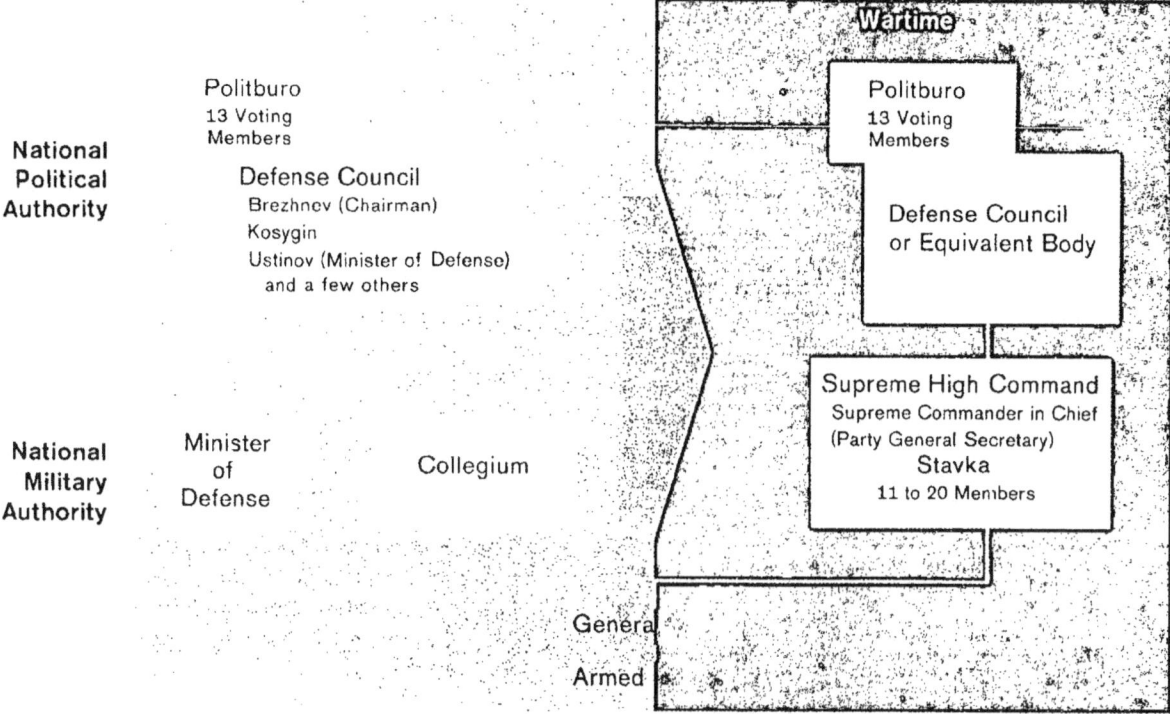

Soviet Command Authorities: Transition to Wartime — Figure III-2

include numerous separate combat and combat-support elements such as tank, artillery, missile, and air defense units. Large service-support elements would provide the front with transport, maintenance, engineering, supply, and medical support. The Soviet front in East Germany could total more than 500,000 men after full mobilization; a more typical front would have some 300,000 to 400,000 men.

11. The Pact has made advance preparations to man front headquarters in wartime. Since the late 1960s, Soviet military district staffs have been augmented in order to be able to provide staff for front headquarters when created. East European front staffs have been predesignated in Poland, Czechoslovakia, and probably Bulgaria. These front command and control elements are routinely under national control in peacetime.

Armies and Divisions

12. The headquarters staffs and communications support elements of armies and divisions also routinely participate in exercises. When these commands are activated, their signal support units establish the communications for their command posts. Most armies and independent divisions would be subordinate to fronts, but some may be withheld as strategic reserves under the control of the VGK or theater commanders. All Soviet armies have direct communications with the General Staff and normally receive communications support from signal units of the Committee of State Security (KGB) and of the Reserves of the Supreme High Command (RVGK).[3]

III-5

Possible Warsaw Pact Theaters of Military Operations (TVDs) in Europe Figure III-4

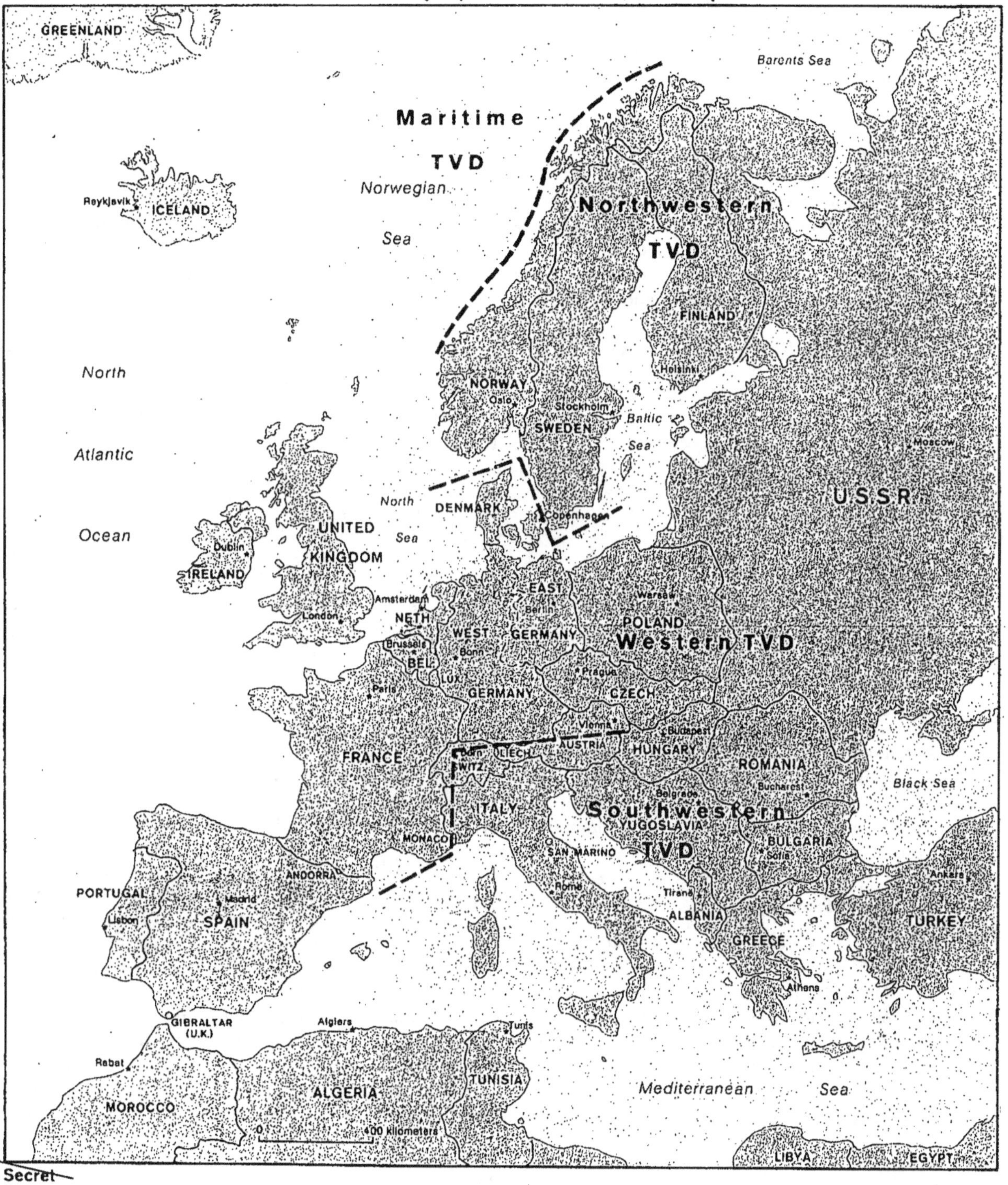

~~Secret~~
577636 1-79 CIA

Fleets

13. In wartime, the Pact would have two combined fleets opposite NATO: the Baltic and Black Sea Combined Fleets, both under Soviet Command. The Combined Baltic Fleet would consist of elements from the Soviet Baltic Fleet and from the Polish and East German Navies. The Combined Black Sea Fleet would be formed from the Soviet Black Sea Fleet and the Romanian and Bulgarian Navies. The Soviets' Northern Fleet and the Soviet Fifth Squadron (*Eskadra*) in the Mediterranean would support Pact operations under the control of the Main Naval Staff in Moscow, although in some cases control might be exercised by continental theater-level commands.

B. Measures for Control of Combined Operations

14. The Soviets intend to maintain centralized control of all Pact military operations. To this end they have devised a variety of mechanisms to facilitate their control over Pact planning, training, and communications.

War Plans

15. The Soviet General Staff develops strategic objectives for the Pact, and assigns specific missions and planning guidelines to Soviet commands and to the General Staffs of the non-Soviet Warsaw Pact (NSWP) countries. In turn, these commands and staffs prepare detailed operational plans and NSWP planners obtain national approval. The Soviet General Staff reviews and gives final approval to all plans to ensure that operations are fully integrated throughout the theater and consistent with the accomplishment of Soviet objectives.

Standardization

16. The adoption of Soviet military doctrine in the NSWP forces has produced a high degree of standardization in training and command and control procedures. This doctrine is propagated by frequent exercises and by training NSWP officers in Soviet military academies. It is reinforced by the use of Russian as the official language for combined Pact military operations and by various standard operating procedures and formats that minimize language difficulties.

17. Pact standardization is being increasingly reflected in communications equipment and in automated command and staff information support systems. Common radio equipment of various types is being fielded. Some common computer programs are being used for logistics and battle management support at army level and above.

Representatives of Command

18. Soviet military writings indicate that, at times, the actions of theater commands (High Commands) and front commands would be coordinated and monitored by representatives of the VGK and General Staff deployed from Moscow to the field. These representatives would interpret the VGK's orders, report on progress and problems, and help the commanders obtain support from Moscow command authorities.

19. Representatives of the Headquarters of the Warsaw Pact—all Soviet officers—provide liaison between Pact headquarters and national general staffs and monitor NSWP forces to ensure conformity with Soviet requirements. Except in Romania, these representatives appear to have access to most aspects of NSWP military decisionmaking, planning, and operations. They have large staffs to assist them and special communications that provide access to key NSWP leaders as well as to the Pact's Headquarters and the Soviet General Staff. Also, senior Soviet officers are assigned to all major NSWP command elements and, at least in East Germany, down to division level. We expect these officers would remain at their posts during wartime.

Operations Groups

20. The use of operations groups to perform liaison and control functions is central to Soviet control and integration of Pact military operations. Such groups were used during World War II to integrate Soviet and East European operations and are widely used in contemporary exercises. Officers and supporting communications elements are sent from service headquarters to major field commands, from superior to subordinate echelons, and laterally between commands to facilitate coordination. In the Pact context, perhaps the most important operations groups would be those sent to NSWP fronts by local Soviet headquarters to integrate those NSWP fronts into the overall Soviet General Staff command system.

D. Effectiveness of Pact Command and Control

28. The Pact's command and control system appears adequate to alert forces and control mobilization and to control combat operations. The first-echelon Central Front (Soviet Group of Forces in East Germany) and Southwestern Front (Czechoslovak and Soviet forces in Czechoslovakia) could deploy and activate their command and control network in 24 to 48 hours. In a rapidly developing crisis, deploying and activating the Pact's entire wartime command and control system would require about a week.

29. We believe that the Pact's command and control system for theater operations has important strengths:

— Soviet dominance of the Pact allows the USSR to control almost all aspects of Pact operations.

— The Pact has a standardized command and control doctrine.

— The Pact has a significant degree of flexibility in the resubordination of ground armies and divisions from one command to another, including resubordination of these units from one nation to the command of another.

— Each echelon of command has the capability to control both its immediate and second-echelon

— The Pact command and control system is characterized by redundancy, hardening, mobility, and dispersal. This provides a high degree of survivability.

— Pact forces have a high degree of communications security, both in operating practices and in security devices.

— The Pact is demonstrating an increasing degree of interoperability in communications equipment.

— Pact mobile signal units have backup communications equipment to replace that damaged or destroyed.

30. Problems noted include instances of poor-quality staff and communications personnel; low Russian-language proficiency on the part of some Pact staffs; shortcomings in quantity, capacity, interoperability, maintainability, and security of communications equipment; and failure to fulfill doctrinal requirements for camouflage and distance between communications centers and command posts.

CHAPTER IV

WARSAW PACT STRATEGY FOR INITIAL CONVENTIONAL OPERATIONS AGAINST NATO

1. This chapter summarizes our understanding of how the Warsaw Pact would organize and prosecute initial, conventional military operations in a full-scale conflict with NATO. We do not have access to the Pact's war plans, but we can deduce their general nature, at least for the opening phases of a war, from military exercises, from Pact writings on military tactics and strategy, and from the current disposition of Pact forces.

2. The USSR's geographic position as a major continental power in Europe and Asia, and the Soviet perception that potentially hostile neighbors confront the USSR and its allies on virtually every side, have led it to develop contingency plans for military operations on all Pact land frontiers. Our information on Soviet concepts for military operations is best for offensive operations that would be directed against NATO, especially in Central Europe. The Soviets clearly expect Central Europe to be the decisive arena in a war with NATO and assign it the highest priority in the allocation of military manpower and equipment.

3. The Soviets also have plans for offensive action in other NATO regions.

4. We have little direct evidence on the Pact's view of the timing of these flank offensives in relation to an offensive in Central Europe. We judge, however, that the Pact would be unlikely to start a war by mounting major ground offensives against all NATO sectors simultaneously. To do so would unnecessarily extend available Pact forces, airlift, and air and logistic support and would complicate command and control at the General Staff and Supreme High Command levels. The planned Pact air offensive in Central Europe would tie up the bulk of the Pact's tactical air forces and Soviet intermediate-range bomber forces for at least the first week, and the Soviet airlift could not simultaneously support two major airborne operations such as those contemplated against the Danish and Turkish Straits. Moreover, there could be political considerations that would lead the Soviets to defer attacks on some NATO countries in the hope of encouraging their nonbelligerence.

5. We believe, however, that the need for unfettered naval operations from their Northern Fleet bases would almost certainly cause the Soviets to strike NATO facilities in northern Norway, and probably to attempt to occupy some territory there, and that the urgency of this need would lead them to do so concurrently with starting an attack in Central Europe. We also would expect attacks on NATO naval forces in the Mediterranean to occur at the onset of hostilities in Central Europe. None of the other potential flank offensives appear to have this degree of urgency, although the Pact would be likely to move against the Turkish Straits early in a war. Even if they did not begin ground offensives immediately in some flank areas, the Pact would almost certainly conduct feints or holding actions intended to keep NATO from shifting forces from the flanks to Central Europe, compel commitment of NATO reserves, and weaken NATO forces on the flanks in anticipation of further operations.

6. We have considered the question of whether the Soviets could rely on their Warsaw Pact allies to participate willingly and effectively in hostilities against NATO and have concluded that no categorical answer is possible. The extent of reliability in non-Soviet Warsaw Pact (NSWP) countries would depend chiefly upon the circumstances under which NSWP forces became engaged in war with NATO. The period of tension before hostilities would allow the Soviets to manipulate popular attitudes and political leaders. In addition, the Pact's mobilization would be set in motion and its momentum would carry military preparations forward. Refusal on the part of an NSWP country to participate at this stage could be dealt with by force. In sum, the East Europeans would feel they had little choice but to fight on behalf of the Pact.

A. The Initial Campaign in the Western Theater of Military Operations

The Ground Offensive

7. Soviet military strategy calls for a massive and rapid ground offensive into NATO territory in Central Europe to defeat NATO forces, disrupt mobilization, and seize or destroy ports and airfields to prevent reinforcement. Because this strategy envisions a highly fluid battlefield and high rates of advance, Pact planners hope to overrun, penetrate, or bypass NATO forward defenses rapidly to prevent the Western Alliance from strengthening its defenses and using the time gained for mobilization and reinforcement. The Soviets hope that the shock and suddenness of the initial Pact offensive would interrupt NATO's mobilization, forestall reinforcements, and prevent a prolonged period of positional warfare. But they recognize that this strategy would be complicated by a period of political crisis and tension that almost certainly would precede a war and provide impetus to NATO preparations.

8. To achieve the force ratios deemed necessary to accomplish its objectives, the Pact has evolved mobilization and attack concepts that are intended to maximize initial combat power, on the assumption that a war in Europe would be short and, therefore, decided largely by forces in being or quickly available. (See table IV-1.) Accordingly, the Soviets plan against the contingency that Pact forces based in Central Europe, about half of them East European, might be required to initiate a Pact offensive campaign and, bypassing strong resistance, carry the campaign well into NATO territory before reinforcements would arrive from the western USSR.

9. Pact planning for the Western Theater of Military Operations evidently envisions offensives along axes of advance in three distinct areas—central, northern, and southwestern. (See figure IV-1.) The Pact probably would seek to organize its initial attack forces in this theater of military operations (TVD) into three fronts which would correspond to these areas of responsibility:

— **Central.** The Soviet–East German front responsible for this area would be the largest in terms of forces and would be expected to carry out the main effort. It could be made up of as many as 28 divisions, including all Soviet forces in East Germany and Poland and all six of East Germany's ground force divisions. It would have the

Table IV-1

Warsaw Pact Ground Force Divisions Available for Initial Use in the Western Theater of Military Operations
January 1979

	In Central Europe [a]		In the Western USSR [b]	Total [c]
	Soviet	NSWP		
Availability by Type:				
Tank	14	12	14	40
Motorized Rifle	13	17	15	45
Assault Landing	—	1	—	1
Airborne [d]	—	1	—	1
Total	27	31	29	87
Available Over Time:				
M-Day + 24 Hours	7–12	3	—	10–15
M-Day + 96 Hours	27	13	—	40
M-Day + 8 Days	27	31	—	58
M-Day + 14 Days	27	31	29	87

[a] Soviet and non-Soviet Warsaw Pact forces in East Germany, Poland, and Czechoslovakia.

[b] Forces in the Baltic, Belorussian, and Carpathian Military Districts.

[c] In some circumstances the four Soviet and six Hungarian divisions in Hungary, as well as the 11 divisions in the Kiev Military District of the USSR, could also be used in the Western Theater of Military Operations.

[d] The Soviets also have eight airborne divisions (including one training division) in the USSR which could be used against NATO in one or more theaters. Three of these divisions are located in the Baltic and Belorussian Military Districts.

Illustrative Warsaw Pact Ground Force Campaign in the Western TVD

Figure IV-1

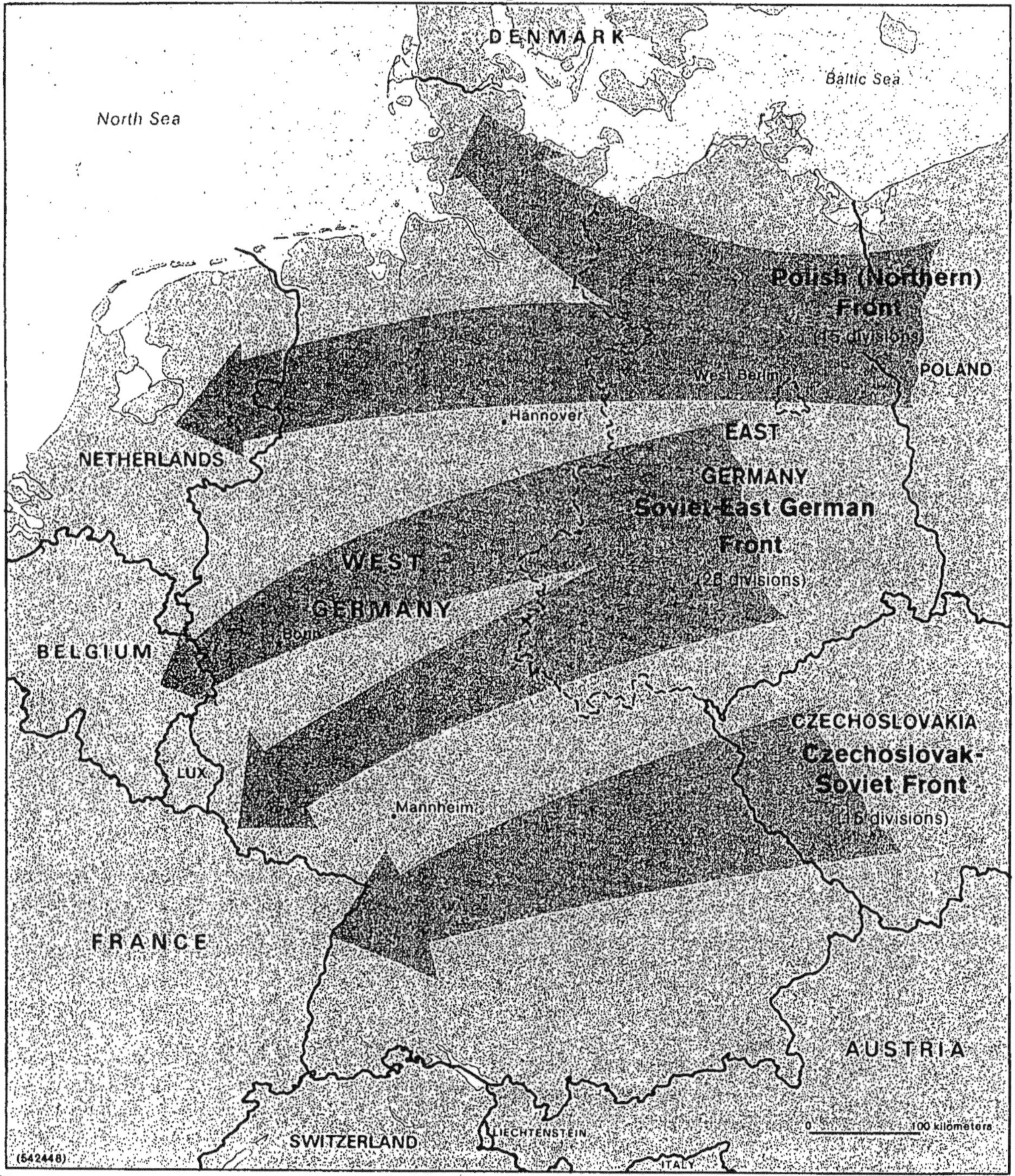

~~Secret~~
577637 1-79 CIA

task of destroying NATO forces in West Germany roughly between Hannover in the north and Mannheim in the south. It could engage forces from as many as six of NATO's eight corps areas.

— **Northern.** Pact forces here would be responsible for engaging NATO forces in the areas of the two northernmost corps of the NATO Central Region, as well as in Denmark. Pact writings and exercises indicate that the Polish front, including some 15 divisions, would be primarily responsible for this area, but Soviet and East German forces would be expected to assume defensive responsibility for the area temporarily until Polish forces arrived.

— **Southwestern.** The majority of the forces in the front assuming responsibility for this area would be Czechoslovak, but they would include the five Soviet divisions in the Group of Forces in Czechoslovakia. This front, with some 15 divisions in all, would have the responsibility of attacking toward the Rhine in an area roughly between Mannheim and the Swiss border.

10. In NIE 4-1-78 (*Warsaw Pact Capabilities for Going to War in Europe: Implications for NATO Warning of War*), we evaluated various attack options which the Warsaw Pact might consider for launching offensives in Central Europe, should it decide to start a war with NATO. These options defined alternative ways in which the Pact might organize the 87-division force described above. In paragraphs 11-22 which follow, we summarize the conclusions of that evaluation.

11. *Option I—The Standing-Start Attack.* There is no evidence of Soviet or Pact military literature, doctrine, plans, or exercises which feature an unprepared, standing-start attack on NATO from a peacetime force posture. The Soviets, however, do have the capability to attack NATO units using ground and air combat forces garrisoned near the inter-German border. As many as 10 to 15 Soviet divisions and perhaps several East German divisions could reach initial combat points and lead or support such an attack in the Central Region in somewhat less than 24 hours. By dint of surprise and local force superiority, Soviet planners would expect—and might achieve—some early ground and air victories.

12. These initial successes would likely be the only advantage that would accrue to such an attack, however. The considerations that weigh against initiating a war from a standing start are persuasive, and we judge that there is virtually no chance the Soviets would initiate a war against NATO with an attack from a standing start. The Soviets would have to expect that the standing-start attack would cause NATO to initiate massive and rapid mobilization, almost simultaneously with the Pact, and the local force superiority which would accrue in such an attack probably could not be maintained if NATO forces reacted effectively. The Soviets, considering their conservative view of NATO rapid mobilization capabilities, might well conclude that the attacking force could face an adverse situation before reinforcements could be committed. The attack would initially have to rely on incomplete lines of communication. The Soviets would not have time to establish a front-level command, control, and communications structure or to prepare the Soviet or East European populace or national economies for warfare—both basic requirements posed in Soviet military literature. Finally, the standing-start attack would leave other Pact strategic and general purpose forces—as well as the national economy—unprepared for expanded hostilities. In particular the Soviets would be concerned about the threat of NATO escalation to nuclear war.

13. *Option II—Attack With Two Fronts.* Extensive analysis of Pact exercises and doctrine leads us to conclude that the smallest force the Pact would use to start theater offensive operations would consist of two fronts. (See figure IV-2.) This force would be composed essentially of all Soviet ground and tactical air force units in East Germany, Poland, and Czechoslovakia together with most of the East German and Czechoslovak units which are active in peacetime—a total of some 40 ground divisions, plus support and tactical air units.

14. Extensive study of ▓▓▓▓▓▓▓▓▓▓▓▓ the Pact's theoretical capability to organize, deploy, and prepare forces for war in Europe, indicates that, in the most urgent circumstances, the Pact would need about four days to prepare a two-front force. While initiation of an attack with slightly less than four full days of preparation is possible, the complexity and magnitude of the operation and the risks attending insufficient preparation would be likely to cause the Soviets to take more than four days to prepare this two-front force. These preparations would be made using a compressed buildup procedure that would exacerbate the confusion and disruptions inherent in a transition to a war footing and, at least initially, would yield combat units—and especially combat support units—with less than full

Warsaw Pact Options
for Initial Attack Force in the Central Region

Option II: Two Fronts

The smallest force the Pact might use to start theater offensive operations probably would consist of two fronts—a total of some 40 ground divisions plus support and tactical air units. In the most urgent circumstances, the Pact would need about four days to prepare this force. Attack with slightly less than four days is possible, but the complexity of the operation and the risks attending insufficient preparation would likely cause the Soviets to take more than four days to prepare this force.

Option III: Three Fronts

The Warsaw Pact envisions a basic force of three fronts as the first echelon of an attack on NATO. As depicted in Pact doctrine and exercises, this three-front force includes 50 to 60 ground divisions plus support and tactical air units. About eight days would be needed to prepare this force.

Option IV: Five Fronts

Establishment of a five-front posture—some 80 to 90 ground divisions—before initiating an offensive against NATO would fulfill Soviet conservative doctrinal preferences to the extent possible in practical terms and would take about two weeks to achieve.

PAGE LEFT BLANK INTENTIONALLY

capabilities to undertake or sustain combat operations. Preparations which, in a less demanding operation, would be undertaken in a phased or sequential pattern would have to occur simultaneously.

15. By waiting to establish a two-front attack force, the Pact would diminish many of the critical deficiencies of the standing-start attack. Naval capabilities would be substantially improved, and the minimal essentials of the command and control system could be functioning.

16. Still, initiating hostilities after only these minimum preparations were made would entail serious risks for the Pact and would be extremely unlikely except in the most urgent circumstances. The attacking force itself would lack some front-level elements and would have to cover the broad sector from the Baltic to Austria. Command and control capabilities, particularly at the theater level, would remain incomplete. Pact mobilization would not have proceeded far enough to ensure immediate followup forces and supplies for the attack in Central Europe and effective participation in the war by major forces in other areas.

17. We are agreed that it is extremely unlikely that the Pact would initiate war from this two-front posture in other than extraordinarily time-urgent circumstances. On this point there are two views. One holds that the only circumstances which would cause the Pact to initiate theaterwide offensive operations against NATO from this posture with only four days of preparation would be the Soviet perception of the threat of imminent NATO attack. Although NATO mobilization would be viewed as a serious threat and would almost certainly cause the Pact to make counterpreparations, the Soviets would be particularly averse to initiating an attack with a force not fully prepared against NATO forces which enjoyed some advantages of prior preparation or mobilization—unless threat of imminent NATO attack was clear.[1]

18. The other view holds that the Soviets might choose to attack with the two-front force in a variety of urgent contingencies. For example, during a serious East-West political dispute, the NATO countries (particularly the United States and West Germany) might undertake a degree of mobilization and other military preparations to improve their defensive postures and to demonstrate will in support of the diplomatic bargaining. The Soviets, of course, might see this as weakening their own bargaining position, in particular by threatening to upset the political advantage afforded them by superiority in forces-in-being in Central Europe. In such a contingency, and if they perceived truly vital interests at risk, the Soviets might set in motion the option for rapid buildup and early attack. Their efforts would be intended to preempt NATO defensive and diplomatic preparations, not an immediate threat of NATO attack.[2]

19. *Option III—Attack With Three Fronts.* The third and fourth options are ones in which Soviet planners, under a less urgent need to defend or attack, would elect to bring the Pact to full readiness via a more efficient, phased buildup procedure and to attack when the force available for initial operations totaled three fronts (Option III) or five fronts (Option IV). The same evidence cited earlier on Pact buildup planning and procedures indicates that, in these circumstances, the Pact would require, at a minimum, about eight days to achieve a three-front force.

20. The Pact preference for a larger-than-two-front attack is well supported in Soviet writings and by analysis of Pact exercises. The phased buildup to three fronts—a total of some 50 to 60 divisions plus support and tactical air units—would offer a reasonable expectation of an orderly and efficient transition to an attack posture affording force superiority, sustainability, and precautions against the risks of a wider war. addition, this option would provide opportunity for significantly more naval forces to deploy. Accordingly, we judge that, except in extraordinarily urgent circumstances (as described above in paragraphs 17 and 18), the Pact would prefer to prepare at least a three-front force before initiating hostilities.

21. *Option IV—Attack With Five Fronts.* The Pact might elect to build up even greater forces in Eastern Europe prior to initiating hostilities against NATO, depending on its assessment of the political and military situation at the time. A five-front posture—about 90 ground divisions plus support and tactical air units and with additional naval units at sea—would fulfill Soviet conservative doctrinal preferences to the extent possible in practical terms and would take about two weeks to achieve.

22. In summary, the following judgments are unanimous within the Intelligence Community

---

[1] *The holders of this view are the Central Intelligence Agency and the Director, Bureau of Intelligence and Research, Department of State.*

[2] *The holders of this view are the Director, Defense Intelligence Agency; the Director, National Security Agency; and the Senior Intelligence Officers of each of the military services.*

— The Pact would begin to organize at least five fronts for use in Central Europe from the time of the decision to go to full readiness.

— There is virtually no chance that the Soviets would attack from a standing start.

— The smallest force the Pact would use to begin a theater offensive would consist of two fronts, requiring about four days of preparation; except in an extraordinarily time-urgent circumstance, it is extremely unlikely the Pact would initiate war from this posture.

— The Pact would prefer, before attacking, to prepare at least a three-front force, which would require, at a minimum, about eight days of preparation.

— Circumstances permitting, the Pact would build up even greater forces in Eastern Europe before initiating hostilities against NATO.

23. *Soviet Views of NATO Defenses.* Soviet planners would anticipate a quick, strong NATO reaction to any attack. ▢▢▢▢▢▢▢▢▢▢▢▢▢▢▢▢ the Soviets have good data on NATO's order of battle, alert procedures, readiness categories, and mobilization times and ▢ they interpret this information in a prudent, conservative manner. ▢▢▢▢▢

— Launch almost 10 percent of tactical nuclear missiles within five minutes.

— Emplace some nuclear mine barriers within two and a half hours and the remainder within 11 hours.

— Complete the air deployment to Europe from the United States of two divisions in three days.

24. *Concepts for the Offensive.* The tactics employed by the Pact to overcome NATO defenses will be based on its perceptions of how strong those defenses are. The Pact would prefer to employ forces on multiple axes, moving in tactical march columns to penetrate defense positions through gaps, weak points, and open flanks, relying heavily on speed and maneuver. In areas where the Pact believed that it must penetrate strong, continuous NATO defenses it would mount breakthrough operations on each principal axis of advance. Depending on the importance of the axis of advance to the overall theater offensive plan and the strength of the defense, a breakthrough attempt might involve the major forces of either a front or an army.

25. According to Soviet doctrinical writings, in a conventional assault against well-prepared defense, the commander of a Soviet wartime front with three to five subordinate armies probably would hold his tank armies in reserve and commit the combined arms for the initial breakthrough of NATO's defensive positions. The tank armies would then be committed to exploit penetrations or weakened sectors of the defense. A modern combined-arms army with three to five motorized rifle and tank divisions would usually have an offensive operational zone 70 kilometers or so wide. An individual army commander in a breakthrough attempt would mass the bulk of his forces along a front of less than 10 kilometers, leaving enough forces in other sectors to hold against a NATO counterattack or to initiate diversionary thrusts.

26. ▢▢▢▢▢▢▢▢▢▢▢▢▢▢▢▢▢▢▢▢▢ Pact doctrine for overcoming strong, fixed defenses, ▢▢▢▢▢▢▢▢▢▢▢▢▢ calls for combined-arms armies to concentrate their attacks on narrow frontages to overcome the defenses and create gaps for the tank armies to exploit. ▢

motorized rifle divisions—as conducting the initial assault and breaking through the defenses with multiple penetrations on a broad frontage. According to the doctrinal writings, this type of assault configuration would be optimally suited for attacking hastily constructed, weak defenses or for keeping pressure on retreating NATO forces, not for breaking through a well-prepared defense.

27. In the Pact exercises, NATO is the aggressor, either launching an attack or preparing to do so. In the first case, Pact forces counterattack and are pursuing a retreating NATO force when they cross the border. In the second case, the Pact crosses the border to preempt the impending NATO attack. In neither case does the Pact encounter a well-prepared NATO defense. Nonetheless, Pact planners probably are aware that actual NATO strategy envisages the Pact as the aggressor with NATO forces in prepared forward defenses awaiting the Pact assault.

28. *The Dilemma of the Nuclear Transition.* Soviet military writings confirm that Warsaw Pact planners see a dilemma in the prospect that a war with NATO could be nonnuclear in the beginning and escalate rapidly to large-scale nuclear war. On the one hand, if faced with strong, continuous NATO defenses, the Pact planners would have to mass large concentrations of forces in places of their choosing to attempt breakthroughs. On the other hand, they fear that NATO might take advantage of their vulnerability while massing for an attack and launch a nuclear strike. The dilemma has led the Soviets to plan a large-scale nonnuclear air attack on NATO's air and nuclear facilities—to which they would commit the bulk of the Warsaw Pact tactical air force and much of the Soviet LRA bomber force—in an attempt to eliminate most of NATO's theater nuclear potential at the very outset of hostilities.

29. The Pact's plans to reduce the vulnerability of its attacking ground forces during a breakthrough effort call for dispersed units to converge rapidly near the point of contact with NATO forces, attack, achieve a breakthrough, and then disperse, continuing the advance or exploitation along a number of different axes. This tactic is designed to minimize the time during which Pact forces would be exposed to nuclear strikes. It is also intended to complicate NATO's use of nuclear weapons by having the Pact units come together for the assault at a point as close as possible to NATO lines so that NATO cannot effectively employ nuclear weapons without endangering its own troops. The Soviets recognize, however, that the breakthrough operation is a complex and risky maneuver.

30. The Soviets place considerable stress on efforts to anticipate NATO's intention to use nuclear weapons on a large scale and to anticipate it in time to launch a Pact preemptive attack. To this end, they expect to keep their own nuclear delivery systems in a high state of readiness and to conduct a vigorous reconnaissance and intelligence-collecting campaign against NATO's nuclear units and facilities, as well as its communications networks, to detect signs which might presage the imminent use of nuclear weapons.

31. *Tanks Versus Antitank Weapons.* Because the type of offensive the Pact planners envision in Central Europe is highly dependent on the mobility and shock effect provided by large numbers of tanks, the Pact is concerned that the proliferation in NATO forces of improved antitank weapons has greatly increased NATO's capability to stop Pact armor. As a result, the Pact has modified its tactics and initiated several force improvement programs in an effort to cope with NATO's antitank threat.

32. Pact doctrine has traditionally stressed the role of artillery on the conventional battlefield, and the Pact now has in Central Europe more than twice as many artillery pieces as NATO. Pact artillery doctrine stresses preplanned, massed barrages, which provides the high volume of fire required in nonnuclear breakthrough operations against relatively static defenses, especially against forward antitank defenses. The large number of multiple rocket launchers deployed with Pact forces could be particularly effective in this role.

33. In accordance with Pact doctrine, defensive positions on these axes would be subjected before a major assault to a 40-to-50-minute bombardment by artillery and possibly by tactical air forces. During the barrage, the assaulting infantry and tank units, using terrain to minimize exposure to NATO's weapons, would try to position themselves for a rapid assault against NATO's defenses. Smoke from shells and smoke generated by devices on the tanks would also be used to mask the assault. Antitank strongpoints which were not destroyed or suppressed by the preparatory

barrage would then be engaged and overrun by assaulting infantry and tanks.

34. Work to reduce the vulnerability of tanks to antitank guided missiles (ATGMs) has been under way in the Soviet Union since at least the early 1960s, most of it directed at defeating the high-explosive antitank (HEAT) warheads which virtually all infantry antitank weapons in both NATO and the Warsaw Pact employ. To provide better protection, particularly against HEAT ammunition, the Soviets have incorporated composite or laminated armor arrays in their new T-64 and T-72 tanks. The additional tanks which the Soviets have assigned to their divisions in the past decade (see paragraph 12 in chapter II) may be intended to compensate for the heavier losses that Soviet planners expect to sustain from improved antitank defenses and to enable assaulting units to overwhelm these defenses by sheer numbers. The addition of an independent tank battalion to a motorized rifle division provides the division commander with an additional maneuver force to commit at a critical point in the battle.

35. *Subsequent Operations.* If a major breakthrough were accomplished by the forces of the Soviet-East German front, the three tank armies of this front probably would launch rapid thrusts—perhaps aided by airborne assaults—in an attempt to secure crossings over the Rhine near Essen, Frankfurt, and similar points, and continue the advance to at least the French border. The Polish front, upon breaking through initial defenses in its area, would be responsible for advancing both into Denmark and across northern Germany into the Netherlands. The Soviet-Czechoslovak front would move into southern West Germany, and advance toward crossings over the Rhine south of Mannheim.

36. The roles of the reinforcing fronts from the western USSR would depend on the progress of the initial offensive. major elements—two or three armies—from one or two Soviet fronts from the western USSR transiting Central Europe in time to enter combat by the end of the first week of fighting. The origins of the initial reinforcements and their exact areas of responsibility when committed to battle are variously depicted forces in the Belorussian and Carpathian Military Districts are used most frequently. When the front from the Baltic Military District is committed, it usually enters the battle between the Soviet-East German and Polish fronts

37. During initial and subsequent operations, Pact commanders would implement their doctrine for radioelectronic combat to locate and either jam or destroy NATO communication and radar links. (See section F, beginning at paragraph 197, in chapter II.) Ground force jamming units, located on the flanks during the breakthrough operation and with the advance echelons during the subsequent exploitation phase, would attempt to jam NATO's command and control and combat support communication links. These links would also be targeted for destruction by Pact artillery and tactical aircraft.

38. *Replacement Concepts.* The Pact structures and employs its ground forces in ways significantly different from the US approach. In large measure, these differences account for the different means adopted by the Pact and the United States for replacing personnel and equipment expended in combat. Generally speaking, the Pact designs its combat units with leaner man-to-equipment ratios and with more modest levels of service support. Pact combat-ready divisions have roughly the same number of tanks and artillery as comparable US divisions, but only about half as many men. For example, a Soviet tank division at combat strength has about 9,500 men, 322 medium tanks, 60 howitzers, and 18 multiple-round rocket launchers; a US armored division at full strength has around 17,000 men, 324 medium tanks, and 66 howitzers.

39. In Pact doctrine, divisions and, to some extent armies would be committed to intensive first-echelon combat missions for relatively short periods of time, after which they would be rotated into second echelon or reserve. Respites from combat would be used to restore the units' effectiveness by replacing personnel losses and repairing or replacing unserviceable or missing equipment. This contrasts with US practice of designing combat units with the idea of sustaining them in combat for long periods and keeping them more or less continuously replenished with personnel and equipment.

40. Thus, Pact and US replacement concepts are consistent with their respective force structures and employment practices and confer no particular advantage. The Soviets stress unit rather than individual replacements for combat units under engagement in both conventional and nuclear war and probably would confine individual replacements mainly to combat units in second echelon or reserve. The United States plans for unit replacement in nuclear war but would generally stress individual replacements in conventional war.

41. *Reliability of NSWP Forces.* While the USSR regards most of its allies with habitual distrust—and at one time or another most of them have merited distrust by rebellion or political instability—it has nevertheless entrusted them to carry out wartime functions potentially critical to the Pact's prospects for success in a conflict with NATO. The East Europeans provide more than half the Pact combat divisions in Central Europe, and the Soviets count on attacks by Polish units in the north and Czechoslovak units in the south to tie down large NATO forces and permit the concentration of Soviet and East German forces in the critical central sector. The major lines of communication from the USSR run through Poland, East Germany, and Czechoslovakia, and nationals of these countries are chiefly responsible for operating and maintaining them. Non-Soviet Warsaw Pact air defenses are intended to provide forward air defense for the western USSR and to protect the Pact's logistic and rear area support. All of this suggests that the Soviets have reconciled themselves to whatever reliability problems they envision and have made a calculated decision to rely on effective NSWP performance in the contingencies for which they plan military operations.

42. Many features of the Pact tend to assure the reliability of the NSWP allies. The Pact is dominated by Soviet officers, and major Soviet forces are stationed in four key counties. Allegiance is sought by the integration of NSWP officers into the Pact command structure, where they participate on a controlled basis. Promising, NSWP officers are schooled in the Soviet Union and indoctrinated with Soviet views and attitudes. Most officers and about half the noncommissioned officers are members of Communist parties or organizations; unreliable officers are dismissed. The missions assigned to the NSWP forces are intended to ensure their early involvement in a war. East German forces are interleaved with the Soviets, to ensure their reliability even against other Germans. The missions assigned the Polish and Czechoslovak forces are initially against their traditional enemies, the Germans.

The Air Offensive in Central Europe

43. Pact planners regard NATO's tactical air forces in Central Europe as a formidable threat to Pact ground, air, and nuclear forces during the initial, conventional phase of war, and as one of NATO's principal means for delivering nuclear strikes in Europe. Consequently, they consider the early attainment of air superiority and destruction of much of NATO's tactical nuclear forces to be critical to the Pact's chances for victory in the theater. The Soviets regard air superiority as a condition in which NATO's air and air defense forces would cease to pose a serious threat to the operations of Pact ground, air, and naval forces. The Pact plans to achieve these objectives by conducting a large-scale, theaterwide conventional air offensive during the first several days of hostilities. The Soviets refer to this offensive as the Air Operation (see inset).

THE AIR OPERATION

This is a Soviet concept denoting the temporary use of air forces belonging to different organizations in a large-scale coordinated effort to achieve a specific objective. Attainment of the objectives of an Air Operation is seen as having a potentially decisive effect on the outcome of a campaign or of the war itself. In World War II the Soviets mounted a number of Air Operations with the aim of destroying enemy air forces. These operations lasted an average of four to five days and their initiation usually coincided with the start of a major Soviet, or anticipated German, ground offensive. In a NATO-Pact conflict the Air Operation concept would govern the employment of the Pact's strategic and tactical air forces during the first few days of conventional hostilities. The objective of an Air Operation in Central Europe would be to destroy as much of NATO's air and theater nuclear forces as possible.

---

44. The goals and principal characteristics of the Air Operation have been ascertained from classified writings, human sources, and exercise scenarios:

— The Pact would commit most of its tactical aircraft and a large number of its Long Range Aviation (LRA) bombers to a series of air assaults designed to achieve tactical surprise at the outset of hostilities and lasting for the first two to four days of combat.

— Each assault, consisting of two or three waves of aircraft, would begin with a concerted effort to destroy or suppress air defenses in corridors through which attacking aircraft would proceed to strike airfields, nuclear-weapons-associated facilities, and command, control, and communications facilities.

— LRA bombers would constitute the primary force for attacking airfields. Most tactical air forces would be used to suppress air defenses, especially HAWK batteries. They would also be expected to provide fighter cover for attack aircraft, to provide reconnaissance and radioelectronic combat (REC) support, and to attack surface-to-surface missile units and some NATO airfields. Non-Soviet Warsaw Pact national air defense fighters would escort Soviet bombers over Pact territory and provide strategic air defense of their homelands.

— Some fighter-bomber and bomber aircraft would be withheld for use in nuclear operations, and a small number of tactical aircraft would be available for direct support of the ground forces.

45. Pact planners would regard attacks against NATO airfields as the principal way of gaining air superiority. They would intend such attacks to damage runways and other airfield facilities and thus degrade NATO's ability to operate its air forces effectively. They would also expect airfield attacks to account for most of the aircraft NATO would lose during the Air Operation. Pact fighter and ground-based air defenses would be expected, however, to contribute to the battle for air superiority by inflicting significant losses on NATO's air forces in the air.

46. In its effort to achieve nuclear superiority, the Pact would probably concentrate its attacks on those bases from which NATO nuclear delivery aircraft would operate. Tactical missile launchers would also be high-priority targets, but they would be difficult to locate and we believe that operations against them would not involve large numbers of aircraft.

47. *Forces.* The Pact has approximately 3,000 tactical aircraft, 775 national air defense fighters, and 525 LRA bombers available for use in Central Europe. (See table IV-2.) Pact writings and exercise scenarios lead us to estimate that, of these aircraft, about 350 LRA bombers and 1,200 to 2,100 tactical aircraft would be made available for use in the Air Operation. The remaining aircraft would be used to defend Pact territory and to provide direct combat support to Pact ground forces. Some of the remaining aircraft would also be kept in readiness for the transition to nuclear war.

48. The number of aircraft available for the initial assault of an Air Operation would vary according to the extent to which the Pact mobilized and moved additional tactical air units within range of NATO targets. Following are three illustrative postures from which the Pact could launch an Air Operation and an estimate of the number of aircraft that would be available in each after the Pact had made provision (as shown in table IV-3) for possible nuclear escalation and air support of its ground forces:

— *Forces in Place.* Aircraft allocated to the Air Operations in this posture would be limited to those considered by Pact air force planners to have a combat radius that would enable the aircraft to strike targets from, and return to, their home bases. Some 1,565 aircraft—350 USSR-based LRA bombers and 1,215 tactical aircraft belonging to Soviet and NSWP units in Central Europe—would fall into this category. Soviet

Table IV-2

Warsaw Pact Combat Aircraft Available for Use in the Western Theater of Military Operations [a]

	In Central Europe [b]			In the USSR			Grand Total
	Soviet	NSWP	Total	Tactical [c]	LRA [d]	Total	
Tactical Aircraft							
Fighters	630	235	865	360	—	360	1,225
Fighter-Bombers	405	465	870	435	—	435	1,305
Light Bombers	—	—	—	30	—	30	30
Reconnaissance/Electronic Warfare Aircraft	140	190	330	105	—	105	435
Total	1,175	890	2,065	930	—	930	2,995
National Air Defense Interceptors	—	775	775	—	—	—	775
Long Range Aviation Bombers	—	—	—	—	525	525	525
Total	1,175	1,665	2,840	930	525	1,455	4,295

[a] Combat aircraft in combat units. Excludes all trainers and combat aircraft in training or flying-school units.
[b] Pact air forces in East Germany, Poland, and Czechoslovakia.
[c] Tactical air forces in the Baltic, Belorussian, and Carpathian Military Districts.
[d] TU-16 Badgers, TU-22 Blinders, and Backfires in the Northwest and Southwest Bomber Commands.

SECRET

Table IV-3

Illustrative Allocation of Pact Combat Aircraft for Initial Use in the Western Theater of Military Operations
January 1979

	Illustrative Deployment Postures		
	Forces in Place	Limited Reinforcement [a]	Full Reinforcement [b]
Total Aircraft Available [c]	2,995	3,505	4,295
Of Which for:			
Air Operations,[d] Including	1,565	1,890	2,450
LRA	350	350	350
Tactical Combat	970	1,210	1,740
Tactical Reconnaissance/Electronic Warfare	245	330	360
Ground Support,[d] Including	300	385	515
Tactical Combat	240	305	425
Tactical Reconnaissance/Electronic Warfare	60	80	90
National Air Defense [e]	775	775	775
Nuclear Reserve,[f] Including	355	455	555
LRA	175	175	175
Tactical	180	280	380

[a] Includes aircraft in place plus the deployment forward of an East German wing (35 aircraft), one Czechoslovak regiment (35 aircraft), seven Polish regiments (335 aircraft), and three Soviet fighter/light-bomber regiments (105 aircraft) from the USSR.

[b] Includes aircraft in "limited reinforcement" category plus about 800 additional aircraft from the USSR.

[c] Normally only about 85 percent of these totals would be available for sustained operations.

[d] Allocation of tactical combat aircraft between ground forces support and the Air Operation is based on a 20-80 split after nuclear alert forces are withheld. This allocation is based on documentary evidence. Although we have no direct evidence, a 20-80 allocation between ground support and the Air Operation was also applied to tactical reconnaissance and electronic warfare aircraft.

[e] Allocation is based on national air defense subordination.

[f] A nuclear reserve in LRA of one-third of its forces is estimated from documentary evidence. The number of tactical aircraft withheld in the "forces in place" option is based on exercise evidence, while each of the reinforcement options assumes an additional allocation of 100 and 200 aircraft.

tactical aircraft based in the western USSR are not included in this illustrative posture.[3]

— **Limited Reinforcement.** Forces allocated to the Air Operation in this posture—some 1,890 aircraft—would include those described above and an additional 220 NSWP aircraft belonging to units which would be moved to within range of NATO targets and about 105 aircraft moved into East Germany from the Baltic Military District of the USSR.

— **Full Reinforcement.** Aircraft allocated to the Air Operation in this posture would total about 2,450. They would include all those noted in the "limited reinforcement" illustration and additional tactical aircraft that would be moved forward from the western USSR.

49. The Pact probably has contingency plans for initiating the Air Operation from any of the postures described above. Such plans probably involve various schemes for timing the movement of additional aircraft to bases within striking range of NATO targets. For example, the Pact could undertake such move-

---

[3] *The Director, Defense Intelligence Agency, and the Assistant Chief of Staff, Intelligence, Department of the Air Force, believe that, this illustrative posture notwithstanding, some tactical aircraft based in the USSR—for example, SU-24 Fencers—could be launched directly from their home bases in an Air Operation. See figures II-13 and II-14 of chapter II for detailed information on the combat performance of Soviet tactical aircraft.*

ment prior to, coincidental with, or after launching the initial assault. The Pact could also expand the area of employment of some of its tactical aircraft based deep in Pact territory by having the aircraft recover at bases closer to the West German border. This would avoid alerting NATO by deploying units forward before launching airstrikes but would strain the resources of the recovering airfields unless provision was made for augmenting logistical support.

50. The reequipment of Pact air forces in recent years with newer, longer range aircraft has resulted in a significant increase in the number of aircraft that could participate in an initial assault without first deploying forward. Pact planning continues to reflect initiation of the Air Operation from a deployment posture such as that illustrated in the "limited reinforcement" option. This evidence reflects an intent to move the Polish tactical air army closer to NATO territory and to introduce a Soviet light bomber division from the Baltic Military District into East Germany before hostilities start. The Polish tactical air force is still largely equipped with obsolescent short-range aircraft that cannot reach NATO targets and return to their home bases.

51. the size of the force illustrated in the "limited reinforcement" case—some 1,900 aircraft—would be sufficient to target in a single attack all NATO airfields in Central Europe which currently support nuclear strike units, as well as 40 percent of NATO's HAWK sites and 30 percent of NATO's primary air defense early warning and control radars. The 800 or so tactical aircraft that would remain in the western USSR after a limited reinforcement was carried out would probably serve as an immediately available reserve force. The forward deployment of these aircraft before hostilitites would enable the Pact to strike a greater number of targets in an initial air assault. These aircraft, however, would be exposed to NATO strikes because the Pact does not have enough shelters to accommodate them, and doubling up aircraft in existing shelter space, though possible, would not be practicable for combat operations.

52. **Preparations.** We estimate that it would take a minimum of 48 hours for the Pact air armies in Central Europe to deploy their wartime command post structure and establish the command and control required to engage in offensive air combat operations in support of a front commander. We believe, however, that it would take a total of about 72 hours to make the command and control preparations (including the updating of battle plans) needed to support a coordinated theaterwide air offensive, including LRA, against NATO airfields, nuclear weapon sites, and other priority targets as envisaged in Pact plans.

53. The other requisite preparations for a major offensive action could probably be accomplished within the time specified above. These would include the callup of reservists, final maintenance and the arming and fueling of aircraft, and the activation of additional airfields for dispersal or recovery purposes. Should the Soviets decide to deploy aircraft from the western USSR into the forward area, they probably could complete this deployment within 72 hours of the decision to do so.

54. Acquiring and processing timely intelligence on NATO forces also would be required before beginning the Air Operation, especially if NATO had been alerted. The Pact would almost certainly attempt to learn the location of air defense and surface-to-surface tactical missile units which had moved to wartime positions. An effort would also be mounted to identify airfields used for dispersal, particularly by nuclear-capable aircraft.

55. **Combat Operations.** The initial objective of the Air Operation would be to suppress NATO's air defenses—especially HAWK missile batteries—in several corridors. (See figure IV-3.) The creation of corridors would obviate the need to suppress all 84 of NATO's HAWK batteries currently in Central Europe and allow more tactical aircraft to be employed against primary targets such as airfields, surface-to-surface missile sites, and command and control facilities. If, for example, three corridors were established, an estimatsd 30 to 35 HAWK sites would have to be suppressed or eliminated. this number of sites could be suppressed by about 200 fighter-bombers. NATO's Nike-Hercules sites would not be subject to a major suppression effort.

Illustrative Penetration Corridors for a Warsaw Pact Air Operation Against the NATO Central Region

Figure IV-3

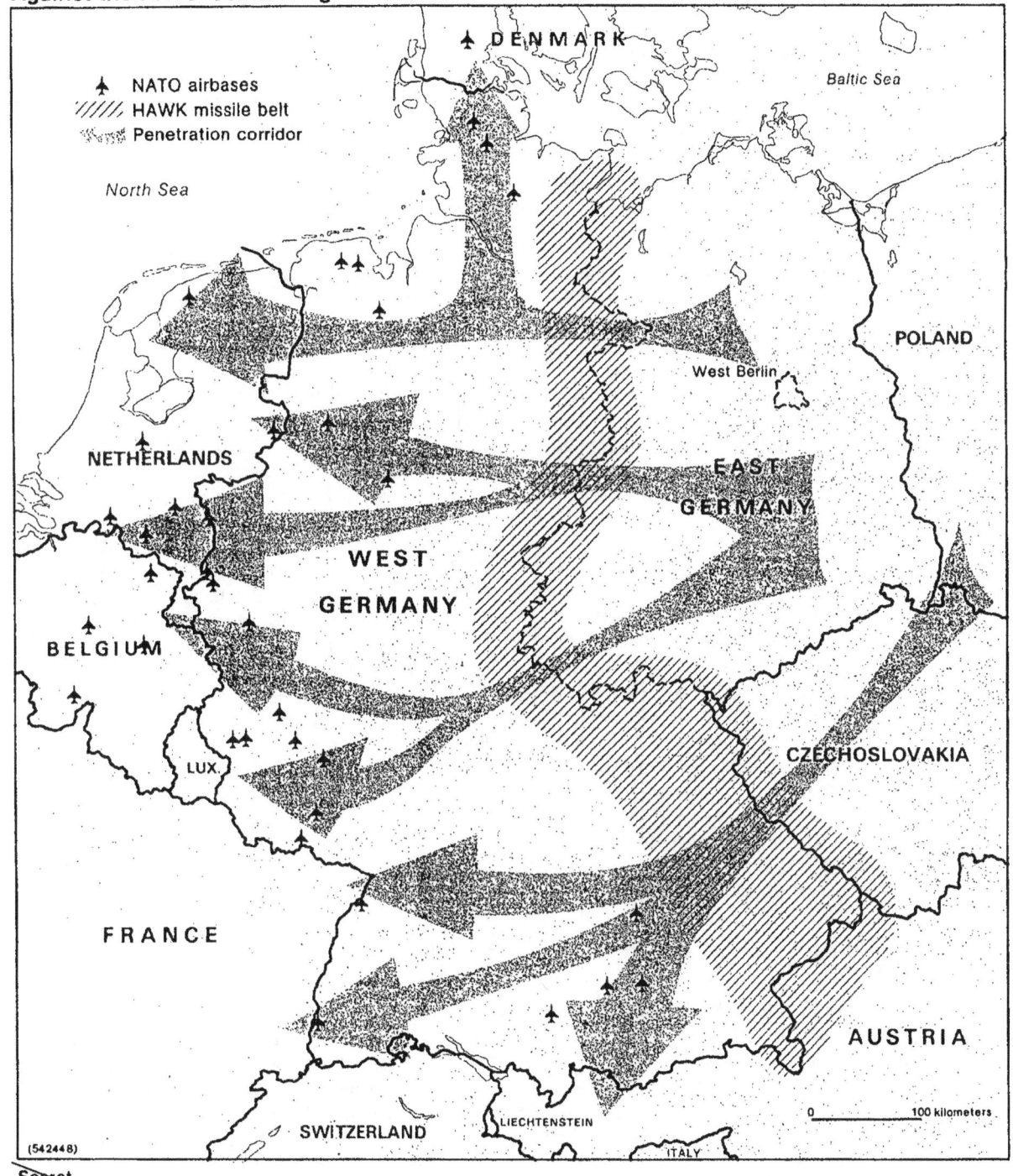

56. Tactical aircraft attacking HAWK units would seek to destroy their fire control radars and associated electronics vans by using cannon fire and unguided bombs and rockets. Area denial weapons such as cluster bomb units are also known to be in the Pact inventory and would facilitate an attack on dispersed targets. Pact tactical aircraft could also use the AS-7 Kerry tactical air-to-surface missile, but its effectiveness is limited by its small warhead, poor accuracy, and the vulnerability it imposes on the delivery aircraft because of the requirement to guide it to the target. Some attacks might also be carried out by tactical aircraft equipped with AS-10 laser-guided or AS-9 antiradiation missiles.

57. In recent years, LRA bombers may have simulated attacks against NATO's Air Defense Ground Environment (NADGE) radars using longer range antiradiation missiles. It would be logical for an attack on these major air defense radar sites, and on the field-transportable tactical air control system (TACS) radars, to precede the main defense suppression effort. Some missile-equipped LRA bombers could also be used against NATO air defense missile sites, especially those protecting important LRA targets in the NATO rear areas.

58. A related aspect of the Air Operation would be a large-scale, coordinated jamming effort aimed at disrupting NATO's air defense radars and communications links. The Pact is expected to depend heavily on airborne as well as ground-based electronic countermeasures (ECM) to facilitate penetration of NATO airspace. Techniques are expected to include the employment of both chaff and broadband noise jamming. The operating frequencies of current NATO air defense radars are well known and are covered by existing Pact noise jammers. Pact ground force ECM units would probably concentrate on the ultrahigh-frequency (UHF) ground-to-air and air-to-air communications used to control NATO interceptor operations. Line-of-sight considerations, however, would probably limit their effectiveness against NATO air defense radars.

59. Jamming of NATO's various early warning, ground-controlled intercept, and acquisition radars would be the responsibility of airborne electronic-warfare-equipped aircraft such as the AN-12 Cub C/D. This aircraft, carrying up to 20 transmitters, can jam all NATO aircraft control and warning radar frequencies. Because of its vulnerability, the Cub C/D would probably be used in a standoff jamming role. We estimate, for example, that as few as 10 of these aircraft, orbiting over East Germany and Czechoslovakia at 6,000 meters, could cover most NATO ground-based radars throughout West Germany.

60. Escort jamming for the main strike force would be provided by LRA's specialized ECM aircraft, which carry both jammers and chaff. About 20 percent of the LRA Badger force opposite NATO (65 Badger H/J aircraft) currently has a dedicated ECM role. About 40 Brewer E aircraft in Soviet Frontal Aviation are also available to provide standoff or escort jamming support. All Soviet bombers and a few types of Pact fighters are equipped with onboard jammers for use against air intercept and surface-to-air missile radars. Large numbers of Pact tactical aircraft can also be equipped with ECM pods, but this would reduce their weapons-carrying capability.

61. The main strike force would follow closely the defense suppression raids carried out by tactical air units and would be intended to deliver the brunt of the attack against NATO airfields, command and control facilities, and nuclear-related targets. LRA bombers would constitute the primary attacking force. Soviet planning factors indicate that the bomber force is large enough to attack simultaneously all 11 airfields in Central Europe which support NATO's nuclear delivery aircraft in peacetime. Some tactical fighter-bombers would also be used to attack airfields. The increased combat radius, payloads, and improved munitions of late-model Pact fighter-bombers enhance their effectiveness in this role.

63. Aerial reconnaissance would be conducted during the Air Operation, primarily by tactical aircraft, to provide Pact commanders with intelligence needed for subsequent targeting and to determine the number and scope of succeeding assaults. The Pact has three primary types of tactical aircraft available for reconnaissance: the MIG-25 Foxbat B/D, the YAK-28R Brewer D, and MIG-21R Fishbed H. Foxbats would probably photograph results of strikes against airfields

deep in NATO territory, while Fishbed and Brewer aircraft would cover targets closer to Pact borders.

64. *Potential Effectiveness.* We have no direct evidence of Pact expectations regarding aircraft losses during the Air Operation. We believe, however, that the Pact probably would not measure the success of the Air Operation in these terms. Substantial Pact losses might be viewed as tolerable to Pact planners contemplating a short, decisive conflict, even if the Air Operation managed only to keep NATO's air forces preoccupied with fending for their own survival during the first few days of hostilities. With their attention so diverted, NATO's air forces could have difficulty countering Pact ground forces during the most critical phases of their initial operations—the breakthrough and penetration of NATO's forward defenses.

65. How the Pact would measure the degree to which the Air Operation would contribute to Pact nuclear superiority is even less clear. Pact strategists may regard this objective as being subsumed under that of air superiority because they view NATO's air forces as the principal component of NATO's theater nuclear capability.

66. The ability of the Pact's air forces to reduce significantly the effectiveness of NATO's air and theater nuclear forces would be affected by a variety of factors. Chief among these factors are Pact capabilities to achieve surprise, effectively coordinate the employment of large numbers of aircraft, suppress NATO's air defenses and destroy aircraft, and crater runways and taxiways at NATO's airfields. Other important factors include the proficiency of Pact aircrews and the ability of Pact air forces to perform their primary missions in poor flying weather.

67. *Surprise.* Complete, or strategic, surprise by the Pact would be unlikely, in view of the extensive preparations it almost certainly would feel compelled to make to enhance the prospects for success of a general offensive in Central Europe and—above all—to reduce the risks posed by the threat of escalation. For these purposes the Pact, in addition to readying its air forces, would take steps to mobilize and move its ground and naval forces, and to put its political, economic, and civil defense systems on a war footing.

68. Soviet planners think more in terms of tactical surprise, or the sort of surprise which is attained in selecting the place, timing, and weight of an attack. This same analysis evinces a keen appreciation of NATO's ability to detect preparations, especially the movement of aircraft, and react quickly.

69. Surprise would affect the Pact's chances of pinning down aircraft at NATO's bases more than it would the Pact's ability to destroy aircraft. NATO has concrete shelters available for the protection of about 70 percent of the combat aircraft it normally maintains in Central Europe. Consequently, until the Pact equips its air forces with large numbers of precision guided munitions suitable for attacking shelters, most of NATO's aircraft would have considerable protection from conventional weapons. The advantage of surprise, therefore, lies in reducing the number of aircraft which NATO can get airborne by cratering the runways and taxiways.

70. The Soviets have considered minimizing NATO's warning time with a preemptive attack in which Pact air forces take off from their home bases and fly the most direct route to their targets. more NATO aircraft would be caught on the ground using this tactic because of the reduction in the Pact's flight time to NATO airfields. the Pact would also stand to lose more aircraft because of their greater exposure to NATO ground defenses. In the final analysis, the corridor approach would be the preferred method of attacking NATO's air defenses during the Air Operation.

71. *Management and Coordination.* The Pact's ability to orchestrate an Air Operation requiring precisely timed, multiple sorties by Soviet bombers flying out of the USSR and the tactical and national air defense forces of several different nationalities operating from within Eastern Europe is open to question. Although the Pact is believed to have the command, control, and communications necessary for such an operation, the full system has never been tested. There is some evidence which indicates that the Pact's ability to coordinate such an undertaking continues to be deficient.

[___] these problems probably concerned coordinating the employment of large numbers of aircraft from different Pact air forces.

72. Command and control deficiencies might not seriously affect the execution of the initial assault of the Air Operation because the participating air forces could perform according to a variety of preplanned options. Serious difficulties could arise in the execution of subsequent assaults, however, especially if the results of the first assault warranted drastic changes in Pact targeting or tactics and the aircrews could not be notified in a timely fashion.

73. An additional potential drawback in the Pact's ability to employ its air forces effectively deep within NATO territory lies in the dependency of Pact tactical aircraft on ground control stations for navigation. These aircraft would have to fly to remain within line-of-sight of these control stations and thus would become more vulnerable to NATO's air defenses; or fly low, where they would have a better chance of surviving but would be more likely to lose contact with their ground control stations. The only Pact ground attack aircraft that can effectively navigate without such assistance are the Fencer A, the Flogger D, and the Fitter C/D. These aircraft currently constitute about 40 percent of the ground attack aircraft the Pact has for operations in Central Europe.

74. Pact air forces generally are dependent on electronic control systems both for navigating to distant targets and for conducting aerial intercepts, and thus are vulnerable to electronic countermeasures. Pact electronic systems susceptible to jamming include radars used to vector aircraft in air-to-air engagements, short-range navigation systems, ground-to-air communications systems, Doppler navigation systems aboard the Flogger D and Fitter D, and bomb/navigation systems on Soviet bombers.

75. *Defense Suppression: HAWKs.* The number of LRA bombers able to reach NATO airfields, the principal objectives of an Air Operation assault, would depend primarily on the effectiveness of Pact efforts to suppress NATO air defenses, especially HAWKs. Since the tactical aircraft assigned this responsibility are currently equipped mainly with direct attack weapons, the HAWKS would have to be visually identified by Pact aircrews before they could be struck. The difficulty of this task would be compounded considerably if NATO were alerted and the HAWKs were moved from their peacetime dispositions. Moreover, because the HAWKs are mobile, the Pact would probably have to revalidate their location for each successive defense suppression assault.

76. Recent improvements in Pact reconnaissance capabilities should increase the speed with which strike aircraft could react to exploit intelligence giving the location of HAWK batteries. Soviet reconnaissance units in Central Europe, for example, now have aircraft equipped with television (Brewer D and Fishbed H). These aircraft types also have a realtime communications link to ground control stations that could direct strike aircraft to newly identified targets. To collect the requisite data, however, the Brewers and Fishbeds would have to overfly NATO territory and expose themselves to NATO air defenses, including the HAWKS. Aircraft equipped with sidelooking radar, such as the Foxbat D, are also available and could partially alleviate this problem by remaining in Pact airspace. We believe these aircraft would have to land, however, in order for the data to be processed and exploited.

77. *Defense Suppression: NADGE and TACS.* NATO's 17 NADGE radar sites in Central Europe, which are fixed and soft, would be highly vulnerable to attack during the Air Operation. Attacks against the US TACS radars, however, would be more difficult because they are field transportable and camouflaged. Munitions which the Pact would be likely to use against either NADGE or TACS sites include unguided bombs, rockets, and antiradiation missiles.

78. *Airfield Attack.* Whatever success the Pact would have in eliminating NATO airpower as an obstacle to a Pact victory would hinge largely on Pact capabilities to destroy aircraft protected by shelters or to put runways and taxiways at NATO airfields out of commission. The Pact's current capability to achieve the objectives it has set for the Air Operation through airfield attacks is judged to be limited for two reasons. One is the size of the force the Pact apparently intends to commit to this task. The other is the tactics the Pact apparently intends to employ.

79. We calculate that about 15 of the 43 main operating bases which NATO normally maintains in peacetime could be attacked in a single assault during the Air Operation. This assessment is based on the number of LRA and tactical air regiments the Pact would be likely to commit to airfield attacks and on Pact planning factors which indicate that one regiment of aircraft would be assigned to attack a single NATO airfield. In conducting the Air Operation, therefore, Pact strategists would face a difficult choice. They could attack each of NATO's major bases once or

conduct repeated attacks against fewer airfields, concentrating on those where nuclear delivery aircraft are based. The Pact's desire to reduce NATO's nuclear strike potential leads us to believe that the Pact would select the latter alternative. NATO maintains 11 airfields in Central Europe where nuclear strike aircraft are based in peacetime. Should NATO disperse its nuclear strike aircraft, however, the Pact's targeting problem would be compounded.

80. Pact tactics do not appear to maximize the potential effectiveness of the force committed to attacking airfields. Evidence [redacted] reflects a Pact tendency to commit the attacking force against both shelters and runways instead of concentrating the attack on one or the other [redacted]

81. *Aircrew Proficiency.* By US standards, Pact tactical aircrews generally are not well trained for combat in the hostile environment they would likely encounter in executing the Air Operation. The training Pact aircrews receive is largely stereotyped, lacks realism, and does not prepare them to exploit the full potential of their aircraft and its weapons systems. Pact aircrews are not exposed to the sorts of tactics NATO pilots would be expected to employ, nor do they practice ground attacks in a realistically simulated hostile air defense environment.[4]

82. A key potential drawback affecting the Pact's ability to execute the Air Operation effectively could be the dearth of training Pact aircrews receive for flying combat missions at low altitudes or over long distances, and their inexperience in operating independently. Peacetime training for Pact aircrews is conducted under strict ground control, which compensates for the rudimentary navigation instrumentation of most Pact tactical aircraft. Operations over NATO territory beyond the range of Pact control stations, therefore, would be flown by aircrews little prepared to seek out and attack airborne NATO aircraft or targets on the ground.

83. The Pact's ability to provide sufficient numbers of proficient pilots would be further constrained by the Pact's requirement to maintain a portion of its force on alert for nuclear operations. Manning this force probably requires up to 200 of the Pact's most experienced tactical aviation aircrews, which would be unavailable for conventional Air Operations. Of the 1,500 tactical aircrews that would be needed to fly the aircraft made available for an initial assault, some 25 to 35 percent would be third-class pilots, who by Pact standards are not qualified to fly combat missions in darkness or in adverse daytime conditions.

84. *Weather.* Because only a small percentage of the Pact's tactical aircraft are equipped to navigate at low altitude or to attack targets in poor weather, good weather with visibilities in excess of several thousand meters would be imperative for the success of the Air Operation. Only Fencer and Backfire aircraft, which are estimated to have full inertial navigation systems and terrain-avoidance and bomb-navigation radars, would have any appreciable capability to conduct operations in poor visibility. Further, crews operating the Badger bombers would also need good visibility, especially if the Badger bombers were to attempt penetrating NATO airspace at low altitude, because they lack a terrain avoidance radar. Once in the target area, however, weather would not be a critical factor because the Badger is capable of radar-directed bombing.

85. *Summary Assessment.* Some in the Intelligence Community believe that, on balance, a Pact Air Operation would do considerable damage to NATO's air and air defense forces, but probably would not be so effective as to prevent NATO's air forces from being able to deliver nuclear weapons on a large scale.[5] This conclusion is based on the evaluation of Pact deficiencies and weaknesses contained in paragraphs 67-84, above. Others believe that no judgment with any useful level of confidence on the effectiveness of an Air Operation is possible at this time.[6] They believe that such a conclusion should of necessity be based on a rigorous analysis of the factors involved which apply to both NATO and the Pact, and the interaction of the forces of both sides. They observe that no such analysis has been offered to support the conclusion. They further believe that the sensitivity of any such analysis to assumptions which have to be based on meager evidence—Pact weapon allocation and delivery tactics, for example—would leave the validity of such an analysis open to question.

---

[4] See chapter II, paragraphs 69-71, for a further discussion of Pact aircrew training.

[5] *The holders of this view are the Central Intelligence Agency and the Director, Bureau of Intelligence and Research, Department of State.*

[6] *The holders of this view are the Director, Defense Intelligence Agency, and the Assistant Chief of Staff, Intelligence, Department of the Air Force.*

Naval Operations in the Baltic

86. Warsaw Pact naval operations in the Baltic would be conducted in the context of the overall campaign in the Western Theater of Military Operations in Central Europe, and would conform with the timing and objectives of the Pact's ground and air forces, in particular those of the Polish, or Northern, Front of that TVD. This front, composed primarily of Polish forces, but with the support of the Combined Baltic Fleet, would be initially responsible for capturing northern West Germany and Denmark.

87. The broad objectives of Pact naval operations would be to gain complete control of the Baltic Sea and access to the North Sea to sever NATO's lines of communication in the North Sea, and deprive NATO of potential launch areas for carrier strikes against Pact air and ground forces in the Central Region. (See figure IV-4.) Control of the Baltic Sea would also facilitate subsequent amphibious operations against Denmark and West Germany, act as a defensive buffer for Pact territory, and defend Pact sea lines of communication from NATO attack. The major Pact forces involved would consist of the Soviet Baltic Fleet reinforced by the naval forces of East Germany and Poland (see table IV-4), the Soviet Baltic Fleet Air Force, Long Range Aviation, and elements of the Pact's national air defense and tactical air forces.

88. *Antiship and Antisubmarine Warfare.* A main objective of the Pact's initial naval operations in the Baltic would be to destroy NATO submarines, fast patrol boats, and mine warfare units because they could interfere with Pact ship movements, especially west of Bornholm Island, and amphibious operations. Pact planners recognize that the elimination of these forces in the Baltic would be a difficult task. ing to operational availability information reported to the Danes and West Germans probably would have 23 diesel-powered submarines and 40 fast patrol boats, 23 of the latter missile armed, after two to four days of preparation. Obviously, it would be preferable for the Pact to destroy these ships at their bases, but a period of tension would provide time for them to deploy and disperse, requiring the Pact to locate and destroy them at sea or in concealed anchorages. This would require effective coordination of all Pact forces,

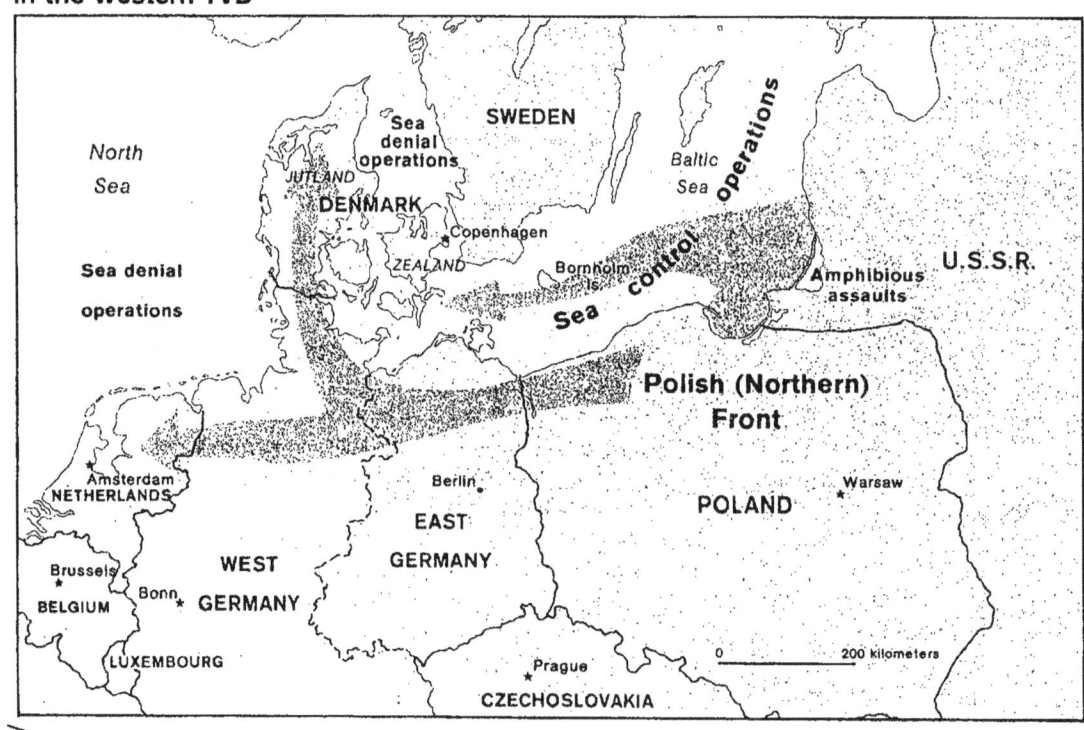

Illustrative Warsaw Pact Naval and Amphibious Operations in the Western TVD

Figure IV-4

Table IV-4

Warsaw Pact General Purpose Naval Forces Estimated To Be Available for Use in the Western Theater of Military Operations
January 1979 [a]

	Soviet [b]	NSWP [c]	Total
General Purpose Submarines			
Cruise Missile Units	1	—	1
Torpedo Attack Units	14	2	16
Principal Surface Combatants			
Cruisers	3	—	3
Destroyers	8	1	9
Frigates	24	2	26
Amphibious Ships	14	23	37
Naval Aircraft [d]			
Strike Aircraft	78	—	78
Reconnaissance/Electronic Warfare Aircraft	12	9	21
Tankers	18	—	18
Fighters/Fighter-Bombers	32	44	76
ASW Fixed-Wing Aircraft	18	—	18
ASW/Reconnaissance Helicopters	26	36	62

[a] Assumes that 60 percent of general purpose submarines, 70 percent of surface combatants, and 85 percent of naval aircraft would be available given four days of preparation. See paragraphs 102 and 103 and table II-8 in chapter II for information concerning normal peacetime availability of Soviet naval forces.

[b] The Soviet Baltic Sea Fleet. Not included are minor surface combatants or 10 reserve ships and 52 reserve submarines.

[c] The East German and Polish Navies. Does not include minor surface combatants.

[d] Operations of naval aircraft in the Western TVD would be augmented by those of Pact national air defense forces, Frontal Aviation, and Soviet Long Range Aviation.

89. The Soviets probably would find it difficult to deal with West German and Danish submarines in the Baltic, particularly if these forces were well coordinated. NATO boats have good shallow-water operating capabilities, are quiet, and have well-trained crews. Moreover, the Soviets would find it difficult to conduct antisubmarine warfare (ASW) operations without air superiority. Under the difficult hydrological conditions that generally characterize the Baltic, we believe that Pact ASW sensors would be inadequate to detect submarines at useful ranges except possibly in harbor entrances and a few close-in coastal areas.

90. *Air Operations.* Air superiority would be a critical ingredient to Pact Baltic Sea operations. As part of the effort to gain overall theater air superiority at the outset of a conflict in Central Europe, initial Pact air operations in the Baltic would be directed against West German and Danish naval bases and airfields and against NATO naval units already present in the area in an attempt to establish sea control and air superiority for the protection of subsequent Pact amphibious operations. Pact air forces probably would also operate against NATO naval forces in the North Sea. Initial strikes by Baltic Fleet bombers against NATO air defenses in Denmark and northern West Germany might be part of air operations in Central Europe or at least would be coordinated with those operations. Such strikes would facilitate the overflight of Soviet naval aircraft en route to NATO naval targets in the North Sea.

91. Achievement of air superiority over the Baltic would depend largely on the success of the Pact's critical offensive air operations in Central Europe. In addition, Pact naval forces would benefit from effective operations by the national air defense forces. Pact tactical aircraft supporting ground troops in coastal areas could also contribute to the contest for air superiority. Fighter cover for surface ships operating in the western Baltic would be at the expense of other missions related to the major air and land battle in the Central Region, however.

92. About 15 of the major Soviet Baltic Fleet warships, one East German frigate, and one Polish destroyer have surface-to-air missile systems. These

systems were designed for self-defense and the protection of other ships in close company, however, and do not have a wide-area defense capability. Pact air superiority in the Baltic would thus be enhanced only to the extent that these ships defended the airspace overhead, forced NATO aircraft into inefficient attack patterns, and possibly caused some attrition among the attacking formations. The Pact probably views the 60 F-104 fighter-bombers (armed with short-range anti-ship cruise missiles) of the West German naval air arm as constituting a primary threat to its surface forces in the Baltic.

93. Most major Soviet warships have some capability to control air defense aircraft in simple airborne intercepts. The Soviets occasionally practice such operations in the Baltic, but most, if not all, air intercept operations in the area probably would be controlled from land-based facilities. Moreover, shipborne controllers generally are not proficient.

94. Soviet plans for coordinating the air defense operations of the various forces in the Baltic to prevent mutual interference are unclear. [ ] we would expect a theater air defense commander to coordinate the air defense operations throughout the Western TVD, [ ] Lack of training could lead to major failures in the air defense system there.

95. *Amphibious Operations.* [ ] we believe that if initial sea control and air superiority operations were successful, Pact forces in the Baltic would then concentrate on supporting the Polish (Northern) Front's offensive across northern West Germany and into Jutland. Combined amphibious and airborne landings are planned against the Danish islands. The Soviets consider seizure of these islands, especially Zealand, to be necessary to prevent naval use of the Baltic by NATO, to permit passage of Soviet naval forces to and from the North Sea, and to be able to carry out subsequent amphibious operations against southern Norway. Early airborne or amphibious operations are also planned against Bornholm Island to neutralize NATO intelligence collection facilities there and prevent its subsequent use by NATO combat forces.

96. Amphibious operations in the Baltic would involve ships from the Soviet, Polish, and East German Navies, plus mobilized merchant ships. Assault forces would be drawn from the Soviet Baltic Fleet naval infantry regiment, the Polish sea landing division, and a specially trained regiment of an East German motorized rifle division. A Polish mechanized division which has received some amphibious training and Soviet motorized rifle divisions from the USSR could be included in follow-on landings. The amphibious landings would be coordinated with the ground offensive in Jutland and with airborne landings by a Polish division and perhaps Soviet airborne troops.

97. The overall direction of Baltic amphibious operations would be from the command post of the Western Theater of Military Operations (the TVD staff would include a TVD deputy commander for naval forces). Front and fleet staffs would perform battle management functions. We also expect that the front would deploy an operations group to control the amphibious operation ashore and that the front and fleet would exchange operations groups to facilitate coordination. Interservice coordination and control probably would be the responsibility of the TVD deputy commander for naval forces.

98. [ ] operations to weaken NATO defenses in the amphibious landing area would be conducted by Pact tactical aircraft, including helicopters, and naval gunfire. These operations might be augmented by naval bombers of the Baltic Fleet Air Force. The regiment of SU-17 Fitter fighter-bombers of the Baltic Fleet Air Force also could provide direct support of Pact amphibious operations. This regiment might also attack other land targets in the Baltic such as NATO naval bases, ports, and air defense installations, and be used for countering the large number of Danish and West German fast patrol boats.

99. Because of a shortage of NSWP landing craft, some Polish and East German amphibious assault forces probably would use Soviet lift in the initial assault. East Germany's current production of amphibious ships, however, will soon provide sufficient lift for its specially trained motorized rifle regiment. Although the two remaining regiments of the East German motorized rifle division are not trained for amphibious operations, we have evidence that they would be lifted by merchant ships as a followup force. Because of the relatively short distances between the Danish islands and Pact territory, the shortage of landing craft for rapid reinforcement and resupply of the landing forces on the islands could be alleviated to some extent by a shuttle using conventional landing craft, air-cushion vehicles, and possibly helicopters.

100. The Pact clearly is aware that the success of its Baltic amphibious operation would depend on the attainment of air superiority and sea control of at least

the area west of Bornholm Island. Pact planners also recognize that the operation would require the multinational integration of a variety of forces, including tactical aircraft and mine-warfare, ASW, gunfire support, and logistic ships. This continues to be a problem for the Pact in its combined Baltic Sea amphibious exercises.

101. We conclude that failure to attain air superiority and sea control of the western Baltic, especially in conventional war, would almost certainly cause the Pact to reconsider the feasibility of its planned amphibious operations. If the amphibious assaults were canceled, Pact planners would also have to decide if any airborne operations could be conducted independently.

102. *Mine Warfare.* Pact planners believe that a key element in all Baltic operations would be to thwart NATO minelaying operations by destroying mine stockpiles and minelaying ships before they deploy. Both Denmark and West Germany possess large stocks of mines (approximately 10,000 for the Germans and 6,000 for the Danes), and more could be introduced into the area by other NATO members. Soviet doctrine and probably Pact planning emphasize the need to locate NATO mine stockpiles in peacetime so that, in the event NATO did not deploy them before the outbreak of hostilities, the mines could be destroyed early in the war.

103. We have reliable evidence that Pact planners would consider NATO minefields off the Danish and German coasts to be a serious threat to their amphibious operations. The task of clearing paths through large fields of contact and influence mines, particularly if opposed by NATO air and naval forces, would be viewed by the Pact as extremely difficult and potentially quite costly. In addition, Pact mine-clearing forces have not demonstrated a high level of proficiency in exercises or other peacetime operations such as in the Gulf of Suez.

104. Nonetheless, Pact naval forces in the Baltic have approximately 175 mine warfare ships and craft of all types and routinely train in mine-clearing operations. In addition, the use of air-cushion vehicles (the Soviets have 15 to 20 in the Baltic) could reduce to a limited extent the vulnerability of some light amphibious elements to NATO mines.

105. The Soviets consider that sea transportation is important for maintaining a high rate of advance along a coastal axis and that, under some conditions, it may be the principal means of resupply. The number of ships assigned to protect Baltic sea lines would be affected by the demands of competing tasks and by Pact success in gaining sea control and air superiority during the initial phase of operations. In the event of continued antiship operations by NATO submarines and fast patrol boats, both of which could also be used to lay mines, the Pact might feel it necessary to allocate a significant portion of the smaller ships to the protection of the Baltic Sea supply lines. They also could route convoys to take advantage of coastal defense coverage. Pact planners seem to feel it necessary to use far larger forces to escort convoys than would Western navies.

106. *Operations in the North Sea.* In addition to the initial naval operations in the Baltic itself, other operations would be conducted in the North Sea to destroy important NATO maritime targets, especially aircraft carrier or amphibious forces, to prevent NATO naval reinforcements from entering the Baltic and to sever the lines of communication through the North Sea to the European continent.

107. Evidence indicates that anti-surface-ship air operations in the North Sea and its approaches would be conducted primarily by missile-equipped aircraft of the Baltic Fleet and possibly some from the Northern Fleet. Pact planners envision that operations from Baltic airfields probably would require the establishment of safe flight corridors—probably using some of these same missile-equipped aircraft—across Denmark or northern West Germany. They also probably believe that airstrikes by way of the Norwegian Sea would require suppression of Norwegian- and UK-based air defenses. If the Pact's initial air defense suppression operations were successful, those surviving strike aircraft not on nuclear alert would then be available to attack NATO forces in the North Sea. Initially, in a period of conventional warfare, as much as one-third of the Baltic and Northern fleet naval aircraft probably would be withheld for nuclear operations.

108. _____ the Soviets intend to deploy a few Baltic and Northern Fleet submarines to the North Sea before the outbreak of hostilities to complement the antiship operations of Pact aircraft. A deployment from the Baltic, however, would provide warning indications to NATO. We believe that deployments of surface ships into the North Sea prior to hostilities would be unlikely because the Pact would lack air cover there early in a war.

109. *Summary Assessment.* According to one view in the Intelligence Community, the allocation of most Pact tactical and LRA bomber aircraft to a large-scale Air Operation in West Germany and the Benelux countries would severely reduce the probability of the Pact's achieving air superiority over the Baltic in the initial stage of a war with NATO.[7] Without air superiority the Pact would have a low probability of sweeping NATO's mines or of successfully defending the amphibious force against NATO missile-armed fast patrol boats. It is further believed that Pact ASW forces probably would be unable to prevent NATO submarine attacks against the amphibious forces. These conclusions are based on the judgments contained in paragraphs 88-94, above.

110. An alternative view holds that the Warsaw Pact's achievement of air superiority over the Baltic would depend on many factors, including the allocation of Pact naval aviation aircraft to suppression of NATO air capabilities in the Baltic area, the degree of success the Pact forces might achieve in these air operations, and the speed with which they achieved it.[8] The holders of this view believe that the conclusions expressed above would be highly sensitive to a number of additional factors, including assumptions about the interaction of NATO and Pact surface and subsurface forces as well as about the timing and urgency which the Pact attached to prosecution of the amphibious operations. They observe that analysis of all these factors has not been sufficient to support any conclusions, explicit or implied, as to the probability of success or failure of Pact amphibious operations, or the degree to which the Pact could defeat NATO submarine operations, in the Baltic.

111. A third view holds that the achievement of air superiority is but one of a number of key factors which, taken together, will determine the outcome of the Pact's Baltic campaign.[9] The holder of this view considers that allocation of considerable air assets to the Pact's Baltic campaign is likely but believes that other factors of equally critical importance include the extent of Pact success in countering NATO mining and submarine operations in the approaches to the Danish Straits.

---

[7] *The holders of this view are the Central Intelligence Agency; the Director, Bureau of Intelligence and Research, Department of State; and the Director, National Security Agency.*

[8] *The holders of this view are the Director, Defense Intelligence Agency, and the Assistant Chief of Staff, Intelligence, Department of the Air Force.*

[9] *The holder of this view is the Director of Naval Intelligence, Department of the Navy.*

B. The Initial Campaign in the Southwestern Theater of Military Operations

112. ▢ the Soviets are concerned about the sizable groupings of NATO forces in the south and especially the threat of air and nuclear strikes which they expect would be launched against Eastern Europe and the USSR by the US 6th Fleet during a NATO–Warsaw Pact war. Accordingly, the Soviets assign high priority to the destruction of Western ballistic missile submarines (SSBNs) and aircraft carriers in the Mediterranean early in a war. They also place great importance on capturing the Turkish Straits—the Bosporus and the Dardanelles.

113. The Pact views early seizure of the Turkish Straits as crucial to the success of its maritime strategy in the Southwestern TVD for the following reasons:

— It would be necessary for wartime augmentation of Soviet naval forces in the Mediterranean by naval forces from the Black Sea. It also would permit the return of ships to the Black Sea for repairs and resupply.

— It would deny entry into the Black Sea of additional NATO ships and submarines.

— It would deny NATO use of the Straits area for launching any attacks against the USSR or Pact forces in the Black Sea, and permit Pact use of the area to support attacks into the Mediterranean.

114. ▢ Soviet ▢ stress the strategic importance of Austria as a link between the Western and the Southwestern TVDs and cite the importance of being prepared to counter any NATO threat launched across Austrian territory. There is also evidence that the Pact has plans for a major attack on northern Italy and deep offensives into Greece and Turkey.

115. ▢ in the Southwestern TVD have ▢ the Pact launching multifront offensives in response to NATO attacks against all these objectives simultaneously with the Central European campaign. We believe that to achieve its more important objectives, however, the Pact would confine its initial ground operations to the Straits area, Austria, and possibly eastern Turkey. In addition, at the onset of a war, air and naval attacks would almost certainly be mounted against NATO forces in these areas and in the Mediterranean.

Initial Ground Operations

116. ▭ the Pact has contingency plans for offensive operations in the south directed against Austria, possibly northern Italy, the Bosporus, the Dardanelles, Greece, eastern Turkey, and possibly Iran. ▭ conceivably the Pact might attempt to advance through Yugoslavia to attack northern Italy. The success of such a move would depend primarily on the attitude and political position of the Yugoslav Government. If the government authorized the transit of Pact forces through Yugoslav territory, the Pact would have shorter and quicker access to northern Italy. If Yugoslavia remained neutral, any Pact incursion probably would prompt armed resistance and defense of the homeland by the Yugoslav armed forces, which could seriously detract from the Pact's main efforts in Central Europe. On balance, we judge it unlikely that Yugoslavia would grant the Pact permission to use its territory or that the Pact would use force to advance through Yugoslavia to attack northern Italy. This judgment is qualified, however, by our uncertainty concerning future political attitudes and developments in Yugoslavia in the post-Tito era.

117. *Against Austria and Italy.* In wartime, the four Soviet divisions in the Southern Group of Forces (SGF) and the six divisions of the Hungarian Army would be subordinate to the Danube Front. (See table IV-5 and figure IV-5.) ▭ this

Table IV-5
Warsaw Pact Ground Force Divisions and Brigades Available for Use in the Southwestern Theater of Military Operations
January 1979

	In the Balkans[a]		In the Southwestern USSR[b]	Total
	Soviet	NSWP		
Divisions				
Tank	2	3	8	13
Motorized Rifle	2	19	27	48
Brigades	--	9 [c]	--	9

[a] Soviet divisions in Hungary (Southern Group of Forces) and ground forces in the Hungarian, Romanian, and Bulgarian Armies.

[b] Soviet tank and motorized rifle divisions in the Odessa, Kiev, North Caucasus, and Transcaucasus Military Districts. The Soviets also have two airborne divisions in these military districts which could be used against NATO in one or more theaters.

[c] Two of these brigades are designated for wartime expansion to motorized rifle divisions.

front would move into Austria to protect the flank of the Western TVD and to destroy any NATO forces that might have entered Austrian territory. In exercises, this invasion is preceded by either a West German or an Italian incursion into Austria. In any case, we believe that the Pact would invade Austria at the start of a war to secure the southern flank of the Western TVD.

118. ▭ the Pact expects it would take about two weeks to defeat the main bodies of Austrian and NATO forces in Austria and be in a position to advance into northern Italy. Given this timing, we believe that the Pact sees an invasion of Italy primarily as a possible followup operation and not essential to the success of the initial campaign against NATO. Moreover, an early move toward Italy could present a difficult problem for Pact commanders in that the main objective of the Danube Front, at least during the first week of the war, would be to protect the flank of the Western TVD.

119. *Against the Dardanelles and the Bosporus.* Before initiating an assault against the Straits, the Soviets plan to move ground and air forces from the Odessa Military District into Bulgaria, with most of these forces transiting Romania. These forces, probably augmented by NSWP forces, would form the Maritime (or Odessa) Front, consisting of as many as 12 divisions. This front's objectives would be to destroy Turkish forces in eastern Thrace, to break through the fortifications protecting the land approaches to the Turkish Straits, and to seize the Straits. Exercises indicate that Soviet forces in the Kiev Military District also have contingency roles as second-echelon forces in this or other areas of the Southwestern TVD.

120. Amphibious and airborne operations, using primarily Soviet forces—probably one motorized rifle regiment and one naval infantry regiment—and a Bulgarian naval infantry battalion, would probably be conducted to support a forced crossing of the Bosporus by elements of the Maritime Front. The Pact would coordinate the timing and location of amphibious landings with both airborne operations and the movement of the Maritime Front along the southwestern littoral of the Black Sea. Soviet surface naval forces would almost certainly be used to establish sea lines of communication to augment the relatively poor landlines supporting the Maritime Front.

121. Timing the seizure of the Straits would present Pact planners with the following special problems:

— Operations to seize the Straits would require Soviet ground forces from the Odessa Military

Illustrative Warsaw Pact Operations in the Southwestern TVD

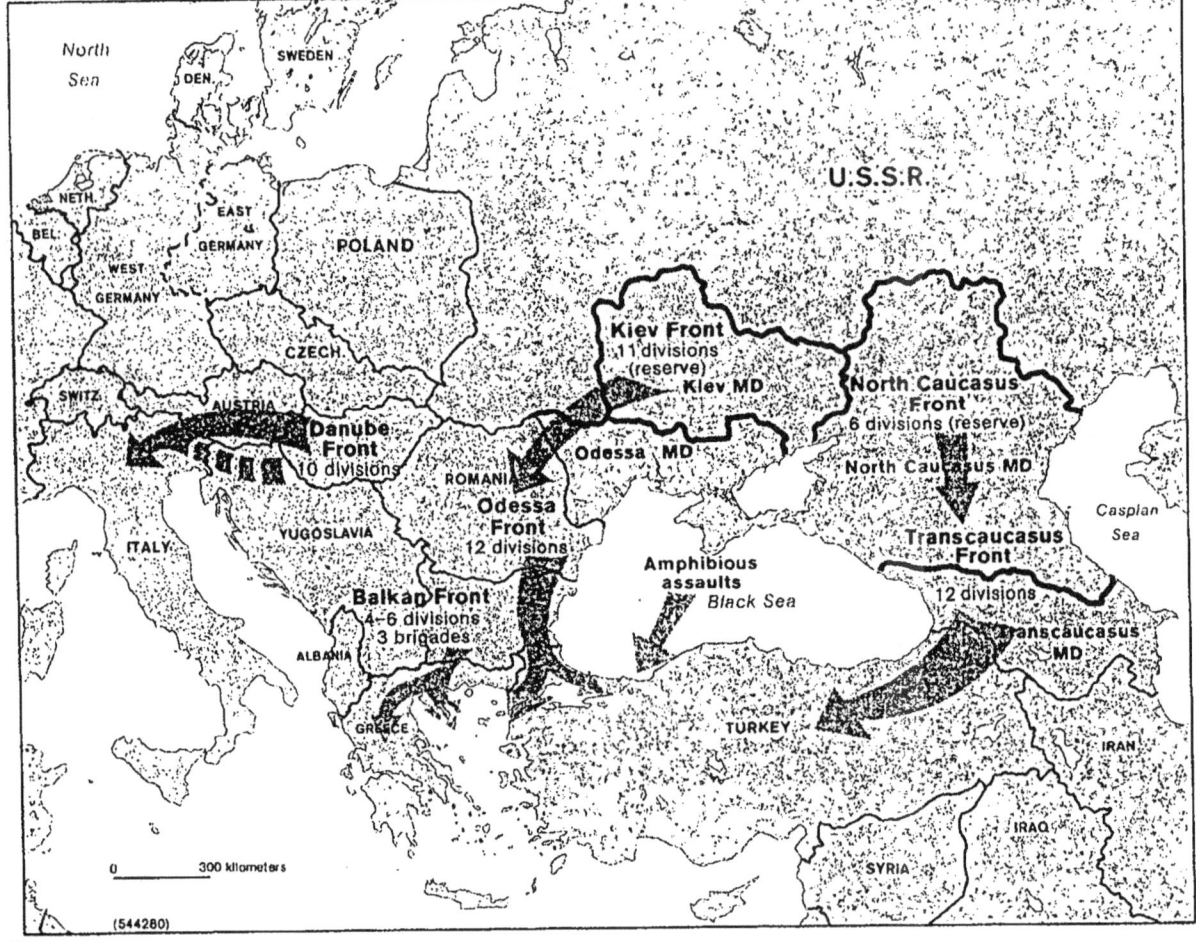

Figure IV-5

District. Once these forces were mobilized, we estimate that they would require about a week to be in position to launch an attack from Bulgaria. If they were to move before the start of a war, this movement would provide warning to NATO in the Southwestern Theater and elsewhere as well.

— The ground campaign to seize the Straits would be difficult and time consuming and would provide NATO time to obstruct the Straits and thus deny their immediate use after seizure.

— The Soviets probably would consider that the airborne division and naval infantry regiment which would be available for joint amphibious and airborne assaults would not be large enough to overcome Turkish defenses and secure the area without timely linkup with the Maritime Front. Airborne operations in this theater would also have to compete for lift resources with operations planned in the Western TVD and thus have to await the accomplishment of these operations.

122. *Against Greece.* On the western flank of the Maritime Front, the remaining two Bulgarian armies, consisting of four to six motorized rifle divisions and three tank brigades, would essentially form the Balkan Front. This front could also include some Romanian forces, although it is more likely that the Romanians would constitute their own national front in the TVD's second echelon. ▢ the mission of the Balkan Front is to break through Greek fortifications and to advance to the Aegean Sea and from there into

IV-26

the main part of Greece. However, considering the size of the Balkan Front and the questionable commitment of Romanian forces to the offensive, we believe that the Balkan Front would probably confine its actual wartime operations to engaging Greek forces in the Thrace area and to defending the western flank of the Maritime Front's forces attacking the Turkish Straits.

123. *Against Eastern Turkey.* While the Soviets might launch a limited offensive into eastern Turkey, we have no evidence that they would undertake operations against Iran during an initial phase of the war. During Soviet exercises, forces from the Transcaucasus Military District have formed a front which—following Turkish and Iranian attacks—conducted operations into eastern Turkey and Iran. In these exercises six Soviet divisions notionally advance between the Turkish Black Sea coast and Lake Van in the direction of Ankara, and a Soviet army of four divisions moves into Iran. Other Soviet divisions, including some from the North Caucasus Military District, form a reserve force—possibly under the control of a North Caucasus Front.

124. There are important constraints on initial Pact ground operations in the Southwestern TVD:

— The Pact probably would not be able to achieve general air superiority or cripple NATO's nuclear war-fighting capability in the theater during conventional conflict. In the Balkans the Pact lacks sufficient ground attack aircraft for simultaneous air attacks against aircraft carriers, NATO airfields, and important air defense, nuclear, and command and control targets.

— The Pact would also face difficult terrain in most of the Southwestern TVD which would impede rapid force deployment and resupply and facilitate NATO defense.

— Soviet forces are at a considerable distance from their wartime areas of operation. Prehostilities deployment of forces would alert NATO and permit defensive preparations, not only in this secondary theater, but in Central Europe as well.

— Romanian forces, as well as Romanian operation and defense of lines of communication, would be vital to sustaining Pact offensive operations against Greece and western Turkey. Romanian reliability is thus a key to sustained Pact offensive operations in the area.

125. Nevertheless, Pact land operations in these areas, if successful, would offer potential benefits. Seizure of the Straits would give the Pact flexibility in committing units from the Black Sea Fleet and provide a more secure line of communication for the Mediterranean Squadron. A Pact advance into Austria would threaten NATO forces in southern Germany and northern Italy, while an offensive into eastern Turkey would tie down Turkish forces in the area.

Initial Naval Operations in the Black Sea

126. [redacted] as part of the offensive by the Pact's Maritime Front, the Soviet Black Sea Fleet would attempt to secure control of the Black Sea, support the movement of Pact ground forces along the western littoral, and assist in seizing the Turkish Straits. Bulgarian and Romanian naval forces in the Black Sea would be primarily responsible for coastal ASW and other forms of coastal and port defense, including the use of guns and missiles. Table IV-6 shows Pact naval forces available for use in the Black Sea and Mediterranean.

127. Initial Pact naval operations in the Black Sea would be opposed primarily by Turkish forces, particularly air units (possibly with some US augmentation) and a Turkish submarine force of some seven to eight available diesel-powered submarines. The Greek and Turkish Air Forces would oppose Pact surface forces in the Black Sea and the eastern Mediterranean and Soviet naval and LRA aircraft overflying Turkish territory or the Aegean Sea to conduct strikes in the Mediterranean.

128. Pact air and sea superiority in the Black Sea would be particularly critical to the Pact's capability to provide air and ASW defense for the amphibious force designated to aid in seizing the Turkish Straits. To assist in the achievement of air and sea superiority and to protect the amphibious force, the Soviets probably would retain in the Black Sea at least some of their available larger combatants equipped for ASW and air defense—such as Moskvas, Karas, Kashins, and Krivaks. If none of these newer and more capable Soviet units were available to support Pact naval operations in support of the ground offensive, Pact capabilities to defend these operations against NATO might prove inadequate.

Table IV-6

Warsaw Pact General Purpose Naval Forces Estimated To Be Available For Use in the Southwestern Theater of Military Operations [a]
January 1979

	Soviet [b]	NSWP [c]	Total
Submarines			
Cruise Missile Units	4	—	4
Torpedo Attack Units	16	2	18
Principal Surface Combatants			
Helicopter Ships	1	—	1
Cruisers	8	—	8
Destroyers	18	—	18
Frigates	29	1	30
Amphibious Ships	19 [d]	—	19
Naval Aircraft			
Strike Aircraft	78	—	78
Reconnaissance/Electronic Warfare Aircraft	10	—	10
Tankers	11	—	11
Fighters/Fighter-Bombers	17	—	17
ASW Fixed-Wing Aircraft	21	—	21
ASW/Reconnaissance Helicopters	54	5	59

[a] Assumes that 60 percent of general purpose submarines, 70 percent of surface combatants, and 85 percent of naval aircraft would be available with four days of preparation. See paragraphs 102 and 103 and table II-8 in chapter II for information concerning the normal peacetime availability of Soviet naval forces.

[b] The Black Sea Fleet and the Mediterranean Squadron, including some eight torpedo attack and two cruise missile submarines normally deployed to the Mediterranean from the Northern Fleet. Not included are minor surface combatants, six reserve ships, and 32 reserve submarines.

[c] The Bulgarian and Romanian Navies. Does not include minor surface combatants.

[d] Includes eight available units assigned to the Caspian Sea flotilla.

SECRET

129. Even with these more modern ships, the Soviet fleet would be vulnerable to low-altitude attacks. The current lack of emphasis on collective defense in training exercises suggests that Soviet naval air defense is based primarily on individual ship self-defense, although missile-equipped ships probably are expected to provide protection for less capable ships in close company, as well as for themselves. Individual SAM-equipped ships probably would be able to defend against a few attackers at medium and high altitudes. Their defenses could be saturated, however, if many aircraft attacked simultaneously from different directions.

Initial Air and Naval Operations in the Mediterranean

130. An important initial mission of Pact tactical air forces would be to suppress NATO's forward air defenses in southern Europe, thus permitting the overflight of Long Range Aviation and naval aircraft heading for the Mediterranean. The Pact may also have plans to conduct a conventional air operation using tactical and LRA aircraft against NATO airfields in the Mediterranean area, but their ability to conduct such an operation would be constrained by the concurrent requirement for LRA bombers to conduct an air offensive in Central Europe and by the limited number of Pact fighter-bombers in the Southwestern TVD. (See table IV-7.) Pact air support of the ground forces would probably be largely confined to key areas, such as the Turkish Straits.

131. Soviet naval operations in the Mediterranean would begin at the start of a war and would be aimed primarily at the destruction of Western SSBNs and aircraft carriers. Forces used would consist of surface and submarine units in the Mediterranean at the outset of hostilities, as well as Soviet naval and perhaps LRA aircraft operating from bases in the Soviet Union and possibly from NSWP countries.

132. Soviet naval deployment patterns indicate that the Soviets expect most activity by their surface forces to be concentrated in the Mediterranean east of Sicily. the initial attacks by Soviet ships and submarines of the Mediterranean Squadron almost certainly would not occur before Pact operations began in other areas of the theater. The Black Sea Fleet Air Force would follow with strikes using air-to-surface missiles (ASMs), while free-fall bombers of Soviet Naval Aviation (SNA) and tactical aircraft were suppressing NATO air defenses. Some LRA aircraft, especially missile-armed Blinders and Backfires, might participate in raids against carriers, although most of these aircraft probably would be committed against Central Europe.

133. Soviet surface and submarine forces continuously monitor the positions of NATO carriers in the Mediterranean in peacetime. Judging by Soviet exercises and reactions in crises, we would expect the Soviets to intensify their surveillance before the outbreak of hostilities and be prepared to attack immediately after war broke out. Although not seen in exercises for several years, there is evidence that the Soviets perceive the value of simultaneously executing a missile attack from aircraft and surface ships and a missile and torpedo attack from submarines. They believe that such an attack would divide NATO defenses, bring the highest concentration of fire to bear, and provide the greatest probability of success.

Table IV-7

Warsaw Pact Tactical Aircraft Available for Use in the
Southwestern Theater of Military Operations
January 1979

	In the Balkans [a]		In the Southwestern USSR [b]	Total
	Soviet	NSWP		
Fighters	135	60	315	510
Fighter-Bombers	45	165	125	335
Light Bombers	30	—	—	30
Reconnaissance/Electronic Warfare Aircraft	35	60	105	200
Total	245	285	545	1,075

[a] Soviet tactical air forces in Hungary and the tactical air components of the Romanian and Bulgarian Air Forces. An additional 435 interceptor aircraft are assigned to the Hungarian, Romanian, and Bulgarian National Air Defense Commands.

[b] Soviet tactical aircraft based in the Odessa, Kiev, and Transcaucasus Military Districts.

134. The Soviets no doubt realize, however, that the advantages of such an attack are largely offset by the fact that Soviet strike aircraft would have to take off several hours in advance of the attack. Soviet ships, moreover, depend on centralized command and control from shore and would generate a high volume of specialized communications. These actions could alert NATO naval forces in the Mediterranean of the impending operations. ▒▒▒ forces in a position to attack aircraft carriers should not await the arrival of other forces.

135. *Operations by Naval Aircraft in the Mediterranean.* While the most immediate threat would come from Soviet ships and submarines already deployed in the Mediterranean, numerically the most sizable threat to NATO's naval forces there would come from missile-equipped Soviet strike aircraft, despite the fact that they would be operating without fighter escort. In a conventional war the USSR-based Black Sea Air Force could sortie about 40 ASM-carrying strike aircraft, with as many as 80 missiles, which could attack throughout the eastern Mediterranean. The Soviets would probably hold another 20 ASM carriers with 40 missiles in reserve as a hedge against escalation to nuclear war. Soviet exercises and training indicates that any reinforcement of the Black Sea Air Force would most likely come from the Baltic Sea Fleet, although reinforcement from the Northern Fleet is also possible.

136. Backfire strike aircraft can cover virtually the entire Mediterranean from Black Sea airfields.[10] Badger aircraft can carry out attacks in most of the eastern Mediterranean from Black Sea or NSWP airfields. The availability of airfields in a friendly North African country to stage or recovery would allow the Soviets to improve the effectiveness of air operations in the entire Mediterranean. At the present time, however, no North African airfields are available to the Soviets.

137. ▒▒▒ whenever possible, the Soviets would use 20 to 40 aircraft to attack an important target such as an aircraft carrier task group. This number would be designed to overwhelm NATO air defenses and achieve the six to 10 hits which the Soviets believe are necessary to disable an aircraft carrier using conventional warheads.

138. *Submarine Operations in the Mediterranean.* The Soviets normally keep eight to 10 submarines, including two cruise missile units, in the Mediterranean in peacetime. The cruise missile submarines usually keep a Western aircraft carrier within range of their missiles and probably would be in a position to

---

[10] See paragraphs 178 and 179 of chapter II for a discussion of the Backfire's capabilities.

attack at the outset of hostilities. In wartime the other submarines probably could monitor Western naval movements near major choke points and possibly near some of the main NATO naval bases.

139. By itself, however, the submarine force normally deployed in the Mediterranean is not large enough to attack all Western aircraft carriers and other potential NATO naval targets there at one time. Reinforcement from the Northern Fleet would take almost two weeks for nuclear-powered submarines—over three weeks for diesels—and provide NATO with warning indications if conducted before war broke out. Because of competing tasks elsewhere, limitations on the availability of submarines, and logistical constraints, we estimate that the submarine formation in the Mediterranean probably would not be reinforced before the outbreak of hostilities.

140. There is evidence that Soviet submarines in the Mediterranean would expend torpedoes only in self-defense or against high-value targets, especially aircraft carrier task groups, amphibious task groups, and US nuclear-powered submarines. Soviet submarines, because of their lack of survivable replenishment points, would probably not, as a matter of course, fire their torpedoes against merchant ships in the Mediterranean until they had succeeded in their attacks on high-value targets or were returning to base.

141. *Operations by Surface Ships in the Mediterranean.* Soviet surface forces normally in the Mediterranean consist of seven to nine combatants and 25 auxiliaries. These forces would conduct ASW operations and serve as target spotters and trackers for strikes by submarines, aircraft, and other surface ships. They would also provide command and control support for Soviet submarines and aircraft. Typically, the forces include one or two ships armed with cruise missiles. The remaining ships are armed with guns of 76-mm to 152-mm caliber and torpedoes. Many have air defense missiles which can be used in an antiship mode. In addition, all are equipped with a variety of ASW sensors and weapons. These ships almost certainly would be operating in an environment in which NATO had air superiority, however, and, together with Soviet submarines, would be the targets for some 30 NATO submarines.

142. There are divergent views within the Intelligence Community on whether or the extent to which the Soviets would augment their surface forces in the Mediterranean during a period of tension preceding the outbreak of hostilities. All agree that the intelligence evidence and other considerations which bear on this question include the following:

— We have no evidence of plans to augment the surface force in the Mediterranean during a period of tension before the outbreak of hostilities.

— Of some 60 principal surface combatants typically available in the Black Sea Fleet, seven to nine are normally deployed to the Mediterranean.

— The Soviets have sortied major surface warships from the Black Sea to augment the Mediterranean Squadron during major fleet exercises and in times of crisis. Following the 1973 Arab-Israeli war, for example, the Soviets almost doubled the size of the Mediterranean force and demonstrated the capability to augment the force quickly.

— Such an act would be a clear warning indicator, and it could be counterproductive, depending on NATO's reaction. On the other hand, it might be viewed by the Soviets as a way to demonstrate their resolve during a crisis.

— The Soviets recognize NATO's capability to block the Turkish Straits, and must consider that such operations could occur early in a war. Consequently, Soviet planners could not count on unobstructed passage to or from the Mediterranean after the outbreak of hostilities.

143. Some believe [11] that the Mediterranean Squadron probably would be augmented by at least a few, and possibly up to 12, of the large surface combatants in the Black Sea—such as Moskvas, Karas, Kyndas, and Kashins—before the outbreak of hostilities. Others believe [12] that the Soviets would deploy no more than a

---

[11] *The holders of this view are the Director, Defense Intelligence Agency; the Director, National Security Agency; and the Director of Naval Intelligence, Department of the Navy.*

[12] *The holders of this view are the Central Intelligence Agency and the Director, Bureau of Intelligence and Research, Department of State.*

few, if any, large combatants from the Black Sea before the outbreak of hostilities. The difference in judgment turns on whether the main purpose of the Black Sea Fleet is to provide air and ASW defense for operations against the Turkish Straits, or whether it is to augment the Mediterranean Squadron.

144. The holders of the first view believe the Fleet is in excess of requirements for the defense of local waters in the Black Sea and for offensive operations against Turkey and judge that, in any event, augmentation of the Mediterranean Squadron would not jeopardize an assault on the Straits. They argue that the time required to seize and clear the Straits and general uncertainty attending such an operation militate against the Pact's holding its forces in the Black Sea, risking their exclusion from use in the Mediterranean. The holders of the second view, on the other hand, point out that naval units sortied during periods of tension could be trapped in the Mediterranean, where they would be highly vulnerable to attack. They judge that Pact planners would view seizure of the Straits as more important than a modest augmentation of the Mediterranean Squadron.

C. The Initial Campaign in the Northwestern Theater of Military Operations

145. Initial Soviet objectives in the Northwestern TVD center on ensuring freedom of action and uninhibited access to the open ocean for the Soviet naval ships and aircraft and maintaining the forward defense of the extensive complex of naval bases and strategic installations located on the Kola Peninsula. (See figure IV-6.) Initial operations by Soviet land forces probably would be limited to northern Norway. We have no evidence indicating that the Soviets plan for a general offensive against Finland or Sweden early in a war. The Leningrad Military District—with its wartime front organization—is intended to defend the city of Leningrad and related areas in the Baltic, in addition to the operations in the north discussed in this section.

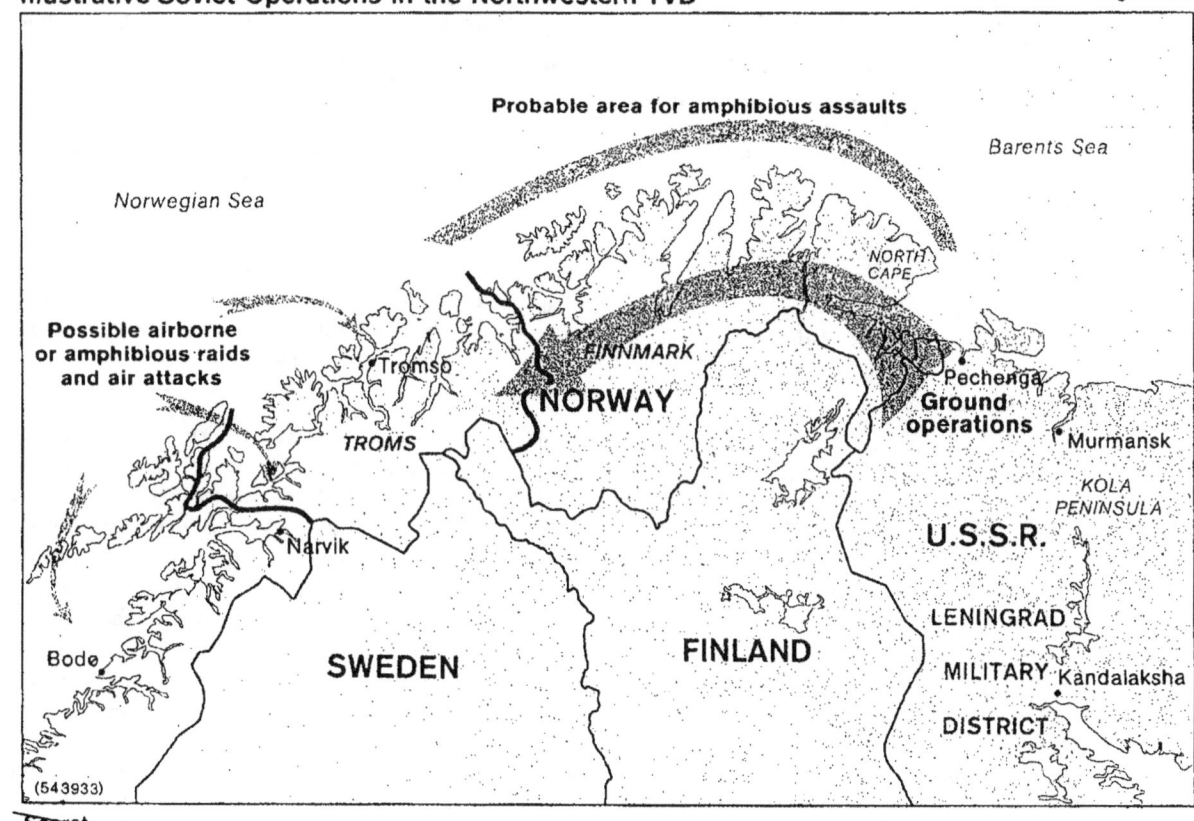

Illustrative Soviet Operations in the Northwestern TVD — Figure IV-6

Naval Operations

146. During a period of tension before a war with NATO, the Soviet Northern Fleet would establish surface, submarine, and air patrols in the Norwegian and Barents Seas and attempt to detect and track Western forces in nearby waters. As the likelihood of a conflict increased, defensive minefields probably would be established along the sea approaches to the Soviet coast.

147. ▒▒▒▒▒▒▒▒▒▒▒▒▒▒▒▒ with the opening of hostilities, the Northern Fleet would attack Western submarines, aircraft carriers, and amphibious task forces detected approaching the Barents and Norwegian Seas.[13] Some LRA bombers and Frontal Aviation fighter-bombers—supplemented by naval bombers, when available—probably would strike NATO naval facilities, airbases, communications sites and surveillance posts in northern Norway. Table IV-8 shows those Soviet theater forces which are likely to be allocated for operations in the Northwestern TVD.

148. Soviet amphibious ships carrying up to a regiment of Soviet naval infantry probably would attempt to seize limited objectives along the northern Norwegian coast. After the naval infantry had secured a suitable port, followup Soviet ground forces from the Pechenga area could be landed from merchant vessels.

149. We do not anticipate any large-scale amphibious operations because the Soviets are limited in their assault lift capacity and their capability to overcome determined resistance from the beach. Initial amphibious operations probably would be confided to the coast of Finnmark, under conditions suitable for an early linkup with the ground forces. The Soviets, however, would probably commit a large number of smaller combatants to an escort role in support of operations in northern Norway.

---

[13] Section D of this chapter, beginning at paragraph 157, discusses Soviet naval operations in these areas.

Table IV-8

Soviet Theater Forces Estimated To Be Available for Use in the Northwestern Theater of Military Operations [a]
January 1979

Divisions [b]	
Tank	—
Motorized Rifle	8
Tactical Aircraft	
Fighter-Bomber	90
Reconnaissance/Electronic Warfare	30
General Purpose Naval Forces [c]	
Amphibious Ships [d]	10
Naval Infantry Regiments	1

[a] Includes Soviet ground and air forces in the Leningrad Military District and those of the Soviet Northern Fleet which might be used in the Northwestern TVD. Some LRA and naval aircraft could also be diverted from operations in other areas for use in this theater.

[b] One airborne division located in the Leningrad Military District could be used in this theater or in other theaters.

[c] Assumes that 70 percent of the amphibious ships would be available given four days of preparation. See paragraphs 102 and 103 and table II-8 in chapter II for information concerning the normal peacetime availability of Soviet naval forces.

[d] Some general purpose submarines, surface combatants, and naval aircraft from the Soviet Northern Fleet would be used to support operations in the Northwestern TVD, but most would be used against NATO forces in the North Atlantic. (See table IV-9.)

Ground Operations in Northern Norway

150. Because of the limited availability of ground forces and tactical aircraft in the northern Leningrad Military District and the high priority given to naval missions against NATO naval strike forces, we believe an initial Soviet ground offensive would be limited to the Finnmark area. Potentially strong NATO resistance beyond Finnmark and the risk of drawing in far greater forces than exist in the Kola Peninsula area would probably deter major Soviet ground offensives in the north until an acceptable outcome in Central Europe had been achieved. Moreover, the better defended—and more defensible—Norwegian territory south of Finnmark is at the extreme limits of Soviet tactical air coverage.

151. ▒▒▒▒▒▒▒▒▒▒▒▒▒▒▒▒ initial ground operations against northern Norway probably would be limited to the Finnmark area and would be made by elements of the two Soviet divisions at Pechenga and Kandalaksha. We believe that subsequent operations could extend as far south as Tromso and Narvik. Seizure of Norwegian bases in the Troms area early in the war would be important to the Soviets because it would provide greater flank security for their naval forces in the Norwegian Sea. Initially, we could expect small-scale airborne or amphibious raids against these bases in an attempt to disrupt NATO operations. We would also expect bombing attacks against them by available LRA and Navy bombers. But we do not expect initial large-scale airborne or amphibious assaults in this area because of the lack of adequate air cover, airlift, and amphibious lift, and because of the

doubtful ability of ground forces advancing across Finnmark to effect early linkup. The Troms area is more heavily defended, the terrain is more difficult than in Finnmark, and larger forces would be required to seize and hold it. Sealifted ground forces could reinforce airborne and amphibious assault elements ashore, but suitable port facilities would be required and the transport of these reinforcements from bases in the northern Leningrad Military District would take two to three days and would need naval escort.

152. Some 10,000 to 20,000 men in Soviet naval infantry, ground forces, and small airborne units would be likely to participate in operations against northern Norway during the first week of conflict. This force could be reinforced, but the movement of additional Soviet ground forces northward has not been evident in Soviet exercise activity in the northwest.

153. The Soviet motorized rifle regiments from the two northern divisions are specially structured and equipped for operations in the Arctic. Although these units can easily traverse the terrain in northern Norway, lines of communication over land would be difficult to maintain because only one major road runs through the area. There is some evidence indicating that the Soviets plan to alleviate this shortcoming by resupplying ground forces by sea.

154. We do not believe that the Soviets would attempt a large-scale airborne assault in northern Norway because the demands for air transport elsewhere against NATO probably would preclude early use of a formation as large as a complete airborne division. The Soviets, however, might attempt to insert small teams to sabotage transportation, communications, and intelligence facilities.

Air Operations

155. Air support for the Soviet ground forces in Finnmark would come primarily from the some 120 Frontal Aviation ground attack and reconnaissance aircraft in the Leningrad Military District. Although none of these tactical aircraft are based in the north, they have deployed during exercises to bases in the Murmansk area. There are no Frontal Aviation fighter regiments in the Leningrad Military District, although fighters from three regiments of the Soviet strategic air defense forces on the Kola Peninsula could provide air cover to a distance of about 200 kilometers over Norway.

156. We have some evidence that the Soviets would use LRA bombers in an attempt to destroy or suppress land-based NATO air defense forces in northern and central Norway, probably to clear a path for naval strike, reconnaissance, and ASW aircraft flying against NATO carrier forces and submarines in the Norwegian Sea. If the Soviets chose to avoid Norwegian-based air defenses, they would route transiting aircraft north of North Cape and then down the center of the Norwegian Sea. Such routing would reduce the exposure of the aircraft to land-based air defenses, but it would decrease significantly the combat radius of the aircraft, the time they could spend in their operating areas, and the promptness of anticarrier strikes. It seems unlikely that many LRA bombers or even tactical aircraft would be made available for strikes against Norwegian air defenses, given the large requirement for these aircraft in the Central Region.

D. Naval Operations in the North Atlantic

157. In wartime the Soviets evidently expect NATO to deploy aircraft carriers, ballistic missile submarines, and large numbers of attack submarines against Soviet surface and submarine forces operating in the North Atlantic. In addition, they believe NATO would attempt amphibious landings in northern Norway and use the Norwegian Sea as a launch zone for carrier-based strikes against the USSR. They also expect NATO to establish antisubmarine barriers in the Greenland-Iceland-United Kingdom (G-I-UK) gap and off northern Norway to prevent passage of Soviet submarines.

158. The Norwegian Sea, especially its southern half ending at the G-I-UK gap, is central to Soviet naval strategy in the Atlantic. While the Soviets clearly expect naval engagements throughout the North Atlantic, they reckon that by far the heaviest combat would occur near and inside a maritime theater of military operations (MTVD) which they evidently would establish north of the G-I-UK gap. Soviet operations in this MTVD would be intended to prevent NATO naval incursions into an ocean area the Soviets consider critical to successful defense of their homeland, especially the Kola Peninsula.

159. Soviet strategy calls for the early establishment of control of the Norwegian and Barents Seas and their approaches. Operations farther into the North Atlantic to prevent transit of NATO carriers and amphibious task groups and to divert NATO naval strength are probably also planned. The Soviets would attempt to

neutralize Western SSBNs near their bases and in the Norwegian Sea before they could launch their missiles.

160. The establishment of control of the Norwegian and Barents Seas and their approaches probably would involve most of the Northern Fleet's submarines and virtually all of the surface forces and aircraft in an effort to exclude NATO forces from the area. The Soviets probably also plan submarine and air operations against NATO naval forces as they exit their bases in Europe and possibly against SSBNs from US bases as well. In addition, at least some submarines would attack shipping engaged in resupply and reinforcement of Europe early in a war.[14]

161. Soviet plans for controlling the Norwegian and Barents Seas and their approaches apparently consist of a deployment in depth. ▢ the Soviets plan to weaken or defeat NATO's naval forces in the Norwegian Sea or approaching the area from the United States and the United Kingdom by successive and coordinated assaults by submarines, strike aircraft, and surface combatant ships.

162. Soviet naval operations in the Norwegian Sea, its approaches, and other Atlantic Ocean areas would probably be preceded by deployments before the onset of hostilities in Central Europe, although the extent of such deployments is not clear. If the Soviets optimized for covertness, they would risk not having most of their units in position when hostilities began. If forces were optimized for maximum D-day impact, however, the Soviet Navy would give NATO early and clear indications of coming conflict, possibly to the detriment of Pact operations in Central Europe. In addition, the Soviets no doubt recognize that NATO naval bases in the United Kingdom are located closer than those of the Northern Fleet to the most important choke points, such as the G-I-UK gap, and that NATO aviation reinforcement to Iceland and Norway could be accomplished more quickly than Soviet naval forces could move to their intended operational areas.

163. There appears to be a conflict between the Soviet desire to strike preemptively every major NATO naval formation in the North Atlantic and the strong possibility that war would begin before Soviet Northern Fleet preparations were complete. Most Soviet exercises since 1970 reflect the latter expectation. The difficulties of coordinating such an attack using submarine, surface, and air forces simultaneously—together with the problems of coordination with the land and strategic forces—all act to reduce drastically the likelihood of a major, preemptive attack by the Northern Fleet against all major NATO naval formations throughout the North Atlantic. As a result, the schedule for prehostilities deployment and the level of deployment would probably be a compromise between the requirements for stealth and those for war-fighting effectiveness.

164. Because of range and time-on-station constraints on naval strike aircraft and the vulnerability of Soviet surface combatants when operating out of area, the Soviet attack submarine force would be the principal element for sustained operations in the North Atlantic. The Soviets have about 130 operational cruise missile and torpedo attack submarines in the Northern Fleet, but about 40 percent are in various stages of repair or workup at any one time. Thus, about 80 submarines (with varying degrees of combat effectiveness) would be available for operations at the outset of hostilities. If about 10 of these submarines continued to be committed to operations in the Mediterranean and the Soviets did not augment their forces there during a period of rising tension, some 70 submarines would be available for operations in the Atlantic. (See table IV-9.) This force would be subjected to heavy demands in wartime, and the Soviets probably would not have as many attack submarines as they deem necessary to perform all important naval missions.

Strategy and Operations

165. We do not know precisely how the Soviets would apportion their naval forces among their several tasks in the initial stages of a war with NATO. ▢ We recognize that Soviet naval deployments could be largely contingent on NATO operations at the outset of hostilities. If the Soviets were to perceive that NATO did not intend to send aircraft carriers into or near the Norwegian Sea, for example, large numbers of submarines could be dedicated to missions elsewhere. Even if NATO carriers deployed into or near the Norwegian Sea, Soviet force allocations could shift, depending on the outcome of the initial engagements. For example, successful Soviet attacks early in a war on NATO carriers and amphibious task groups operating north of the G-I-UK gap might encourage the Soviets to take a more active subsequent role in the Atlantic south of Iceland. On the other hand, should their forces suffer a serious reverse, they would likely

---

[14] See paragraphs 142-149 of chapter II and paragraphs 168 and 169 of this chapter for differing agency views on Soviet plans and capabilities for interdiction of sea lines of communication.

Table IV-9

Soviet General Purpose Naval Forces Estimated To Be Available for Use in the North Atlantic Ocean *

January 1979

Cruise Missile Submarines	
Nuclear	15
Diesel	7
Total	22
Torpedo Attack Submarines	
Nuclear	19
Diesel	32
Total	51
Principal Surface Combatants	
Aircraft Carriers	1
Missile Cruisers	6
Cruisers	1
Missile Destroyers	4
Destroyers	4
Missile Frigates	4
Frigates	28
Total	48
Naval Aircraft	
Strike Aircraft	58
Reconnaissance/Electronic Warfare Aircraft	49
Tankers	19
Fighters/Fighter-Bombers	11
ASW Fixed-Wing Aircraft	48
ASW/Reconnaissance Helicopters	48
Total	233

* General purpose forces assigned to the Soviet Northern Fleet. Assumes that 60 percent of general purpose submarines, 70 percent of surface combatants, and 85 percent of naval aircraft would be available after four days of preparation. See paragraphs 102 and 103 and table II-8 in chapter II for information concerning the normal peacetime availability of Soviet naval forces. Some of these units could also be used in support of operations against northern Norway. Does not include two cruise missile and eight torpedo attack submarines normally deployed to the Mediterranean Sea.

SECRET

continue to concentrate their efforts in the Norwegian and Barents Sea.[15]

166. *Operations South of Iceland.* the Soviets

[15] In view of the foregoing, the Director, Defense Intelligence Agency, notes that the allocation of specific numbers and classes of Soviet submarines to specific tasks and ocean areas in paragraphs 166-190 does not necessarily represent a high-confidence judgment of most probable Soviet courses of action. The inherent flexibility of naval warfare and the range of options available to a force as large as the Soviet Navy leads him to caution that other initial force allocations may be equally likely.

probably would allocate many of their best submarines for antisubmarine warfare—those of the V-class—to operations in the area south of the G-I-UK gap and off the four NATO SSBN bases in the Atlantic. (See figure IV-7.) Furthermore, some of these ASW submarines might also provide tactical support to Y-class SSBNs, which have to pass south of the gap to cover targets in the eastern United States. These tasks would require some two-thirds (six to 10 units) of those V-class submarines available for even minimal coverage.

167. Soviets might also want to commit some C-class submarines to operations south of the gap, in the vicinity of Great Britain, and along the carrier transit routes to the Norwegian and Mediterranean Seas. They probably would attempt to use these submarines to intercept and trail Western aircraft carriers, amphibious task forces, and other important targets as war became imminent, and to attack them at the outset of hostilities. Almost all of the available C-class submarines (five to seven units) would be needed for minimal coverage of these areas.

168. There is disagreement regarding the likely number and role of other Soviet submarines which would be deployed south of Iceland. According to one view,[16] about 10 other submarines would probably be deployed south of Iceland and consist mostly of long-range diesel torpedo attack units. These submarines probably would be dispersed in North Atlantic shipping lanes for reconnaissance and attacks on NATO shipping and naval targets of opportunity. Alternatively a few might lay mines in confined waters near NATO naval bases and ports. Others might patrol off major NATO naval bases to report on NATO movements and attack major warships.

169. Another view[17] holds that, in a typical initial wartime deployment, some 20 submarines would probably be positioned in the Atlantic astride NATO's sea lines of communication to attack NATO warships and those convoys or ships carrying equipment for US Army divisions in the initial phase of a war. The number of Soviet submarines dedicated to this effort would depend upon the number of carriers which the Soviets would believe likely to deploy to the Norwe-

[16] The holders of this view are the Central Intelligence Agency; the Director, Bureau of Intelligence and Research, Department of State; and the Director, National Security Agency.

[17] The holders of this view are the Director, Defense Intelligence Agency, and the Director of Naval Intelligence, Department of the Navy.

Initial Soviet Operating Areas in the North Atlantic

Figure IV-7

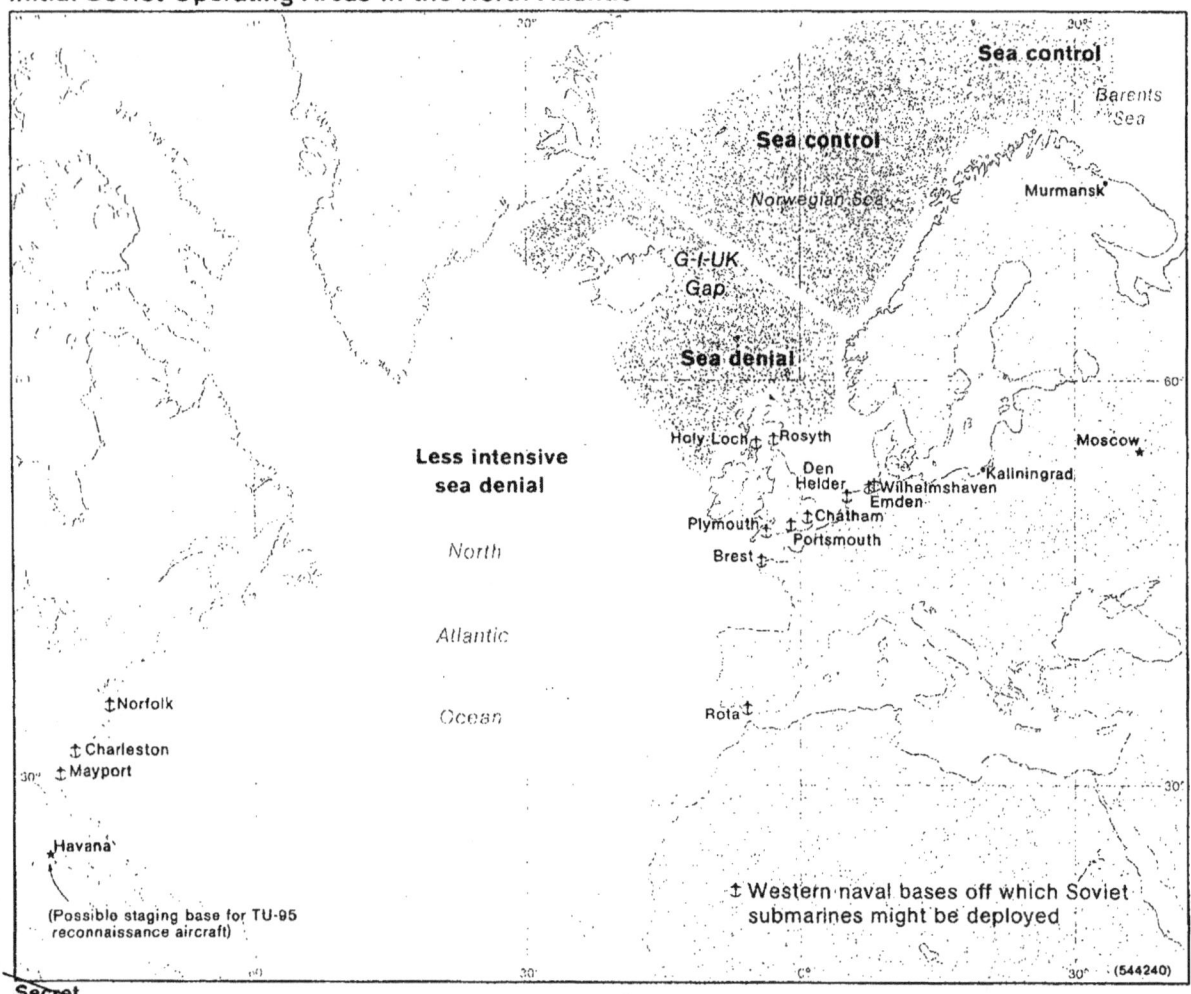

gian Sea. This view is based on a differing interpretation of the evidence as reflected in paragraphs 142-149 of chapter II. These agencies consider that the Soviets view interdiction of US reinforcements to Europe to be of such significance and their submarine inventory of sufficient depth to warrant use of larger numbers of attack submarines in this effort while maintaining adequate forces near the G-I-UK gap and in the Norwegian Sea. Accordingly, the number of attack submarines would be correspondingly lower than the 10 torpedo attack submarines postulated for deployment near the G-I-UK gap in paragraph 173 below, or the 10 or so torpedo attack submarines postulated for the central Norwegian Sea in paragraph 183.

170. Submarine ASW operations in the North Atlantic could be augmented by TU-142 Bear F long-range ASW aircraft of Soviet Naval Aviation. These aircraft frequently exercise in the area south of Iceland and in the G-I-UK gap and could operate there for at least several hours before returning to base. Operations by ASW aircraft probably would be restricted to the Norwegian Sea north of the G-I-UK gap, however, because ASW aircraft are highly vulnerable to Western air defenses and probably would not be able to operate safely near the G-I-UK gap once hostilities began. Similarly, Soviet surface combatant ships probably would not deploy south of Iceland for initial wartime operations because NATO would likely have air superiority there.

171. In addition to submarines, Soviet naval reconnaissance forces in the Atlantic would include intelligence collection ships and TU-95 long-range reconnaissance aircraft operating from Northern Fleet airfields, and possibly Cuba and Angola. Long-range

reconnaissance aircraft and intelligence collection ships are important elements of Soviet ocean surveillance because they can monitor the disposition of NATO naval surface forces in distant areas without relying on NATO electronic emissions. Once hostilities began, however, these forces probably would suffer heavy attrition. TU-95 reconnaissance operations probably would then be restricted primarily to the Norwegian Sea, with occasional sorties into the North Atlantic.

172. *Operations in the G-I-UK Gap.* ▨ the Soviets probably would plan for their first large-scale strikes on NATO surface forces to occur in the G-I-UK gap area. These strikes probably would be conducted mainly by cruise missile submarines patrolling 150 to 200 nautical miles north of the gap, although some strikes by naval aircraft, and perhaps LRA aircraft, would probably also be made in the area of the gap.

173. The Soviets evidently do not plan on stationing large naval forces in the G-I-UK gap itself. Exercises and military writings indicate that the Soviets believe this area would almost certainly be dominated early in a war by NATO air and ASW forces. Nonetheless, the Soviets stress the utility of placing submarines, particularly diesel units, in geographically constricted waters where their chances of acquiring targets are greater. They could deploy one-half (about 10) of the available long-range diesel submarines in or near the gap, where they would serve in both reconnaissance and attack roles. The Soviets might also deploy some C-class nuclear-powered submarines to attack aircraft carriers in the gap area. Concentrating C-class submarines in these relatively constricted waters would reduce the C-class's open-ocean disadvantages of slow speed relative to strike carriers. All these submarines could also conduct ASW searches while patrolling in the area.

174. The Soviets probably could not establish a comprehensive submarine ASW barrier across the G-I-UK gap, even if NATO ASW forces were not a consideration. US experience shows that such a barrier would require 30 or more nuclear-powered attack submarines or twice as many diesel units. Because of their inferior detection capabilities, considerably more Soviet submarines would be required to perform the same task. However, only about 17 nuclear and 28 diesel-powered torpedo attack submarines from Northern Fleet bases would be available for deployment in the entire Atlantic.

175. The Soviets could more easily cover the G-I-UK gap against Western aircraft carriers by using submarines armed with long-range cruise missiles. If positioned 150 nautical miles north of the gap and provided with externally derived targeting support, three or four E-II-class submarines could theoretically cover the approaches to the Norwegian Sea. Our knowledge of Soviet planning factors indicates that they probably would regard the level of coverage provided by this number of submarines as barely adequate in nuclear war, however, and clearly insufficient for a conventional conflict. They may also assume that some of these units would be destroyed by NATO ASW forces before they could launch their missiles and that NATO would send more than a single carrier into a strongly contested area such as the Norwegian Sea.

176. We believe that the Soviets would deploy most or all of the available 10 E-II-class cruise missile submarines to positions within 200 nm of the G-I-UK gap. This number of submarines would provide the concentration of conventional fire throughout the area which Soviet planning factors indicate is required to disable aircraft carriers—some six to 10 hits each. Some J-class units could also be used, but they carry only half the number of missiles as the E-II-class units.

177. Antiship attacks by submarines in the G-I-UK gap probably would be supplemented by strikes by aircraft of Soviet Naval Aviation and possibly Long Range Aviation. From Northern Fleet airfields, the Backfire bomber and some TU-16 Badgers with aerial refueling could reach targets throughout the G-I-UK gap and the northern approaches to the North Sea. From Baltic Fleet airfields, SNA aircraft could strike targets between Iceland and Great Britain and in the approaches to the North Sea.

178. Airstrikes in the G-I-UK gap would be especially hazardous for Soviet aircraft because of NATO land-based air defenses in the area. (See figure IV-8.) The Soviets probably believe that NATO would augment these air defenses with additional fighters in time of war. Consequently, the Soviets would be likely to limit antiship attacks by strike aircraft in the G-I-UK gap to NATO aircraft carrier and amphibious task groups in the approaches to the North Sea which pose a direct threat to the Western TVD. Strike aircraft might also attack NATO antisubmarine forces which were in a position to impede the movement of Soviet submarines to and from their patrol areas.

179. We have tenuous evidence of Soviet plans for strikes by LRA Bears against NATO bases in Norway, Great Britain, and Iceland. Such strikes early in a war could be constrained, however, by the commitment of

IV-38
Top Secret

LRA bombers to operations elsewhere. Attacks could also be conducted against NATO radar installations by Northern Fleet naval aircraft using antiradiation missiles.

180. It is unlikely that any Soviet surface combatant ships would be concentrated initially near the G-I-UK gap because they would be vulnerable to air attacks if NATO maintained air superiority in the area. In addition, fighter air cover for Soviet surface ships would be unavailable there because of the distances from Warsaw Pact airfields. YAK-36 V/STOL (vertical/short takeoff and landing) aircraft operating from the Kiev aircraft carrier probably would be unable to cope effectively with NATO high-performance fighters.

181. *Operations in the Central Norwegian Sea.* From the central Norwegian Sea north to the Barents Sea, the Soviets would attempt to establish total sea control. They probably would deploy most of the remaining Northern Fleet submarines plus some major surface combatant task groups to the central Norwegian Sea. ASW aircraft probably would conduct area searches in coordination with the surface ships and attack submarines to find and destroy NATO SSBNs and attack submarines. Antiship strikes by naval and LRA aircraft would be conducted in conjunction with those of surface ships and submarines.

182. A NATO naval task force entering the central Norwegian Sea would have to deal with continuous attacks by Soviet strike aircraft, submarines, and surface ships. Some of these attacks would be massive and highly coordinated. In coordinated attacks involving mixed forces, all forces would not necessarily strike simultaneously. Exercises evidently have shown the Soviets that simultaneous strikes by aircraft, submarines, and surface ships would be infeasible in most situations because of the problems in bringing all forces to bear at the same time. Coordinated attacks probably would be keyed to a prescribed time or attack sequence. An individual attacking unit or group would attack at its appointed time without waiting for confirmation that other forces were ready for the attack.

183. The naval forces deployed in the central Norwegian Sea probably would include about one-fourth of the Northern Fleet's available cruise missile and torpedo attack submarines (about 18 units). These could include most (about five) of the J-class diesel submarines armed with long-range cruise missiles and the remaining third (fewer than five) of the V-class attack submarine fleet. Some of these submarines could form a second line of defense against Western strike forces which penetrated into the Norwegian Sea, and some probably would assist in securing the operating areas of Soviet D-class SSBNs from Western ASW ships and submarines.

184. About 18 of the available major surface combatant ships in the Northern Fleet, including a Kiev aircraft carrier, six guided-missile cruisers, four guided-missile destroyers, and seven destroyers and frigates probably would also be used in the central Norwegian Sea. Although the primary purpose of these forces would be ASW, they would have a secondary mission of antiship attack. The Kiev probably carries a mix of YAK-36 V/STOL aircraft for reconnaissance strikes against surface ships and limited air defense and Hormone helicopters for antisubmarine warfare. Another 13 major surface combatants in the Northern Fleet, including a Sverdlov heavy cruiser, probably would operate in the northern Norwegian Sea in support of Soviet amphibious operations against Norway.

185. In the central Norwegian Sea, attacks by strike aircraft operating from Northern Fleet airbases would be more massive and more frequent than those conducted farther to the south. This fact, coupled with the expected higher force levels of surface combatants and submarines in the central Norwegian Sea, would increase the probability of successful antiship strikes. There are about 56 TU-16 Badger air-to-surface antiship missile carriers available in the Northern Fleet. During a period of conventional attacks, about one-third of this strike force would probably be held in readiness for rapid transition to nuclear operations. Assuming no reinforcement by other fleet air forces and minimal combat attrition, we would expect the remaining aircraft to conduct an average of about 1.5 sorties per aircraft per day for the first three days of combat. After this initial surge period, crew fatigue, mechanical problems, the repair of combat damage, and to a significant degree the status of potential targets, would impact on sortie rates—probably decreasing them substantially.

186. Northern Fleet strike aircraft could be augmented with LRA bombers and naval strike aircraft redeployed from other fleets. In a NATO–Warsaw Pact war, however, most LRA and Baltic and Black Sea Fleet aircraft might be unavailable for operations in the Atlantic because of commitments in the Western and Southwestern TVDs. Also, if the Soviets perceived the threat in the Pacific to remain high, Pacific Fleet aircraft would be unavailable for re-

deployment to the Northern Fleet. On the other hand, if the Soviets perceived a reduced threat in the Pacific—for example, if the United States moved several aircraft carriers from the Pacific to the Atlantic—they probably would send one or two regiments of Pacific Fleet strike aircraft to the western USSR. The Soviets maintain four strike regiments in the Pacific Fleet, with some 95 ASM-carrying aircraft.

187. About 17 TU-142 Bear F and 18 IL-38 May fixed-wing ASW aircraft are also part of the Northern Fleet, and about 15 of each probably would be available for patrols throughout the Norwegian Sea. The TU-142s probably would conduct missions in southern portions of the Norwegian Sea to take advantage of their greater endurance, while the IL-38s would patrol farther north. If the TU-142s in this force spent about five hours on station and suffered no combat attrition, the force could mount about nine missions per day for the first three days of combat, and about seven missions per day thereafter. Under the same conditions in the central area the IL-38 force could average about 10 missions per day for the first three days and about eight missions per day thereafter.

188. The Soviets would also have 21 TU-95 long-range and 17 TU-16 medium-range reconnaissance aircraft available for comprehensive surveillance of the Norwegian Sea. Four of the TU-95s could be deployed to Cuba and Angola, although they would be extremely vulnerable if they attempted to operate from these countries in wartime. Some TU-95 sorties to the North Atlantic through the G-I-UK gap probably would be attempted to verify intelligence information on important targets, such as aircraft carriers heading toward the Norwegian Sea or North Sea. If TU-95s flew to their maximum endurance of about 19 hours, the TU-95 force could average some six missions per day for the first three days of combat, and five missions per day thereafter. If the TU-16s flew to their maximum endurance of about seven hours, the force could average some 15 missions per day for the first three days, and 12 missions per day thereafter.

189. Several NATO aircraft carrier task groups entering the Norwegian Sea at the same time would complicate the situation for Soviet anticarrier forces because they would divide Soviet firepower. The Soviets probably hope that hostile carrier task groups would be weakened sufficiently by initial submarine attacks in the G-I-UK area so that their destruction could be completed in the central Norwegian Sea with the forces available. If the Soviets were certain that NATO was about to send more than two carrier task groups to the Norwegian Sea and not to the North Sea, they almost certainly would reinforce their forces there with one or more regiments of naval strike aircraft from the other fleets, plus some LRA bombers if they could be spared from operations in Central Europe.

190. *Operations in the Barents Sea.* If Soviet defenses in the Norwegian Sea were penetrated by NATO naval forces, large Soviet forces would be available to confront them in the Barents Sea. In addition to available naval strike aircraft, these forces could include 10 submarines (nearly 15 percent of those available). These would be mostly medium-range torpedo attack units, possibly supplemented by one or two J-class cruise missile submarines. In addition, about 17 destroyers and frigates, plus about 20 missile patrol boats, about 19 short-range ASW fixed-wing aircraft, and about 40 ASW helicopters probably would be available for operations in the approaches to the Barents. Some tactical aircraft supporting land operations in the area might also be made available for antiship attacks. The seaward approaches to the Murmansk area can be covered by the long-range cruise missiles of the Soviet Navy's coastal missile and artillery force.

Potential Effectiveness [18]

191. *Submarines.* In conducting these operations, Soviet submarines would be present in large numbers, but they would be limited by their poor detection capability against Western ballistic missile and attack submarines. This makes it unlikely that Soviet submarines would be able to solve the initial ASW problem of target location and would make it difficult to protect themselves from NATO submarines.

192. The Soviets consider that a key but difficult task for their attack submarines during the conventional phase of a war would be the protection of Soviet SSBNs from NATO ASW forces, particularly nuclear attack submarines (SSNs). The Y-class, for example, not only is much noisier than Western nuclear submarines, but also, in order for its SS-N-6 missiles to reach targets in the United States, must operate in areas where it is subject to detection by the US sound surveillance system (SOSUS) and where it would have little or no support from other Soviet forces. The Soviets therefore probably would assign a few of their

---

[18] *See paragraphs 198-200, setting forth an alternative view of the Director, Defense Intelligence Agency, and the Director of Naval Intelligence, Department of the Navy, regarding paragraphs 191-197.*

best attack submarines to provide escort for Y-class SSBNs. Because Western SSNs can launch torpedoes outside the detection envelope of V- and Y-class submarines, the Soviets probably could not prevent at least some of their SSBNs from being destroyed.

193. For anticarrier warfare, the Soviets' reliance on external targeting support could effectively restrict the operating areas of their long-range cruise missile submarines, such as the E-II and the J-class, to areas within range of the Bear D aircraft. In addition, these submarines must surface to launch their missiles and hence would be vulnerable. The more modern C-class would pose a more serious threat in distant waters, but these submarines probably would not be able to keep up with fast-moving carrier strike forces. Moreover, Soviet cruise-missile-armed submarines normally carry a mixed load of nuclear and conventionally armed missiles, thereby reducing the number available for conventional strikes.

194. *Aircraft.* The success of antiship attacks by naval or LRA aircraft would hinge primarily on the capabilities of the aircraft and their cruise missiles to penetrate a series of NATO land-based and fleet air defenses. These defenses include land- and ship-based aircraft, surface-to-air missile systems, and electronic countermeasures systems to confuse, decoy, or disrupt the sensors of incoming aircraft or cruise missiles. At medium and high altitudes, NATO radars and land-based interceptors or surface-to-air missile systems can cover virtually all approaches to the Norwegian and North Seas and the G-I-UK gap, except for flights around northern Norway to the important northern and central Norwegian Sea areas. If Soviet strike aircraft successfully penetrated or avoided NATO land-based air defenses, they then would have to deal with formidable fleet air defenses.

195. The first line of fleet air defense typically would be an outer zone defended by carrier-based early warning aircraft and interceptors. It could extend more than 400 nm from the fleet, well beyond the 200-nm maximum missile launch range of the best Soviet air-to-surface missiles. A Soviet airstrike against a NATO task group including two US aircraft carriers, for example, might have to confront more than 30 carrier-based interceptors. Soviet strike aircraft, especially the TU-16s, would be highly vulnerable to attacks by interceptors as they maneuvered to launch their ASMs. Although individual TU-16s would be vulnerable because of their slow speed and lack of extensive ECM (electronic countermeasures) equipment for self-defense, one or more Badger ECM aircraft probably would be part of each attack formation. The Backfire would be better able to survive because of its high-speed capability—near Mach 2 at high altitude—and modern ECM equipment, although both Badger and Backfire aircraft have large radar cross sections which would make them easily detectable. Cruise missiles, flying at speeds of Mach 2.5 to 3.5 and launched by aircraft which successfully penetrated the interceptor zone, would face shipborne surface-to-air missile, gun, and ECM systems.

196. *Surface Forces.* The effectiveness of Soviet surface combatants in the Norwegian Sea would be a function not only of their capabilities as individual ships, but also of their cooperation with each other and with submarines and aircraft. As individual units, Soviet surface ships are particularly weak in providing area air defense against US and UK attacking aircraft and protection against low-flying aircraft and cruise missiles. Their ASW capability suffers particularly from a limited sensor range. The ranges at which they can reliably detect attacking submarines are less than the range at which the submarine can detect and attack the surface ship. ASW sensor range is also less than that of such primary ASW weapons as the SS-N-14, making it extremely difficult for an individual Soviet ship without ASW helicopters to exploit the potential of such weapons fully.

197. The weaknesses of individual ships are overcome to some extent when ships, submarines, and aircraft operate in concert, as they presumably would in the Norwegian Sea, supporting and complementing one another with sensor and weapons coverage. The presence of a Kiev, with its multiple sensors, weapon systems, and command and control capabilities, would provide a significant addition to the capability of the other surface forces. For example, operations by the Kiev's V/STOL aircraft would be valuable in thwarting fair-weather attacks from slower NATO aircraft such as the P-3 and in limiting the operations of AWACS (airborne warning and control systems) aircraft.

198. According to an alternative view, paragraphs 191-197 should convey a more balanced appraisal of potential effectiveness, in substance as well as in tone.[19] The holders of this view believe these paragraphs tend to overstress weaknesses inherent in Soviet platforms, such as the relative noisiness of submarines, without offsetting consideration of inherent strengths,

---

[19] *The holders of this view are the Director, Defense Intelligence Agency, and the Director of Naval Intelligence, Department of the Navy.*

such as their relatively high speeds. They further note that any assessment of the potential effectiveness of Soviet submarines, naval aircraft, and surface ships should include consideration of their operation as a mutually supportive force; they feel that this is only partially achieved in paragraph 197.

199. According to this view, paragraphs 191-197, in addition to an essentially negative treatment of Soviet platforms, assess their effectiveness in tactical contexts which convey an impression of NATO capabilities that is maximal and unrealistic. Realistically, the potential effectiveness of Soviet strike aircraft should be measured in terms of a radar coverage, as well as fighter coverage, that would have suffered some degradation in the early stages of hostilities. Likewise, the US sound surveillance system should be expected to suffer early degradation, especially in view of the detailed Soviet knowledge of and concern about its capabilities. Indeed, even during peacetime, important links of the SOSUS have, on a number of occasions, been cut and temporarily disabled by unknown shipping.

200. Finally, the holders of this view note that these paragraphs reflect insufficient regard for evidence of demonstrated Soviet naval effectiveness.

CHAPTER V

THEATER NUCLEAR OPERATIONS

1. Pact nuclear operations against NATO in the European theater could involve:

   — Tactical nuclear weapons assigned to Soviet ground and air forces in Eastern Europe and in the USSR and to Soviet naval forces in the three western Fleets.

   — Soviet strategic systems (mainly medium- and intermediate-range ballistic missiles, bombers of Long Range Aviation, and some ballistic missile submarines) which are based in the USSR and intended chiefly for use against NATO.

3. The scope and specific targets of Pact nuclear operations would depend on Soviet campaign objectives, the scale of NATO's nuclear use, and other circumstances. The following discussion is confined to the likely general characteristics of large-scale theater nuclear operations by the Pact.

A. Tactical Nuclear Operations

4. The Pact tactical nuclear arsenal consists of aircraft, missiles, artillery, submarines, and surface ships. Although nuclear weapons are normally carried aboard Soviet submarines and some surface ships during peacetime deployments, the Soviets do not maintain nuclear-armed tactical missiles or aircraft on alert during peacetime. During the period of tension that probably would precede a war in Europe, however, and during any initial conventional phase of such a war, the Pact would take steps to ready its tactical air and missile delivery systems for nuclear operations. Warheads and bombs probably would be dispersed from storage sites to delivery units. Nuclear warheads probably would be mated to most tactical ballistic missiles at the start of a war and up to one-fourth of Soviet tactical aircraft probably would be withheld from conventional operations as a nuclear alert force.

5. Once the decision to use nuclear weapons was made, all tactical systems probably would come into play and the timing and targeting of tactical strikes would be planned to take advantage of the special characteristics of each system. The primary objective in Soviet tactical nuclear planning appears to be the assured destruction of military targets. Limiting collateral damage does not appear to be a main concern.

9. During a coordinated, large-scale initial strike, many tactical missiles probably would be targeted against air defense systems. Tactical missile strikes could precede strikes by tactical aircraft by 15 to 20 minutes. [   ] the Soviets would use aircraft mainly in battlefield strikes in close proximity to Pact forces, presumably because tactical aircraft are more versatile and better able to locate mobile targets than missiles and because the Pact currently does not have nuclear artillery in Eastern Europe. The mix of low- and high-yield bombs allocated to Soviet Frontal Aviation [   ] is about equal, while heavier warheads predominate in the mix of such weapons allocated to tactical missile units. Following the initial strikes, when the effectiveness of the air defense systems presumably would be reduced, the Soviets clearly place increasing reliance on air-delivered weapons.

10. [   ] the USSR would be unlikely to initiate the use of nuclear weapons at sea while a war was being fought with only conventional weapons against NATO in Europe. [   ] the clear predilection of Soviet military policymakers to focus decisions on the developing situation in Central Europe and to avoid actions elsewhere that would jeopardize the campaign there or that would cause an escalation to nuclear warfare. Nevertheless, Soviet general purpose naval forces are normally armed with nuclear weapons during peacetime deployments and would be prepared at the outset of hostilities to conduct nuclear operations if a decision were made to do so. Once authorized, these operations would be directed mainly against important NATO surface ships, submarines, and possibly selected land targets.

11. An alternate view * maintains that Soviet nuclear operations at sea would not necessarily await employment of nuclear weapons on land. Should the Soviets perceive a major threat to their security interests or military objectives from NATO carrier forma-

---
* The holder of this view is the Director of Naval Intelligence, Department of the Navy.

tions, they might launch a nuclear attack at sea in the expectation that it could be confined to the sea campaign and would not precipitate the employment of tactical nuclear weapons in the ground campaign.

B. Nuclear Strikes Against NATO by Soviet Strategic Forces

14. Our understanding of Soviet concepts for the employment of strategic forces against European NATO is hampered by a lack of precise information regarding: what the Soviets see as the specific numbers, locations, and vulnerabilities of potential targets; how the Soviets allocate strategic weapons among NATO military, political, and economic targets; and how the Soviets view the capabilities and limitations of their own weapon systems and forces. Despite these uncertainties, technical analysis of Soviet strategic systems, evidence from Pact exercises and military writings, and our knowledge of Western targets permit some conjecture as to how Soviet strategic strike forces might be used against NATO.

15. We believe that Soviet doctrine emphasizes counterforce rather than countervalue strikes. The prime objective of Soviet nuclear forces in wartime

would be to destroy NATO's means for waging nuclear war. Accordingly, a typical target list for the Soviet strategic forces would include NATO nuclear missile sites; airfields used by nuclear delivery aircraft; nuclear weapons storage sites; and command, control, and communications facilities. Other airfields, air defense facilities, large troop concentrations, and conventional storage depots probably are also targeted, as well as some political and economic centers. In all instances, strikes by the strategic forces would be coordinated with those by the Pact's tactical nuclear forces.

16. In Europe there are several thousand military, political, and economic targets in these categories which the Soviets might wish to cover. Military targets range from those that have been extensively hardened to those that are highly vulnerable. We estimate that there are fewer than 300 hardened targets of significant military value in the European NATO countries. About half of these are slightly hardened installations—such as nuclear weapons storage facilities, some POL storage facilities, and ground force depots. The remainder are moderately hard installations such as command posts and the French intermediate-range missile silos. The great majority of potential targets in Europe are soft area targets, including NATO airfields, ports, and air defense facilities.

17. The Soviet Strategic Rocket Forces would have a key role during large-scale nuclear operations. Although the SRF's medium- and intermediate-range ballistic missiles would be assigned a variety of strategic targets, some sources have indicated they would be primarily used to destroy NATO airfields, air defenses, and command and control facilities beyond the reach of the Pact's forward-based tactical systems. In addition to the MRBMs and IRBMs, some of the Soviet ICBMs might be used against NATO targets in Europe. Ballistic missiles launched from the G- and H-class submarines are not as accurate as most of the land-based missiles and probably would be used against large targets such as ports.

18. The Long Range Aviation bomber force would also be used both during the initial nuclear strike and for followup strikes against targets not already destroyed or attacked. As much as one-third of the LRA bomber force would be withheld from use in conventional operations in anticipation of escalation to nuclear conflict. All LRA bombers based in the western USSR could reach most potential NATO targets directly from their home airfields carrying either bombs or air-to-surface missiles. For most of these targets, the unrefueled combat radius of the LRA bombers is sufficient to permit the use of indirect routing and low-level flight profiles to evade NATO air defenses.

CHAPTER VI

FUTURE FORCES

1. As we have noted in chapter II, the past decade was marked by vigorous modernization of Soviet theater forces facing NATO. This modernization was accompanied by some increase in the manpower strength of the forces—especially in the late 1960s and early 1970s—as the number of weapons in units was increased and as support requirements grew to accommodate more, increasingly sophisticated hardware. Modernization of the Soviet theater forces is evidently continuing at much the same pace, along with modest, commensurate growth in manpower. The non-Soviet Warsaw Pact (NSWP) forces have shared in the Soviet buildup, although at a slower pace and with uneven results, especially in the more expensive tactical air and missile forces and in ground force armor replacement programs.

A. Factors Affecting Future Forces

2. In this Estimate we do not provide a detailed analysis of the factors that motivate the Soviets' military policy toward Europe and the development of their theater forces. These factors are discussed in detail in NIE 11-4-78, *Soviet Goals and Expectations in the Global Power Arena*. We proceed from the premise that the developments we currently observe in Warsaw Pact theater forces opposite NATO represent the sorts of activities necessary to maintain and gradually improve the capabilities of these large standing forces. They are the activities necessary to replace obsolete or wornout equipment and to incorporate new weapons and tactics which flow from a vigorous Soviet research and development program. They portend no large, short-term change in the general size or character of these forces.

3. Although we believe this to be a valid premise, we have examined a number of factors which conceivably could alter it. This examination is summarized in the following paragraphs.

Soviet Perceptions of NATO's Military Capabilities

4. The Soviets have a keen perception of NATO's forces and military programs and regard NATO's capabilities as substantial and technologically challenging. We believe that they will see current developments in NATO as portending a continuing strong NATO defense posture with good prospects for improvement, especially in the critical Central European area. They are likely to be especially concerned with expected improvements in NATO's precision weapons and nuclear systems. Nothing in NATO's current or near-term defense programs, however, is likely to precipitate any major change in the level of Pact efforts. Over the longer term, the large-scale deployment by NATO of a new theater nuclear delivery system, such as ground-launched cruise missiles, could cause an upswing in Pact efforts, especially in air defense.

Soviet Leadership

5. Change in Soviet leadership within the period of this Estimate is inevitable. At least in its early phase, however, the change is unlikely to alter the priority given to theater forces. The new leaders, whoever they may be, will undoubtedly emerge from the ranks of the present leadership which are responsible for creating current Pact forces and which are committed to maintaining Soviet military strength in Europe. The new leaders will likely seek to avoid moves that would antagonize large segments of the military.

Economic Considerations

6. Since 1970, total Soviet defense spending, which accounts for 11 to 12 percent of the USSR's gross national product, has grown at an average annual rate of 4 to 5 percent. Spending for Soviet theater forces opposite NATO has grown at roughly the same rate and probably will continue to grow into the 1980s. This judgment is supported by several trends in Soviet defense programs, the increasing costs of new, more complex military hardware, the large number of weapons development programs currently under way, and the continuing capital investment in defense industries.

7. We have taken note of the decline in Soviet economic performance and the economic difficulties of such NSWP countries as Poland and Czechoslovakia. Despite these difficulties, we find no evidence

that suggests the Soviets anticipate cutbacks in allocating resources to theater forces. Indeed, we have good evidence that some NSWP countries plan modest increases.

Demographic Factors

8. In every Warsaw Pact country the military manpower procurement system depends on conscription. Conscripts provide up to 75 percent of the manpower assigned to the regular armed forces, the border guards, and some elements of the internal security forces. During the next decade, however, the number of young men reaching draft age each year will decline in most Pact countries, a trend that will complicate the allocation of manpower between the armed forces and industry.

9. Pact military manpower requirements are expected to increase only modestly in the next 10 years. Even so, there may be shortfalls in available military manpower. The Pact countries could meet such shortfalls by changes in their manpower procurement systems. They could grant fewer deferments, extend the term of conscript service, increase the use of women in the armed forces, and supplement the number of full-time soldiers by recalling reservists to active duty for short periods. They might also attempt to persuade more conscripts to extend their service.[1]

10. We do not believe that the manpower squeeze will lead to any decline in future Pact military manpower. We expect that most Pact countries, the USSR included, will meet their projected military manpower needs by some combination of the options mentioned above. Some are already calling previously exempted reservists to active duty for up to six months. Fewer deferments are being granted, and the grounds for medical exemption have been defined more clearly and strictly. In a few Pact countries, those persons found unfit for combat duties are being placed in sedentary military positions rather than being exempted.

Technology

11. We foresee no technological breakthrough that could lead to a major change in either the size or character of the Pact theater forces during the period of this Estimate. New technology, whether developed, purchased, or illegally acquired, is expected to lead to improvements in individual Pact systems and help redress major deficiencies, but no one development or even a combination of technological developments in the foreseeable future is expected to revolutionize modern warfare or provide a decided advantage to Pact forces.

Sino-Soviet Relations

12. The size of the Soviet forces opposite China—nearly 25 percent of the total theater forces—suggests a potential for some impact on the forces facing NATO. There is no evidence, however, that the burden of maintaining forces against China has seriously constrained Soviet military posture in the West in recent years, and we do not anticipate such an effect in the foreseeable future. Short of a rapprochement with China, which could release some resources for defense in the West, or a war with China, which would, at a minimum, absorb much of the Soviet troop and logistical reserves in the western and central USSR, we believe the Soviets can continue to support both efforts at present or even modestly greater levels.

B. Trends in the Size and Composition of Future Forces

13. In this section we estimate likely changes in the size and composition of the Warsaw Pact's theater forces during the next five to 10 years. These estimates are based on our knowledge of ongoing Soviet weapons production and deployment programs and new weapons which we have identified in research and development or testing. We have also considered evidence relating to gaps which the Soviets perceive in Pact weapons capabilities and Pact production and technological capabilities.

General

14. Although the expansion in manpower which characterized Pact theater forces during the mid-1960s and early 1970s has slowed, we expect some gradual increase in manpower in Pact ground and air combat units opposite NATO over the next decade as ongoing programs are implemented. The overall number of ground and air combat units opposite NATO is expected to remain at or near its current level, while a modest decline is anticipated in the number of general purpose naval ships and submarines.

15. Warsaw Pact nations will continue to improve the weapons and equipment in their theater forces opposite NATO. Major weapon production and deployment programs which are clearly in midstream are expected to continue. In addition, the Soviets will

---

[1] See paragraphs 44 and 45 in chapter II for differing agency views on Pact extended-service programs.

no doubt seek to develop some entirely new weapons and support systems. Certain of these systems, such as laser- or television-guided munitions, are already in testing. Still other Pact weapons—such as enhanced radiation weapons and advanced cruise missiles—may emerge in reaction to NATO weapons programs or force improvements.

16. As the modernization of the Pact's theater forces equipment progresses, we expect continuing standardization problems. For example, the Soviets are currently producing three different medium tanks while retaining older models in the inventory. This situation leads to other problems for Pact planners in that the mix and growing technical complexity of models in the forces requires additional mechanic and operator training and more elaborate logistic arrangements.

Ground Forces

17. Barring an agreement on mutual and balanced force reductions (MBFR), the number and disposition of Pact ground force divisions opposite NATO are likely to remain stable during the period of this Estimate, although expanded divisional organizations and the formation of new nondivisional units probably will account for moderate increases in manpower and equipment. We foresee no development over the next several years which would appreciably alter the basic Pact strategy of an armor-heavy offensive against NATO in Central Europe. Despite NATO's substantial and growing capability for antitank warfare, Pact planners will continue to regard the tank as the backbone of their ground assault forces. Considerable emphasis will be placed throughout the 1980s on modernizing the tank forces.

18. Improvements in other Pact forces probably will also be stressed over the next decade to give their armored forces a better chance to survive on the modern battlefield. These almost certainly will include new artillery and air defense weapons. The increased use of smoke and aerosols to interfere with optical and electro-optical surveillance and tracking devices of NATO antitank weapons is also expected. Against antitank helicopters the Pact probably will enlarge its use of tactical surface-to-air missiles (SAMs), antiaircraft artillery, and other helicopters.

19. We are monitoring one development in particular with potentially significant implications for the Soviet ground forces during the upcoming decade. Over the past year the Soviets have reconfigured two divisions, each of which has three tank regiments that have been augmented with organic infantry and artillery battalions. The divisions' motorized rifle regiments have been disbanded and other subordinate units have been modified. The changes will improve the combined-arms capabilities of the tank regiments and increase their firepower. The overall personnel requirement for the new structure probably will not greatly exceed that of the 9,500 men in a standard Soviet tank division.

20. We have no evidence regarding the extent to which the Soviets intend to so restructure additional divisions. We also note that the Soviets are engaged in a program to expand some standard tank divisions by adding infantry and artillery to the tank regiments, but without disbanding the division's motorized rifle regiment. At best, therefore, our evidence thus far indicates only that the Soviets are experimenting with differing ways of improving the tank-infantry-artillery balance in their tank divisions but have not yet settled on which alternative, or combination thereof, will be emphasized during the 1980s.

21. *Tanks.* Production of the T-72 medium tank will continue well into the 1980s, accompanied by the gradual phasing out of the active Soviet inventory of the T-54/55 and T-62. We expect Soviet production of the T-55 and T-64 to end within the next few years. A new tank, designated the T-80, is expected to enter service by the early 1980s, but our evidence on its current status is fragmentary. The NSWP armies will remain largely standardized on the T-55, but some NSWP countries are expected to begin production of the T-72 for their forces in the early 1980s. The new Romanian medium tank, an improved version of the T-55, has been developed and could be fielded soon. Overall, the total number of tanks in Pact ground force units opposite NATO could increase somewhat—perhaps by as much as 10 percent—as tank battalions in Soviet divisions in the USSR are expanded to the tank strength which characterizes Soviet divisions in Eastern Europe.

22. There is little evidence of advanced antiarmor countermeasures programs in the USSR. The Soviets apparently have experimented with infrared absorbing and reflecting paints and electro-optical countermeasures. Such coatings and systems could be developed and applied to existing systems without a significant reequipment program. Because all present and projected NATO antitank guided missiles (ATGMs) rely on high-explosive (shaped-charge) warheads for their kill mechanism, the Soviets can be expected to continue their heavy R&D emphasis on developing armor to defeat these weapons.

23. ***Artillery.*** Pact concern with increasing conventional firepower in general and with the neutralization of NATO antitank defense in particular is expected to result in continued increases in numbers of artillery pieces as well as improvements in weapons, target acquisition capabilities, and ammunition. The upgrading of the artillery battery in the Soviet motorized rifle regiment to an artillery battalion—a measure already well under way—has improved the regiment's capability to suppress or neutralize antitank weapons as well as other targets. As towed artillery is replaced by self-propelled (SP) models (with their own armored command and reconnaissance vehicles) this capability will grow further because the newer systems have better mobility, are more responsive, and provide better crew protection. By the early 1980s, battalions of 122-mm SP weapons probably will be found in all Soviet BMP-equipped motorized rifle regiments and may also appear in some BTR-equipped regiments and division artillery regiments.

24. Deployment of other SP artillery weapons will also proceed over the next decade. The new nuclear SP heavy artillery (203-mm guns and 240-mm mortars) will continue to replace older towed weapons in Soviet heavy artillery brigades and may supplement or replace lighter weapons in army artillery regiments and in artillery divisions. If the new heavy artillery pieces are deployed to the Soviet groups of forces, as we believe likely, it would break NATO's monopoly on nuclear tube artillery in Central Europe and provide the Pact with a capability to respond in kind to NATO's use of nuclear tube artillery and to provide close-in nuclear strikes in support of ground forces.

25. NSWP artillery improvements will lag behind those of the Soviets. Only a few batteries of the new SP guns and no heavy artillery are in service in the NSWP forces. The number of SP guns in the East German, Czechoslovak, and Polish Armies will increase, but towed models will continue to predominate.

26. We have fair evidence that the Soviets are working toward development of improved conventional munitions (ICMs) for their tube artillery systems. The Soviets have the technology to develop ICMs for their artillery pieces of 152-mm or larger caliber, but we have not observed them in testing. We estimate, however, that by the mid-1980s the Soviets will field ICMs with their larger caliber weapons. The new 240-mm multiple rocket launcher (M-1977) is well suited for the delivery of ICMs, and we believe that it is so equipped. The Soviets probably have the technological base to produce artillery-delivered scatterable mines and, while it is unlikely that such mines are currently with Pact artillery units, we believe that they will be introduced by the mid-1980s.

27. ***Antitank Weapons.*** Soviet R&D programs for antitank weapons are being directed toward development of missile systems incorporating semiautomatic or automatic guidance to relieve the gunner of guidance responsibility, thereby increasing hit probabilities and reducing gunner vulnerability. These programs are expected to result in the fielding of a short-to-medium-range man-portable system by the mid-1980s and a similar heliborne system somewhat earlier. These systems probably will have increased accuracy and warhead effectiveness. The heliborne system probably will have a supersonic velocity.

28. ***Armored Personnel Carriers.*** Production of both the BMP and the BTR-60 is expected to continue at a steady pace. Soviet motorized rifle divisions are expected to standardize during the 1980s on a mix of one motorized rifle regiment equipped with the BMP and two with the BTR-60PB. The motorized rifle regiment in tank divisions will be equipped with the BMP. The East German Army has this same organization, while the Czechoslovaks have one field army equipped according to the Soviet pattern and another in process. Poland has only about 300 BMPs and is expected to equip no more than one additional motorized rifle regiment per year with them. The remainder will continue to use older models. A follow-on to the BTR-60PB, designated the BTR-70, is in production and is being assigned to units. These changes will improve the general mobility of Pact ground forces, as well as their capabilities for operating in a chemical, biological, or radiological environment.

29. ***Ground Force Air Defense Systems.*** The Soviets are likely to continue the advances which they have made in air defense weapons over the last decade. Existing systems will no doubt undergo modification and improvements. The SA-9, for example, currently mounted on a scout car chassis, will probably be deployed on a light tracked amphibious carrier that would increase its mobility as well as provide more internal storage space for refire missiles.

30. A follow-on to the ZSU-23/4 is expected in the next decade, but probably not before the mid-1980s. This new system, with a caliber estimated at 30 to 40 mm, will probably have a greater effective range than its predecessor.

31. We also expect deployment of a successor to the SA-6, the SA-X-11, probably within the next year. Its

main improvements over the SA-6 will be the integration of the target-tracking radar and missile launcher in a single unit, greater mobility, better capabilities for electronic counter-countermeasures (ECCM), and a multiple-target-handling capability. A possible follow-on to the SA-4 is also being tested and is expected to enter series production within the next three or four years. It probably will also have a multiple-target-handling capability.

32. *Tactical Ballistic Missiles.* Surface-to-surface ballistic missiles are expected to play an increasingly important role in Warsaw Pact planning for conventional combat during the period of this Estimate. New missiles such as the SS-21 have characteristics that give them a significant conventional capability. The SS-21, for example, could be used effectively with improved conventional munitions in an air defense suppression role. In such a role, tactical missiles offer the advantages of tactical surprise and assured penetrability, but they require timely and accurate reconnaissance data. Near the end of the period of this Estimate, tactical ballistic missiles equipped with terminal guidance and conventional, earth-penetrating munitions could pose a serious threat to NATO airfields.

33. By the mid-1980s the Soviets could introduce tactical ballistic missiles equipped with terminal homing systems. We lack information on the specific types of terminal guidance systems the Soviets might develop, but at ranges of 1,000 kilometers or less, they should be able to achieve accuracies with a CEP (circular error probable) of about 50 meters or less. We believe that the Soviets will introduce terminal homing in their division-level missiles first, possibly in a modification to the SS-21, because Soviet terminal homing technology is believed to be more advanced for these shorter range systems.

Air Forces

34. We believe that the number of fixed-wing aircraft in Soviet Frontal Aviation opposite NATO will remain essentially unchanged over the next decade. Efforts to improve the quality of Soviet tactical aircraft and munitions are likely to continue, although the rate of new aircraft deployment is expected to slow as the Soviets meet their current force objectives. Furthermore, we expect the Soviets to continue improving their support and subsidiary systems such as command and control, radioelectronic combat (REC), and reconnaissance data link systems. No major changes are expected in the number of fixed-wing aircraft in the NSWP air forces. NSWP equipment modernization will continue to proceed gradually and be driven largely by economic considerations.

35. *Fighters.* Production of the MIG-23 Flogger probably will continue well into the 1980s. A variant of the Flogger with an improved radar designed to give it a better low-altitude intercept capability is being developed and could be deployed with the Soviet tactical air forces by the early 1980s. Production of MIG-21 Fishbed variants is also expected to continue at least into the early 1980s. NSWP tactical fighter units are expected to receive mainly Floggers and late-model Fishbeds over the next decade.

36. Longer term improvements in Soviet fighter capabilities could arise from the introduction of a totally new aircraft. The Soviets are testing at least three new or highly modified fighter-type aircraft, one of which is intended for deployment with the Soviet strategic air defense forces. Should either or both of the other aircraft be deployed with the tactical forces, they would not be available in significant numbers before the mid-1980s.

37. *Ground Attack Aircraft.* We expect deployment of a new ground attack aircraft—designated the SU-25—with the Soviet Air Force by 1980 and believe that it will be purchased by some NSWP countries. The SU-25 is a twin-engine, subsonic, heavily armored aircraft, presumably designed for close air support of ground forces. The aircraft apparently does not incorporate advanced technology and is considerably slower and has a shorter combat radius than the SU-17 Fitter C/D and MIG-27 Flogger D. But it will be armed with guns, rockets, bombs, and tactical air-to-surface missiles, and will almost certainly handle better at low speeds than the other Pact fighter-bombers.

38. Soviet ground attack units opposite NATO will be totally equipped with newer aircraft—SU-25, Flogger D, Fitter C/D, and Fencer—by the early 1980s. Within five years over one-half of the aircraft in NSWP ground attack units probably will be more modern types. The SU-25 and Flogger will be the main ground attack aircraft in NSWP air forces by the end of the next decade.

39. We have evidence that the Soviets are testing an air-to-air refueling capability for the SU-24 Fencer and future variants of this aircraft, and possibly others could be so equipped. No operational Soviet tactical aircraft are currently capable of in-flight refueling, nor do the Soviets have an adequate tanker force to support large-scale use of air-to-air refueling by their tactical air forces. Moreover, none of the new model

aircraft currently being tested are known to have such a capability. Whatever in-flight refueling capability the Soviets develop for their tactical aircraft during the period of this Estimate, therefore, is likely to be confined to only a small portion of the force.

40. The Soviets will no doubt pursue improvements in the range and all-weather, day or night, low-level attack capabilities of the Pact's ground attack forces. We also expect increased use of ECM (electronic countermeasures) pods and other ECM equipment, which should enhance survivability in hostile airspace.

41. *Reconnaissance.* Modernization in the reconnaissance component of the Pact's tactical air forces will continue during the next few years. Deployment of Foxbat B/D aircraft to Soviet reconnaissance units will proceed, and reconnaissance variants of the Flogger and Fencer could appear in the early 1980s. Improved systems for data processing and transmission are also expected.

42. *Helicopter Forces.* We expect in the next decade that several additional Soviet, Czechoslovak, Polish, and East German combat helicopter regiments, primarily for ground attack, will be formed. The NSWP regiments probably will be patterned after Soviet regiments and may be equipped with MI-24 Hind armed helicopters. The Romanians may also organize a combat helicopter regiment in the next five years, using attack and transport helicopters of French design.

43. The Soviets are applying their latest technology in avionics and air ordnance to helicopter platforms. This could result in improvements to their weapon systems to increase standoff ranges and enhance the survivability of the helicopter in an advanced air defense environment. In addition to assigning broader ground attack roles to helicopters, the Soviets are expected to equip them to a greater extent for command and control and electronic warfare missions. The Soviets are also increasing the air-to-air combat training of MI-24 Hind crews.

44. The Soviets are developing a new heavy lift helicopter, the Halo A. This helicopter is assessed to have almost twice the payload of the current Hook and Harke heavy lift helicopters. The new helicopter has twin engines and an eight-blade main rotor, and could be operational by the early 1980s.

45. *Air Munitions.* The Soviets also are developing more advanced air-to-air missiles, tactical air-to-surface missiles, and precision guided bombs. Programs directed toward fielding advanced air-launched cruise missiles for delivery by Soviet Long Range Aviation bombers are also under way.

46. We have no evidence that the Soviets have operational precision guided bombs but they are conducting tests of unpowered, airdropped vehicles that exhibit precision-delivery characteristics. These tests indicate that a guided bomb employing a laser illuminator mounted on board the launch aircraft could be available in the near future, and that a TV-guided bomb could become operational in the early 1980s. These systems would be accurate within 10 to 20 meters.

47. The Soviets are developing a minimum of two new tactical air-to-surface missiles, the AS-X-11 and AS-X-12, with operational ranges of about 40 to 30 kilometers respectively. These new antiradiation homing missiles will probably be deployed by 1980. They will have improved accuracy—within 12 meters—and are expected to lock on targets more quickly than previous systems. The AS-X-11 can be targeted against EW/ECI and ground-based air defense (SAM) radars. The AS-X-12 can be targeted only against ground-based air defense (SAM) radars. The Soviets are also expected to begin testing a TV-guided version of their AS-10 in the near future.

48. We have no evidence that the Soviets are developing a new air-to-air missile for their tactical fighters. Development of new missiles for the strategic air defense forces, however, could have some future applications in the tactical air forces.

49. *Military Air Transport.* Soviet Military Transport Aviation (VTA) will continue to be modernized with newer aircraft, but the size of the force will not appreciably change. Although overall lift capacity will increase, the Soviets do not appear to be building a force capable of simultaneously lifting much more than one airborne division or the assault elements of two divisions.

50. The AN-12 Cub medium-range transport will remain the mainstay of the airlift force, at least into the mid-1980s, although its numbers will continue to decrease as the IL-76 Candid enters the force. The Soviets will continue to rely on the AN-22 Cock, which is no longer in production, to lift outsized military equipment. We also expect the Soviets to continue relying on Aeroflot for airlift augmentation, and this capability will increase as the civil air fleet is modernized.

51. A new transport, the AN-72, will probably be operational in Frontal Aviation units in the early 1980s. This aircraft, which is optimized for short-haul operations from unimproved airfields, will enable cargo and personnel to be delivered close to deployed field forces.

52. **NSWP National Air Defense.**[2] We have good evidence that non-Soviet Warsaw Pact countries plan to undertake a major program to reequip their national air defense forces. The program is scheduled to run into the mid-1980s and is designed to remedy what the Pact considers to be the growing obsolescence of its surface-to-air missile and interceptor forces. Though intended primarily to improve defense against low-altitude targets, the modernization effort would also entail the introduction of systems that would extend the range and ceilings at which targets could be engaged.

53. The Pact's early warning network is scheduled to be reequipped with newer radars having improved capabilities for target information handling and data transmission and greater resistance to electronic countermeasures. Some Pact countries might also receive radar-equipped ships or possibly aircraft to extend early warning coverage over water approaches to Pact territory. NSWP SA-2 and SA-3 systems are to be upgraded with equipment more resistant to electronic jamming and possessing better capabilities to engage targets with small radar cross-sections. The SA-5, a long-range SAM system that has heretofore been deployed only in the USSR, is also being considered for deployment in some NSWP countries. The most notable development affecting Pact interceptor forces would be the continued introduction of Floggers equipped with a fire-control radar providing a limited lookdown/shootdown capability. While this aircraft and late-model Fishbeds will be the mainstay of the force, Pact planners are also considering equipping some NSWP interceptor units with the MIG-25 Foxbat.

54. Our evidence of Pact plans to deploy the Foxbat and SA-5 with the NSWP air defense forces indicates that both would be intended primarily to counter the growing capabilities of NATO's air forces for standoff air-to-surface missile attack. The evidence also suggests that these systems might be used to engage such NATO aircraft as the E-3A AWACS (airborne warning and control system).

---

[2] See NIE 11-3/8-78 for a discussion of the Soviet strategic air defense forces.

General Purpose Naval Forces

55. During the next decade, developments in the Soviet Navy will produce a force with improved capabilities to perform its peacetime and wartime missions. The Soviets will also press forward with programs to correct shortcomings in submarine detection, fleet air defense, logistic support, and communications. Indeed, developments over the past decade have been so rapid that a period of time may be required to integrate and consolidate advances and ensure that combat potentials are fully realized. We expect a modest decline in the overall number of Soviet general purpose naval ships and submarines but newer and more capable units will be replacing older and less effective ones.

56. We expect the Soviet Navy within the next decade to continue concentrating on the missions outlined in chapter II. We also anticipate that its current roles of sea control in limited areas and support of Soviet overseas policies will continue to evolve. Improvements in antiship, amphibious, and antisubmarine warfare (ASW) capabilities are also likely. Moreover, we foresee that by the mid-1980s the Soviets will have made some progress in such current problem areas as logistic support and the ability to conduct sustained operations. The result of this process will be a somewhat more capable Navy which will remain an integral element of Pact planning for war in Europe. We believe, however, the Soviets will continue to have problems in detecting enemy submarines, in defending their surface ships against air attack, in providing targeting assistance for the effective use of many ASW and antiship weapons, and in replenishing ships at sea.

57. The Soviet Navy will also continue to devote resources and develop tactics for preventing the approach of NATO's carrier task forces or other major surface ship formations into waters contiguous to the European theater. As new cruise-missile-equipped ships, submarines, and aircraft replace less capable units and the technology of cruise missiles is advanced, we expect the Soviet capabilities against those NATO forces to improve. Reliance on external targeting will, however, remain a serious deficiency in beyond-the-horizon attacks.

58. Antisubmarine warfare will remain a serious concern of the Soviet naval leadership. Soviet ASW capabilities will improve somewhat with the acquisition of new classes of surface ships, submarines, and aircraft and as new technology and better operating techniques take hold. These capabilities will continue,

however, to be greater in areas closer to the Soviet homeland than in the open ocean. Although there are gaps in our knowledge of Soviet ASW developments, we have no evidence of any major breakthrough that would give the Soviets confidence in their ability to neutralize Western submarines in the open ocean.

59. The Soviets are also committed to protecting their own submarines from NATO naval forces, particularly their D-class SSBNs operating in the Barents and Norwegian Seas and other areas. We expect the Soviets to continue working to improve their capabilities to support and protect their SSBNs.

60. Support for ground forces in the context of a general European war will continue to be an important mission of the Soviet Navy's general purpose forces. In addition to protecting the seaward flanks of the ground forces from attack by enemy sea-based air or naval forces or by enemy amphibious assaults, the Navy has the role of providing gunfire support for ground forces and launching amphibious operations against enemy flanks. This role will have some influence, albeit limited, on the future composition and force levels of the fleets. Some older units will be retained and some new systems, including air-cushion vehicles and hydrofoils, will be allocated to these flank support missions.

61. Soviet capabilities to interdict NATO's sea lines of communication (SLOC) by attacking ships at sea and by mining and airstrikes against European port facilities probably also will improve. This will result from the increased capabilities that will likely exist in future Soviet general purpose submarines, mine warfare ships, and naval aircraft. Some agencies believe, however, that Soviet capabilities to perform this mission will nonetheless remain limited. Other agencies believe that Soviet capabilities for SLOC interdiction currently are and will continue to be significant.[3]

62. *General Purpose Submarines.* During the past few years, Soviet construction programs for torpedo attack and cruise missile submarines have produced an average of about five units per year, which is below estimated shipyard capacity. Because older submarines have been retired at a greater rate than new ones have been produced, overall force levels have been declining. We estimate, however, that overall general purpose submarine output will increase to at least eight and possibly 10 units annually over the next few years as newly identified construction programs proceed and some ballistic missile units are converted to attack submarines.

63. These new programs probably will include follow-ons to the C-II nuclear-powered guided-missile submarine (SSGN), the V-II nuclear-powered attack submarine (SSN), and possibly the A-class SSN. If pressure hulls are fabricated from HY-130 equivalent steel, the operational depth limit for the new SSNs probably will be to as much as 470 meters, as compared with about 360 meters for present classes. If titanium hulls are used, the operational depth limit could reach about 600 meters. According to one intelligence estimate,[4] the maximum speeds for some of the new SSN and SSGN classes could reach 37 knots. Another view[5] holds that these submarines will be capable of speeds of up to 33 knots. We believe the classes projected for the late 1970s or early 1980s will not be significantly quieter than current submarines.

64. Many operational diesel torpedo and cruise missile units will be reaching the end of their useful age by about 1980. We believe the T-class diesel submarines will remain in production for several years, gradually replacing the F-class in open-ocean operations.

65. During the next decade we estimate that the number of diesel submarines will decrease from about 170 to about 85 as older units are replaced on a less than one-for-one basis; nuclear attack submarines will increase from 43 to about 75; nuclear cruise missile submarines will increase from 44 to about 55. Thus, the total number of general purpose submarines will decrease by about 15 percent—from 257 to about 215. Because a greater proportion of the force will be nuclear, however, there will be a significant increase in overall capabilities.

66. *Principal Surface Combatants.* The Soviets currently have at least six construction programs under way for principal surface combatants, including aircraft carriers. The principal surface combatants are expected to decrease in number over the next decade but to grow in firepower and in capability for prolonged deployment and combat. While most warships produced in the USSR to date appear to be optimized

---

[3] For a discussion of differing views on Soviet intentions and capabilities to interdict NATO's sea lines of communications, see paragraphs 142-149 of chapter II and 168 and 169 of chapter IV.

[4] *This estimate was made by the Director, Defense Intelligence Agency, and the Director of Naval Intelligence, Department of the Navy.*

[5] *The holder of this view is the Central Intelligence Agency.*

for short, intense engagements, some future construction programs probably will feature ships of larger displacement which carry more fuel, ammunition, provisions, and perhaps more crew space.

67. Two Kiev-class carriers are operational, and a third has been launched and will probably become operational in 1981. A fourth carrier of this class is being built. We also have some information suggesting that upon completion of the Kiev-class program the Soviets will begin construction of a new and larger class of aircraft carrier, possibly incorporating an arrested landing capability.

68. The Kiev clearly has capabilities in ASW and in other areas of naval warfare such as antiship strike, area air defense, and perhaps support for amphibious attack. We do not know how the Soviets assess the overall value of the Kiev inasmuch as the capabilities of its aircraft are limited. It will take a long time for Soviet crews to become proficient in the complex procedures of carrier flight operations and to develop appropriate tactics for carrier operations in conjunction with other ships. It is apparent that the Soviets have made a commitment to the construction of aircraft carriers, although general purpose submarine construction will absorb well over half of what the Central Intelligence Agency projects will be total Soviet expenditures for general purpose ships and submarines through the mid-1980s.

69. There is disagreement within the Intelligence Community regarding the extent to which the Kiev enhances current Soviet military effectiveness and regarding the impact of Soviet acquisition of carriers upon the evolution of naval missions. According to one view,[6] the introduction of the Kiev may constitute a major turning point in the development of the Soviet Navy, but it is premature to judge the impact of the acquisition of carriers upon the evolution of naval missions. Some holders of this view [7] further believe that one, two, or three ships of this class, because of their limited capabilities to detect NATO submarines beyond torpedo attack range and to defend against NATO air attack, do not by themselves represent a significant improvement in Soviet capabilities to fight a war with NATO. It is apparent to the holders of this view that the Soviet naval leadership has chosen an option which is more significant for the future of the structure of the Navy than for the enhancement of current military effectiveness.

70. According to an alternative view,[8] the acquisition of carriers with introduction of the Kiev clearly constitutes a major watershed in the development of the Soviet Navy. The holders of this view further believe that the Kiev already has influenced the acquisition of other future surface combatants, and enhances Soviet antiship, ASW, and other capabilities to an extent that could have significant influence on Pact naval operations in a NATO–Warsaw Pact war. The construction of the Kiev class and possibly a larger carrier class in the 1980s will provide added impetus to the Soviet Navy's gradually expanding role in achieving sea control and in providing support to amphibious operations.

71. There also is disagreement within the Intelligence Community regarding a large combatant—some 25,000 tons—which was launched in 1977 and is currently being fitted out at the Baltic shipyard in Leningrad. A keel, probably for the second unit of the class, has been laid. According to one view,[9] the ship is probably a nuclear-powered cruiser which will carry a vertical-launch air defense missile system and a variety of other antiship, antiair, and ASW weapons, possibly including the SS-N-12. Another view [10] holds that the evidence is still too ambiguous to classify the ship as to propulsion.

72. A new cruiser program has begun at the Zhdanov shipyard in Leningrad. At least four ships of this class, slightly larger than the Kresta, are under construction. There are indications that this class will mount large-caliber guns for gunfire support. The lead unit should become operational in 1981.

73. The Soviets probably will continue to build Kara-class missile cruisers or heavily modified versions of this class at a rate of about one per year. The Krivak-class missile frigate probably will be produced at two or three per year until at least the early 1980s, when its follow-on is expected. Grisha-class light frigates are being built at four per year, and the program is expected to continue through 1980. In addition,

---

[6] The holders of this view are the Central Intelligence Agency; the Director, Bureau of Intelligence and Research, Department of State; and the Director, National Security Agency.

[7] The Central Intelligence Agency and the Director, Bureau of Intelligence and Research, Department of State.

[8] The holders of this view are the Director, Defense Intelligence Agency, and the Director of Naval Intelligence, Department of the Navy.

[9] The holders of this view are the Director, Defense Intelligence Agency, and the Director of Naval Intelligence, Department of the Navy.

[10] The holder of this view is the Central Intelligence Agency.

some Kashin-class destroyers probably will continue to be converted to the Modified Kashin class, being armed with the SS-N-2c cruise missile.

74. *Patrol Combatants and Mine Warfare Units.* The capabilities and flexibility of minor combatants have been improved with the introduction of the newer classes. Construction of the Nanuchka-class guided-missile patrol boat (PGG) probably will end in about 1980, at which time a new PGG class probably will be introduced. Construction of the Matka-class missile hydrofoils will probably continue at least through the 1980s. Construction of the Turya class (also a hydrofoil) of submarine chaser probably will end in 1979, with a follow-on expected. New classes of both are forecast for introduction in the early 1980s. We also believe that torpedo and patrol boats will be gradually phased out of the Soviet Navy in favor of small antiship missile and ASW combatants.

75. *Amphibious Warfare.* Current Soviet amphibious ship programs include the new Ivan Rogov class of amphibious landing ship and dock (LPD) and continued acquisition of the Polish-built Ropucha-class tank landing ship (LST). The 12,500-ton LPD can lift a 500-man battalion landing team with its equipment and carry about six helicopters and two or three air cushion vehicles, while the 4,500-ton Ropucha probably can carry about 250 men and 16 tanks. At current construction rates, the Soviets would add three or four of the new LPDs and about six Ropuchas by the mid-1980s. During this same period, we expect the Soviet inventory of Polnocny-class medium landing ships (LSMs) to diminish by some 10 units, primarily by transfer to other navies. In addition, East Germany is building the 2,700-ton Frosch-class LST at the rate of about three per year and the Soviets continue to produce air cushion vehicles for use in amphibious assault.

76. We do not believe that these programs will have a major impact on Soviet amphibious lift capabilities until the mid-1980s. By that time, however, Pact capabilities to lift amphibious forces in support of land operations in Europe will significantly improve.

77. *Auxiliaries.* The Soviets are working to improve their underway replenishment capabilities. The introduction of a new underway-replenishment ship of 35,000 tons, for example, should improve the situation somewhat. This ship, which now is operational, has a helicopter pad which also allows replenishment by air. In addition, a new type of cargo ship and a submarine tender are under construction, and production of earlier types is continuing, including a water tender, an ammunition support ship, and a repair ship. The pace of these programs, however, still lags the modernization of the surface combat fleet and will continue to be a factor retarding extended operations.

78. *Strike Aircraft.* During the next several years TU-16 Badger aircraft armed with air-to-surface missiles will remain numerically the greatest threat to surface ships operating within 1,000 to 1,500 nautical miles of the Soviet landmass. The Backfire, using a variable flight profile and speeds near Mach 1.5 at high altitude, has a penetration capability against aircraft carrier defenses significantly superior to that of the Badger. The Backfire is currently being produced at a rate of between two and three per month, and to date deployment has been nearly equal between the Navy and Long Range Aviation. We project that production of the Backfire will continue into the 1980s. A reconnaissance/ECM version could enter service by the early 1980s,[11] as could a new tanker based on the IL-76 Candid, which could be capable of supporting the Backfire. We believe that Soviet Naval Aviation in the three western fleets will have about 160 Backfires by 1988.

79. *Fixed-Wing ASW Aircraft.* The TU-142 Bear F is the only fixed-wing antisubmarine warfare aircraft currently in production. We have evidence that a variant, incorporating airframe modifications seen on several earlier models, may be nearing deployment. Given the effort placed on advanced marine vehicles operating in the surface effects zone, the Soviet Navy may also be planning to use the wing-in-ground (WIG) concept in an ASW application. A WIG ASW vehicle could enter naval service in the early 1980s.

80. *Fighter/Attack Aircraft.* Approximately two to three YAK-36 Forger V/STOL (vertical and short takeoff and landing) aircraft are being produced per month, and production probably will continue until about 1980. A new or extensively modified V/STOL aircraft will probably enter production some time in the early 1980s. SU-17 Fitters are still in production, and some of these attack aircraft have been assigned to the Baltic Fleet. We believe that the Navy will receive about 60 SU-17s by 1983, and some of these may be assigned to the Black Sea Fleet.

81. *Helicopters.* The MI-14 Haze is the only naval helicopter in production today. Its use aboard ships is limited, however, because it does not have folding rotors. The Soviets also lack an ASW helicopter which can conduct dipping sonar operations at night or in

---

[11] See NIE 11-3/8-78 for a detailed discussion of present and future Backfire production.

bad weather. Therefore, we estimate that a new helicopter with folding rotors and perhaps an all-weather capability will start to enter the force by the mid-1980s.

82. *Tactical ASW Missiles.* The SS-NX-16 is an ASW weapon which uses a solid-fuel motor that ignites under water. In testing it has carried a homing torpedo on a ballistic trajectory to a maximum range of 54 nautical miles (100 km). The missile has been in testing since the early 1970s and could become operational at any time. We expect it to be carried on board the V-II-class attack submarine. Submarines of the C-II, T, and A classes are other possible platforms for this weapon.

83. *Antiship Missiles.* We estimate that, by the early 1980s, the Soviets probably will introduce improved cruise missiles as follow-ons to those developed during the late 1960s. Work is currently under way on new surface- and submarine-launched missiles, possibly combining improved home-on-jam, infrared, and antiradiation seeker capabilities.

84. We have limited evidence that by 1985 a follow-on to the SS-N-9 will be available for the Nanuchka class and the projected PGG. This system probably will also be available in a submerged-launch version for use on C-class submarines and their follow-ons. In addition, the Soviets have in development a submerged-launched antiship cruise missile with an estimated range of 270 nm (500 km). It could be available by the mid-1980s, but would require a new and as yet unidentified submarine. The SS-N-12 cruise missile system, which has a range of 300 nm (550 km), will likely be installed in some additional E-II-class submarines—perhaps one-half the force—during normal overhaul periods. It is also possible that some J-class submarines and additional large surface combatants will receive the SS-N-12.

85. We have no evidence that the Soviets are testing a new antiship air-to-surface missile (ASM), although they continue to test versions of the AS-4 and AS-6. Given past trends, however, the Soviets probably will develop a new antiship ASM for the Backfire during the next several years.

86. *Air Defense Systems.* Gatling gun systems and the 6-nm (11-km) SA-N-4 missile probably will continue to be installed on most new naval ships for point defense against aircraft and antiship missiles. These weapons were even placed on board the new replenishment oiler that became operational in late 1977, the first time an auxiliary has been equipped with a SAM system.

87. The Soviets are testing several new surface-to-air missile systems, some of which could have naval applications. The Soviet Navy needs a long-range SAM for defense beyond 20 nm, as well as more advanced shorter range systems for individual ship defense against low-altitude aircraft and cruise missiles. There is evidence that the SA-X-10 land-launched SAM is being adapted for naval use. It would improve Soviet fleet air defenses against the low-altitude threat and may provide a significant improvement in range over current naval systems.

88. *ASW Detection Systems.* The Soviets will no doubt make additional efforts to improve their surface ship, submarine, and helicopter-borne sonars by decreasing operating frequencies of passive systems, improving the signal structures of active systems and improving the signal processing capabilities of both. The Soviets also are investigating various nonacoustic methods to detect a submarine by the effects caused by its passage through the water or by contaminants from the submarine itself. These efforts include development of air and shipborne sensors for detection of surface thermal effects, detection of radioisotopes in the wake of submarines, detection of the wake itself, and exploitation of low-frequency, electromagnetic radiations from submarines. We do not believe, however, that they will achieve any near-term technical solution to their relative inability to locate Western submarines in the open ocean.

89. *Ocean Surveillance.* A new ELINT ocean reconnaissance satellite (Eorsat) is now becoming operational. It has a direction-finding capability with an estimated accuracy of 2 to 20 nm (4 to 37 km), depending upon target location vis-a-vis the satellite. It can transmit near-real-time tactical data to some Soviet ships and submarines operating in the same general geographic area as the target. Western ships operating under conditions of electronic silence cannot be detected by this system. The Soviets can use a radar satellite (Rorsat) in conjunction with the Eorsat system. The Rorsat is not affected by electronic silence but has only a limited area search capability and is unable to identify contacts. Neither system is kept continuously in orbit. These two satellites probably will undergo future development; the Soviets may be exploring alternative power sources to replace the nuclear one used on the Rorsat system.

Theater Nuclear Forces

90. Over the next decade the Soviets will continue their ongoing programs to improve their peripheral

strategic strike forces and to eliminate the imbalance in battlefield nuclear capabilities they perceive in the European theater. Force improvements carried out to date and ongoing deployment of new systems are increasing the flexibility with which the Soviets can employ their theater nuclear forces. In particular, they are acquiring low-yield tactical nuclear weapons and delivery systems with sufficient accuracy to permit employment in close proximity to Pact forces.

91. *Tactical Nuclear Forces.* The Soviets will continue to improve the quality of their tactical ballistic missile forces by deploying new missiles, introducing improved guidance systems, and increasing the number of weapons in tactical units. Deployment of the SS-21, the replacement for the FROG division-level weapon, will continue at least through the mid-1980s; its deployment with Soviet forces in Eastern Europe could occur at any time. The deployment of the SS-22 as a replacement for the SS-12 front-level missile system also is probably under way and will continue until all 12 SS-12 brigades are reequipped.

92. Increases in Soviet tactical missile forces opposite NATO are expected over the next several years. Three Soviet Scud brigades in East Germany have already been increased from 12 to 18 launchers. If all Soviet Scud brigades in Eastern Europe are similarly augmented—as probably will be the case—the force will have an additional 66 launchers, bringing the total there to 198 Scud launchers. We are unable to predict whether Scud brigades in the USSR will also be expanded. We have recent evidence that the Soviets plan to increase the number of tactical missile launchers in their divisions from four to six as the SS-21 replaces the FROG system. The increases in both Scud and SS-21 launchers would provide the Soviets with greater firepower and flexibility during conventional and nuclear operations.

93. A probable replacement for the Scud, the SS-X-23, is in an early stage of development. The first flight test of this missile was observed in October 1977. This system, which is expected to have improved accuracy and reduced reaction time over the current Scud systems, could reach operational status by 1982.

94. In the Pact tactical air forces, the potential for nuclear delivery is expected to grow as the aircraft modernization programs progress over the next decade. In addition, the availability of low-yield warheads and improved air-to-surface missile guidance systems could induce the Soviets to field an air-delivered tactical missile with a nuclear capability during the next few years.

95. The number of pilots in Soviet units qualified to drop nuclear bombs is also expected to grow, particularly in the fighter-bomber regiments, as the level of pilot experience and proficiency increases and nuclear delivery training is broadened. We do not expect the number of such pilots in the NSWP units to grow, however, because nuclear delivery training probably will continue to be confined to a few specially designated units.

96. The Soviets are expected to continue reequipping their heavy artillery brigades in the USSR with the nuclear-capable 203-mm self-propelled guns and 240-mm self-propelled mortars. All six such brigades opposite NATO are expected to complete the reequipping process within the next several years. It also seems likely that the Soviets will deploy some nuclear artillery to Eastern Europe during the period of this Estimate. The Soviets probably have the technological capability to develop a 152-mm nuclear artillery round, but we have no reliable evidence that they intend to develop and field such a weapon.

97. *Peripheral Strategic Forces.* The Soviets will continue to rely heavily on land-based ballistic missiles to conduct strategic nuclear strikes in the areas surrounding the USSR. Some intercontinental ballistic missiles probably will continue to have peripheral missions, but the SS-20 intermediate-range ballistic missile will be the backbone of the peripheral force. There is evidence that in late 1975 the Soviets were considering a plan to field a force of up to 28 SS-20 regiments. Satellite photography of the support bases currently under construction indicates that eventually there will be at least nine SS-20 launchers per regiment. We project a total force of 250 to 300 launchers, and we estimate that such a force could be fully deployed by the early 1980s. We also project that the Soviets will begin fielding a modified version with a more flexible payload and improved accuracy shortly thereafter. As a result, we project a total force of about 300 mobile IRBM launchers from 1984 onward. About 200 of these will be deployed in areas opposite NATO. (See table VI-1.)

98. Our force projections assume that the size of the Long Range Aviation bomber force with a peripheral attack mission will remain about the same as at present. Some aging Badgers and Blinders probably will be retired as Backfires are assigned to LRA in increasing numbers. By the late 1980s about 270 Backfires could be in service with LRA if the rate of production increases as projected. One constraint being considered at the strategic arms limitation talks is a

Table VI-1

Projected Soviet Peripheral Strike Forces Opposite NATO [a]
1979, 1983, and 1988

	1979	1983	1988
MRBMs and IRBMs			
SS-4 Launchers	384	140	0
Silo	64	56	0
Aboveground	320	84	0
SS-5 Launchers	61	51	0
Silo	27	27	0
Aboveground	34	24	0
SS-20	45-63	171	27
SS-20 Mod B	0	9	171
Bombers of Long Range Aviation			
TU-16 Badgers	325	300	250
TU-22 Blinders	155	140	100
Backfires	45	115	160
Ballistic Missile Submarines/Launchers [b]			
SS-N-4 (G-I)	1/3	0	0
SS-N-5 (G-II)	6/18	3/9	0
SS-N-5 (H-II)	4/12	0	0

[a] For a more detailed treatment of the peripheral strike forces, the implications and possible constraints of a SALT agreement, and alternative projections of future peripheral strike forces, see NIE 11-6-78, *Soviet Strategic Forces for Peripheral Attack*.

[b] Some of the modern Y-class submarines probably have contingency missions for peripheral strike. As the number of older ballistic missile submarines with peripheral missions declines, some of their target coverage may be assumed by modern ballistic missile submarines.

limitation on the rate of Backfire production. If this enters into effect, LRA could have almost 200 Backfires in 1988, of which about 160 would be deployed opposite NATO. In the near term, we expect Backfires to be deployed primarily with LRA units in the European USSR, enabling some Badgers, especially those capable of delivering both bombs and air-to-surface missiles, to be transferred to the Soviet Far East.

99. The number of older ballistic missile submarines for peripheral strike probably will decline during the period of our projections. The Soviets probably will continue to convert their G-I submarines to attack or special-purpose submarines or retire them. We estimate that some of the G-II submarines, which are targeted against the peripheral areas, will be in the force until the mid-1980s, but the last G-II probably will be deactivated before 1988. The future of the H-II submarine as a ballistic missile system is in doubt because of the limitations of a prospective SALT agreement.

100. As the number of older ballistic missile submarines with peripheral missions declines, some of their target coverage may be assumed by modern ballistic missile submarines. The range of the missiles carried by these modern SSBNs gives them greater targeting flexibility than the G- or H-classes.

Support Systems and Forces

101. *Command, Control, and Communications.* We estimate that, currently, about one week would be required before the Pact's wartime communications links could be established to theater-level headquarters and to supporting strategic commands. Communications, between Moscow and the fronts and within the fronts, to control combat operations by divisions and armies could be effectively established within a few days. However, the Pact has two programs under way—the creation of a centralized command structure and the establishment of a unified communications system—which, during the period of this Estimate, could shorten the time required by the Pact to get its command and control system prepared for war. The two programs are intended to establish in peacetime the theater-level (High Command) resources needed to control Pact forces once they are released from national control. We estimate that the centralized

command structure could be complete by the early 1980s. The unified communications system could begin to improve the Pact's command capabilities by the mid-1980s, but it is not scheduled for completion until 1990.

102. While the Pact is expected to achieve a more centralized command system through the creation of permanent theater commands, the Soviets probably will not control the day-to-day peacetime operations of non-Soviet Warsaw Pact forces. The centralized control structure would, however, enable them more quickly to assume wartime control of Pact forces, once authorized by NSWP leaders. The theater commands would also plan wartime operations and control forces during exercises. Hardened command and communications centers which could be used by theater commands have already been constructed, and more are planned.

103. The Pact made the decision in 1974 to create by 1990 an integrated communications system to provide high-capacity communications for Pact forces, to include theater commands. This new system—referred to by the Russian acronym VAKSS—is a civilian network which also will provide the Pact with its first integrated communications system with the increased communications capability and connectivity necessary to support the developing centralized command structure. The VAKSS program is an ambitious one, however, and may meet some resistance from NSWP countries—particularly Romania—that could delay completion, even though most of the developments specified for VAKSS probably are within the Soviet and NSWP technological capabilities.

104. When completed, the VAKSS system—primarily using buried cables—will become the Pact's principal communications system for use between major fixed headquarters.

105. Improved mobile communications equipment also has been provided to Soviet signal units supporting theater, front, army, and lower echelons of command. This equipment provides increased channel capacity and better communications security devices, and it can be set up quicker than the equipment it is replacing. These developments are expected to continue and spread to the NSWP forces.

106. We expect these developments over the next decade to improve the Pact's ability to:

— Alert multinational Pact forces during periods of international tension.

— Transfer forces from national to Pact operational control.

— Control mobilization and the deployment forward of reinforcements.

— Better coordinate Pact forces and allocations of resources.

— Simplify planning, reallocation of resources, and logistic support for the command and control system through the standardization of communications equipment, computers, and software.

— Coordinate the mobilization and initial movements of the various national fronts and the allocation of resources among them.

107. *Radioelectronic Combat.* Pact electronic warfare capabilities are also expected to be improved with the deployment of additional existing equipment and the acquisition of some advanced electronic equipment. Some of this advanced electronic equipment would likely include jammers with a higher power output and more capability to respond in a rapidly changing target environment. Some additional capabilities in radiofrequency coverage and target-handling capacity could also be realized,

108. *Logistic Support.* Improvements in the logistic support field are also likely, although we have little evidence regarding the extent of Pact plans in this area. There probably will be increased mechanization of material-handling procedures, including the computerization of supply and repair parts depots and automated inventory and requisition control systems. There may also be improvements in transportation, including greater containerization of supplies and equipment, as well as increases in the capacities of cargo carriers, particularly in the fields of tactical motor transport.

ANNEX A

SOVIET MILITARY OPERATIONS OUTSIDE THE EUROPEAN THEATER DURING A NATO–WARSAW PACT WAR

1. In this annex we briefly consider some possible Soviet military operations in distant areas during the early phase of a conventional European conflict, and the factors which would impinge on Soviet decisions. Only major ground, air, or naval operations are considered. Isolated commando-type raids or small-scale naval and air actions are beyond the scope of this Estimate.

2. Although Soviet leaders would prefer not to fight a war in Europe and Asia at the same time, they evidently believe that there is a serious possibility of simultaneous hostilities in both theaters and are preparing for this contingency. The Soviets maintain large forces, independently controlled and supported, directly opposite both NATO and China and could sustain large-scale combat in both theaters concurrently. However, the great distances from the European part of the USSR, the poorly developed transportation network in the Asiatic part, and the enormous frontages which would have to be defended would severely strain Soviet capabilities to support forces in Asia if a war should be prolonged.

3. We judge that the Soviets would not initiate operations which would impair their ability to achieve a quick victory in Europe. Undertaking large-scale military operations in distant areas would be circumscribed for the Soviet Union by two interrelated factors—geography and logistics—and shaped by its leaders' perception of objectives, threats, and timing. Despite increasing Soviet strategic concern with China and the major military buildup they have conducted in the Far Eastern USSR, the preponderance of evidence indicates that their main concern is still with the West. In the main body of this Estimate, we conclude that the Soviets desire a quick victory in Europe. We therefore believe that their objectives in Western Europe would take precedence over objectives elsewhere during a war with NATO.

4. An important factor affecting the development and capabilities of Soviet ground forces is that they are located within the USSR or its contiguous areas of influence. In addition, both the European and Far Eastern theaters are contiguous to the Soviet Union and, except for naval units, operations there would not require transfer of combat or support forces overseas or through exposed areas. Soviet ground forces attempting to conduct operations in noncontiguous areas probably would have to contend with hostile forces in transit. Exterior lines of communication would have to be established and maintained by force, and any prepositioned Soviet forces would be exposed to hostile forces and subject to interdiction. These factors would also constrain any significant Soviet support for operations by friendly forces.

Operations Against China

5. The major buildup of Soviet forces in Asia began in the mid-1960s, and currently some 47 divisions composed of almost 500,000 men, one-fourth to one-third of the USSR's ground and air forces, are deployed there (see annex B for order-of-battle information). The Soviet ground and supporting tactical air forces in Asia are deployed primarily along the Sino-Soviet border. Soviet strategic attack, air defense, and naval forces in the Far East support the Soviet military posture against the United States and its allies and against China. Soviet exercises usually portray war against China as the result of a Chinese attack before or during a war with NATO. We have no knowledge of Chinese plans to attack the USSR during a NATO-Pact war, however, and tend to believe that the Chinese would monitor the early course of such a war before deciding on any action.

6. The Soviets probably would not see it in their interest to initiate offensive military operations against China during a NATO–Warsaw Pact war unless the Chinese had massed forces on the border and the Soviets concluded that a Chinese attack was imminent. Chinese forces normally are well back from the frontier, heavily dug in, and could rely on almost infinite reinforcement on interior lines of communication. The Soviets would also have to consider that an

attack on China could develop into a long-term, large-scale commitment of manpower and materiel which could degrade their European war effort, especially in a prolonged conflict.

7. A two-front war with China and NATO would represent the worst case situation for the Soviets. It would involve major ground and tactical air units in Asia and, depending on military developments, could require the Soviets to draw upon their strategic reserve force. Soviet reinforcements would be required to defeat a large Chinese conventional attack or to permit the Soviets any chance of overrunning all of northern China. If the Soviets were able to maintain their forward or defensive positions against China, the leadership probably would continue to give priority consideration to the Western theater. Major Chinese advances into Soviet territory during the early stages of a European war, as the Soviets have simulated in exercises, would be likely to cause Moscow to send some reserves to Asia.

8. We have little evidence of Soviet strategy in the event of prolonged conflict with either NATO or China. Although the Soviets have sufficient resources to fight major conventional battles in both theaters concurrently, they could hardly count on being able to mount the massive offensive campaigns against the various NATO theaters which we describe in chapter IV, while at the same time prosecuting a war aimed at the defeat of China. We are unable to predict, however, the circumstances in which the Soviets would shift forces from one theater to the other during a prolonged two-front war.

Operations Against South Korea

9. The Soviets probably would regard Korea as a potential problem during a NATO–Warsaw Pact war. Although they recognize that the South Koreans pose no direct threat to the USSR, they no doubt realize that the US facilities and some forces in the Republic of Korea (South Korea) could be used to support a war against them. Whether hostilities are initiated against South Korea would be primarily a North Korean decision, although the Soviets could encourage the North Koreans to attack the South. In any event, Moscow would probably provide logistic support to North Korea if war broke out on the Korean Peninsula in the hope that a major conventional war on the Korean Peninsula would pin down US forces there and reduce the US ability to reinforce Europe or strike targets in the Soviet Far East.

10. The Soviets could elect to provide combat forces to support an attack on South Korea by North Korea. If the Soviets adopted this strategy, they would have to consider whether it would provoke a US attack on Soviet port facilities and the Pacific Fleet; and whether a military action against South Korea would provoke the Japanese into a more active role in the area. They would also have to consider whether supporting a North Korean attack on the South would precipitate Chinese military action along the Sino-Soviet border. At the same time, the Soviets know that US nuclear weapons are located in South Korea and would have to weigh the risk that a North Korean attack would provoke an escalatory response there from the United States and perhaps the eventual introduction of nuclear weapons into the conflict worldwide. The Soviets probably would consider that the risks attending direct military support of a North Korean attack would far outweigh the possible benefits of tying up the US forces committed to defending South Korea.

Operations in the Pacific

11. The Soviet Pacific Fleet is a large force primarily made up of submarines, surface ships, and aircraft. The submarine force consists of 106 submarines, of which 32 are ballistic missile and 78 cruise missile or torpedo attack units. The surface fleet is made up of 35 cruisers, destroyers, and Krivak-class missile frigates in addition to numerous smaller combatants. Nearly all of the fleet is based either in Vladivostok or Petropavlovsk. Soviet naval airpower in the area includes about 175 strike, reconnaissance, and tanker aircraft, about 65 fixed-wing and about 55 helicopter antisubmarine warfare (ASW) aircraft. Most aircraft are based in the vicinity of Vladivostok, some strike aircraft are based farther north, and some reconnaissance and ASW aircraft are based in Petropavlovsk. A naval infantry force of about 6,000 men is based near Vladivostok. (See tables B-4, B-5, and B-6 of annex B for a detailed order of battle of the Soviet Pacific Fleet.)

12. The Pacific Fleet conducts routine operations and the great majority of its training in the Sea of Japan, along the Kuril Islands, and off the Kamchatka Peninsula. Except for Indian Ocean deployments and annual ASW exercises in the Philippine Sea, surface combatants do not normally operate in the open ocean areas of the Pacific. Intelligence collection patrols are routinely maintained off some US naval facilities in the Pacific and periodically conducted in the

Tsushima, Tsugaru, and La Perouse Straits to provide fleet commanders with surveillance of the major passages into the Sea of Japan.

13. The possibility of becoming embroiled in a two-front war against the United States, Japan, and China in the Far East while fighting NATO in Europe would weigh heavily in Moscow's decision whether to initiate combat operations in the Pacific. Nonetheless, the Soviets clearly regard the US Pacific Fleet as a dangerous adversary to be kept outside of striking distance of the USSR. Soviet sea control capabilities against US carrier and amphibious task groups are considerable in the area within about 1,000 to 1,500 nautical miles of the USSR. US naval forces based out of Japan ordinarily are located in areas where Soviet sea control operations would be likely. If military considerations alone pertained, the Soviets almost certainly would strike US forces within 1,000 to 1,500 nm of the USSR.

14. There is disagreement within the Intelligence Community, however, regarding the extent to which larger, strategic considerations would influence initial Soviet naval actions in the Pacific during a war in Europe. According to one view,[1] the possibility of avoiding general two-front conflict would be paramount. Moscow would seek to avoid conflict in the Far East because the prospects for early victory are far from certain, but the risks of involving massive amounts of men and equipment are great. Until it believed conflict were unavoidable, such as if a US carrier task force entered the Sea of Japan or approached to within its striking range of the USSR, Moscow probably would direct its forces to assume a posture of preparedness for conflict which would fall short of provoking conflict. Nonetheless, it would be difficult, in the context of a war with NATO, for the Soviets to control events in the Far East, and it seems likely that they would be unable to avoid hostilities there.

15. According to an alternative view,[2] the Soviets would not seek to avoid a conflict with the United States in the Pacific to such an extent that they would refrain from attacking any US naval forces entering the Sea of Japan, the Sea of Okhotsk, or the approaches to Petropavlovsk. Additionally, the holders of this view believe that the Soviets would consider it necessary to deploy attack submarines and conduct air reconnaissance within the western Pacific out to 1,000 to 1,500 nm from the USSR to maintain their readiness to attack major US naval surface forces, especially carriers. The holders of this view believe that Soviet attacks at the onset of hostilities against any carriers operating in this area are likely because the Soviets would view the presence of US carriers operating in proximity to areas from which they can launch attacks against the USSR as a military threat of sufficient gravity to require an early Soviet counteraction. The holders of this view, furthermore, believe that the Soviets would not consider such actions against US forces in the Pacific, by themselves, as directly causing wider hostilities with China or Japan.

16. All agree that once hostilities began in the east a main task of the Pacific Fleet would be the establishment of sea and air control in the waters adjacent to the Soviet Union—the Sea of Japan, the Sea of Okhotsk, and the Pacific off Petropavlovsk—and limited sea denial tasks against carrier and amphibious task groups in the approaches. Operations outside those waters would depend in large part on US strategy, and on whether the USSR was simultaneously at war with China or involved with supporting the North Koreans in a war on the Korean Peninsula.

17. The Soviets would be concerned about any US combat aircraft based at airfields in Japan (including Okinawa). Aircraft from these bases would pose a major threat to the Soviet fleet operating in the Sea of Japan and to naval air reconnaissance and ASW missions. The Soviets undoubtedly would bring strong pressure on Japan to deny the United States the use of these bases during a war and undoubtedly there would be strong Japanese domestic pressures as well. If these pressures were successful, the Soviets would probably take no military action against the bases. If it appeared that they would be used to mount an attack on the USSR or its military forces, the Soviets would almost certainly strike them.

18. The Soviets do not have the capability to mount large-scale ground force attacks in the Aleutians and the Alaskan mainland. US surveillance, missile tracking, and air and naval facilities located in Alaska would be attractive targets for airstrikes during a conflict in the Pacific. In deciding whether to attack these targets, however, the Soviets would have to weigh the risks attending any attacks on US soil, and in any event such targets probably would not receive high priority

---

[1] *The holder of this view is the Central Intelligence Agency.*

[2] *The holders of this view are the Director, Bureau of Intelligence and Research, Department of State; the Director, Defense Intelligence Agency; the Director, National Security Agency; and the Director of Naval Intelligence, Department of the Navy.*

Operations in the Indian Ocean

19. The Soviet Navy maintains a small force in the Indian Ocean, normally consisting of six to eight surface combatants, a diesel-powered torpedo attack submarine, and 10 to 12 support ships drawn mainly from the Pacific Fleet. This force has been occasionally augmented during the past few years in reaction to crises and during interfleet transits. The Soviet ouster from Somalia deprived the Indian Ocean Squadron of its shore support facilities in Somalia, but it has subsequently acquired access to the Ethiopian ports of Assab and Massawa and increased its use of the PDRY (South Yemen) port of Aden. We do not expect a large-scale augmentation of Soviet naval forces in the Indian Ocean during the initial period of a NATO–Warsaw Pact war.

20. Currently, Western naval forces in the Indian Ocean far outnumber Soviet naval combatants. The US force usually consists of two destroyers and a command support ship. Three or four times a year this force is augmented for about six weeks by a US naval force led by a cruiser or an aircraft carrier. The French maintain the largest naval force in the Indian Ocean—usually consisting of two destroyers, five frigates, and four corvettes—and keep a fighter-bomber squadron at Djibouti. This force is occasionally augmented by an aircraft carrier. The British Royal Navy does not keep a permanent force in the area, but occasionally deploys four or five frigates there for short visits en route to the Far East. In addition to these Western forces, both India and Iran maintain naval forces in the area.

21. Because of its small size, the Soviet Indian Ocean force would be unable to exercise sea control in the area against the combined Western forces. In peacetime, the force performs primarily a political/psychological function to enhance the USSR's prestige along the littoral. The most lucrative naval targets in the area are the sea lines of communication that connect the oilfields of the Middle East with Western Europe, the United States, and Japan. This route is highly vulnerable to disruption, but the overall balance of forces in the area and the relative lack of Soviet submarines there raise doubts as to whether even the Soviets would expect their Indian Ocean forces to initiate and maintain a significant interdiction campaign. They might seek, however, to disrupt Western shipping by mining straits and choke points or by other means.

22. The Soviets might question whether an interdiction campaign would be felt soon enough to have any effect during a short European war. If a NATO-Pact war were prolonged and if continued Western access to Middle Eastern oil were to become a factor, the Soviets might attempt to increase their submarine operations in the area. However, because of the long distances between naval bases in the USSR and the Indian Ocean, the Soviets would probably concentrate any such increased submarine operations on areas closer to the ports of destination. At the same time they might attempt to cut off the flow by attacking the oilfields in the Middle East with other forces.

Operations in the Middle East

23. Soviet operations in the Middle East during a Pact-NATO war would almost certainly be intended to interrupt the supply of oil to the West, inasmuch as there is no viable military threat to the USSR from the area. While the prospect of denying Middle East oil to the West would be tempting to the Soviets, we do not believe that they would undertake major ground or airborne operations in the Persian Gulf area during the early stages of a Pact-NATO war because to do so would involve the use of forces which could be needed against NATO. In addition, the Soviets probably would consider operations in the Persian Gulf to be impractical during a NATO-Pact war, because their forces could not be safely transported by sea or air to the area in significant numbers and would be very difficult to maintain. Although ground operations through Iran would be feasible, we have no evidence that the Soviets would undertake such operations during the initial phase of a war and believe that the Soviets would prefer instead to reserve most of their forces in the Transcaucasus Military District for use against Turkey. Soviet capabilities for airstrikes in the area, however, are much greater and such attacks might occur if aircraft were available.[3]

Operations in the South Atlantic

24. Soviet naval forces in the South Atlantic lack air cover and are not prepared for extended wartime operations there. The Soviet force normally comprises

---

[3] *The Assistant Chief of Staff for Intelligence, Department of the Army, would note that, while the Soviets probably would not undertake major ground or airborne operations in the Persian Gulf during the early stages of a NATO-Pact war, they would probably consider such operations subsequently. The objective of these operations would be the securing of Middle East oil sources, rather than only interdicting the flow of oil to the West. Under these circumstances, Soviet forces in the Transcaucasus, North Caucasus, and Turkestan Military Districts, for example, might well be employed in ground and airborne operations through Iran into the Persian Gulf area.*

a few surface combatants, a torpedo-attack submarine, and several auxiliaries. In addition, a number of Soviet naval auxiliaries regularly deploy to the South Atlantic for intelligence collection and research operations. Soviet surface combatants on patrol off Guinea and occasionally some units en route to the Indian Ocean reprovision at Conakry, but Soviet use of support facilities ashore there remains limited. The Soviet Navy also uses port facilities in Benin and Angola but could not rely on their availability during a war. Soviet Bear D long-range reconnaissance aircraft occasionally deploy to Angola. Use of these aircraft, in conjunction with others operating from Cuba, could provide the Soviets with a reconnaissance capability in the South Atlantic in the opening stages of a war, but they could not count on continued access during a war.

Operations in the Caribbean

25. The Soviets have military advisers in Cuba and send some personnel there to train, but they have no ground, air, or naval units permanently stationed there. Naval deployments of about 30 days are made approximately every six months, mostly from the Northern and Baltic Fleets. A typical force consists of two surface combatants, one or two submarines, and a logistic ship. The force makes port calls in Havana and Cienfuegos for provisioning and crew rest, and some units exercise with the Cuban Navy and make brief excursions into the Gulf of Mexico. Bear D reconnaissance aircraft regularly deploy to Havana, sometimes coincident with visits of Soviet naval ships. The Soviets would probably consider any major operations in the Caribbean infeasible.

26. Whether Cuba would initiate hostilities against the United States during the early stages of a European war would be primarily Havana's decision. In our view, however, the Soviets would be unlikely to expect a significant Cuban military contribution in support of the Warsaw Pact. Cuba lacks the resources to transport large forces overseas, and those already deployed abroad would require support which the Soviets would find extremely difficult to provide. While the Cuban armed forces have been equipped for many years with some naval and air force weapons (including a few recently introduced Flogger interceptor and ground attack aircraft) capable of striking the southern United States or US forces in the Caribbean, Castro would have to consider that offensive actions against the United States during the early stages of a NATO–Warsaw Pact war could result in decisive US retaliation.[4]

---

[4] *The Assistant Chief of Staff for Intelligence, Department of the Army, would note that another important aspect of the recent introduction of Flogger ground attack aircraft lies in the fact that it could presage the introduction of these aircraft in more significant numbers. In the context of a NATO-Pact war, these aircraft, flown by Soviet pilots, could conceivably be used in attacks against ground targets throughout the Caribbean basin, to include the southeastern United States. While the Soviets would have to calculate the response such attacks would incur, the prospect that they are developing such a capability should not be overlooked.*

ANNEX B

DISPOSITION OF WARSAW PACT
GENERAL PURPOSE FORCES,
1 JANUARY 1979

PAGE LEFT BLANK INTENTIONALLY

Table B-1

Disposition of Warsaw Pact Ground Forces
January 1979

	Category I				Category II				Category III				Total	
	TD	MRD	Abn	Bde	TD	MRD	Abn	Bde	TD	MRD	Abn	Bde	Div	Bde
Divisions Opposite NATO Central Region														
East European														
East Germany	2	4	—	—	—	—	—	—	—	—	—	—	6	—
Poland	5	3	1	—	—	3	—	—	—	2	—	—	15 a	—
Czechoslovakia	3	4	—	—	—	1	—	—	2	—	—	—	10	—
Total East European	10	11	1	—	—	4	—	—	2	2	—	—	31 a	—
Soviet														
GSFG (East Germany)	10	10	—	—	—	—	—	—	—	—	—	—	20	—
NGF (Poland)	2	—	—	—	—	—	—	—	—	—	—	—	2	—
CGF (Czechoslovakia)	2	3	—	—	—	—	—	—	—	—	—	—	5	—
Baltic MD	—	—	1	—	2	1	—	—	1	4	1	—	10	—
Belorussian MD	—	1	1	—	—	—	—	—	8	1	—	—	11	—
Carpathian MD	—	—	—	—	1 b	2	—	—	2	6	—	—	11	—
Total Soviet	14	14	2	—	3	3	—	—	11	11	1	—	59	—
Total Opposite Central Region	24	25	3	—	3	7	—	—	13	13	1	—	90 a	—
Divisions on NATO's Flanks														
East European														
Hungary	1	2	—	—	—	1	—	—	—	2	—	—	6	—
Bulgaria	—	3	—	6 c	—	3	—	1 d	—	—	—	—	6	7
Romania	2	5	—	2 e	—	3	—	—	—	—	—	—	10	2
Total East European	3	10	—	8	—	7	—	1	—	2	—	—	22	9
Soviet														
SGF (Hungary)	2	2	—	—	—	—	—	—	—	—	—	—	4	—
Odessa MD	—	—	1	—	—	1	—	—	—	6	—	—	8	—
Kiev MD	—	—	—	—	1	—	—	—	6	4	—	—	11	—
North Caucasus MD	—	—	—	—	1	—	—	—	—	5	—	—	6	—
Transcaucasus MD	—	—	1	—	—	2	—	—	—	9	—	—	12	—
Leningrad MD	—	1	1	—	—	1	—	—	—	6	—	—	9	—
Total Soviet	2	3	3	—	2	4	—	—	6	30	—	—	50	—
Total on NATO Flanks	5	13	3	8	2	11	—	1	6	32	—	—	72	9
Other Soviet Divisions														
In the Eastern USSR and Mongolia														
Soviet Forces in Mongolia	1	1	—	—	1	—	—	—	—	—	—	—	3	—
Central Asia MD	1	1	—	—	—	2	—	—	—	3	—	—	7	—
Siberian MD	—	—	—	—	—	1	—	—	—	4	—	—	5	—
Transbaykal MD	1	3	—	—	—	2	—	—	1	3	—	—	10	—
Far East MD	—	5	—	—	1 b	6	—	—	—	10 f	—	—	22 g	—
Total in Eastern USSR and Mongolia	3	10	—	—	2	11	—	—	1	20	—	—	47	—
Elsewhere														
Moscow MD	—	—	1	—	1	1	—	—	1	3	—	—	7	—
Ural MD	—	—	—	—	—	—	—	—	1	2	—	—	3	—
Volga MD	—	—	—	—	—	—	—	—	—	3	—	—	3	—
Turkestan MD	—	—	1	—	—	1	—	—	—	3	—	—	5	—
Total Elsewhere	—	—	2	—	1	2	—	—	2	11	—	—	18	—
Total Other Soviet Divisions	3	10	2	—	3	13	—	—	3	31	—	—	65	—
Total Warsaw Pact	32	48	8	8	8	31	—	1	22	76	1	—	227 a	9
Of which:														
Soviet	19	27	8	—	7	20	—	—	20	71	1	—	174	—
East European	13	21	1	8	—	11	—	1	2	5	—	—	53 a	9

a Includes a Category I Polish sea landing division of some 4,400 men which is not listed in category columns.
b This division does not conform to the standard TO&E of a tank division and may be experimental.
c Five tank brigades and one training brigade, the latter designated for wartime expansion to a motorized rifle division.
d Peacetime training brigade designated for wartime expansion to motorized rifle division.
e Mountain rifle brigades.
f Includes one division which is in the process of being upgraded from a mobilization (second-generation) division to an active one.
g Includes three motorized rifle divisions of the Far East Military District which, because of their remote locations in Sakhalin and Kamchatka, are not considered to be deployed opposite China.

PAGE LEFT BLANK INTENTIONALLY

Top Secret RUFF UMBRA

Table B-2

Disposition of Warsaw Pact Tactical Air Forces [a]
January 1979

	Fighters					Fighter Bombers/Light Bombers							Aircraft for Reconnaissance/Electronic Warfare										Total [b]		
	MIG-23	MIG-21	MIG-17	MIG-19	MIG	MIG-21	MIG-17	MIG-15	SU-17	SU-7	SU-24	YAK-28	MIG-25	MIG-21	MIG-15	IL-28	YAK-25	L-39	L-29	IL-14	IL-20	AN-30	Soviet	East European	Total
Aircraft Opposite NATO Central Region																									
East European																									
East Germany	—	—	—	—	—	—	35	—	—	—	—	—	—	10	—	—	—	—	—	4	—	—	—	49	49
Poland	—	100	10	—	—	—	195	10	30	30	—	—	—	35	35	15	—	—	—	4	—	—	—	464	464
Czechoslovakia	—	125	—	—	—	45	—	40	—	75	—	—	—	35	—	—	—	10	30	10	—	—	—	374	374
Total East European	—	225	10	—	—	45	230	50	30	105	—	—	—	80	35	15	—	10	30	18	—	—	—	887	887
Soviet																									
GSFG (East Germany)	150	225	—	—	90	45	—	—	90	45	—	—	15	35	—	—	40	—	—	—	2	—	767	—	767
NGF (Poland)	45	90	—	—	45	45	—	—	45	—	—	—	15	10	—	—	10	—	—	—	—	—	305	—	305
CGF (Czechoslovakia)	45	45	—	—	—	—	—	—	—	—	—	—	—	15	—	—	—	—	—	—	—	—	105	—	105
Baltic MD	45	45	—	—	—	45	—	—	—	70	30	—	—	15	—	—	20	—	—	—	—	—	270	—	270
Belorussian MD	90	45	—	—	—	45	—	—	—	45	35	—	15	15	—	—	—	—	—	—	—	—	290	—	290
Carpathian MD	90	45	—	—	45	—	—	—	45	—	105	—	10	15	—	—	15	—	—	—	—	—	370	—	370
Total Soviet	495	495	—	—	180	150	—	—	180	90	210	30	55	105	—	—	85	—	—	—	2	—	2,107	—	2,107
Total Opposite Central Region	495	720	10	—	180	225	230	50	210	195	210	30	55	185	35	15	85	10	30	18	2	—	2,107	887	2,994
Aircraft on NATO's Flanks																									
East European																									
Hungary	—	—	—	—	—	—	—	—	—	—	—	—	—	—	—	—	—	—	—	—	—	—	—	—	—
Bulgaria	7	20	25	10	15	—	65	—	—	—	—	—	—	10	25	—	—	—	—	—	—	1	—	178	178
Romania	—	—	—	—	—	—	25	60	—	—	—	—	—	—	—	20	—	—	—	—	—	3	—	108	108
Total East European	7	20	25	10	15	—	90	60	—	—	—	—	—	10	25	20	—	—	—	—	—	4	—	286	286
Soviet																									
SGF (Hungary)	45	90	—	—	—	—	—	—	45	—	—	30	—	15	—	—	20	—	—	—	—	—	245	—	245
Odessa MD	90	45	—	—	45	—	—	—	—	—	—	—	15	15	—	—	20	—	—	—	—	—	230	—	230
Kiev MD	—	45	—	—	—	—	—	—	—	—	—	—	—	—	—	—	—	—	—	—	—	—	45	—	45
Transcaucasus MD	90	45	—	—	—	—	—	—	45	—	35	—	10	30	—	—	15	—	—	—	1	—	271	—	271
Leningrad MD	—	—	—	—	45	—	—	—	45	—	—	—	15	15	—	—	—	—	—	—	2	—	122	—	122
Total Soviet	225	225	—	—	90	—	—	—	135	—	35	30	40	75	—	—	55	—	—	—	3	—	913	—	913
Total on NATO Flanks	232	245	25	10	105	—	90	60	135	—	35	30	40	85	25	20	55	—	—	—	3	4	913	286	1,199
Other Soviet Aircraft																									
In the Eastern USSR and Mongolia																									
Soviet Forces in Mongolia	45	45	—	—	—	45	—	—	45	—	—	—	—	—	—	—	—	—	—	—	—	—	180	—	180
Central Asian MD	—	90	—	—	15	80	—	—	—	—	—	30	10	30	—	—	20	—	—	—	2	—	277	—	277
Transbaykal MD	45	45	—	—	45	—	—	—	135	35	—	—	15	15	—	—	15	—	—	—	—	—	350	—	350
Far East MD	90	45	—	—	45	45	—	—	90	35	—	—	15	50	—	20	20	—	—	—	2	—	457	—	457
Total in Eastern USSR and Mongolia	180	225	—	—	105	170	—	—	270	70	—	30	40	95	—	20	55	—	—	—	4	—	1,264	—	1,264
Elsewhere																									
Moscow MD	45	45	—	—	—	—	—	—	45	—	—	—	15	—	—	—	15	—	—	—	—	—	165	—	165
Turkestan MD	—	45	—	—	—	45	—	—	—	—	—	—	—	15	—	—	15	—	—	—	—	—	120	—	120
Total in General Reserve	45	90	—	—	—	45	—	—	45	—	—	—	15	15	—	—	30	—	—	—	—	—	285	—	285
Total Elsewhere	225	315	—	—	105	215	—	—	315	—	70	30	55	110	—	20	85	—	—	—	4	—	1,549	—	1,549
Total Warsaw Pact	952	1,290	35	10	394	440	320	110	660	195	315	90	150	380	60	55	225	10	30	18	9	4	4,569	1,173	5,742
Of which:																									
Soviet	945	1,035	—	—	375	395	—	—	630	90	315	90	150	290	—	20	225	—	—	—	9	—	4,569	—	4,569
East European	7	245	35	10	19	45	320	110	30	105	—	—	—	90	60	35	—	10	30	18	—	4	—	1,173	1,173

[a] Includes all combat aircraft (except trainers) assigned to what the Pact calls frontal aviation, or air forces for the support of fronts. It does not include some 2,800 Soviet and 1,200 East European fighter aircraft that are subordinate to the national air defense commands with the primary mission of strategic air defense over the territories of the Warsaw Pact countries. In an emergency, limited numbers of these aircraft—particularly East European—might be assigned tactical air defense missions. Aircraft models of the Soviet strategic air defense forces (PVO Strany), however, are different from those of the tactical air forces and for the most part would not constitute a suitable replacement pool without special logistic arrangements.

[b] All figures in this table represent the number of operationally available (OA) aircraft that are assigned to active combat units of the Warsaw Pact tactical air forces. In most units this would include a few aircraft above the normal unit equipment (UE). The figures do not include some 900 combat-capable trainers that are in Pact tactical air units or some 2,500 aircraft assigned to Pact (mainly Soviet) operational conversion units and pilot training schools. These aircraft probably could serve as maintenance and attrition replacements during hostilities. The table does not include aircraft in storage.

SECRET

PAGE LEFT BLANK INTENTIONALLY

Table B-3

Disposition of Warsaw Pact Tactical Helicopter Forces [a]
January 1979

	Combat Helicopters									Support Helicopters [d]											
	Ground Attack [b]			Assault Transport [c]																	
	MI-8	MI-24	Total Ground Attack	MI-1/2	MI-4	MI-8	MI-6	MI-10	Alouette III	Total Assault Transport	MI-1/2	MI-4	MI-8	KA-26	Alouette III	Puma	MI-6	MI-10	Total Support	Total Soviet	Total East European	Grand Total
Opposite NATO Central Region																						
East European	25	--	25	225	110	75	--	--	--	410	50	20	5	--	--	--	--	--	75	--	510	510
Soviet	15	230	245	5	25	295	95	5	--	425	330	25	160	--	--	--	45	--	560	1,230	--	1,230
Total Opposite Central Region	40	230	270	230	135	370	95	5	--	835	380	45	165	--	--	--	45	--	635	1,230	510	1,740
Helicopters on NATO's Flanks																						
East European	--	--	--	40	30	60	--	--	15	145	10	5	5	15	5	10	--	--	50	--	195	195
Soviet	--	40	40	--	20	250	135	--	--	405	155	10	65	--	--	--	5	--	235	680	--	680
Total on NATO's Flanks	--	40	40	40	50	310	135	--	15	550	165	15	70	15	5	10	5	--	285	680	195	875
Other Soviet Helicopters																						
In Eastern USSR	--	115	115	15	65	295	95	5	--	475	175	40	120	--	--	--	20	5	360	950	--	950
Elsewhere	--	25	25	5	10	125	55	--	--	195	30	15	30	--	--	--	5	--	80	300	--	300
Total Other Soviet Helos	--	140	140	20	75	420	150	5	--	670	205	55	150	--	--	--	25	5	440	1,250	--	1,250
Total Warsaw Pact	40	410	450	290	260	1,100	380	10	15	2,055	750	115	385	15	5	10	75	5	1,360	3,160	705	3,865
Of which																						
Soviet	15	410	425	25	120	965	380	10	--	1,500	690	90	375	--	--	--	75	5	1,235	3,160	--	3,160
East European	25	--	25	265	140	135	--	--	15	555	60	25	10	15	5	10	--	--	125	--	705	705

[a] Includes all helicopters (except those used as trainers, in storage, in maintenance, or in repair depots) assigned to Warsaw Pact tactical air forces. Does not include helicopters assigned to national air defense and naval forces.

[b] Includes only those helicopters assigned to units which have a primary mission of attacking ground targets with rockets, bombs, and/or guns. This designation does not necessarily exclude the capability to perform other combat or support missions.

[c] Includes only those helicopters assigned to units which have a primary mission of transporting assault troops and their associated cargo into an objective area. This designation does not necessarily exclude the capability to perform other combat or support missions.

[d] Includes only those helicopters assigned to units which have primary missions of support to combat operations by providing services such as logistic support, reconnaissance, artillery spotting, medical evacuation, communications relay, electronic warfare, or airborne command posts. This designation does not necessarily exclude the capability to perform combat missions.

PAGE LEFT BLANK INTENTIONALLY

Table B-4

Soviet General Purpose Submarines, by Fleet Area[a]
January 1979

	Antiship Missile Tubes per Unit	Northern	Baltic	Black Sea	Pacific	Total	Missile Tubes
Cruise Missile Submarines							
Nuclear-Powered (SSGN)							
E-II-Class	8 SS-N-3/12	15	—	—	14	29	232
C-I-Class	8 SS-N-7	7	—	—	4	11	88
C-II-Class	8 SS-N-9	3	—	—	—	3	24
P-Class	10 poss. SS-N-9	1	—	—	—	1	10
Diesel-Powered (SSG)							
J-Class	4 SS-N-3	12	—	—	4	16	64
W-Class	4 SS-N-3	—	2	1	2	5	20
W-Class	2 SS-N-3	—	—	2	—	2	4
Total Cruise Missile		38	2	3	24	67	442
Torpedo Attack Submarines							
Nuclear-Powered (SSN)							
N-Class		8	—	—	4	12	
E-Class		—	—	—	5	5	
V-I-Class		12	—	—	3	15	
V-II-Class		6	—	—	—	6	
V-III-Class		1	—	—	1	2	
A-Class		3	—	—	—	3	
Diesel-powered (SS)							
W-Class		5	15	10	15	45	
F-Class		36	5	—	19	60	
Z-Class		3	4	1	5	13	
R-Class		10	—	2	—	12	
B-Class		1	—	2	1	4	
T-Class		6	—	4	—	10	
G-Class		1	—	—	2	3	
Total Torpedo Attack		92	24	19	55	190	
Total G. P. Submarines		130	26	22	79	257	
Of which nuclear		56	—	—	31	87	

[a] Does not include submarines in reserve status but does include units in both short- and long-term overhaul or conversion, or on sea trials. Two Y-class SSBNs are being converted to SSNs, but are not likely to become operational this year.

Table B-5

Selected Soviet Surface Combatants and Carriers by Fleet Area [a]
January 1979

	Northern	Baltic	Black Sea [b]	Pacific	Total
Aircraft Carriers					
Kiev CVSG	1	—	1 [c]	—	2
Helicopter Ships					
Moskva CHG	—	—	2	—	2
Missile Cruisers					
Kynda CG	—	—	2	2	4
Kresta-I CG	3	—	—	1	4
Kresta-II CG	6	1	—	3	10
Kara CG	—	—	6	—	6
Sverdlov CG	—	—	1	—	1
Total	9	1	9	6	25
Cruisers					
Chapayev CL	—	1	—	—	1
Sverdlov CL	2	2	2	3	9
Total	2	3	2	3	10
Missile Destroyers					
Kanin DDG	3	1	—	3	7
Kashin DDG	—	1	9	4	14
Mod Kashin DDG	2	1	2	—	5
Kotlin DDG	1	1	3	2	7
Kildin DDG	—	—	—	1	1
Total	6	4	14	10	34
Destroyers					
Kotlin/Mod Kotlin DD	3	2	3	6	14
Skoryy/Mod Skoryy DD	3	4	7	5	19
Mod Kildin DD	—	1	2	—	3
Total	6	7	12	11	36
Missile Frigates					
Krivak I/II FFG	5	11	3	5	24
Total	5	11	3	5	24
Frigates					
Kola FF	—	—	1	—	1
Mirka FFL	—	14	6	—	20
Petya-I FFL	3	2	3	3	11
Petya-II FFL	11	—	5	11	27
Mod Petya-I FFL	3	1	1	3	8
Riga FF	8	5	8	11	32
Koni FF	—	1	1	—	2
Grisha FFL/WFFL	15	—	14	9	38
Total	40	23	39	37	139
Total Principal Surface Combatants	69	49	82	72	272

[a] Does not include ships in reserve status but does include ships undergoing short- or long-term overhaul or conversion and on sea trials.
[b] Includes one Kola and two Rigas assigned to the Caspian Sea Flotilla.
[c] Expected to transfer to Pacific Fleet.

Table B-6

Soviet Naval Combat Aircraft, by Fleet Area
January 1979

	Northern	Baltic	Black Sea	Pacific	Total [a]
Aircraft for Reconnaissance/Electronic Warfare					
TU-95 Bear D [b]	25	—	—	20	45
TU-22 Blinder C [c]	—	3	3	—	6
TU-16 Badger D/E/F/K [d]	20	—	—	17	37
TU-16 Badger H/J [e]	11	9	7	12	39
AN-12 Cub B [f]	2	2	2	2	8
Total	58	14	12	51	135
Strike Aircraft					
Backfire B [g]	—	24	17	—	41
TU-16 Badger C [h]	68	28	46	51	193
TU-16 Badger G [i]	—	22	8	47	77
TU-22 Blinder A [j]	—	20	21	—	41
Total	68	94	92	98	352
Tankers					
TU-16 Badger	22	21	13	27	83
Fighters/Fighter-Bombers					
SU-17 Fitter C/D	—	38	—	—	38
YAK-36 Forger V/STOL [k]	13	—	20	—	33
Total	13	38	20	—	71
ASW Fixed-Wing Aircraft					
BE-12 Mail [l]	22	12	25	34	93
IL-38 May	18	9	—	20	47
TU-142 Bear F	19	—	—	12	31
Total	59	21	25	66	171
ASW/Reconnaissance Helicopters					
MI-4 Hound	—	—	—	5	5
MI-14 Haze	16	16	—	12	44
KA-25 Hormone A	34	10	70	38	152
KA-25 Hormone B [b]	6	5	7	8	26
Total	56	31	77	63	227
Grand Total Naval Combat Aircraft	276	219	239	305	1,039

[a] Does not include some 70 aircraft of numerous types in a training role—primarily in Black Sea area or about 120 transport aircraft and 105 transport helicopters which support Soviet Naval Aviation.
[b] Configured for surface surveillance and target acquisition support for Soviet cruise missile ships and submarines.
[c] Configured for PHOTINT.
[d] Configured for PHOTINT or ELINT.
[e] Configured for ECM.
[f] Configured for SIGINT.
[g] Carries bombs or one, two, and possibly three AS-4 ASMs.
[h] Carries one AS-2 ASM, or 2 AS-5 or AS-6 ASMs.
[i] Carries bombs and/or two AS-5 or AS-6 ASMs.
[j] Free-fall bombers only.
[k] Carried aboard Kiev-class carriers.
[l] Amphibian.

DISSEMINATION NOTICE

1. This document was disseminated by the National Foreign Assessment Center. This copy is for the information and use of the recipient and of persons under his or her jurisdiction on a need-to-know basis. Additional essential dissemination may be authorized by the following officials within their respective departments:

    a. Director of Intelligence and Research, for the Department of State
    b. Director, Defense Intelligence Agency, for the Office of the Secretary of Defense and the organization of the Joint Chiefs of Staff
    c. Assistant Chief of Staff for Intelligence, for the Department of the Army
    d. Director of Naval Intelligence, for the Department of the Navy
    e. Assistant Chief of Staff, Intelligence, for the Department of the Air Force
    f. Deputy Assistant Administrator for National Security, for the Department of Energy
    g. Assistant Director, FBI, for the Federal Bureau of Investigation
    h. Director of NSA, for the National Security Agency
    i. Special Assistant to the Secretary for National Security, for the Department of the Treasury
    j. The Deputy Director for National Foreign Assessment, for any other Department or Agency

2. This document may be retained, or destroyed by burning in accordance with applicable security regulations, or returned to the National Foreign Assessment Center.

3. When this document is disseminated overseas, the overseas recipients may retain it for a period not in excess of one year. At the end of this period, the document should be destroyed or returned to the forwarding agency, or permission should be requested of the forwarding agency to retain it in accordance with IAC-D-69/2, 22 June 1953.

4. The title of this document when used separately from the text should be classified: CONFIDENTIAL.

Top Secret

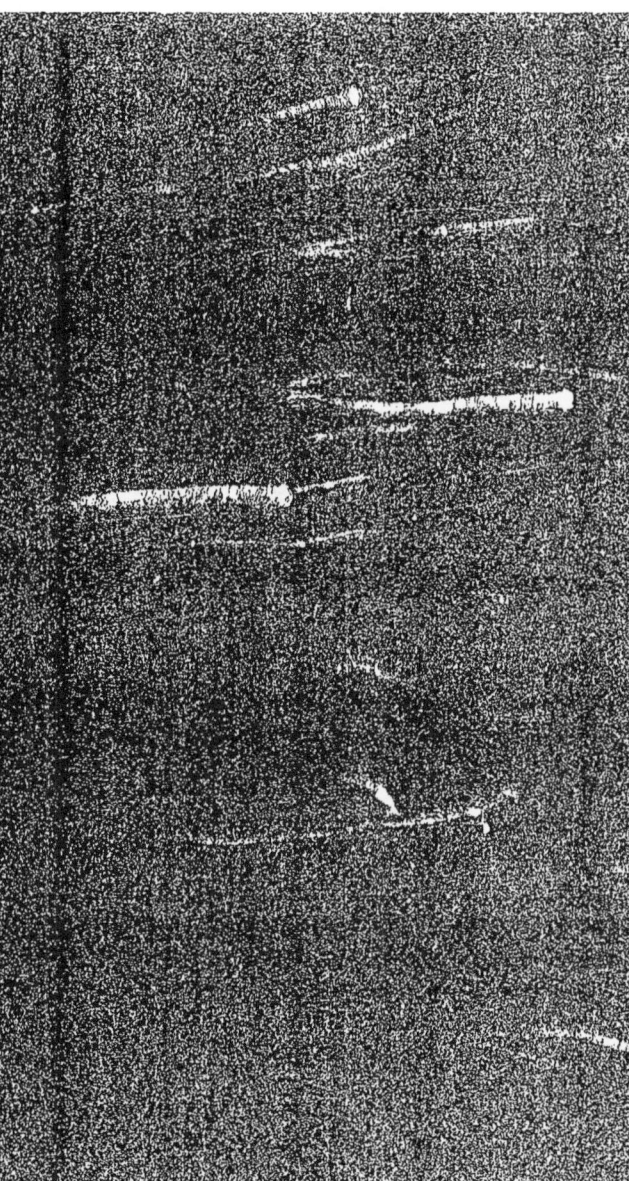

Top Secret

www.ingramcontent.com/pod-product-compliance
Lightning Source LLC
Chambersburg PA
CBHW082117230426
43671CB00015B/2722